Memories of 1968

International Perspectives

Ingo Cornils and Sarah Waters (eds)

PETER LANG

Oxford · Bern · Berlin · Bruxelles · Frankfurt am Main · New York · Wien

Bibliographic information published by Die Deutsche Nationalbibliothek
Die Deutsche Nationalbibliothek lists this publication in the Deutsche Nationalbibliografie;
detailed bibliographic data is available on the Internet at http://dnb.d-nb.de.

A catalogue record for this book is available from The British Library.

Library of Congress Cataloging-in-Publication Data:

Memories of 1968 / [edited by] Ingo Cornils and Sarah Waters.
    p. cm. -- (Cultural history and literary imagination ; v. 16)
  The papers collected in this volume are selected from the proceedings
of a conference entitled 'Memories of 1968: International Perspectives'
that was held at the University of Leeds in 2008
  Includes bibliographical references and index.
  ISBN 978-3-03911-931-8 (alk. paper)
  1. Nineteen sixty-eight, A.D.--Congresses. 2. Nineteen sixty-eight,
A.D.--Historiography--Congresses. 3. Social change--History--20th
century--Congresses. 4. Social history--1960-1970--Congresses. 5.
Collective memory--Congresses. I. Cornils, Ingo. II. Waters, Sarah,
1966-
  D848.M46 2010
  909.82'6--dc22
                            2010009558

ISSN 1660-6205
ISBN 978-3-03911-931-8

© Peter Lang AG, International Academic Publishers, Bern 2010
Hochfeldstrasse 32, CH-3012 Bern, Switzerland
info@peterlang.com, www.peterlang.com, www.peterlang.net

Memories of 1968

CULTURAL HISTORY AND LITERARY IMAGINATION

EDITED BY CHRISTIAN EMDEN & DAVID MIDGLEY

VOL. 16

PETER LANG

Oxford · Bern · Berlin · Bruxelles · Frankfurt am Main · New York · Wien

Contents

vi

Acknowledgements

The idea for this volume came out of a research group on '1968' in the School of Modern Languages and Cultures at the University of Leeds. The editors would like to thank Frank Finlay and Margaret Atack for their support and encouragement.

We would like to thank all those who took part in the 'Memories of 1968' conference at Leeds in April 2008, on which this volume is based, and particularly our co-organiser Alan O'Leary, and the conference administrators Mercedes de Birch and Ed Kirby.

The conference was generously supported by the Association for the Study of Modern and Contemporary France, the Brazilian Embassy and the French Embassy in London, the Goethe Institute in Manchester, the Italian Cultural Institute, the Leeds Humanities Research Institute and the Universities' China Committee in London.

Our gratitude is extended to all the contributors to the present volume for their professionalism and dedication in bringing the book to its conclusion. We are very grateful to the School of Modern Languages and Cultures, University of Leeds and to the French Embassy in London, which both supported the publication of this volume.

Shortly before this volume went to press, we received the sad news that Daniel Bensaïd had passed away. We respectfully dedicate this book to his memory.

Ingo Cornils and Sarah Waters
Leeds
February 2010

SARAH WATERS

Introduction: 1968 in Memory and Place

1. A contested memory

Forty years after the events denoted by the term '1968', the memorialisa-tion of this 'first global rebellion'[1] reached a climax in 2008. All around the world, on television and radio, in the print media, exhibitions, public debates, literature readings and film showings, the experiences of '1968' were dissected, discussed and probed for their continuing relevance or remaining toxicity.[2] While it was unclear what this collective production of increasingly nostalgic reflections was supposed to achieve, the debates ignited by the anniversary signalled that '1968' continues to be a currency in public debates across the world. The cause of this surprising longevity is the tension between two forces of memory that are oddly out of synch: historicisation ('objective') and memorialisation ('subjective').[3]

On the one hand, there have been widespread efforts, across different national cultures, to historicise '1968', to locate it within a recent past and to assign it a definitive and objective meaning. 1968 is now often seen as

1   Wolfgang Kraushaar, *1968 als Mythos, Chiffre und Zäsur* (Hamburg: Hamburger Edition 2000), 19.
2   In the United Kingdom, the BBC turned the 40th anniversary of '1968' into a test case of modern popular remembrance, merging the images and sounds of global events with the experiences of the viewers and listeners on interactive websites.
3   For the French sociologist Maurice Halbwachs, whose work has helped to define a field of 'memory studies', history and memory were opposing forces: whilst memory was grounded in lived experience, as a kind of past within the present, history, as an objective study of the past, took over when memory died out. See Maurice Halbwachs, *La Mémoire collective* (Paris: Albin Michel, 1997)

sufficiently distant to be summoned up as an object of history, one that is open to objective historical enquiry and research.[4] There may be disagreements about the interpretation of the era (Mark Kurlansky describes the global event as 'the year that rocked the world', while Gerard DeGroot doubts that the dominant narrative about 1968 reflects the historical truth),[5] but many observers argue that the proper place of the 'ideas of 68' is now in the history books, preferably within a broader post-war context. Many younger historians in different countries have set out to challenge the 'myth' of 1968 propagated by former activists by subjecting this period to serious historical scrutiny. Some of the most innovative recent research has sought to open up 1968 to new historical assessment, accessing new archives and sources and situating the events within a broader chronological context or *longue durée*. Thus, recent comparative studies use a wide historical lens, taking 1968 as a symbol for a far larger moment in time. For Arthur Marwick, in *The Sixties*, this period saw its first stirrings in 1958, accelerating during the period from 1964 to 1969, before concluding in 1974, whereas for Gerd-Rainer Horn in *The Spirit of '68*, the student movement stretched across the two decades between 1956 and 1976.[6] Other comparative studies have used innovative historical methods in their quest to locate the origins and consequences of the 1968 years. For instance, Ronald Fraser's classic

4   See for instance the programmatically titled studies David Farber, *The Sixties. From Memory to History* (Chapel Hill / London: University of Carolina Press, 1994); and Ingrid Gilcher-Holthey (ed.), *1968 vom Ereignis zum Gegenstand der Geschichtswissenschaft* (Göttingen: Vandenhoeck & Ruprecht, 1998).

5   Mark Kurlansky, *1968. The Year that Rocked the World* (London: Jonathan Cape, 2004); Gerard DeGroot, *1968 Unplugged* (London: Macmillan, 2008).

6   Arthur Marwick, *The Sixties: Cultural Revolution in Britain, France, Italy, and the United States* (Oxford: Oxford University Press, 1998) and Gerd-Rainer Horn, *The Spirit of '68. Rebellion in Western Europe and North America, 1956–1976* (Oxford: Oxford University Press, 2007). In France, new historical research on 1968 includes Michelle Zancarini-Fournel, Geneviève Dreyfus-Armand, Robert Frank and Marie-Françoise Lévy (eds), *Les années 68. Le temps de la contestation* (Brussels: Editions Complexe, 2000). See also the recent collaborative volume by French historians, Philippe Artières and Michelle Zancarini-Fournel (eds), *68 Une histoire collective [1962–1981]* (Paris: La Découverte, 2008).

study of the student movement in six different countries drew on 230 interviews with former participants in order to produce an international oral history of the period.[7]

Other forces have sought to historicise 1968, not in the interests of objective academic research, but as an exercise in a much more contemporary cause, that of vested political interests. In political debates across the world, '1968' is often treated as finished history, as a closed chapter in the trajectory of post-war societies. Here, it has often been a question of consigning 1968 to the past, of severing its links with the present and of stemming any repercussions for the future. In Germany, this happened in 2005 when the red-green coalition government of Gerhard Schröder and Joschka Fischer imploded, thus ending the German 68ers' 'long march through the institutions'. In France, Nicolas Sarkozy described the era and its protagonists as a spent force during his election campaign in 2007 and urged the French people to close the chapter on the 'events'. In the United States the sixties were officially over when Hillary Clinton lost the race for the nomination of the Democratic Party, thus ending the dominance of the baby-boomer generation.[8] No matter whether '1968' is repressed, reevaluated, reintegrated or redeemed, it is now seen by the political majority in most countries as safely in the past and as no longer contagious.

At the same time, '1968' is still very much part of our recent past. It is the cherished or reviled object of memory, hotly contested by people who have living memories of or a vested interest in the era. Some feel that its utopian promise has not been fulfilled, while others believe that one must get rid of the utopian ideas to return to moral certainties that existed before. Recent debates have contributed to a 'memorialisation' of 1968 which

7 Ronald Fraser et al. *1968. A Student Generation in Revolt* (London: Chatto & Windus, 1988). Other comparative histories of 1968 include Carole Fink, Philipp Gassert and Detlef Junker (eds), *1968: The World Transformed* (Washington: Cambridge University Press, 1998); Martin Klimke and Joachim Scharloth (eds), *1968 in Europe. A History of Protest and Activism, 1956–1977* (Basingstoke: Palgrave Macmillan, 2008) and Jeremy Suri, *Power and Protest: Global Revolution and the Rise of Détente* (Cambridge, MA: Harvard University Press, 2003).

8 Joe Queenan, *Balsamic Dreams* (New York: Picador 2001), 11.

places precedence on the lived experience of these events, through a vast plethora of personal testimonies, autobiographies and partisan accounts. Former activists may wish to re-live their days of glory or atone for what they now perceive as the sins of their youth. In any event, '1968' is alive in many people's memory, though these memories differ widely. '1968' has become a site for what Anne Fuchs, Mary Cosgrove and Georg Grote have defined as *memory contests*, where former activists and observers are often pitted against one another and different interpretations of the movement itself clash: 'Memory contests are highly dynamic public engagements with the past that are triggered by an event that is perceived as a massive disturbance of a community's self-understanding.'[9] Thus, in France, reformed gauchistes such as André Glucksmann and Bernard Kouchner renounced the 'excesses' of their youth, criticised the radicalism of the student movement and threw their support behind Sarkozy's right-wing majority (in Kouchner's case by joining his government as Minister for Foreign Affairs), while former activist Daniel Bensaïd continued to support 1968's radical leftist legacy and remained, until his recent death, a key figure within the Trotskyist left.[10]

Although in Europe former activists in different countries have pitted their own versions of 1968 against those of others, in Mexico, the memories of former student leaders are evoked to challenge state silence and repression in relation to the events of that year. Here 1968 is remembered primarily for the massacre at Tlatelolco Square on 2 October 1968 when troops opened fire on students gathered at a demonstration. In the face of the government's refusal to acknowledge or to accept responsibility for these events, journalists, writers and film-makers have sought to vindicate the memories of the students, to demand truth and justice and to confront state-led repression.[11]

---

9   Anne Fuchs, Mary Cosgrove, Georg Grote (eds), *German Memory Contests. The Quest for Identity in Literature, Film, and Discourse since 1990* (Rochester: Camden House 2006), 2.

10   See Daniel Bensaïd's chapter in this volume.

11   See chapters by Brewster and Fenoglio in this volume.

Such testimonies, whether objectifying and historicising or reviving personal memories, have shaped and reshaped the events to such an extent that many of today's notions of what 1968 was all about have to be seen as constructs of subsequent interpretations. Thus in the European context, Martin Klimke and Joachim Scharloth emphasise the importance of 'myth-making' in our understanding of what 1968 was about: 'in almost all European countries, the actual historical events have been transformed by subsequent narratives illustrating a vast array of nostalgia, condemnation, and myth-making.'[12] Similarly, Kristin Ross has noted that the meaning of 1968 in France has now been overtaken by its subsequent representations or 'afterlives.'[13]

Over the past twenty years, the theme of 'memory' has been the object of a new vogue within the academic field with a vast production of literature across various academic disciplines, including history, cultural studies, literary studies and the social sciences. According to the authors of one recent volume, 'memories, identities and heritage have become the new holy trinity for contemporary academic research.'[14] On the one hand, there are studies which link memory to identity and to the search for forms of tradition, community and belonging in the present day. Here 'memory' concerns a quest to retrieve a shared past that can reaffirm social bonds and restore cultural affinities at a time of rapid change and internationalisation. Thus Pierre Nora's seminal work, *Les Lieux de mémoires* was prompted by a sense of loss at the disappearance of collective repositories of memory and at the decline of a unified model of identity: 'People talk so much about memory because it no longer exists.' As identity has become more fragmented and differentiated, Nora believed it was essential to reconstruct the foundations of Frenchness through a diversity of fragments from the past, such

---

12   Martin Klimke and Joachim Scharloth (eds), *1968 in Europe. A History of Protest and Activism, 1956–1977* (New York: Palgrave Macmillan, 2009), 7.

13   Kristin Ross, *May '68 and its Afterlives* (Chicago: University of Chicago Press, 2002).

14   S. Blowen, M. Demossier and J. Picard (eds), *Recollections of France. Memories, Identities and Heritage in Contemporary France* (New York & Oxford: Berghahn Books, 2000), 1.

as monuments, rituals, customs, physical objects, historic sites: 'The rapid disappearance of our national memory today calls for an inventory of the places in which it has been selectively embodied.'[15]

On the other hand, there are studies that link memory to the legacy of traumatic experiences within national or international history and their impact on social and cultural experience in the present day. Here the theme of memory signifies the individual or collective effort to come to terms with painful experiences from the past and to find a place for them within collective memory. Thus, much of the literature within memory studies has focused on the historical experience of the Second World War and the Holocaust, examining their legacy and significance within the public and private sphere. These events have produced a veritable 'memory industry' in contemporary scholarship which re-interprets, examines and locates the traumas of this period.[16]

Earlier theoretical work that can help to inform our approach to the memory of 1968 is that of the French philosopher and sociologist Maurice Halbwachs who introduced the notion of a 'social framework of memory' (*cadre social de la mémoire*). Halbwachs stressed how strongly social processes influence not only an individual's memory but a community's shared memory of the past. The memories we have and the form they take are strongly influenced by the present and by the social context that we inhabit. Memory is constructed in time and space but always by social groups. It is the social group to which an individual belongs that determines what is memorable and what our memory brings to mind in the present: 'In a word, memory is impossible outside the frameworks which men living in society use to fix and locate their memories.'[17] Given that memory is always imbricated in social and historical processes, is a transnational memory

---

15   Pierre Nora (ed.), *Les Lieux de mémoire* vol. 1. (Paris: Gallimard, 1984), 23 and back-cover of the new paperback edition.

16   In the American context, see for instance Peter Novick, *The Holocaust in American Life* (Boston: Houghton Mifflin, 1999) and Norman Finkelstein, *The Holocaust Industry* (London: Verso, 2000).

17   Maurice Halbwachs, *Les Cadres sociaux de la mémoire* (Paris: Albin Michel, 1994), 79.

of 1968 possible? Can a memory of 1968 exist outside the parameters of a nationally defined social context?

2. 1968 and memory studies

1968 has hardly suffered from a lack of attention from scholars over the past forty years, but it is only recently that this has been analysed from the perspective of memory. For instance, a number of recent studies within specific national contexts have set out to reconsider the political, social or cultural significance of 1968 and to examine the way in which it is represented within different spheres of public and private life. These studies are concerned less with the events themselves, with their historical reality, than with the way in which they are framed, narrated and interpreted within different national cultures. Their aim is not to seek the effects of 1968 on subsequent developments, but rather to explore how societies choose to remember 1968 and how they manipulate this memory for political and cultural purposes. In her study of representations of the French May in fiction and film, Margaret Atack refers to a shift from a history to a memory of 1968 and to a growing interest in 'the frame of May as text, and its framing texts, within which it is seen and without which it would be invisible'.[18] Here 1968 becomes a symbolically charged moment that can be imbued with a diverse set of potential meanings, one which is continuously open to interpretation and which has repercussions in the present. We will now turn to look at recent influential studies on the memory of 1968 in the context of France, Italy and Germany respectively.

In her compelling account, *May '68 and its Afterlives*, Kristin Ross inveighs against a dominant public discourse in France, which, in her view, has served only to liquidate, erase and render obscure the history of May

---

18   Margaret Atack, *May 68 in French Fiction and Film. Rethinking Society, Rethinking Representation* (Oxford: Oxford University Press, 1999), 2.

1968. This 'official story' has reduced the greatest general strike in French history to a benign and sympathetic revolt led by 'youth', a non-violent cultural transformation, which has accompanied the transition to today's liberal capitalist society:

> The official story that has been encoded, celebrated publicly in any number of mass media spectacles or commentaries, and handed down to us today, is one of a family or generational drama, stripped of any violence, asperity, or overt political dimensions – a benign transformation of customs and lifestyles that necessarily accompanied France's modernization from an authoritarian bourgeois state to a new liberal, modern financier bourgeoisie.[19]

This official story, constructed by sociologists and penitent ex-student leaders, has, according to Ross, circumscribed the events, reducing them to a particular social group (students), to a specific moment in time (the month of May) and to a given place (the Latin Quarter in Paris). Ross's purpose is therefore to retrieve and reaffirm the profound political and historical significance of the 1968 events in France. She argues that the importance of this period lies in the political possibilities that it opened up – for a brief moment in time, students and workers were able to escape from the usual social categories that bound them to a particular role in society and to rediscover the authentic and dynamic experience of politics and this was about 'a shattering of social identities that allowed politics to take place'.[20] May 1968, Ross suggests, was profoundly political, but this was not about a seizure of power but a radical egalitarianism which broke with existing institutions.

Just as Kristin Ross has challenged the 'official story' of 1968 in France, so Luisa Passerini in Italy has contested a conventional history of 1968, one that in her view ignores the role of personal experience and individual subjectivity. A pioneer in the study of the history of individual subjectivity, Passerini's *Autobiography of a Generation. Italy, 1968* sought to reconstruct a 'collective autobiography' of a post-war generation for whom 1968 signified

---

19   Kristin Ross, op. cit., 5–6.
20   Ibid, 3.

a period of profound political emancipation and a decisive cultural shift. This book combines Passerini's own personal reflections on 1968, the life histories of a generation of activists who took part in student protest in Turin and the author's analysis of this material. Here 'memory' takes the form, not of recordable or objective facts, but of fleeting personal recollections that may drift from the conscious to the unconscious and move across different points in time. Unlike conventional history, this account gives precedence to the complexity, contradictions and ambiguities of individual subjectivity and analyses the relationship between the individual and collective societal change:

> Memory narrates with the vivid tones of actual experience. But what interests me is neither the liveliness of the accounts nor their faithfulness to reality, both of which would make these stories a secondary source for a good social history of Italy after 1945. Rather, what attracts me is memory's insistence on creating history itself, which is much less and perhaps somewhat more than a social history.

Passerini's purpose is to restore 1968 to the present not as an object of history but as a period that profoundly marked the individual lives of an entire post-war generation and forever changed the course of their lives. For her, 1968 was a defining moment in the construction of a collective self, through which the individual sought 'to create him or herself subjectively and to make a unique and inimitable contribution to a shared subjectivity'.[21]

In the German context, the prominent political scientist Wolfgang Kraushaar has also challenged a dominant public discourse on 1968 which, in his view, has romanticised and over-simplified these events. He argues that this public discourse tends to treat 1968 as a foundational myth by contending that West Germany only became a liberal and tolerant society after the rebellion of German students from 1967 to 1969.[22] Kraushaar suggests that the memory of 1968 has become not less but more complex as individual experiences constantly challenge the historical and closed version

---

21   Luisa Passerini, *Autobiography of a Generation. Italy, 1968*, trans. Lisa Erdberg (Middletown, Conn.: Wesleyan University Press, 1996), 60, 23, 68.

22   Wolfgang Kraushaar, *1968 als Mythos, Chiffre und Zäsur* (Hamburg: Hamburger Edition, 2000).

of these events. Every time historicisation tries to 'fix' a moment in time, individual experiences rebel against this 'impertinence', so that it is even more difficult to find a neutral/objective standpoint. [23] However, Kraushaar argues, our views of '1968' are constantly changing anyway, partly because while 68 gave the impetus for change, very little of the change happened in the way it was intended, and partly because every anniversary generates a surge of new interpretations which are dependent on the broader socio-political context.

Expanding on the tension between historicisation and memoriali-sation, Kraushaar touches upon several aspects that further complicate the issue: firstly, the sensationalist/partisan press which drives a wedge between individual and collective memory; and secondly, the attempts to represent '1968' in fiction and film. The latter can be very impressive (see for instance, the re-enactment of the 1967 demonstration in West Berlin in *The Baader-Meinhof Complex*, 2008), but compete with and overlie memories and historical evidence. Kraushaar argues for the precedence of historical facts over memory, given that ex-activists, chroniclers, partici-pants, writers, journalists, and psychologists have created a 'myth of 68' that is difficult to disentangle and looks more like a collage. However, neither those who were present, nor the objective historian can claim a monopoly on the interpretation of the era. In fact, we could argue that it is one of the legacies of 68 that we have learned to question the impartiality of any authority and their motives.

The above studies make a number of important contributions to our understanding of the 'memory' of 1968. Firstly, this memory is highly con-tested – each of the authors, in his or her own way, challenges a prevalent or orthodox discourse on 1968 and seeks to open this up to competing narratives and interpretations. Here, it is not so much a question of con-structing memories of 1968, but rather of contesting established ones and

23   One recent example of this process is the debates surrounding the killing of the German student Benno Ohnesorg who was killed by a policeman in West Berlin on 2 June 1967. This event, more than anything else, was the catalyst for the politi-cisation and radicalisation of West German youth. See 'The gunshot that hoaxed a generation', in: *The Economist*, 28 May 2009.

of challenging the dominant narratives which have held a monopoly over its memory. In the case of 1968, 'memory' is therefore invoked in order to produce alternative representations, dissenting narratives and countervailing experiences of these events. Secondly, each of the authors argues for greater interpretive complexity in our understanding of 1968. Memory needs to negotiate the difficult terrain between personal experience and objective history, between the dominant narratives of past events and what are often 'silent' voices. Whilst it is impossible to reconstruct 'the thing as it was', each of the authors calls for a pluralist and diversified interpretation of 1968 that incorporates different methodological approaches and divergent personal experiences.

Nonetheless, the memory of 1968 in each of these studies is restricted to the national cultural experience and is severed from its wider international context. By delineating and reinterpreting the historical experience of 1968, these authors seek to arrive at a closer understanding of the nature of a given national culture, of its limitations and future possibilities. The memory of 1968 is therefore seen to reflect processes of post-war historical change and modernisation or to mirror the political and intellectual preoccupations of a specific culture. This memory is often mobilised in the service of a broader quest to redefine national historical experience or to locate the threads of a common national identity. Thus, in Germany, 1968 is remembered and understood in relation to the earlier historical experience of the Nazi regime, whereas in France, many see May '68 as a unique and quintessentially French experience.[24] Yet the 1968 events were themselves profoundly international, transcending any given national context and interacting with other movements throughout the world. A whole set of recent studies attest to the international character of 1968, to the way in which the events in one country were inseparable in their logic and development from events occurring elsewhere. Indeed this protest movement 'transcended national borders in its attempt to realize an alternative society

24   See chapters by Kraushaar and Gordon in this volume.

and world order.'[25] Given the international dimension of 1968, how can we isolate representations of these events within a specific national context? Why have these events been reinscribed within national boundaries and harnessed towards the interests of national culture alone?

In this volume, our aim is to open up the memory of 1968 to a more diverse international perspective and therefore to help stimulate further comparative research on representations of 1968 across contemporary societies. How is 1968 narrated, framed, interpreted in different countries across the world? To what extent is there a shared collective memory of 1968 and can this memory cross national boundaries? How does the way 1968 is remembered differ in countries such as France, Germany, Italy, USA, Mexico and China? Is a transnational cultural memory of 1968 possible? The volume draws on selected papers from an international conference held at the University of Leeds on 17 and 18 April 2008 that was organ-ised by a group of lecturers within the School of Modern Languages and Cultures at Leeds. As academics working on different national contexts (France, Germany, Italy) and within different disciplines (politics, litera-ture and film) we nonetheless shared a fascination for 1968 and the way in which these events are conceptualised differently in different places. Our aims in organising the conference were twofold. Firstly, to juxtapose and compare representations of 1968 in different national contexts both within and outside Western Europe and secondly, to bring together specialists on 1968 from across a range of different scholarly disciplines (literature, history, film, politics, cultural studies). In producing an edited volume of selected papers, it is not our intention to define an 'international memory' of 1968 which in any case would be an impossible task to fulfil. Rather, by juxtaposing representations of 1968 from across a range of national cul-tures, we hope to contribute to a more complex and nuanced memory of 1968, one that provides a more authentic and dynamic representation of the international character of the events themselves.

25   Klimke and Scharloth (eds), op. cit., 1. For recent comparative studies on 1968 that emphasise its transnational dimension, see list of works in footnotes 6 and 7.

3. Processes of remembering

In comparing the way that 1968 is remembered across different national cultures, one clear line of demarcation separates public or official memories of 1968, which are typically constructed or endorsed by established institutions, political leaders or economic elites, and private memories or counter-memories that challenge and subvert this public memory and open it up to countervailing representations of the period. Whilst this line of demarcation masks deeper, more complex divisions and fault lines within each category, it does help elucidate some of the key processes by which 1968 is remembered in different places.

Public memories

State repression

The key means by which 1968 was apprehended by the established order in the aftermath of the events was through systematic repression and counter-offensive measures. In a westernised context, this repression often took the form of police brutality against students, a prohibition of leftist groupings, an eviction of strikers and an arrest of student leaders. These counter-offensives were endorsed by a public discourse that sought to discredit, circumscribe and stifle the events and to reassert a narrative of order, authority and stability. By June 1968, the French government had outlawed all the far-left organisations (*groupuscules*) involved in the movement. In West Germany, a 1972 measure (employment ban) prohibited state employees from belonging to any organisation pursuing 'anti-constitutional aims'. In Italy, the massive bomb blast in Milan in December 1969 which killed 17 people was initially blamed by the government on anarchists, although it was in fact the work of the extreme right.

Yet, it is in countries with non-democratic authoritarian regimes that this repression reached particularly violent extremes. Thus in Mexico, the government's brutal repression of the student movement was followed by a systematic denial of all wrongdoing and the construction of an 'official story' that cast the massacre as an instance of self-defence in the face of student provocation. The case of 1968 in China presents a complex and difficult picture as here 1968 was experienced not as a libertarian student movement, but as a state-led 'cultural revolution' with its own repressive ideology. Remembering 1968 in the immediate aftermath of the Cultural Revolution therefore involved exposing the violence and brutalities of this period, accessing previously hidden archives, and vindicating the 'truth' of what occurred. Whilst official discourse since the late 1970s denounced the movement as a 'national catastrophe', recent debates on the internet have challenged this point of view, rehabilitating the movement and defending or even glorifying the role of Mao Tse Tung.[26] Studies published elsewhere have examined the case of the former communist countries of Eastern Europe and the way in which following brutal state repression, a distorted public memory of the events was constructed. Thus in the case of Romania, Corina Petrescu and Serban Pavelescu note that after 1968 'the repressive apparatus was omnipresent and highly effective' which prevented the rise of a subversive anti-establishment discourse in the 1970s.[27] It is this state repression of 1968 and the official discourse which followed that became the main focus for counter-memories of the period, produced by those who sought to bear witness to the events and reject what they saw as a distortion of its memory.

26   See Lan Yang's chapter in this volume.
27   Corina Petrescu and Serban Pavelescu, 'Romania', in Klimke and Scharloth (eds), op. cit., 204.

Political appropriation

If the memory of 1968 has been systematically repressed by the establishment, it has also been appropriated by that same establishment in order to serve vested political interests. One of the ironies of 1968 is that in countries such as France, Germany and the United States, the right has reinstated 1968 for its own specific ends. This vision of 1968 is of a wholly negative and destructive juncture in the recent past, one associated with moral stagnation and social decline and one that is seen as responsible for the many social ills that beset contemporary societies. 1968 is seen to have triggered a spiral of decline, marking the descent from the moral certainties of the post-war period to a new phase of moral turpitude, permissiveness and social violence. In Germany, the political mainstream, baffled by the student insurrection, launched a campaign of disinformation which cast leftist activists as reincarnated Nazis whose political beliefs were highly suspect if not dangerous. This line of criticism continues to prevail within German debates about 1968 as reflected by the recent book by the former activist and historian Götz Aly in which he too argues that a Nazi worldview lurked behind the students' leftist ideology.[28] In France, Nicolas Sarkozy's notorious pre-election speech of 2007 encapsulated this style of political appropriation by a right-wing establishment: 'May 1968 imposed intellectual and moral relativism. The heirs of May 1968 had imposed the belief that anything goes, that there was no longer any difference between good and evil, between true and false, between the beautiful and the ugly. They tried to make us believe that the pupil was equal to the teacher, that one shouldn't give grades for fear of upsetting the weaker pupils, that all classification was to be avoided.' More unsettling still, behind the legacy of 1968 lurked, according to Sarkozy, the spectre of renewed social disorder, anarchy and chaos which at any moment could burst forth and engulf the French Republic: 'It is interesting how the heirs of those who in May 68 shouted CRS=SS now systematically take the side of thugs, hooligans and

28 Götz Aly, *Unser Kampf. 1968 – ein irritierter Blick zurück* (Frankfurt am Main: Fischer, 2008).

fraudsters against the police'.[29] Here 1968 was invoked as a political metaphor, one that could be used to bolster right-wing support, to discredit
the left and justify appeals for a break with the past. For Sarkozy, it was
necessary to close the chapter on 1968 in order to strengthen a weakened
moral fibre, to reassert collective identity and rebuild the foundations of
the French nation.

Commercialisation

1968 is also present in the public domain as an iconic moment of youth
rebellion that is harnessed towards purely commercial ends. It is indeed
ironic that a movement that challenged consumer values and called into
question the capitalist system itself is now often appropriated for purely
consumerist purposes. In their seminal work, *The New Spirit of Capitalism*,
French sociologists Luc Boltanski and Eve Chiapello argued that during
the 1970s 'the ideas of May 1968' were incorporated into a capitalist system
which sought to challenge existing constraints on the freedom of capital
and private enterprise. Whilst 1968 was a high point of social critique and
leftist opposition, it had now been enlisted in the cause of greater economic
liberalism: 'it was by recuperating some of the oppositional themes articulated during the May events that capitalism was to disarm critique, regain
the initiative, and discover a new dynamism'. This new spirit of capitalism
sought to transform the private firm from an oppressive institution into
a site for personal freedom, autonomy and creativity and this opened the
way for 'a new liberated, and even libertarian way of making profit.'[30]

As Martin Klimke shows in this volume, the commodification of youth
counter-culture has facilitated the rise of a cultural memory of 1968 that
transcends national boundaries. Thus 1968 is evoked as a symbol of youth
culture, idealism and liberation that can be used to sell products as diverse

29   Nicolas Sarkozy. Speech at Bercy, 29 April 2007.
30   Luc Boltanski and Eve Chiapello, *The New Spirit of Capitalism*, trans. Gregory Elliot
      (London and New York, 2007), 168, 201.

as trainers, high fashion and fast cars. Yet, this 'radical chic' is less about sustaining a memory of 1968 than reducing it to a pure image, a hollowed out symbol emptied of its political and historical significance.

Private memories

Personal testimonies

Alongside the official 'public memories' of 1968, we find a stream of counter-memories produced by protagonists, eye-witnesses or ordinary people which may find expression in autobiographies, testimonies, partisan accounts, film or literature. Unlike official memories or objective historical analysis, such memories are often imbued with a sense of moral urgency and legitimacy, as they seek to bear witness to events which, in their view, are misrepresented or distorted in public accounts. Thus in Mexico, the 'unofficial literature' on 1968 has been impelled by a profound sense of injustice in relation to the state's denial and misrepresentation of what occurred. Similarly, in Italy, public 'silence' in relation to 1968 and in relation to those who died during the political violence of this period, has been challenged by those who have built 'martyr monuments' in relation to those who died.

Political battles

Representations of 1968 are a site for 'memory battles' amongst those who, depending on their politics, offer very different narratives of this period. Thus in France, the 2008 anniversary gave way to a fierce 'battle of interpretation' amongst former activists of different political persuasions. On the one hand, former leftist activists who had converted to the right, such as André Glucksmann – a Maoist activist in 1968 who became a 'new philosopher' in the 1970s and who threw his support behind Nicolas

Sarkozy's right-wing government in 2007 – railed against the 'errors' of 1968, its misplaced utopianism, its political extremism, its excessive violence. Meanwhile, Daniel Cohn Bendit, once the public face of the French student movement and now a green MEP, urged the public to 'forget '68' which had lost its political and social significance in the present day.[31] In his view, this movement was driven by archaic political ideas which could no longer provide answers to today's problems. On the other hand, leftist activists and intellectuals such as Daniel Bensaïd and Alain Krivine portrayed 1968 as a moment of revolutionary change which challenged a capitalist regime, opened up new political possibilities and which continued to define the political terrain in the present. Echoing Marxist and neo-Marxist analyses from the period, they argued that 1968 was the proof that revolution was still possible in a Europe experiencing generalised modernisation and prosperity. In this, it paved the way for subsequent protest from the 'big strikes' of 1995, to protest against employment contracts in 2006, to more recent anti-globalisation protest.

Marginal voices

Remembering 1968 also involves giving expression to those who were sidelined or eliminated from the dominant narratives of the period. These may include women, often omitted from male-centred accounts, immigrants who do not fit in with national stereotypes of the student or worker and even ordinary citizens who did not actively take part, but whose lives were irrevocably shaped by the events. In her oral history of the 1968 generation in Italy, Luisa Passerini noted during her interviews with former activists some of these glaring omissions: 'The mother goes unmentioned, barely touched on, in these stories, even under the pressure of direct questions.'[32] One set of counter-memories therefore sets out to redress this imbalance, giving voice to the other side of 1968 and shedding a new and alternative

31   Daniel Cohn-Bendit, *Forget 68* (Paris: Editions de l'Aube, 2008).
32   Luisa Passerini, op. cit., 32.

perspective on this period. In Italy, the oral testimony of those on the other side of the barricades – university professors, school teachers, police, lawyers, journalists can shed an interesting light on how ordinary citizens remember 1968. For some of them, 1968 is not remembered as a moment of utopia and idealism, but one of chaos, anarchy and social disorder. In Germany, the experience of those with a dual, transnational identity, who are positioned both inside and outside a national culture, namely Turkish-German writers, challenges dominant narratives of the nation-state and its reconstruction of the past and opens this up to a distinctly transcultural perspective.[33]

Fictional imaginaries

1968 has become a source of inspiration for a new generation of writers and film-makers who have sought to restore this movement and explore its different possibilities in the present. Thus, novels, films, poems, plays and autobiographies have helped to sustain and reconfigure a cultural memory of these events within different countries. Some German writers have revived 1968 as a 'magic moment' of past idealism and youth revolt in relation to which they now experience a palpable sense of nostalgia and loss. Recent autobiographical texts have contributed to a cultural memory of 1968 in Germany as a utopian dream cut short by political violence and tragedy. Yet 1968 is not necessarily remembered as a moment of utopian revolt – recent Mexican literature has taken a conservative turn, depicting 1968 within a narrative of failure and emphasising the violence, madness and futility of all revolutionary acts. In recent films such as the German-language *Edukators*, 1968 is represented as a politically charged moment that can provide a source of inspiration for radicalism and dissent in the present day. This representation challenges what appears to be a prevailing

---

33 See chapters by Hilwig and Rinner in this volume.

consumerist pop-culture which has reduced 1968 to a commodified image, a mere product for passive consumption.[34]

Decentring 1968

Other private memories depict how 1968 was experienced in local places outside the dominant centres of student and worker protest. Such accounts often contest the dominant narratives which have confined this to a few urban centres and which tend to reduce the periphery to a provincial echo of national events. In France, Kristin Ross has criticised the tendency to concentrate the French 1968 in space and time, referring to 'a geographical reduction of the sphere of activity to Paris, more specifically to the Latin Quarter'.[35] There is now growing awareness that local experiences can provide not merely a mirror for national events but a deeper or even contradictory experience. Thus the testimonies of political groups in provincial Italy tend to subvert stereotypical images of 1968 and its relationship with the family.[36] Studies published elsewhere have examined how, in certain cases, the provinces acted as a site of resistance to 1968.[37]

The chapters in this volume combine a discussion of the memory of 1968 within different national cultures with an analysis of processes of remembering that cross different national boundaries. Thus, in the first section, 'Memories and Places', the contributors discuss contemporary debates surrounding the memory of 1968 in different countries, analysing the key narratives and representations and the main lines of division and controversy within these debates. Martin Klimke begins by examining the rise of a transcultural memory of 1968 in Europe and the United States. Subsequent chapters by Daniel Gordon, Wolfgang Kraushaar, John Foot, Timothy Brown and Claire Brewster look at contrasting representations of

34   See chapters by Fenoglio and Homewood in this volume.
35   Kristin Ross, op. cit., 8.
36   See chapter by Serenelli in this volume.
37   See articles by Siân Reynolds and Chris Reynolds in the special issue on 1968 *Modern & Contemporary France*, vol. 16, no. 1, May 2008.

1968 in France, Germany, Italy, United States and Mexico respectively. In the second section, 'Personal Testimonies', Daniel Bensaïd, a leading activist during the May 1968 events in France, reflects on their political and social significance in France today. In the third section, 'Marginal Voices', Susanne Rinner looks at representations of 1968 in recent fiction by Turkish-German writers; Stuart Hilwig considers how the 'other side' remembers 1968 in Italy, in other words, ordinary people who were there at the time but did not march; Lan Yang goes on to examine recent debates on the internet in China which have sought to revise and rehabilitate the legacy of Mao Tse Tung's cultural revolution. In the fourth section, 'Fictional Imaginaries', Ingo Cornils examines the representation of 1968 in recent German fiction; Irene Fenoglio considers fictional representations in Mexico, whilst Chris Homewood goes on to consider the German-language film *The Edukators* and its portrayal of 1968. In the final section, 'Decentring 1968', Sofia Serenelli considers how 1968 is remembered by former leftist activists from the provincial town of Macerata in Italy.

In re-evaluating the way 1968 is remembered in this volume, we are negotiating not only with the past but with present circumstances and future possibilities. Luisa Passerini in her classic work, emphasised the importance of reconstructing the memory of 1968 as a way of mapping future directions: 'there is a vein of '68 acknowledged as a worldwide phenomenon that changed and will change the course of our lives, within a process that is not completed and is thus difficult to grasp. Reconstructing it is a way of continuing it and of detecting the next steps.'[38] In producing this volume, we hope to make a small contribution to this process of remembering, a process which is still ongoing and still incomplete.

38   Luisa Passerini, op. cit., 60.

PART I

Memories and Places

MARTIN KLIMKE

Revisiting the Revolution:
1968 in Transnational Cultural Memory

> The sixties that were seedbeds of fanaticism were the sixties of George Wallace as well as Jerry Rubin, police goons as well as the Black Panther party, napalm as well as flag burning. The interesting, genuinely divisive question is which sixties to embrace and which to criticize.[1]
>
> — TODD GITLIN

> So close to and yet so distant from the present, this era cannot be pressed into simple schemata nor invoked in embellished legends and the banal narratives on the epos of longing and imagination. After all, in this history, on the Latin American side, there is a great deal of blood and a great number of dead. Out of respect for them – and for the truth – we must bear witness to and interpret this age in a responsible manner. We must continue to research, rethink, and retell the history of this period, which is still far from having revealed all of its enigmas.[2]
>
> — HUGO VEZZETTI

If there is a date in post-war history that continues to capture the emotions and imaginations of people around the globe, it is '1968'. Given the prevailing attention this year and, in fact, the whole decade, receive in politics, scholarship and public discourse, one can rightfully label it as a past that does not want to go away. As historian Gerard DeGroot argued in a recent

---

1   Todd Gitlin, 'Afterword', in: Stephen Macedo, ed., *Reassessing the Sixties: Debating the Political and Cultural Legacy* (New York: W.W. Norton, 1997), 290.
2   Hugo Vezzetti, 'Argentina: The Signs of "Revolutionary War"', in: Philipp Gassert and Martin Klimke (eds), *1968: Memories and Legacies of a Global Revolt* (Washington, DC: GHI, 2009), 31.

account of the sixties, 'After the decade died, it rose again as religion.'[3]
According to DeGroot, the followers of this cult of memory

> worship martyred gods (Che, Lennon, Kennedy, King, Lumumba) and seek truth
> in the teachings of an assortment of sometimes competing prophets (Malcolm X,
> Leary, Hoffman, Hendrix, Dylan, Dutschke, Muhammad Ali, et al.). Their reliquary
> includes the incense, hash pipes, beads, buttons, tie-dyed shirts, and Day-Glo posters
> still sold at sacred sites in Berkeley, Greenwich Village, Soho, and Amsterdam. Their
> gospel is peppered with stock slogans from the Heavenly Decade: 'All you need is
> love,' 'Make love not war,' 'Power to the people,' 'Turn on, tune in, drop out.'[4]

The downside of this nostalgic ritualism, in the eyes of DeGroot, is that
it poisoned the political landscape for years to come and obstructed any
sober, historical assessment of a time that is by now clouded in myth and
mystery. After the 40th anniversary of '1968,' the time has come to take
stock and test this assumption.

For anyone trying to analyse the global memory of '1968,' the year
2008 was undoubtedly a field day.[5] The number of conferences, books
and lecture series dealing with '1968' that year and the amount of media
attention this 40th anniversary received were without parallel. Especially
in Europe, it is fully justified to talk about a 'publicistic orgy' that swept
the continent's media outlets that year.[6] Everywhere, the memory of '1968'
went far beyond the level of personal anecdote and public acknowledgement, and became a hotly debated political issue.

3   Gerard J. De Groot, *The Sixties Unplugged: A Kaleidoscopic History of a Disorderly
     Decade* (Cambridge, Mass: Harvard University Press, 2008), 449.
4   Ibid.
5   Whereas '1968' is a much more common metaphor for the events of the decade in
     Europe and other places, references to the 'sixties' or the 'baby-boomers' dominate
     in a North American context.
6   Timothy Garton Ash, 'This Tale of Two Revolutions and Two Anniversaries May Yet
     Have A Twist,' in: *The Guardian* (May 8, 2008). One of the most peculiar publica-
     tions is the book 'Mai 68: Le Pavé,' a chronology and image collection of the protests
     of May 1968 in Paris, which bears the shape and form of an actual cobblestone in
     reminiscence of the street fighting during those times. See De Fetjaine, *Mai 68: le
     pavé* (Paris: Editions Fetjaine, 2007).

What this cacophony of sound bites and reflections about the legacy of '1968' demonstrated was that with regard to a global memory of '1968,' we are still in the middle of an ongoing process that continues to consist of a tremendous amount of political implications and open wounds. Although this process has reached different levels from country to country, there is, in addition to our national recollections, also a transnational pool of memories. In fact, icons, images, references, and experiences associated with '1968' have been circulating across national borders ever since this turbulent decade. They have created a loose, but nonetheless potent generational identity as well as a firm imprint in popular culture that transcends national boundaries. Facilitated by the commercialisation of 1960s counter-culture, they have become part of our communicative memory and are now, more than 40 years after they occurred, at the threshold of being passed into a transnational cultural memory.

Transnational locations of memory

The first systematic, cultural studies about the process of remembering and the creation of a collective memory date back to the 1920s and are connected to the names of Maurice Halbwachs and Aby Warburg. The sociologist and philosopher Halbwachs argued that individual acts of remembering were part of a larger system of social frameworks (*cadres sociaux*) that constitutes our memory.[7] This takes place through interactions with other people, through the media, as well as real and imagined visual expressions. Our individual memory is thus embedded in more comprehensive, social structures of remembrance which form a collective memory (*mémoire collective*). This collective memory displays itself in various shapes and is determined by family, class, ethnicity, religion, etc. It is also essential for situating past events in the framework of a present collective and symbolic order, in

7   Maurice Halbwachs, *Les cadres sociaux de la mémoire* (Paris: Alcan, 1925).

which we all participate. For Halbwachs, the significance of memory thus lay in its dependency on present needs and its selective reconstruction of the past with the help of current events and debates.

In contrast to Halbwachs, the art and cultural historian Aby Warburg emphasised specific cultural forms, images and symbols and their recurring presence in processes of collective memory. According to Warburg, emotionally charged symbols are able to transcend a particular time period and develop new strength and energy in a different historical context.[8] For Warburg, culture is thus defined, among other things, as the memory of a specific set of symbols, which establish our pictorial, collective memory, which he also calls social memory. This social memory is in a constant state of transformation and updating and forms a community of memory, which can easily reach across national borders.

Most theories about memory and remembrance that have been developed in recent years are largely based on the works of these two thinkers, which stress the social interaction and its material manifestations in the constitution of collective memory. But as our social infrastructure has changed over the last 50 years, so has our understanding of memory. The diversity, plurality and diffusion of our collective memory (through migration, technological development, globalisation, etc.) have by now seriously undermined the attachment of our memory to the traditional narratives of nation, race or ethnicity. According to the French historian Pierre Nora, this fragmentation of collective memory has resulted in the fact that previously coherent forms of group memory have now been substituted by locations of memory with no particular hierarchical or narrative order: a so-called memorial topology, from which the individual can almost freely select.[9]

8   See also Richard Woodfield, *Art History as Cultural History: Warburg's Projects* (Amsterdam: G+B Arts International, 2001); Philippe-Alain Michaud, *Aby Warburg and the Image in Motion* (New York: Zone Books, 2004); Mark A. Russell, *Between Tradition and Modernity: Aby Warburg and the Public Purposes of Art in Hamburg, 1896–1918* (New York: Berghahn Books, 2007).

9   Pierre Nora. *Realms of Memory: Rethinking the French Past*, 3 vols. (New York: Columbia University Press, 1996–1998).

The transnational history of '1968'

In recent years, historiography has equally experienced a transnational turn.[10] Fostered by public debates about globalisation, the rise of multinational corporations, and an increasingly global marketplace of goods and ideas, academics have begun to incorporate a new perspective on official state interactions as well as people-to-people relationships between different nations.[11] This paradigm shift also affected the dominant narratives of '1968,' which is now increasingly viewed from an international perspective and classified not only as the 'first global revolution' but also as a 'transnational moment of change.'[12] As Giovanni Arrighi, Terence K. Hopkins, and Immanuel Wallerstein put it, 'There have only been two world revolutions. One took place in 1848, the second took place in 1968. Both were historic failures. Both transformed the world.'[13]

Accordingly, several recent studies of the period have focused on the global and transnational aspects of the protest movements of the 1960s.[14]

10   Akira Iriye, 'The Transnational Turn,' in: *Diplomatic History*, Vol. 31, No. 3 (June 2007), 373–376.

11   See for example Sanjeev Khagram and Peggy Levitt (eds), *The Transnational Studies Reader: Intersections and Innovations* (New York: Routledge, 2008); Akira Iriye, and Pierre-Yves Saunier (eds), *The Palgrave Dictionary of Transnational History* (Basingstoke: Palgrave Macmillan, 2009).

12   Wolfgang Kraushaar, 'Die erste globale Rebellion,' in: idem, *1968 als Mythos, Chiffre und Zäsur* (Hamburger Edition: Hamburg, 2000), 19–52; Gerd-Rainer Horn and Padraic Kenney (eds), *Transnational Moments of Change: Europe 1945, 1968, 1989* (Lanham: Rowman & Littlefield, 2004).

13   Giovanni Arrighi, Terence K. Hopkins, and Immanuel Wallerstein, *Antisystemic Movements* (London: Verso, 1989), 97 (quoted after: Gerd-Rainer Horn, *The Spirit of '68: Rebellion in Western Europe and North America, 1956–1976* (Oxford: Oxford University Press, 2007), 238).

14   George Katsiaficas, *The Imagination of the New Left. A Global Analysis of 1968* (Boston: South End Press, 1987), David Caute, *The Year of the Barricades: A Journey through 1968* (New York: Harper & Row, 1988); Ronald Fraser, *1968: A Student Generation in Revolt* (New York: Pantheon, 1988); Carole Fink et al. (eds), *1968: A World Transformed* (New York: Cambridge University Press, 1998); Arthur Marwick, *The*

Stressing shared intellectual sources, cognitive orientations and processes of cultural exchange between activists, theses studies have begun to portray '1968' as part of yet another phase of globalisation that reached a new quality after the Second World War. The powerful economic upswing of many Western countries in the 1950s, the emergence of a broad-based consumer society and new social freedoms, as well as the discovery of youth as an economic factor were just some of the hallmarks of this historical transformation that was deeply shaped by the global competition of the U.S. and the Soviet Union in the Cold War. In Eastern Europe, post-Stalinist liberalisation and the thaw period also allowed for a limited opening of Communism. In the case of Czechoslovakia, for example, it led to a reform effort from above which was put to an end with the invasion of the country in August of 1968 and the establishment of the Brezhnev doctrine.

Despite these national differences, activists during the late 1960s struggled against what they perceived to be a fundamentally unjust political and economical order, both on a domestic and international level. Although most of the organisational engines of the movements '1968' faltered in the course of the 1970s, their participatory impulses survived and manifested

Sixties. Cultural Revolution in Britain, France, Italy and the United States c.1958–c.1974 (Oxford: Oxford University Press, 1998); Gerard J. DeGroot, ed., Student Protest. The Sixties and After (London: Longman, 1998); Wolfgang Kraushaar, 'Die erste globale Rebellion,' in idem, 1968 als Mythos, Chiffre und Zäsur (Hamburg: Hamburger Edition, 2000), 19–52; Geneviève Dreyfus-Armand, et al., Les années 68: Le temps de la contestation (Brussels: Editions complexe, 2001); Jeremi Suri, Power and Protest: Global Revolution and the Rise of Détente (Cambridge: Harvard University Press, 2003); Horn, The Spirit of '68; Jeremi Suri, ed., The Global Revolutions of 1968 (New York: Norton, 2007); Martin Klimke and Joachim Scharloth, ed., 1968 in Europe. A History of Protest and Activism, 1956–1977 (New York: Palgrave Macmillan, 2008); Norbert Frei, 1968: Jugendrevolte und globaler Protest. (München: Deutscher Taschenbuch Verlag, 2008); Jens Kastner und David Mayer, ed., Weltwende 1968?: Ein Jahr aus Globalgeschichtlicher Perspektive (Wien: Mandelbaum, 2008); Karen Dubinsky, et al., ed., New World Coming: The Sixties and the Shaping of Global Consciousness (Toronto: Between the Lines, 2009); Gassert/ Klimke (eds), 1968: Memories and Legacies. See also the forum in American Historical Review on 'The International 1968, Part I & Part II,' in: idem, Volume 114, Number 1 (February 2009), 42–135; idem, Volume 114, Number 2 (April 2009), 329–404.

themselves in new efforts of grassroots democracy and far-reaching changes in mainstream society and culture.[15] At the same time, their more extreme fringes entered a spiral of violent confrontation with the state that led to terrorist networks that equally stretched across national boundaries.[16] In the end, the protest movements of the 1960/70s can thus be seen both as a first response as well as a catalyst for a new wave of primarily technological and cultural globalisation.

1968 in (Trans-)national memory

As diverse as the national characteristics of '1968' are the national memories and narratives of this time period in various countries. In West Germany or France, the metaphorical year 1968 is seen as a watershed year; in the U.S., on the other hand, it signifies 'the year the dream died.'[17] Similar incongruities apply to other countries. Whereas the public memory of 1960s' protest has been almost erased in Belgium, it has been seamlessly 'integrated into the grand narrative of Scandinavian progressivism' in Northern Europe.[18] In some former countries of the Warsaw Pact, the collective memories have even achieved the rank of a stepping stone for the fall of Communism in 1989, for example as a 'turning point for the country's breakthrough to

15   See also Philipp Gassert, 'Narratives of Democratisation: 1968 in Postwar Europe,' in: Klimke/Scharloth, *1968 in Europe*, 307–324.

16   Dorothea Hauser, 'Deutschland, Italien, Japan. Die ehemaligen Achsenmächte und der Terrorismus der 1970er Jahre,' in: Wolfgang Kraushaar, *Die RAF und der linke Terrorismus* (Hamburg: Hamburger Edition, 2006), 1272–1298.

17   Jules Witcover, *The Year the Dream Died: Revisiting 1968 in America* (New York: Warner Books: 1997); Philipp Gassert, 'Kein annus mirabilis: 1968 in den USA,' in: Auslandsinformationen, Number 24, 2008, 7–36.

18   Louis Vos, 'Belgium,' in: Klimke/Scharloth, *1968 in Europe*, 159 f.; Thomas Ekman Jorgensen, 'Scandinavia,' in: ibid, 249.

democracy' in Poland, or as 'an important marker on the way to the revolution of 1989' in East Germany.[19]

In other cases, the associations with '1968' are vastly overshadowed by government repression and civil unrest. Next to the events in Prague, the 'Massacre of Tlaltelolco', the climax of brutal suppression of the student movement and domestic dissent in Mexico when local police forces opened fire on about 6,000 demonstrators at Tlaltelolco Square in Mexico City on October 2, 1968, certainly stands out here. The killings, which took place only a few days before the opening of the Olympic Games in the country, remained legally unresolved for decades and are only now being honored by a museum and memorial installation that tries to avoid any 'obituary character' as well as any 'non-critical triumphalism and fatalistic defeat'. Instead, the commemoration attempts 'to confront its spectators with the peculiar power of memory while retaining the necessary distance from the dullness of predetermined value judgments. Aimed primarily at human nature, including its contradictions, it construes this power of memory as a creative experience.'[20] Memorialisation of '1968' in Mexico thereby tries to come to terms with the past in a way that does justice to the victims and the larger historical narrative the events of the late 1960s are embedded in.

What unites all these phenomena are the frequent changes in meaning the narrative of '1968' has undergone since the actual historical events. Already during that decade supporters and adversaries of the revolt fought about their historical role, contemporary agenda and future impact of their activism. On both sides, this polarisation of the public debate was expressed not only emotionally but through an extraordinary amount of written material. It also gave rise to a collective identity based on political orientation, socio-cultural allegiance and the vaguely defined image of generational cohort. The immediate aftermath of the decade soon brought

---

19   Stefan Garsztecki, 'Poland', in: Klimke/Scharloth, *1968 in Europe*, 179; Timothy Brown, 'East Germany', in: ibid, 194.
20   Sergio Raúl Arroyo, 'Mexico: The Power of Memory', in: Gassert/Klimke (eds), *1968: Memories and Legacies of a Global Revolt*, 51–55.

about an even greater plethora of contradictory interpretations and narratives. Their emergence, however, varied from country to country, depending on the scale and timing of protest activities. The late '1968' in Greece, namely the occupation of the Polytechnic School of Athens from November 14–17, 1973, for example, instantly gained such a foundational status for the country's post-Junta regime that the first new elections were scheduled precisely one year after the event. As historian Kostis Kornetis argues, 'the memorialisation of the Polytechnic was the major legitimizing incident of the democratisation process' in Greece.[21] In the case of Germany, on the other hand, people did not use the shorthand '1968' to denote the protest movements of the 1960s before the 1980s. Instead, the most formative event of the student movement served as the initial reference point. This event did not occur in 1968 but took place on June 2, 1967, when a West German police officer killed the student Benno Ohnesorg from behind with a shot to the head during a demonstration against the visit of the Shah of Persia.

In many cases, the experience of the terrorism of the 1970s and the state's reaction to it reinforced the generational narrative of '1968.' Caught between solidarity and renunciation, many activists felt the need to differentiate their ideas and actions from terrorist acts. As a result, they strove to clarify the original goals of sixties' activism or simply to take a position in an increasingly hostile, political climate of ideological suspicion and dragnet investigations. In countries like West Germany or Italy, the climax of terrorist violence in 1977/78 thus equally paved the way for a fundamental introspection among former activists on the nature of their revolt, its achievements and shortcomings, as well as its legacy.[22]

The actual term '1968' and its mythological charge often only emerged two decades later in the middle of the culture wars about how to interpret the events that shook the respective country in the late 1960s and the first

21   Kostis Kornetis, 'Spain and Greece', in: Klimke/Scharloth, *1968 in Europe*, 263.

22   On this point, see for example Albrecht von Lucke, *68 oder neues Biedermeier. Der Kampf um die Deutungsmacht* (Berlin: Klaus Wagenbach, 2008), 28–34. For a contemporary example see Peter Mosler, *Was wir wollten, was wir wurden: Studentenrevolte, 10 Jahre danach* (Reinbek, Hamburg: Rowohlt, 1977).

half of the 1970s. It gained full metaphorical force at a time when a new generation of peace activists wanted to distance themselves from their predecessors, who were about to celebrate the twentieth anniversary of their revolt. This second wave of anniversaries in the 1980s set the stage for what the German philosopher Friedrich Nietzsche identified as an antiquarian and monumental access to history; in other words, the first major, public clash between the former participants of the protest movements of the 1960s and their adversaries about how to remember '1968.'[23]

An example of the emotional fervor of this debate was the philosopher Allan Bloom, who in his 1987 book *The Closing of the American Mind* compared the politicisation of U.S. students in the 1960s to National Socialist Germany: 'Whether it be Nuremberg or Woodstock, the principle is the same. As Hegel was said to have died in Germany in 1933, Enlightenment in America came close to breathing its last during the sixties.'[24] For Bloom, the New Left and the counterculture were to blame for almost any social and academic problems of his day. His interpretation also set the tone for a whole host of other, mostly conservative, assessments of the decade. In 1994, Speaker of the House Newt Gingrich, for example, even declared that 'Sixties values [...] cripple human beings, weaken cities, make it difficult for us to, in fact, survive as a country.'[25]

Underlying this drastic notion was the assumption that the activists of the 1960/70s polarised domestic politics, damaged the social peace and cohesiveness, and gave rise to selfish individualism and the yoke of identity politics. After the attacks on the World Trade Center and the Pentagon on 11 September 2001, U.S. conservatives did not even hesitate to evoke badly flawed comparisons between events in the 1960s and contemporary terrorism. According to radical-turned-conservative David Horowitz for example,

---

23   For an application of these categories see Edgar Wolfrum, '"1968" in der gegenwärtigen deutschen Geschichtspolitik', in: *Aus Politik und Zeitgeschichte* (B 22–23/2001), 28–36.

24   Allan Bloom, *The Closing of the American Mind* (New York: Simon & Schuster, 1987), 313 f.

25   Quoted in Alexander Bloom, ed., *Long Time Gone: Sixties America Then and Now* (New York: Oxford University Press, 2001), 3.

the memoir of SDS and Weathermen activist Bill Ayers is 'a text that the bombers of the World Trade Center could have packed in their flight bags.' In his view, tenured radicals and leftists 'have been busy at work for the last two decades seeding our educational culture with anti-American poisons that could one day destroy us.'[26] Incidentally, the Republican campaign for the U.S. Presidency in 2008 chose to take up precisely this sentiment. Although John McCain tried to claim in the final presidential debate that he did not care about 'an old washed-up terrorist,' his campaign managers obviously did since they made Barack Obama's alleged 'socialism' and loose political contacts to Bill Ayers from his time in Chicago one of the central themes in the last weeks of his bid for the White House.[27]

On the other hand, prominent representatives of '1968' in various countries such as Daniel Cohn-Bendit, Tom Hayden, Todd Gitlin, or Tariq Ali offered their own take on the events of the decade at the end of the 1980s mainly through autobiographical lenses or historical narratives.[28] Faced with a resurgence of the Cold War through the nuclear rearmament of the early 1980s, a conservative domestic backlash embodied by politicians such as US President Ronald Reagan and British Prime Minister Margaret Thatcher, as well as West German Chancellor Helmut Kohl, and new forms of grassroots activism, their books sought to retrace the cultural awakening, utopian vision and political agenda that was pursued by sixties activists. In

---

26   David Horowitz, 'Allies in War,' *Frontpage Magazine*, September 17, 2001, http:// www.frontpagemag.com/Articles/ReadArticle.asp?ID=1021 (accessed April 2003), quoted after John McMillian, '"You didn't have to be there": Revisiting the New Left Consensus,' in: McMillian Buhle, *The New Left Revisited*, 7; referring to William Ayers, *Fugitive Days: A Memoir* (Boston, MA: Beacon Press, 2001). Interestingly enough, Ayers makes the question of memory a *leitmotiv* in his 'memory book.' See esp. 76–97.

27   See also the post-election response: William Ayers, 'The Real Bill Ayers,' in: *New York Times* (December 5, 2008).

28   Todd Gitlin, *The Sixties: Years of Hope, Days of Rage* (Toronto: Bantam Books, 1987); Tom Hayden, *Reunion: A Memoir* (New York: Random House, 1988); Luisa Passerini, *Autoritratto di gruppo* (Firenze: Giunti, 1988); Tariq Ali, *Street Fighting Years: An Autobiography of the Sixties* (London: Collins, 1987); Daniel Cohn-Bendit, *Wir haben sie so geliebt, die Revolution* (Frankfurt: Athenaeum, 1987).

this, some of them were able to vary from a defiant, almost hagiographic and 'monumentalist' historical narrative (Nietzsche) to a more balanced, cautious soul-searching. Luisa Passerini's *1968: Autobiography of a Generation*, which appeared in the Italian version in 1988, for example, combined her personal diary written during her own historical research during 1983–1987 with interviews and other narrative segments, thus making the fragmentary and experimental nature of her memoir explicit.

Whereas the 1980s were still characterised by a panorama of interpretations that ranged from hostile critique and condemnation to uncritical appraisal and glorification, the narrative of the 1960s changed remarkably after the fall of Communism in 1989. The year '1968' now acquired the character of a caesura in the history of the Cold War from 1945 to 1989; a turning point that defined two periods in the struggle between the two opposing ideological blocs. Coinciding with that was a greater interest in the academic treatment of the 1960s as a subject of historical inquiry. In other words, '1968' began to move from political utilisation and individual recollection to historical reflection and reconstruction in the 1990s.[29] This did not mean that the subject lost anything of its polarizing quality. While there was, for example, agreement that the African-American civil rights struggle and the women's movement had a profound social impact in the U.S. and elsewhere, the legitimacy of the New Left and its effects remained widely contested.[30]

Nonetheless, a general consensus emerged towards a more balanced view. In the case of the U.S., for example, the history of the New Left and

29   See for example: Ingrid Gilcher-Holtey, *1968: vom Ereignis zum Gegenstand der Geschichtswissenschaft* (Goettingen: Vandenhoeck & Ruprecht, 1998); Jürgen Heideking, ed., *The Sixties Revisited: Culture, Society, Politics* (Heidelberg: Winter, 2001). For a review of existing literature see: Philipp Gassert and Martin Klimke, '1968 from Revolt to Research,' in: Gassert/Klimke (eds), *1968: Memories and Legacies of a Global Revolt*, 5–24.

30   The groups that continued to view the sixties' legacy rather critically included former activists who had given the decade a 'second thought,' see for example: Peter Collier and David Horowitz, *Destructive Generation. Second Thoughts About the Sixties* (New York: Summit Books, 1989); idem, ed., *Second Thoughts. Former Radicals Look Back At The Sixties* (New York: Madison Books, 1989).

its interpretation were now often divided into two parts: the first half of the decade with the theoretical formation of the New Left, the campaign for nuclear disarmament, the African-American civil rights struggle, the Free Speech Movement (FSM) and the early opposition against the Vietnam War were seen as a more or less idyllic phase of legitimate political protest. This was then, however, followed by Third World romanticism, revolutionary fervor and by 'a more guilt-driven politics of confrontation, Marxist-Leninist dogmatism, and countercultural indulgence' in the late 1960s and early 1970s.[31] This perspective began to be reflected in more and more works and tended to replace a one-sided emphasis on either a whole-hearted condemnation of the decade or its liberating and visionary elements alone.[32] Symptomatic of these efforts towards periodisation and greater differentiation was a comment by Paul Lyons in 1998, who noted that '[t]here has already been all too much Sixties bashing and apologia. Perhaps it's time to examine this remarkable decade in all of its contradictoriness, valuing its enormous contributions, recognizing the problems it intensified, and placing it within a framework of time and space that continues to see the project of this short twentieth century as the fulfillment of democratic promise.'[33]

---

31 Paul Lyons, *New Left, New Right and the Legacy of the Sixties* (Philadelphia: Temple University Press, 1996); see also Todd Gitlin, *The Sixties. Years of Hope, Days of Rage* (New York: Bantam Books, 1987); David R. Farber, *The Age of Great Dreams. America in the 1960s* (New York: Hill & Wang, 1994); David Steigerwald, *The Sixties and the End of Modern America* (New York: St. Martin's Press, 1995), 121–147.

32 From the booming literature on the Sixties in the U.S. see the excellent bibliography by David Farber and Beth Baily, ed., *The Columbia Guide to America in the 1960s* (New York: Columbia University Press, 2001). See also: David Farber, ed., *The Sixties: From History to Memory* (Chapel Hill: University of North Carolina Press, 1994); Terry H. Anderson, *The Movement and the Sixties. Protest in America from Greensboro to Wounded Knee* (New York: Oxford University Press, 1995); Douglas C. Rossinow, *The Politics of Authenticity: Liberalism, Christianity, and the New Left in America* (New York: Columbia University Press, 1998); John McMillian and Paul Buhle (eds), *The New Left Revisited* (Philadelphia: Temple University Press, 2003).

33 Lyons, *New Left*, 222.

Although not following Lyons' normative implications, post-1990s research on '1968' has benefited from precisely this diversification and courage to complicate previous narratives. Scholars now seek to demystify the decade by subjecting it to increased historical scrutiny and by questioning the central role of '1968' as a caesura in postwar history. Recent research more often stresses the transitory elements of the decade situating it in a *longue durée* by emphasizing the continuities of both dissent and reform in social transformations that stretched from at least the mid-1950s well into the 1970s and affected all parts of society.[34] In addition, the focus has shifted from the main organisations and location of protest activities to a perspective that includes other social actors, regions and countries.[35] Especially the 'establishment' perspective has now become a vital component of sixties' research.[36] Furthermore, the cultural dimension of protest

34 Axel Schildt and Detlef Siegfried, and Karl Christian Lammers, ed., *Dynamische Zeiten: die 60er Jahre in den beiden deutschen Gesellschaften* (Hamburg: Christians, 2000); Alexander Bloom, ed., *Long Time Gone: Sixties America Then and Now* (New York: Oxford University Press, 2001); Van Gosse and Richard R. Moser, ed., *The World the Sixties Made: Politics and Culture in Recent America* (Philadelphia, PA: Temple University Press, 2003); John Campbell McMillian, and Paul Buhle, ed., *The New Left Revisited* (Philadelphia, PA: Temple University Press, 2003).

35 For recent regional studies see: Rusty L. Monhollon, *This is America?: The Sixties in Lawrence, Kansas* (New York: Palgrave, 2002); Mary Ann Wynkoop, *Dissent in the Heartland: The Sixties at Indiana University* (Bloomington: Indiana University Press, 2002); Paul Lyons, *The People of this Generation: The Rise and Fall of the New Left in Philadelphia* (Philadelphia: University of Pennsylvania Press, 2003); 'The Sixties: Glimpses from Latin America and Beyond,' ReVista, Harvard Review of Latin America, Winter 2009; Samantha M.R. Christiansen and Zachary A. Scarlett, ed., *1968 and the Global South* (New York: Berghahn Books, forthcoming).

36 Suri, *Power and Protest*; Sandra Kraft, 'Vom Autoritätskonflikt zur Machtprobe: Die Studentenproteste der 60er Jahre als Herausforderung für das Establishment in Deutschland und den USA,' PhD diss., University of Heidelberg, 2008; Stuart Hilwig, *Italy and 1968: Youthful Unrest and Democratic Culture* (London: Palgrave Macmillan, 2009); Katja Nagel, 'Die Provinz in Bewegung. Studentenunruhen in Heidelberg, 1967–1973' (Heidelberg: Verlag Regionalkultur, 2009); Kathrin Fahlenbrach, Martin Klimke, Joachim Scharloth, Laura Wong, ed., *The 'Establishment' Responds: Power, Politics and Protest Since 1945* (forthcoming).

and the various facets of its mediatisation have come to the forefront and are often combined with a fresh methodological approach that contests the conventional boundaries of cultural, political and gender history.[37]

In sum, a new generation of scholars has successfully initiated a paradigm change in the academic treatment of the '1968,' emancipating themselves from both eyewitness perspectives and traditional narratives by pursuing new venues of inquiry. Research and teaching on the protest movements of the 1960/70s has thus become institutionalised in the academy and continues to attract a growing number of new students from a variety of disciplines. Asserting that 'no decade has had such an enduring grip on politics, culture and consciousness as the 1960s,' a new journal has even been dedicated to it.[38] Considering these developments, it is fair to say that the discourse on '1968,' and in particular its transnational dimension, is booming and its historiographical and memorial march through the institutions of society and higher learning well underway.

The commercialisation of '1968'

From the very beginning, this march and the story of 1960s was, however, inextricably tied to the economic boom that swept through much of the Western world. Combined with the post-war increase in birth rates, this

---

37 See for example Victoria Langland, 'Birth Control Pills and Molotov Cocktails: Reading Sex and Revolution in 1968 Brazil,' in: Gilbert M. Joseph and Daniela Spenser (eds), *In from the Cold: Latin America's New Encounter with the Cold War* (Durham: Duke University Press, 2008), 308–349; Joachim Scharloth, *1968. Eine Kommunikationsgeschichte* (Munich: Fink, forthcoming 2010). For an overview with regard to the German case see Martin Klimke and Joachim Scharloth, ed., *1968 Handbuch zur Kultur- und Mediengeschichte der Studentenbewegung* (Stuttgart: Metzler, 2007).

38 Michael Foley, John McMillian, and Jeremy Varon (eds), *The Sixties: A Journal of History, Politics and Culture* (New York: Routledge Press, since 2008).

eventually led not only to the rapid rise of university enrolment, but also to
the emergence of a consumer culture particularly geared toward the young
generation.[39] The rebellious spirit of the 1950s, embodied by James Dean,
Marlon Brando and musical innovations such as Rock'n'Roll, was soon
absorbed by a cultural industry that sought to maximise profits by cater-
ing to a youthful audience protesting the status quo through a wide range
of artistic expressions. Style, fashion, music, and even publishing quickly
adjusted itself to this new generation of consumers. The commercialisation
of youth culture was therefore a thread that can be followed throughout
the 1960s and was part and parcel of the articulation, and even more so,
the representation of dissent; not only in the West.[40] As historian Victoria
Langland has shown in her analysis of '1968' in Brazil, for example, the
advertising and fashion industry took up public anxieties about female
(student) activists in the late 1960s by incorporating 'sexualized images
of armed and/or persecuted women' on a large scale. These images then
found their way into the mainstream press and substantially shaped the
perception of women in the political arena.[41] Similar processes of 'framing' the story with the help of a specific media coverage geared to both
sensationalise or polarise can also be observed in other countries and are
particularly visible in the treatment of violence with regard to 1960/70s
protest movements.[42]

39   See Arthur Marwick, *The Sixties*, 45–50.
40   The works of Detlef Siegfried have been groundbreaking in this regard: Axel Schildt
     and Detlef Siegfried, 'Youth, Consumption, and Politics in the Age of Radical
     Change,' in: Axel Schildt/Detlef Siegfried (eds), *Between Marx and Coca-Cola.
     Youth Cultures in Changing European Societies, 1960–1980* (Oxford/New York:
     Berghahn Books, 2005), 1–35; Detlef Siegfried, *Time is on my side: Konsum und
     Politik in der westdeutschen Jugendkultur der 6oer Jahre* (Göttingen: Wallstein, 2006).
     See also Stephan Malinowski and Alexander Sedlmaier, '1968' als Katalysator der
     Konsumgesellschaft: Performative Regelverstösse, kommerzielle Adaptionen und ihre
     gegenseitige Durchdringung, in: *Geschichte und Gesellschaft* 32, 2006, 239–267.
41   Victoria Langland, 'Between Bombs and Bombshells: Student and Sexual Politics in
     1968 Brazil,' in: *ReVista, Harvard Review of Latin America*, Winter 2009, 58–61.
42   See Todd Gitlin, *The Whole World Is Watching: Mass Media in the Making & Unmaking
     of the New Left* (Berkeley: University of California Press, 1980); Martin Steinseifer,

The collective memories of '1968' have thus not only been fundamentally shaped by contesting political narratives of this time, but also, more than we usually acknowledge, by the many audio-visual and commercialised representations of sixties' counter-culture that have flooded the global market place ever since. This becomes even more pronounced in the 1970s and 1980s with the broad-based change of individual lifestyles and value systems as a result of the protest movements. Ironically, this commodification of protest not only kept '1968' alive in collective memory in the following decades, but also turned it into a reference point that people could now connect to across national boundaries and political lines.

In 1987, for the first time in a major television advertisement campaign, the U.S. company Nike adopted one of the most popular songs of the late sixties, the Beatles song 'Revolution,' originally released in the summer of 1968. The seeming abuse of the sixties' spirit to sell a pair of sneakers provoked major dissatisfaction among former activists. Even Paul McCartney objected to its usage, arguing that 'Songs like *Revolution* don't mean a pair of sneakers, they mean *Revolution*.' However, Nike was certainly not the only company that sought to increase its profits by tapping into the feeling of rebellion embodied by the sixties counterculture. In addition to the latest commodification of revolutionary chic in fashion through products such as the Prada-Meinhof collection in reference to the West German terrorist group Red Army Faction ('Baader-Meinhof Group'), the car industry in particular has adopted numerous images, slogans and references from the 'sixties' in the last two decades. Two of the most recent examples are the appearances of Dustin Hoffmann in a 2004 Audi commercial featuring an adaptation of a famous episode from the movie *The Graduate* (1967) or Bob Dylan's advertising campaign for Cadillac in 2007.

As these examples illustrate, the so-called 'cultural revolution' has in many countries been at the forefront of the social construction process of a public and collective memory of '1968.' Through its commercialisation, this

_____

'Zwischen Bombenterror und Baader Story. Terrorismus als Medienereignis,' in: Klimke/Scharloth (eds), *1968. Handbuch zur Kultur- und Mediengeschichte*, 285–301; Hilwig, *Italy and 1968*.

cultural dimension has become even more widespread and internationally perpetuated than it was during the historical decade itself. To speak with Warburg, the emotionally charged symbols of '1968' have entered our collective memory and can now be easily re-activated in a different time and place, whether it be for economic purposes or for political goals.

As part of this iconisation, the events of that time have been almost seamlessly integrated into a teleological story of the spread of freedom, of battles won, obstacles overcome, and youthful rebellion pacified. This one-sided and sanitised narrative of '1968' is epitomised by movies such as 'Forrest Gump' (1994), which provide a harmless quaintness with the decade, gently walking us through its most important historical events; a kind of feel-good history 'lite' which refrains from any deeper political commentary and mainly satisfies the need to create a consensual view of the past with a mainstream appeal.[43] At the same time, such representations put forward the idea that, after the turmoil of the sixties, the world has somehow gone back to a traditional, clear-cut order and business. Recent movies, such as the 'La Meglio gioventù' (*The Best of Youth*, 2003) or 'Die fetten Jahre sind vorbei' (*The Edukators*, 2004) try to complicate this narrative while still trying to provide a similarly accessible account of '1968.' And interestingly enough, the protest movements themselves are also entering the world of cartoon history and animation movies.[44]

But as soon as we leave the counter-cultural aspects of the 'sixties' and enter the strictly political sphere, assuming we can make such a distinction, the narratives become far more controversial. For the longest time, the political narratives have been organised along old battle lines between former activists and their opponents and even the recent trends in historiography have done little to change this. Both groups have offered numerous

---

43   For a most recent example in print and as a movie, see Tom Brokaw, *Boom! Voices of the Sixties* (New York: Random House, 2007).

44   See Harvey Pekar, Gary Dumm, and Paul Buhle, *Students for a Democratic Society: A Graphic History* (New York: Hill and Wang, 2008); Chicago 10 (2007), dir. By Brett Morgen; David Farber, 'The Art of Rebellion: Brett Morgen's *Chicago Ten*,' in: *The Sixties* 2 (December 2008), 239–241; Harvey Pekar, Ed Piskor, and Paul Buhle, *The Beats: A Graphic History* (New York: Hill and Wang, 2009).

fictional, non-fictional, biographical, and academic accounts in which they explain, apologise, condemn, and defend the achievements and failures of the decade; in other words, battle about their very own legacy and place in the history books. Regrettably, this coming to terms with their own biography often stands in stark contrast to the more critical and balanced approach to the past, which sixties' activists in particular called for and, thankfully, institutionalised in many academic disciplines. But why was the 40th anniversary of '1968' so important in this process?

According to the Egyptologist Jan Assmann, there are two important categories when looking at the collective memory of a society: the communicative and the cultural memory.[45] The communicative memory deals with the most recent past and is negotiated in daily, social interactions. It is shaped by individual experiences and eye-witnesses or people who experienced a certain time period and have now become the main carrier group of its memories. As a result, the time span of the communicative memory is about 80–100 years. What is important is that after about 40 years a phase of reflection and reconfirmation sets in, in which people begin to negotiate the 'correct' conservation of past events.

In contrast, the cultural memory includes all symbolic forms and signs of the past. By entering the cultural memory, past events become foundational memories; this means they become crucial elements in the process in which a society tries to establish its own identity through a remembrance of the past. This process can be highly ritualised, through particular holidays or events dedicated to the past, or memorials or plaques, or, in a more narrative way, through media coverage, exhibitions and books. In other words, in the cultural memory individual recollections turn into collective long-term memories, which are being safeguarded by a selected group of experts, such as academics, for example. Based on their training and

---

45   Jan Assmann, *Das kulturelle Gedächtnis. Schrift, Erinnerung und politische Identität in frühen Hochkulturen* (München: Beck, 1992), 50–56. For an early application of this paradigm, see 'Gelebt, erinnert – und erforscht? 1968 auf dem Weg vom Kommunikativen zum Kulturellen Gedächtnis', Conference at the University of Heidelberg, July 9–10, 2009, convened by Martin Klimke and Joachim Scharloth.

knowledge, they try to exercise a particular influence on the canonisation of past events by deciding what to include and what to exclude.

With regard to the global memory of '1968,' we are currently at a crossroads, namely precisely at the end of the 40-year threshold where the individual memories are about to enter our long-term collective memories; or, in Assmann's terms, where our societies negotiate which parts of the communicate memory will make it to our cultural memory. In this selection process the counter-cultural dimension of '1968' has become a far less contested terrain due to its commercialisation and the real social changes in individual lifestyles and value systems in subsequent decades. What we are seeing now, both nationally and trans-nationally, is therefore (1) a celebration of the 1960s as a cultural revolution, (2) a renewed but very limited debate about the political legacy of the decade that is, as always, informed by current events (invasion of Iraq, terrorism, election of Barack Obama, etc.), (3) a massive canonisation of the sixties through extremely high biographical, journalistic, and academic attention, (4) a wave of autobiographical introspection, (5) ritualisations of memories of '1968' in various countries, and (6) the first very cautious steps of coming to terms with establishing a narrative of '1968' in countries with formerly repressive regimes, e.g. in Asia, Eastern Europe or South America.

Historians and academics in general are no innocent bystanders in this process and cannot be. Especially the younger generation that was born after or was still very young during the sixties has begun to interfere in the discourse about '1968' to broaden the picture, enable a plurality of even contradictory narratives and follow previously unexplored venues of research.

In doing so, academic and public narratives gradually move away from only looking at the historical events. Scholars have begun to closely examine the politics of memory that ensued in the aftermath of the sixties. As part of this politics of memory, the metaphorical 'sixties' have become an imaginary space with which to identify or from which to separate and distance oneself. As Kristin Ross has shown in her study of the French May, the actual historical events have long been 'overtaken by subsequent representations.' In other words, the 'afterlives' of '1968' have developed a life of their own.[46] The fierce battles about the political legacy of the 'sixties' have even created, as historian Elizabeth Peifer labeled it, 'a discursive commemoration through contestation which kept 1968 alive in political culture.'[47] Taking it a step further, it seems that both the contestation and commercialisation of '1968' fundamentally shaped (and will continue to shape) the public narratives and imaginaries of this time. In the case of the U.S., for example, the presidential election of 2008 and the candidacies of Barack Obama and Hillary Clinton, as well as Sarah Palin, re-energised the debate about the legacies of the metaphorical 'sixties' and sparked a series of reflections and publications about the election's place in the long history of African-American civil rights and Black Power, as well as the women's movements and the state of modern conservatism.[48]

The task of future scholarship on this time period will thus be to try to lay bare the constructs of '1968' and the 'sixties' as imaginary spaces in order to embrace the complexities and contradictions of this decade. To achieve this, scholars need to take into account the plethora of memories and voices from all sides of the political and social spectrum and diversify traditional narratives that are still dominated by the 'Western' experience of the 1960/70s. We still know far too little about the actual events in Asia, Africa, Eastern Europe, Latin America, and the Middle East, as well as their perception and utilisation by activists worldwide to establish a truly global comparative frame.[49] Only after establishing a truly global perspec-

---

46   Kristin Ross, *May '68 and its afterlives* (Chicago, 2002), 1.

47   Elizabeth Peifer, '1968 in German Political Culture, 1967–1993: From Experience to Myth', Doctoral Dissertation, University of North Carolina, Chapel Hill, 1997, 17.

48   See the forum and special issue 'The Sixties and the 2008 Presidential Election', *The Sixties: A Journal of Politics, History and Culture*, Vol. 2, No. 1, June 2009, 49–78; Tom Hayden, *The Long Sixties: From 1960 to Barack Obama* (Boulder, CO: Paradigm Publishers, 2009).

49   The only studies touching this with respect to the national liberation movements of the Third World are: Van Gosse, *Where the Boys Are: Cuba, Cold War America and the Making of a New Left* (London: Verso, 1993); Ingo Juchler, *Die Studentenbewegungen in den Vereinigten Staaten und der Bundesrepublik der sechziger Jahre. Eine Untersuchung hinsichtlich ihrer Beeinflussung durch Befreiungsbewegungen und –theorien aus der Dritten Welt* (Berlin: Duncker & Humblot, 1996); Max Elbaum, *Revolution in*

tive and taking into account, as historian Tina Mai Chen has demanded, the complex relationship between such ideological concepts as the Cold War, modernisation theory and how 'the Third World operated simulta-neously as a political category of radical promise and of Euro-American discipline in the 1960s' can we arrive at a sufficient understanding of the transnational dimension of '1968' and its global traces in our collective memories.[50]

In contrast to DeGroot's characterisation of the sixties' memorial culture as religion quoted at the beginning, I prefer a different metaphor. Since 1980, a theater play has been performed in Berlin entitled 'A Left History.' It chronicles the biographies of three different people who get to know each other as students during the 1960s and whose lives were shaped by the protest events of this decade. The unique feature of this play is that since its first performance, its story (the life of the three protagonists) has been continually enlarged each year and carried further into the present time, thus now including the protagonists' reactions to the war in Iraq, terrorism and the global justice movements. As the play's own descrip-tion states, '[the] story starts in 1966 and ends today,' with each passing year being incorporated into it. Since the play has been performed for the last 28 years, it is, to my knowledge, the best illustration for the location of '1968' in our collective memory, which is constantly being transformed by current events.

Expanding our perspective on '1968' to include a study of its ongoing memory will not only help us escape the traditional battle lines and offer further avenues for future research. Such an approach will help keep alive

the Air: Sixties Radicals turn to Lenin, Mao and Che (New York: Verso, 2002); Cynthia Ann Young, Soul Power: Culture, Radicalism, and the Making of a U.S. Third World Left. Durham: Duke University Press, 2006; Quinn Slobodian, 'Radical Empathy: The Third World and the New Left in 1960s West Germany,' PhD diss., New York University, 2008; Christiansen/Scarlett, ed., 1968 and the Global South, forthcoming.

50 Tina Mai Chen, 'Epilogue: Third World Possibilities and Problematics: Historical Connections and Critical Frameworks,' in: Dubinsky, et al., ed., New World Coming, 425.

the philosophical, artistic, cultural and political richness of the decade as a significant although at times contradictory site of memory, and not allow it to be turned into a site of partisan strife or forgetfulness; no matter whether we consider the legacies of this time period as progress or backlash. This will eventually contribute to a more inclusive transnational cultural memory of this time, not only bringing us closer on our way to contextualise 'the long sixties' in the larger course of a global history of the Cold War and the twentieth century; but also forcing us to constantly re-think the lessons and legacies of '1968' for the present.

DANIEL A. GORDON

Memories of 1968 in France: Reflections on the 40th Anniversary

Perhaps more than any other moment of that eventful year, the May 'events' in Paris have come to stand in the popular imagination as *the* pivotal image of 1968. While there is a certain strand of polemic that seeks to downplay the importance of events in Paris relative to the Prague Spring,[1] within the spectrum of Western radicalism the French events are generally accepted as central. The major gathering in France's historic rival Britain in 2008 to commemorate 1968, for example, took place on the anniversary not of any event in Britain, such as the Grosvenor Square demonstration, but on 10 May, that of the 'Night of the Barricades' in Paris.[2] Similarly, for a certain generation of American academics, their decision to specialise in the study of France was in part conditioned by May '68: though also experiencing the sixties as left-leaning students in their own country, the French events had an indefinably special quality about them, especially in the context of France's earlier revolutionary history.[3]

In France itself, while the international context of 1968 is by no means unacknowledged, there is a certain view of May '68 as a quintessentially French phenomenon, principally resting on the conjuncture of student and

---

1   For example the conversation reported by Kristin Ross in *May '68 And Its Afterlives* (Chicago: University of Chicago Press, 2002), 19; 'Robert Cooper on Ostpolitik', *Prospect*, 146 (May 2008), 39; Eric Chenoweth, 'The true revolutionaries of 1968', *Democratiya*, 13 (Summer 2008).

2   *1968 and All That*, Conway Hall, London, 10 May 2008.

3   This was the case for five of the autobiographical contributors to Laura Lee Downs and Stéphane Gerson (eds), *Why France? American historians reflect on an enduring fascination* (Ithaca: Cornell University Press, 2007): Hermann Lebovics, Lynn Hunt, Steven Kaplan, Edward Berenson and Herrick Chapman.

worker unrest that seriously threatened the existing political order, and that supposedly happened nowhere else.[4] Nevertheless, just what exactly was the significance and meaning of May '68 has been the subject of myriad controversies over the four decades that followed. This chapter aims to give an overview, including for a comparative audience less familiar with the French case, not of the events themselves, but of how they are remembered in retrospect. The 40th anniversary provides the occasion to reflect on how memories of 1968 continue to shape French views of the country's contemporary history. Beginning with an overview of the classic debates about 1968 as expressed in 1978, 1988 and 1998, the bulk of the chapter analyses what was and was not new in the 2008 commemorations, before suggesting some areas which might be opened up further in future.

Memories of 1968 in the public sphere are dominated by the 10-yearly outbreaks of what has been referred to as 'May pride'.[5] 1978, 1988 and to some extent 1998 were dominated by essay-type books, usually by former participants, offering speculative interpretations of the real meaning behind these events, that often closely reproduced the instant interpretations of the time. Such interpretations ranged from a university crisis, a crisis of youth, a crisis of Western society, a general strike and a revolt through to a revolution betrayed. But the dominant idea became that 1968 was not a political phenomenon but a cultural one that unwittingly paved the way for the libertarian capitalist society of the 1980s by removing the archaic and authoritarian features of the old society. Although this cultural interpretation, which sees 1968 as essentially akin to the Anglo-American 'sixties', can be traced back as early as 1970, its most influential exponents were 1978's *Modest Contribution to the Rites and Ceremonies of the 10th Anniversary* by Régis Debray, formerly a comrade in arms of Che Guevara, 1983's *The Era of Emptiness* by Gilles Lipovetsky, and 1985's *68 Thought* by Alain Renaut

4   Isabelle Sommier, 'Mai 68: sous les pavés d'une histoire officielle', *Sociétés Contemporaines*, no. 20 (1994), 72–73.
5   Chris Reynolds, 'Mai 68 à Brest', *Mai 68: Forty Years On* conference, University of London Institute in Paris, 15 May 2008.

and Luc Ferry, later minister of education.[6] Serious empirical research was thin on the ground, with the exception of lovingly prepared family portraits of, and often by, a certain in-crowd who had all known each other in the Latin Quarter circa 1968. The *locus classicus* of this approach was Hervé Hamon and Patrick Rotman's *Generation*. Published in time for the 20th anniversary of the events, *Generation* fitted the mood of the times, as the re-election of François Mitterrand as President in 1988 on a moderate centrist platform far removed from his radical manifesto of 1981 symbolised the emergence of what commentators referred to as the 'Republic of the Centre', bereft of the ideological passions of yesteryear. Mitterrand's was a new establishment within which many of the 'usual suspects' from 1968 had found their niche – as their contemporary Guy Hocquenghem sardonically put it, *Those Who Passed From Mao Collars to the Rotary Club*.[7] A chief faultline in memories of 1968 is thus between those who see it as essentially cultural and those, especially to be found amongst those 68ers still involved in activist politics, who see it as essentially political.

Yet the dominant cultural view of 1968 involved a triple reduction: chronologically to the sole month of May; geographically France was reduced to Paris, and Paris to the Latin Quarter; and socially the diverse participants in the movement were reduced to 'student riots'.[8] Thus dominance of the phrase 'May '68' has served to elide the broader history of what historians have more recently come to understand as a 'long '68' or the '68 years'[9] stretching over a decade or more. Even amongst specialists

6   For guides through these interpretations, see Keith Reader and Khursheed Wadia, *The May 68 Events in France: reproductions and interpretations* (Basingstoke: Macmillan, 1993); Michelle Zancarini-Fournel, *Le Moment 68: une histoire contestée* (Paris: Seuil, 2008).

7   Hervé Hamon and Patrick Rotman, *Génération*, 2 volumes (Paris: Seuil, 1987–1988); Guy Hocquenghem, *Lettre ouverte à ceux qui sont passés du col Mao au Rotary* (Paris: Albin Michel, 1986).

8   Ross, *May 68 and its afterlives*, 8–10; Christophe Voilliot, talk to *Le mai des ouvriers à Nanterre*, Agora Nanterre, 20 May 2008.

9   Geneviève Dreyfus-Armand, Robert Frank, Marie-Françoise Lévy and Michelle Zancarini-Fournel (eds), *Les 'Années 68'. Le temps de la contestation* (Brussels: Complexe, 2000).

on 1968 in other countries, it is conventional to contrast the French May to
the supposedly earlier start and later finish of 1968 in, for example, Italy.[10]
Yet it is difficult to understand May 68 itself without reference to such
prior developments as opposition to the war in Algeria, the emergence of
new left splits away from both Socialist and Communist parties, and the
revitalisation of Marxist thought in France, as well as a radicalisation of
labour conflicts in the immediate pre-May period. Since the 'events' themselves stretched over two months, they should more accurately be described
as May–June 1968 (indeed in some cases they continued into July). And
nor can 1968 be easily separated from the new social movements, far left
parties and considerable agitation inspired by it that flourished into the
mid-1970s and defined important aspects of the political landscape right
up to the left's return to power in 1981. Similarly, the narrative of events
was overwhelmingly concentrated on Paris, and especially its student areas,
to the detriment of the rest of France, and even its own industrial suburbs.
68 veterans in regional cities such as Brest feel that their experiences of a
non-violent, united movement with concrete demands, linking students
and workers, are excluded by the official emphasis on the utopian 'student
'68' of Paris.[11] Finally the Parisian events were seen very much through the
eyes of the students, eliding the way the student unrest of early May sparked
a much wider social crisis. Emphasis was made on the essential failure of
the ephemeral dream of student-worker unity. The idea that there was no
real meeting between students and workers was often expressed with reference to the symbolic closing of the gates by trade unions to the students
at the Renault factory at Boulogne-Billancourt on 18 May,[12] preventing
serious exploration of the many other places where such encounters did
take place. Outside the labour movement's own institutions, dominated
by the Communist Party's line on events as a general strike rather than a

10   For example, Toby Abse, 'Italy 1967–1969', talk to *1968 and All That*, Conway Hall,
     London, 10 May 2008.
11   Chris Reynolds, 'Understanding 1968 – the Case of Brest', *Modern and Contemporary
     France*, 16, 2 (May 2008), 209–222.
12   Contemporary television footage suggests that, though differences of opinion cer-
     tainly existed, discussions did take place even on this incident, in nearby cafés.

revolution, the strikes of 1968 were little remembered considering they constituted the largest labour uprising in French history – reflecting both a decline in labour history and of the labour movement itself.

So where does the renewed outpouring of words and images for the 40th anniversary leave the French memory of 68? Has the dominant narrative been reproduced, challenged or surpassed? Commemorating and debating its own past is an activity at which France seems to excel. The sheer quantity of memorialisation of 1968 – the number of books and special issues of magazines published,[13] of debates taking place in the media, in public, in private – in 2008 was remarkable. Even academic specialists on 1968 sometimes claimed half-jokingly to be suffering from '1968 fatigue'. Indeed one magazine columnist, the historian Jacques Julliard, ironically complained that insufficient preparation had thus far been made for the 41st anniversary in 2009.[14] It was noticeable that the theoretically more chronologically significant 50th anniversary of the foundation of the Fifth Republic in May 1958 received rather less attention than the 40th anniversary of 1968 with which it coincided.

Did this show that 1968 is regarded as the real founding moment of contemporary France – that, as the historian Max Gallo, not generally known for his sympathy for 1968, declared to television viewers, 'We are all heirs of 68'? The idea that the 68ers are now the establishment has been long established enough to become an inescapable cliché. On the way to one of many conferences on 1968, strolling past the ornate palazzo-style buildings of the Quai d'Orsay, the French foreign ministry, complete with formal plaques to illustrious predecessors like Aristide Briand, one cannot help noticing the irony that inside it is the 68er Bernard Kouchner. The classic 1978/1988 view that 1968 was about cultural rather than political change was still given prominence in the media in 2008. In January, Danny Cohn-Bendit summed up this view by declaring in the televised debate with Gallo 'We won culturally and socially, but fortunately we lost politically'.

13   Aude Lancelin, 'Trop de pavés pour les 40 ans: liquider le merchandising 68?', *Le Nouvel Observateur*, 8–14 May 2008.

14   Jacques Julliard, 'Mai, la gâteuse', *Le Nouvel Observateur*, 22–28 May 2008.

The same programme used the classic image of the gates at Boulogne-
Billancourt to emphasise the student/worker divide.[15]

Yet if 1968 has an 'official' history, it is, as befits the nature of the events,
a deeply contested one, and one without, in contrast to other similarly controversial areas of twentieth century French history, its formal plaques and
state commemorations. The other side of the coin to the 'official' version is
that there remains a greater sense than in the English-speaking world that
1968 retains a subversive power to energise and enthuse political and social
movements in the present. Among the most frequently cited interventions
in the debate about the memory of 1968 is Kristin Ross' *May '68 And Its
Afterlives* (2002). Ross argues that the memory of '68 was retrospectively
rewritten by former 68ers, such as Kouchner, or the 'New Philosophers' of
the 1970s, so as to expunge its central political messages of anti-capitalism
and anti-imperialism. While specialists both in the English-speaking world
and France, if often welcoming its general thrust as a breath of fresh air,
have criticised Ross on many points of detail,[16] the book has been very
well received by a broad public in France, comparatively unusually for a
work on France by an Anglo-Saxon author. The 2005 French translation
sold very well[17] – perhaps because it tells the still substantial leftist reader-
ship in France, fed up with 1968 being belittled, broadly what it wants to
hear: that 1968 was an important political and social movement, and its
heritage was betrayed by prominent intellectuals among its participants
who subsequently moved to the right. The context of 1968 remembrance
changed after the strike movement of November–December 1995, since

15   *Droit d'inventaire: Mai 68*, broadcast France 3, 22 January 2008. I am grateful to
     Chris Reynolds for supplying me with a copy of this programme.
16   For example, Michael Seidman, *H France Book Reviews*, December 2002, http://
     www3.uakron.edu/hfrance/reviews/seidman2.html, and *The Imaginary Revolution*
     (Oxford: Berghahn, 2004); Chris Warne, 'Bringing Counterculture to France: *Actuel*
     Magazine and the Legacy of May '68', *Modern and Contemporary France*, 15, 3 (August
     2007), 309–324; reviews by Daniel Bensaïd, *Radical Philosophy*, 119 (May–June
     2003), 1–4 and Christelle Dormoy, *Le Mouvement Social* (April–June 2008).
17   Dormoy, op. cit; http://www.amazon.fr/Mai-68-ses-vies-ult%C3%A9rieures/
     dp/2804800202/ref=cm_cr_pr_pb_t states that its sales on Amazon are the sev-
     enth best of any book on the history of the Fifth Republic.

when social movements, questions of inequality and class, and even the far left have returned in significant proportions to the present-day agenda in France for the first time since the '68 years'. It was significant that the French edition of *May '68 And Its Afterlives* was co-published by *Le Monde Diplomatique*, the leftist analysis of international affairs whose growth in the late 1990s was often cited as evidence of the large audience in France for anti-capitalist arguments. The alter-globalisation movement in France, to which *Le Monde Diplomatique* has links, contains many activists who are either veterans of the '68 years' themselves,[18] or would at least identify positively with them. The very popularity of Ross' book suggests that to say there is a caricatured 'official' history of 1968, while containing an important part of the truth, is itself something of a caricature that may not fully do justice to the multiple ways 1968 is remembered.

A walk through the urban landscape of Nantes in May 2008 bore out this contradictory nature of the memorial traces of 1968. On the one hand, clearly the appropriation of 1968 for commercial ends is present in France as elsewhere.[19] The FNAC chain of music and bookshops, for example, used the anniversary to sell not only the weighty tomes of new and old books on '68, but also 68-related comic books, posters and DVDs, and CDs of music first recorded in 1968, and hosted some 25 1968-related author events in its stores nationwide. Customers could take home their purchases in a special *68 Is Still Running* plastic bag made for the occasion. Similarly, a local bookshop also decked out its front window display entirely in 1968 imagery. One expensive clothes shop even took advantage of the merely chronological fact that it had been founded in 1968 to use the slogan *May 68 – May 2008* to sell dresses at 220 euros. But just around the corner, could be seen a poster against education cuts featuring the banner 'Do we need a new May '68?', and elsewhere posters used 1968 clenched fist imagery to invite citizens to a May Day march. This after all was the city whose 1968

18 Eric Agrikiolansky, Olivier Fillieule and Nonna Mayer, *L'Altermondialisme en France: la longue histoire d'une nouvelle cause* (Paris: Flammarion, 2005).

19 Already in June 1968 Atelier Populaire posters were on sale in New York: Martin Adeney, *The Guardian*, 27 June 1968, reproduced in *Le Courrier International*, 7–14 May 2008.

occupied a special place in leftist memories, as the site of the first occupied factory and the 'Nantes Commune' where strikers were held to have
effectively taken over the running of the city. On the one hand the history
of 1968 now appears more respectable and institutionalised, part of the
national and local heritage industries: the Chateau of the Dukes of Britanny
was the incongruous surroundings for an exhibition about 1968, while a
local magazine inevitably celebrated Nantes' role in the events. (Likewise,
one British newspaper invited its readers to download a podcast tour of
1968 Paris).[20] Yet on the other, posters appeared around Nantes using 1968
imagery to make a subversive point in the present. Based on the 1968 poster
Be Young and Shut Up, featuring a silhouette of Charles de Gaulle with
his hand over a youth's mouth to silence him, the new posters replaced
the silhouette of de Gaulle with one of Nicolas Sarkozy, and amended the
slogan to *Be Stupid and Shut Up*.

Lying behind many of these contradictions is the ironic context that the
40th anniversary commemorations were effectively started a year early in
2007 by a man who professes to despise 1968, indeed to wish to 'liquidate'
its heritage, with his successful use of the memory of 1968 to be elected
president. Yet Sarkozy's assault is not new: in part it can be explained in
terms of the trajectory of a generation of politicians who reached adulthood in the immediate aftermath of 1968.[21] More broadly, what both
Serge Audier (emphasising the intellectual field) and myself (emphasising the political field) have independently labelled 'Anti-68 Thought'[22] is

20   *68 Court Toujours*, sales brochure distributed in FNAC; Yannick Guin, *La Commune
      de Nantes* (Paris: Maspero, 1969), was influential on the image of the Nantes '68;
      'Dossier: Mai 68: de la mémoire à l'histoire', *Place Publique. Nantes / St Nazaire. La
      revue urbaine*, 9, May–June 2008; Agnès Poirier, 'Sous le pavé, le Podtour', http://
      commentisfree.guardian.co.uk/agnes_poirier/2008/04/le_podtour_may_68_1.
      html, 12 April 2008.
21   Daniel Gordon, 'Liquidating May 68? Generational Trajectories of the 2007
      Presidential Candidates', *Modern and Contemporary France*, 16, 2 (May 2008),
      143–159.
22   Serge Audier, *La Pensée anti-68, enquête sur les origines d'une restauration intellectuelle*,
      Paris, 2008; Serge Audier 'Le discours anti-68', *Les idées de mai 68, Le Magazine
      Littéraire Hors-série*, 13 (April–May 2008), 92–93; Daniel Gordon, 'Controlling the

a feature of political life in France over the last four decades. A strongly anti-1968 discourse was cultivated, for example, among activists in the Club de l'Horloge (a think-tank credited with paving the way for the rise of the National Front), who opposed their contemporaries' rejection of traditional values.[23] But some would detect a certain ambivalence amidst the outpouring of scorn for '68: as a response to Sarkozy's 'liquidating' speech, André Glucksmann, a former Maoist and New Philosopher, wrote together with his son Raphaël Glucksmann a book entitled *May '68 Explained to Nicolas Sarkozy*, to attempt to reconcile their support for Sarkozy's presidential campaign with their defence of 1968: 'Jog fast, comrade president, the old world is behind you.'[24] And while the more consistently anti-68 camp professes to despise the nostalgic commemorations of 1968, it also likes to engage in nostalgia about its own anti-68 activities of the time. The far right magazine *Le Choc du Mois*, for example, devoted its issue for May 2008 to *May 68 Seen From the Right*, on the one hand denouncing 1968 commemorations as a 'trap for fools', yet also featuring accounts of the student days of prominent National Front politicians such as Bruno Gollnisch and Marie-France Stirbois, and interviews with right and far right activists about their 68. Even those who both reject 68 and were not alive at the time feel compelled to engage in commemorative activities of their own: on 1 May 2008, the student wing of Sarkozy's party marked the anniversary by holding an anti-68 picnic in a park in eastern Paris.[25]

But beyond the debates as to whether 68 was a good or a bad thing, another key fault-line in 1968 memorialisation is between those who see 68

Streets in May 1968', in Jessica Wardhaugh (ed.), *Paris and the Right in the Twentieth Century* (Newcastle: Cambridge Scholars Publishing, 2007), 117–120; Gordon, 'Liquidating May 68?', 144.

23   Mette Zølner, *Re-Imagining the Nation: debates on immigrants, identities and memories* (Brussels: European Interuniversity Press, 2000), 125–128.

24   André and Raphaël Glucksmann, *Mai 68 expliqué à Nicolas Sarkozy*, Paris, 2008, p. 234; interview with the Glucksmanns in *Le Point*, 7 February 2008.

25   'Mai 68 vu de droite', *Le Choc du Mois*, May 2008; 'Pique-nique anti-Mai 68', *Charlie Hebdo*, 30 April 2008.

as dead (as Cohn-Bendit starkly put it, 'Forget 68. 68 is finished!'[26]) and
those who see it as alive. At its most caricatured, the anniversary could seem
like a tussle between those who want to forget 1968 and those who think
it is still 1968. But events to mark the 40th anniversary generally divided
into two sorts: detached academic dissection of 68, to try and understand
it as history, which may be taken to imply it is dead, and political celebration, which often vehemently denies a merely nostalgic function, justifying
itself by stressing 68's ongoing power to effect political and social change.
In the latter camp, as a direct riposte to Sarkozy, a broad coalition of leftist journals, publishers and institutions launched the initiative *May 68
It's Still Only the Beginning*, affirming in phraseology borrowed from the
Communist Manifesto that 'A spectre is haunting the established order: the
spectre of May '68.' Seeeking to rescue the commemoration of '68 from
'exorcisms and funeral orations, first class burials and farewell ceremonies',
the organisers of the initiative sought to celebrate (though not uncritically)
1968 for its continuing power to change the world in the present. Some 27
public meetings, 20 film screenings and four exhibitions were organised
in Paris as part of the initiative (itself only a proportion of the total commemorative activity of the anniversary).[27]

    This tension between dead and living 68s was present from as early
as 1968 itself. The social history journal *Le Mouvement Social* marked the
2008 anniversary by publishing interviews about 1968 with historians
associated with the journal. They recount that while several of them were
participants in the movement themselves, they were also as historians,
busy collecting documents from it for posterity. As Michelle Perrot puts
it, this was having 'one foot in the movement and one foot in memory, in
history'. The negative response of students in 1968 to *Le Mouvement Social*'s
publication of documents from the movement is revealing of some of the
issues involved in trying to treat 68 as past history:

26   Daniel Cohn-Bendit, *Forget 68* (Paris: Editions de l'Aube, 2008), 118.
27   'Mai 68 Ce n'est toujours qu'un début', leaflet, c. April 2008 and website, www.mai-68.
      org, to which were added details of many events outside Paris.

The reaction of students was not necessarily enthusiastic. I remember one Trotskyist militant who told me: 'Really you're a *petite-bourgeoise* continuing her work' ... That rather put a dampener on things! But I told myself that she was undoubtedly right and that I needed to come to terms with my situation and carry on my work. All in all, the students thought we were transforming into memory what was still current, present, living history. They had the feeling that we were burying May 68 by making it an object of history. And some of them were upset by it like from a betrayal.[28]

Similarly to this conflict between a mere 'object of history' and an ongoing 'living history', the shadow of 1968 seems to be omnipresent over subsequent social movements, and can work in both positive and negative ways. Participants in the student movement of 1986 rejected the comparison by asserting their independence from the heritage of 1968 with the slogan '68 is old, 86 is better'. While some hailed the strikes of 1995, and the 2006 movement against changes in employment law, as a new 68, others compared them unfavourably, accusing them of being backward-looking and corporatist in contrast to the utopianism of 1968. Thus participants may feel handicapped by being perpetually judged by the 68ers, by the cynical view that it had all been tried before and failed. Hence if the 30th anniversary in 1998 was not simply a repeat of 1978 and 1988, there were indications that the new movements could never quite live up to the standards of 1968.[29] Also symptomatic of this omnipresence of the shadow of 68, thinkers throughout all varieties of the French left, from at one extreme the unapologetically neo-communist Alain Badiou, to at the other what some view as the crypto-neo-conservative Bernard-Henri Lévy, often con-

28 Michelle Perrot, 'Michelle Perrot: entretien avec Nicolas Hatzfeld, 24 janvier 2008', *Le Mouvement Social*, April–June 2008; Jean-Claude and Michelle Perrot, Madeleine Rebérioux and Jean Maitron (eds), *La Sorbonne par elle-même. Mai–juin 68*, special issue of *Le Mouvement Social*, 64 (July–September 1968).
29 Frank Georgi, 'Jeux d'ombres: Mai, le mouvement social et l'autogestion (1968–2007)', *Vingtième Siècle*, 98 (April–June 2008), 29–41; François Cusset, *Contre-discours de mai: ce qu'embaumeurs et fossoyeurs de 68 ne disent pas à ses héritiers* (Paris: Actes Sud, 2008), 42–44, 53–54, 79.

tinue to define their thought and political interventions with references to 1968.[30]

One classic memorial form is the pre-prepared party line, closely reflecting the controversies of the day. Jean-Pierre Duteil, for example, an anarchist prominent in the 22 March Movement at Nanterre University during the run-up to 1968, was presented at the London *1968 and All That*, in a meeting organised by the Anarchist Federation, as solely remaining true to the ideas of 1968, in contrast to the alleged sellouts of his former 22 March comrade, Danny Cohn-Bendit (though as late as 1988 relations had still been cordial enough for Cohn-Bendit to preface a book by Duteil). Eschewing personal reminiscences, Duteil simply gave a political lecture, insisting that 1968 was not only a historical object, but a living social movement, to whose anti-hierarchical and internationalist core we should return in the present.[31] Nevertheless, there are some signs that the passing of time has made the battle lines on 1968 less polarised. A certain self-criticism and distancing from the rhetoric of the era can be detected even on the far left. Also speaking in London, Alain Krivine, the former leader of the Trotskyist Revolutionary Communist League (LCR), while in some respects presenting a classical Trotskyist analysis, candidly admitted that his language of the time did not appeal to the wider society outside an ultra-leftist milieu: 'Yes, we were revolutionaries, but student revolutionaries, with a student language.' In a point also made in his 2006 autobiography *You'll Grow Out of It*, Krivine says that watching his election broadcasts from 1969, the first of two presidential campaigns, he realises now why he was not successful: people calmly watching television eating their soup were startled to hear someone talk of destroying the bourgeois state.[32]

---

30 Eric Aeschimann, 'Oui, Mai!', *Libération*, 1 February 2008.

31 Jean-Pierre Duteil, 'Demanding the Impossible: the reality of May 1968', talk to *1968 and All That*, Conway Hall, London, 10 May 2008; Jean-Pierre Duteil, *Nanterre 1968, vers le mouvement du 22 mars* (Mauléon: Acratie, 1988).

32 Alain Krivine, answer to question I asked him at *1968 and All That*, Conway Hall, London, 10 May 2008; Alain Krivine, *Ca te passera avec l'âge* (Paris: Flammarion, 2006), 183.

Similarly, while it is conventional to stress the hostility of the French Communist Party and its trade union confederation, the General Confederation of Labour (CGT), to 1968 and especially the student movement, Communist memories today are less categorical on this theme. A 40th anniversary special glossy supplement to the Communist daily *L'Humanité* on the one hand emphasised traditional themes in the Communist memory of 1968 by giving prominence to the experiences of workers, and was accompanied by a free DVD of the film *The CGT in May '68*, made in 1969 as an explicit attempt to rebut attacks from the far left.[33] Yet on the other, there were signs of openness: the supplement contained rather more on student, intellectual and cultural sides of 68 than might be expected; included some self-criticism, notably of leading Communist George Marchais's notorious dismissal of Cohn-Bendit as a 'German anarchist',[34] as well as the admission that *L'Humanité* had refused to print an article by one of its journalists about the student movement at Nanterre; and featured an interview with the historian Xavier Vigna which was critical of the CGT's reading of events. Indeed, the title of the magazine placed the Communists clearly in the '68 is still alive' camp: *May 68, No, It's Not Finished*. An official party supplement to *L'Humanité* made use of what would previously have been regarded as petit-bourgeois adventurist slogans such as 'Be realistic, demand the impossible'.[35] Arguably this can be seen in the context of a rapprochement between the party under the leadership of Marie-George Buffet, whose own first demonstration was in 1968, and those social movements associated with alter-globalisation for whom 1968 is a key reference point.[36]

33   Also included was the documentary *Ce jour-là* (1967), whose depiction of young Communists travelling to an anti-Vietnam War demonstration was perhaps intended to suggest that the far left did not have a monopoly on youth or Vietnam protest.

34   Similarly, Cohn-Bendit, *Forget 68*, 41, reports Georges Séguy and other unnamed Communists as having since admitted to him that this was a mistake.

35   *Mai 68: non, ce n'est pas fini*, *L'Humanité Hors-Série*, April 2008; Cédric Clérin, 'Soyons réalistes, exigeons l'impossible', *Communistes*, supplement to *L'Humanité*, 21 May 2008.

36   Gordon, 'Liquidating May 68?', 146–147.

At the level of popular memory, this tension between an older party line and new openness seems to have made it more acceptable within the Communist milieu to valorise 68. Thus one participant at an eyewitness roundtable co-organised by the CGT's social history institute began by emphasising that because of her working class background 1968 meant little to her, but later on in the discussion recounted how the '68 years' had greatly affected her personally, by the CGT's organisation of coaches for women including her to have abortions abroad at a time when this was illegal in France.[37] So beneath the 'official' memory, the memory of 1968 could also be seen as diverse and pluralist. Arguably the situation is not unlike that described by Benjamin Stora about memories of the Algerian War: a series of conflicting private memories, held by different interest groups with competing grievances largely speaking to themselves. Symptomatic of this separation of memories were commemorations in the Paris suburb of Nanterre, triply resonant in recent French history as the university where May '68 began, a classic workers' 'red suburb' and the former site of the largest immigrant shantytown in France. The event, taking place in a municipal cultural centre typical of the historically Communist suburbs, was clearly aimed at the second of these Nanterres: to remember the May of Nanterre the town, rather than Nanterre, the university. Complaints were made about the under-representation in media commemoration of the workers' May (some 50 workplaces in the town had been on strike), and the lack of sites of memory to it. Few members of Nanterre's substantial North African community were present (which was attributed to another meeting taking place the same evening), as were few students. Judging by the age of participants, the meeting's intended aim[38] of transmitting memories to the children and grandchildren of participants did not seem to have met with great success. Yet there were also some signs of a dialogue. While some speakers presented a standard Communist line, an excerpt was also shown from the far-left film *Citroën-Nanterre*, including sharp criticism of

37   Concluding roundtable of *Mai 68: Forty Years On*, Canal 93, Bobigny, 17 May 2008.

38   Advertisement for meeting, *netx.u-paris10.fr/actuelmarx/mai_ouvrier.rtf*

the role of the CGT during the strike at the car factory in Nanterre. The reaction of the audience to such moments was laughter rather than anger, and one Citroën veteran recounted in light-hearted fashion how the hero of the film used to irritate him with his *Little Red Book*. This suggested that the battlelines of yesteryear were no longer felt so sharply. The role of immigrant workers in strikes was acknowledged and discussed in response to questioning. A former student at Nanterre University even dared to ask how the Citroën workers viewed the students.[39]

So perhaps the separate memories are at last engaged in a dialogue. The editors of a special issue of the journal *Esprit* suggested that the 40th anniversary was moving away from the tired self-congratulatory commemorations of former participants, that had dominated since 1988, in favour of a more nuanced, distanced view: 'In a word, we can no longer play an imaginary civil war about May 68. Which amounts to saying that from now on May '68 is part of history.'[40] Serious research has at last been conducted in France on previously marginal areas such as the peasantry,[41] the regions[42] and immigrant workers,[43] while more familiar areas such as the far left *groupuscules*,[44] intellectuals,[45] and industrial unrest[46] have been studied in a properly critical and historical light. The collaboration of some 61 historians on *68: A Collective History [1962–1981]* may prove to be a

39   *Le mai des ouvriers à Nanterre*, Agora Nanterre, 20 May 2008.
40   Marc-Olivier Padis, 'Introduction. 68, au-delà des générations', *Esprit*, May 2008.
41   Jean-Philippe Martin, *Histoire de la nouvelle gauche paysanne* (Paris: La Découverte, 2005).
42   *Mai 68: Forty Years On* featured a panel of four papers on this theme.
43   'Immigration et luttes sociales: filiations et ruptures (1968–2003)', special issue of *Migrance*, 25 (3rd quarter 2005); Ahmed Boubeker and Abdellali Hajjat (eds), *Immigration en luttes. Des travailleurs indigènes aux héritiers de l'immigration post-coloniale* (Paris: Editions Amsterdam, 2008).
44   Jean-Paul Salles, *La Ligue communiste révolutionnaire (1968–1981). Instrument du Grand Soir ou lieu d'apprentissage?* (Rennes: Presses Universitaires de Rennes, 2005).
45   Bernard Brillant, *Les clercs de 68* (Paris: Presses Universitaires de France, 2003).
46   Xavier Vigna, *L'insubordination ouvrière dans les années 68* (Rennes: Presses Universitaires de Rennes), 2007.

landmark in this respect, uniting a variety of generations and intellectual approaches to take a view of the '68 years' that is both broad and long, stretching right from the end of the Algerian War in 1962 to the election of Mitterrand in 1981. Symptomatic of the aim to give a more rounded view was the inclusion in the book of previously unpublished amateur photographs of the '68 years' taken by readers of *L'Humanité*, in place of the usual hackeneyed images.[47]

Despite these advances in historiography, many feel the 2008 media version of 1968 is still too centred on Parisian elites. While some previously marginalised areas, such as the exclusion of women by male activists in 1968, did receive some treatment,[48] other aspects remain marginal. Even the general strike actually became less prominent in school textbooks between 1998 and 2004.[49] There was still an overemphasis on Paris, though France's national audiovisual archives attempted to remedy this by producing a DVD of 1968 television images featuring much regional material.[50] This marginalisation of memory is also experienced from the socio-economically disadvantaged suburbs of the capital itself. From the Seine-Saint-Denis, the northern suburbs that have become synonymous with suburban deprivation, the CGT's social history institute complained that television coverage was too student and Cohn-Bendit-centred. Similarly, Farid Mebarki and Erwan Ruty complained that the suburban uprisings of autumn 2005 are not given parity of memorial treatment with 1968, and the connections between the two unexplored, suggesting that suburban activists should have had the opportunity to debate with 68ers on television about the similarities between the two movements. It took a foreign institution to attempt to link the two: the University of London Institute in Paris symbolically moved for the final day of its 40th anniversary conference from its build-

---

47   *68 Une histoire collective [1962–1981]*, eds Philippe Artières and Michelle Zancarini-Fournel (Paris: La Découverte, 2008).

48   The *Droit d'inventaire* programme featured a film entitled *Mai 68, interdit aux femmes?*.

49   Zancarini-Fournel, *Le moment 68*, 91–94.

50   *Mai 68: les images de la télévision*, 2008.

ing in the very bourgeois 7th arrondissement of Paris to an arts centre in Bobigny, capital of the Seine-Saint-Denis.[51]

Connected to this, there is still a certain francocentricity to the 2008 memory of 1968. While more detailed accounts now widely acknowledge the international nature of 1968,[52] the headline debate about 68 could be characterised as one of the 'Franco-French wars' that have raged over conflicting areas of national memory. In general, concentration on international aspects of '68 is greatest when the memorial venue is the most marginal. The only public memorial event specifically dedicated to the immigrant experience of 1968 in France took place in a squat in eastern Paris and was attended by only 12 people.[53] The CEDETIM,[54] a centre of research and activism on international issues that is one of the few surviving institutions from the '68 years', hosted an engaging debate about international aspects of 1968, attempting to deflate any French self-satisfaction by featuring in one afternoon an Italian ultra-leftist exiled in France, a Czech social democratic former foreign minister and a former leader of the Tunisian League of the Rights of Man, as well as speakers from China, Congo and both North and South America, but it was sparsely attended.[55] As part of a season of films on 1968, one Latin Quarter cinema hosted a film makers' collective showing a triple bill of their films that opened with *Berlin 68*, made on the February 1968 international anti-Vietnam War demonstration in Berlin.

---

51   Alain Lepert, 'Mai 68 caricaturé', *Généraction: IHS 93*, 8 (May 2008), 3; Farid Mebarki and Erwan Ruty, 'Banlieues: Mai 68–Novembre 2005, l'impossible filiation', http://www.rue89.com/2008/06/12/banlieues-mai-68-novembre-2005-l-impossible-filia-tion, 12 June 2008; *Mai 68: Forty Years On* conference plus *Happy Together* musical performance, Canal 93, Bobigny, 17 May 2008.

52   See for example, 'Que reste-t-il de 68?', supplement to *Courrier International*, 20 December 2007 – 1 January 2008; while some 28 of the contributions to *68 Une histoire collective* relate to events outside metropolitan France.

53   *Français-immigrés, même patron, même combat*, La Petite Rockette, Paris, 22 May 2008.

54   At various points in its history, CEDETIM has been called the Centre d'études sur les problèmes du tiers-monde, the Centre socialiste d'études sur les problèmes du tiers-monde and the Centre d'études anti-imperialistes.

55   *1968 dans le monde*, CERI-Sciences-Po, Paris, 14 May 2008.

Discussion emphasised Franco-German exchanges between 1965 and 68, as well as a strike by Moroccan workers at a French factory (Pennaroya) in 1972. However there were no more than 30 people present, and it was clear from the debate afterwards that most were either veterans of the movement or younger 68-o-philes well versed in factual details, rather than a broader public.[56] If the influence of the German movement on France is well known, acknowledgement is starting to be made of how activists crossed not only the Rhine but also the Mediterranean:[57] the student movement in Tunisia, for example, had many links with France.[58] International movement is an element to consider in understanding the lives of many of the French 68ers themselves: Benny Lévy, for example, the leading figure of the Maoist Proletarian Left, was born in Cairo and died in Jerusalem.

In future, a generational reading of 1968 will also have to take account of the perspective of the children of the 68ers. The Swiss director Alain Tanner's humorous cinematic exploration of the various strands of activity carried out by 68ers as the movement declined in the mid-1970s culminates with the image of a child of militant parents, a little boy in dungarees: in the words of the title, *Jonah, Who Will Be 25 in the Year 2000*.[59] So how have Jonah's contemporaries assumed their heritage as heirs of 68? Attitudes might range from an unproblematic celebration of parents' past – Cohn-Bendit's son placed on his father's mobile phone the famous photo of him eyeball-to-eyeball with a policeman, while the filmmaker Phillippe Garrel's actor son Louis starred in the film *Regular Lovers*, as, in effect, his own father in 1968[60] – to rejection. The situation is complicated by the fact

56   *Berlin 68, Comité d'action 13e* and *Reprise*, shown by Arc Collective at Cinéma Grand Action Rue des Ecoles, Paris, 18 May 2008.

57   One weakness in Gerd Rainer-Horn's otherwise promising thesis of a 'Mediterranean New Left' is that within it he only includes movements on the northern shores of the Mediterranean. Gerd Rainer-Horn, *The Spirit of 68: rebellion in Western Europe and North America, 1956–1976* (Oxford: Oxford University Press, 2007), 148–152.

58   Sophie Bessis, 'Perspectives: l'effervesence tunisienne des années 1960', in *68 Une histoire collective*, eds Artières and Zancarini-Fournel, 120–124.

59   *Jonas, qui aura 25 ans dans l'an 2000* (1976), shown at Institut Français, London, 10 May 2008.

60   Cohn-Bendit, *Forget 68*, 19; *Les amants reguliers* (2005).

that later generations might embrace the younger selves of the 68ers, the 'real', exhilarating experience of 68, while denouncing what is seen as their narcissistic self-obsession today, as in François Cusset's lively anniversary polemic *Counter-Discourse of May*. In less polemical tone, one of the most interesting books to emerge from the 40th anniversary was *The Day When My Father Went Silent* by Virginie Linhart, the daughter of the leading Maoist Robert Linhart. Linhart senior, himself the author of an oft-cited memoir about his days on the production line at Citroën, subsequently suffered a breakdown and refuses to talk about his past. *The Day When My Father Went Silent* recounts his daughter's attempts to understand why, a quest that led Linhart to interview the children of many other leading 68ers, discussing such issues as a sense of feeling neglected in favour of their parents' political activities, that led them to an ambivalence to the heritage of 1968 which has nevertheless shaped many of their values today. An accompanying documentary, *68, My Parents and Me* was shown on French television in May 2008.[61]

This difficult transmission of the heritage of 1968 is also illustrated in the film *Code 68*, depicting a twenty-first century young woman's frustrated attempts to make a historical documentary about May '68. At one point Anne, the central protagonist, expresses her exasperation at the continuing control of the memory of 1968 by its participants, exclaiming '68 is a little mafia of forty people'.[62] Difficulties also take place in political families as well as biological ones. Even between those who share an ideology, there is a generational experience missing. Thus in the reflection of the older Alain Krivine on his younger self's television broadcasts, there is also a second dialogue, between generations, as he was comparing himself to the much more successful use of the media today by his successor Olivier Besancenot, the LCR's presidential candidate in 2002 and 2007. Daniel Bensaïd, another historic figure in the LCR, freely acknowledged this generation gap between

---

61   Cusset, *Contre-discours de mai*; Virginie Linhart, *Le jour où mon père s'est tu* (Paris: Seuil, 2008); Robert Linhart, *The Assembly Line*, London, 1981 [1978]; *68, mes parents et moi*, broadcast on Planète, 7 May 2008.
62   *Code 68* (2004).

Besancenot and 68ers like himself, steeped in the labour movement traditions of the mid-twentieth century, who believed themselves to still be in an era opened up by the October Revolution of 1917.[63]

As was noted at the Leeds conference *Memories of 1968*, darker corners of '68, notably the issue of violence and terrorism, remain an area which needs further exploration. As the editors of a new American journal devoted to the history of the sixties, put it, the era included 'traumatic experiences yielding plainly traumatic memories, which are both notoriously fallible and discursively unstable, subject to wild oscillations. Hence the public 'memories' of so many sixties communities – whether veterans of foreign and essentially civil wars or survivors of all kinds of limit experiences – display odd mixes of defensiveness, reaffirmation, disavowal and anguish.'[64] How, then, might such issues be explored in a French context? In general, it seems that violence is played down in French memories of the period, particularly those emphasising soft, cultural change. It has often been claimed, for example, that no one was killed during the events, when in fact at least seven people were, as well as 1798 injured badly enough to require hospital treatment.[65] There seems to be a lapse in memory about many of the deaths. There is no real equivalent to the crafted memorials which remember those killed during the Italian 'years of lead', or the 'battle of numbers' which has raged over the Algerian demonstrators killed in Paris on 17 October 1961.[66] Names such as those of Pierre Beylot and Henri Blanchet, carworkers killed when police stormed the Peugeot fac-

---

63   François Bazin, 'Le point de vue de Daniel Bensaïd', *Le Nouvel Observateur*, 8–14 May 2008, 54–55.

64   Jeremy Varon, Michael S. Foley and John McMillian, 'Time is an ocean: the past and future of the sixties', *The sixties*, 1, 1 (June 2008), 4.

65   Ross, *May '68 and its Afterlives*, 19; Zancarini-Fournel, *Le Moment 68*, 67; Arthur Marwick, *The sixties* (Oxford: Oxford University Press, 1998), p. 617, puts the number of deaths at eight; while by including deaths only loosely attributable to the events, Alain Delale and Gilles Ragache, *La France de 68* (Paris: Seuil, 1978), placed the figure as high as 19.

66   Jim House and Neil McMaster, *Paris 1961: Algerians, State Terror and Memory* (Oxford: Oxford University Press, 2006). Nevertheless, since some historians would date the sixties as beginning as early as 1956, arguably any discussion of violence in the

tory at Sochaux on 11 June, remain largely forgotten today. Slightly better known ones include Gilles Tautin, a 17 year old Maoist schoolboy who was drowned whilst attempting to flee police during fighting around the Renault factory at Flins, to the west of Paris on 10 June, and the policeman René Lacroix, who died in Lyons on 24 May. Lacroix's death, which used to be attributed to a lorry sent careering into police lines by rioters, was the subject of some controversy in the years after 1968: it has recently been established, as was known locally at the time, that Lacroix in fact died in hospital of a heart attack.[67]

On the one hand this may appear paradoxical, since photographs of rioting in the Latin Quarter remain some of the most widely known images of the events. Yet in retrospect violence is often reduced to mere play, symbolism and psychodrama. In cinematic depictions, Bernardo Bertolucci's *The Dreamers* (2003) was typical of the depoliticised, soft 68, revolving around the sex lives of bourgeois youth who do not even attend a demonstration until the closing scene of the film. When Phillippe Garrel announced that he was making a film about '68 as a riposte to Bertolucci,[68] it might have been expected that *Regular Lovers* would be a harder edged, political portrayal. Yet while political conflict, including police brutality, features more prominently in *Regular Lovers* than in *The Dreamers*, this is not saying much: there is a distinctively dreamlike quality to Garrel's barricades scenes, in which the central protagonist actually falls asleep.[69] Indeed, the prime example of May '68 kitsch are replicas of the *pavé* or

---

'1968 years' should include the police killings on 17 October 1961, and at Charonne metro station in February 1962, within it.

67   Nicolas Hatzeld, 'Les morts de Flins et Sochaux: de la grève à la violence politique', in *68 Une histoire collective*, eds Artières and Zancarini-Fornel, 322; Michelle Zancarini-Fournel, 'Jeux d'échelle: local-regional-national', paper to *Mai 68: Forty Years On* conference, University of London Institute in Paris, 15 May 2008; Laurent Burlet, 'Mai 68: mystères autour de la mort du commissaire Lacroix', www.lyoncapitale.fr, 1 May 2008.

68   Interview with Garrel at the Venice Film Festival on DVD of *Les amants reguliers*.

69   Julian Bourg, 'Tempered Nostalgia in Recent French Films on les années 68', paper to *Mai 68: Forty Years On* conference, University of London Institute in Paris, 16 May 2008.

typical Parisian paving stone, as thrown by Latin Quarter demonstrators at the police. As early as June 1968, paving stones already served an apparently trivial memorial function: when arrested with one in his pocket, an American poet claimed it was a souvenir paperweight for his father's secretary. Today one humorous cartoon of stereotypes of French right- and left-wing men depicts a paving stone resting on the bookshelves of a typical middle aged leftist academic with the following caption: 'Even in the most bourgeoisified homes on the left, one always finds a touch of fantasy: "The first paving stone I threw in May '68!"'[70]

Another aspect of the downplaying of violence is the way Maurice Grimaud, Paris Prefect of Police in May 1968, is near-universally celebrated for his role in avoiding the worst. Especially by contrast to his predecessor Maurice Papon, later convicted of complicity in crimes against humanity, and also to international examples of police killings in 1968 such as in the United States and Mexico, Grimaud is held up as the model of a republican official, with the good sense to steer his men away from violent excess. Thus in 2008, Max Gallo attributed the restraint of Grimaud on one side of the barricades and student leaders on the other to 'the national republican tradition' and 'the encrustation in the citizens' soul in France of democratic principles'. This de-emphasis on violence is made easier by the fact that none of the deaths took place in the Latin Quarter itself, with the exception of one young man on 24 May, about whom it is hard to find anything in the historiography: curiously, one of the few people to mention his death is Grimaud himself, who suggests that he was forgotten because he was not a member of any 'extremist group'.[71] The emphasis on Grimaud arguably obscures the more repressive side of state responses, as Grimaud was frequently under pressure from ministers urging a tougher line. When the issue of violence in 68 was explored in 2008, on the tele-

---

70   *Paris-Presse L'Intransigeant*, 16–17 June 1968; *France-Soir*, 16–17 June 1968; Du Peloux, Schmurl and Antilogus, *Quel homme choisir? De gauche ou de droite?* (Paris: Jungle, 2007), 12.

71   Jean-Marc Leclerc, 'Le préfet Grimaud, de la gauche à Mai 68', *Le Figaro*, 16 May 2008; Cohn-Bendit, *Forget 68*, 22–23; Gallo speaking on *Droit d'inventaire: Mai 68*.

vision show *Droit d'inventaire*, it largely took the form of an attempt to rehabilitate the French riot police, the CRS – depicted at the time in the famous slogan as 'CRS-SS' – as the 'real heroes of 68'.[72]

Similarly, the predominant view in France about 1970s terrorism is a rather self-congratulatory emphasis on its avoidance of the violence produced elsewhere, with limited analysis of why this was the case, or acknowledgement of grey areas.[73] As *Paris-Match* put it: 'Sweet France! Apart from a few attacks by Action Directe, our country avoided the terrorist wave which affected Germany, Italy and Japan.' The ultra-left terrorist group Action Directe is easily excluded from the French memory of 1968, perhaps because of a combination of its chronologically late period of activity (1979–1987) and its links to more successful groups elsewhere, which allowed it to be dismissed at the time as a relatively insignificant offshoot of Middle Eastern or 'Euroterrorism'.[74] The total number of deaths attributed to the group was 15, small in comparison to their Italian and West German counterparts. Nevertheless it is hard to explain the genesis of Action Directe without drawing links to certain strands of post-1968 leftism, notably the violent rhetoric of the Proletarian Left:[75] one can therefore see how 68ers would be reluctant to draw such links. Public controversies in France today around post-1968 terrorism more often relate to countries other than France, especially Italy – thereby giving the impression that real, serious violence is something external to France. Since in 2002 the government of Jean-Pierre Raffarin reversed the 1985 'Mitterrand doctrine', whereby those accused by the Italian authorities of involvement in terrorism had effectively

72 Laurent Joffrin, *Mai 68*, Paris, 1998, 26–27 and passim; *CRS, stars de 68*, part of *Droit d'inventaire: Mai 68*.

73 See Sommier, 'Sous les pavés', 70–74.

74 Jean-Pierre Bouyxou and Pierre Delannoy, in *Paris Match*, 3–9 January 2008; for the latter point, Jörg Requate and Phillipp Zessin, 'Comment sortir du "terrorisme"? La violence politique et les conditions de sa disparition en France et en République Fédérale d'Allemagne en comparaison 1970–années 1990', *European Review of History: Revue Européene d'Histoire*, 14, 3 (September 2007), 440.

75 Michael Dartnell, *Action Directe: ultra-left terrorism in France, 1979–1987* (London: Frank Cass, 1995), 47–72.

been granted asylum in France, controversies have ranged over attempts to extradite Italians. Individual cases, notably that of Cesare Battisti in 2004 and Marina Petrella in 2008, have become front-page news. Battisti's case attracted widespread mobilisation in his support from many veterans of the 1968-era far left, the novelist Fred Vargas, and even centre-left politicians such as Bertrand Delanoë and François Hollande. Outrage at the government's behaviour, often expressed in rather consensual, republican terms of the Republic going back on its word, and condemnation of the deficiencies of the Italian legal system, took the place of a more detached examination of the period. And while Nicolas Sarkozy's divorce and remarriage to Carla Bruni was much commented on, including by Danny Cohn-Bendit, as evidence of the president conducting his private life in *soixante-huitard* fashion, it also provided a link to the Italian 'years of lead'. While Bruni's wealthy parents had originally come to France to avoid kidnap by the Red Brigades, her sister Valeria Bruni Tedeschi personally intervened against Petrella's extradition.[76] By comparison, the memory of Action Directe is relatively low-key: while a few posters calling for the release of Action Directe prisoners could be seen in Avignon in spring 2007, a leading figure from the group, Nathalie Ménignon, was released with little controversy in July 2008.[77]

At an academic level there has been some more rigorous discussion of the issue of non-terrorism (or at least low levels of it) in France, though this is still relatively marginal within studies of 1968. Yaïr Auron points to the prominent role of activists of Jewish origin in the French movement, generating a less intense hatred of their parents (and a greater sensitivity to the complexities of the Arab-Israeli conflict) than was evident in Germany. Another factor that could be explored further is how the French ultra-left continued to place the French working class on a pedestal, still semi-

76   http://cesarebattisti.free.fr/archives/archives.html; Franck Johannès, 'En grève de la vie', *Le Monde*, 1 July 2008; Fred Vargas, ed, *La vérité sur Cesare Battisti*, 2004; Dominique Simonot, 'Hollande visite Cesare Battisti à la Santé', *Libération*, 24 February 2004; Cohn-Bendit, *Forget 68*, 43–44; *The Observer*, 27 July 2008.

77   Alain Salles, 'Libération conditionelle pour Nathalie Ménignon', *Le Monde*, 19 July 2008.

trapped as they were within the mythologies of French Communism even as they criticised the party from the left – though this is a contrast that explains the difference with Germany better than the difference with Italy. On the latter, Isabelle Sommier contrasts the fragility of the Italian state to the more secure nature of its French counterpart, thus avoiding the need for severe repression and provocation. Julian Bourg critiques Sommier's argument on the grounds there was real repression in France, in the shape of infringements to the classic freedoms of the press and from arbitrary arrest: over a thousand people were imprisoned for politically motivated offences between 1968 and 1972.[78] While this scarcely equates with the security services conspiring with neofascists to place bombs in the street, as in Italy, it points to a more menacing side to state responses that is under-memorialised in public. As Maurice Rajsfus described at the time of the 30th anniversary, the real element of state repression that continued for years after 1968, with political parties and newspapers banned and censored, activists imprisoned, youth harassed, and foreigners deported, has been somewhat forgotten.[79] On the other side of the barricades, it must be admitted that relatively low level violence against property and against the police was a fairly widespread aspect of political activism. In particular, the use of crash helmets, iron bars, and, on occasion, Molotov cocktails, was characteristic of a certain subculture of young male activist on both far left and far right during the period. In 1984, the French Senate counted more than five thousand incidents of political violence in France over the preceding nine years.[80] Though the majority of these related to regionalist groups rather than extreme right or left, many of the former also bore some relationship to 1968.

78 Yaïr Auron, *Les juifs d'extrême gauche en mai 68* (Paris: Albin Michel, 1998); Dartnell, *Action Directe*, 161; Isabelle Sommier, *La Violence politique et son deuil: l'après-68 en France et en Italie* (Rennes: Presses Universitaires de Rennes, 1998); Julian Bourg, *From Revolution to Ethics; May 1968 and contemporary French thought* (Montreal: McGill-Queens University Press, 2007).

79 Maurice Rajsfus, *Mai 68. Sous les pavés, la répression* (Paris: Cherche Midi, 1998).

80 Dartnell, *Action Directe*, 161.

Is 1968, then, remembered as a revolution without martyrs? This would be an odd situation in a country with a past culture valorising revolutionary violence. It would also contrast with 1968's opponents on the far right: Jean-Marie Le Pen still leads an annual pilgrimage of National Front supporters to the grave of François Duprat, the ideologue credited with being the brains behind the formation of the National Front, who was a key figure in far right student politics in the sixties before being assassinated by a car bomb in 1978.[81] The only two leftist 'martyrs' from the '68 years' whose names would be widely recognised today in France are Pierre Overney and Pierre Goldman. Overney, a young Maoist worker, was shot dead by a security guard outside the gates of the Renault factory at Boulogne-Billancourt on 25 February 1972. Overney's funeral, attended by an astonishing 200,000 people, and its aftershocks, are generally seen as the emblematic endpoint to *68-era leftism*, because this was the crucial stage at which the movement in France teetered on the brink of plunging into terrorism, but held back. The New Popular Resistance (NRP), an offshoot of the Proletarian Left, staged its first and only, half-hearted, act of terrorism, by in revenge kidnapping Renault's deputy head of human resources, and then changed their minds, releasing him unharmed. Traumatised by the experience, and by the failure of the 'popular masses' to join them, both the NRP and its parent organisation disbanded themselves. Many ex-Maoists radically changed direction in the mid-1970s to become anti-totalitarian 'New Philosophers', rejecting the whole leftist inheritance.[82] The Overney affair is thus remembered rather more as part of the narrative of the intellectuals' journey from revolution to reform than for Overney's own life – or for the way that Maoist calls to avenge Overney's death inspired the murder of his killer, Jean-Antoine

---

81   Frédéric Charpier, *Génération Occident*, Paris, 2005; an audio recording and photo-
      graphs of Le Pen's speech at the 30th anniversary in 2008 were placed on YouTube at
      http://www.youtube.com/watch?v=oEWjleOGapo. In it Le Pen hailed Duprat as
      'one of the heroes of our fight' and an '*engagé* student' who 'participated passionately
      in the battles against the leftists in 1968'.
82   Hamon and Rotman, *Génération*, vol 2, 383–421; Fausto Giuduce, *Arabicides* (Paris:
      La Découverte, 1992), 56; Kristin Ross, *Fast Cars, Clean Bodies: decolonization and
      the reordering of French culture* (Cambridge, MA: MIT Press, 1996), 16–19.

Tramoni, by the Armed Nuclei for Popular Autonomy in 1977, which as Michelle Zancarini-Fournel argues, puts a question mark over the thesis of French exceptionalism in relation to violence.[83]

The offbeat activist and adventurer Pierre Goldman became something of an icon for the *soixante-huitard* generation after being wrongly convicted in 1974, and acquitted in 1976, of an armed robbery in 1969. In 1979, Goldman was assassinated in a murder that has never been solved, possibly by a far right group. Though not on the same scale as Overney, some 15,000 people marched to Goldman's funeral at Père Lachaise cemetery. Goldman's 1975 autobiography, *Obscure Memories of a Polish Jew Born in France* is regarded as a classic self-portrait of the 68ers, republished most recently in a pocket edition in 2005. Features about Goldman sometimes appear in magazines, and a documentary about his death was broadcast on French television in 2006.[84] While the ongoing interest in Goldman may partly be attributed to the 'whodunnit' detective mystery nature of both the 1969 hold-up and his assassination, and a certain penchant in parts of 68 culture for the world of the criminal and the outlaw,[85] it also suggests a certain fascination with how the dreams of 68 died a decade on. The difficulty of transition, personally and professionally into 'normal' life after the extraordinary ferment of the '68 period, what Robert Gildea has called the 'tragic dimension to 1968',[86] is a fertile area for future exploration, and not only for the best known leaders.[87] As the sociologist Olivier Fillieule has noted in one of the few forays into this area, how people stop being

83 Michelle Zancarini-Founel, 'Changer le monde et changer sa vie' in Artières and Zancarini-Fournel (eds), *68 Une histoire collective*, 429.
84 *Libération*, 28 September 1979; *Le Monde*, 29 September 1979; Pierre Goldman, *Souvenirs obscurs d'un juif polonais né en France*, Paris, 2005 [1975]; *L'Express*, 20 September 2004, on the 25th anniversary of his death; the website of Goldman's brother, the singer Jean-Jacques Goldman, lists nine books about Pierre Goldman, six of which have been published since his death: http://www.parler-de-sa-vie.net/index2.html; *L'Assassinat de Pierre Goldman*, broadcast France 3, 13 January 2006.
85 Bourg, *From Revolution to Ethics*, 198.
86 Robert Gildea, '1968 in 2008', *History Today*, 58, 5 (May 2008), 25.
87 Nicolas Daum, *Mai 68 raconté par des anonymes* (Paris: Editions Amsterdam, 2008), is a comparatively rare attempt to explore the point of view of rank and file activists.

political activists is under-researched compared to how they start.[88] At one
extreme, this could lead to suicide: one of the most celebrated cinematic
depictions of the 1968 generation is *To Die At Thirty*. The film depicts the
life of Michel Recanti, a prominent activist in the LCR, who threw himself under a train in 1978. As Recanti was in charge of the LCR's *service
d'ordre*, who provided security on demonstrations, the film does hint at
the role of violence during 'our period of militarist deviation', including
the events of 21 June 1973, when Recanti's forces threw Molotov cocktails
at the police in an attempt to disrupt a far right meeting, leading to the
temporary banning of the LCR.[89]

So perhaps funerals do play some part in the way that May 68 has
been remembered (or forgotten). The metaphor of burial has sometimes
been used to describe the retreat by former 68ers from their earlier positions: hence the subtitle of François Cusset's polemic: *What Embalmers
and Gravediggers of 68 Don't Tell Their Inheritors*.[90] Looking for a symbolic
burial of grand ideals, some would, following Louis Althusser, place the
end point as early as the funeral of Overney;[91] others would favour that of
Jean-Paul Sartre, a key fellow-traveller of the Maoists, in 1980.[92] In more
recent years, ageing and death is quietly becoming a more general part of the
memorial landscape of 1968. First, reflection on the era has been generated
by the passing of intellectuals of a generation younger than Sartre, but older
than the 68ers themselves, the in-between generation who are sometimes,
if controversially, put under the category of '68 Thought': Pierre Bourdieu
in 2002, Jacques Derrida in 2004, and Jean Baudrillard and André Gorz in

88   Olivier Fillieule, ed, *Le désengagement militant* (Paris: Editions Belin, 2005).
89   *Mourir à trente ans* (1978).
90   Cusset, *Contre-discours de mai*.
91   Louis Althusser, *The Future Lasts a Long Time* (London: Chatto and Windus, 1994
     [1992]), 232; David Macey, *The Lives of Michel Foucault* (London: Hutchinson, 1993),
     315.
92   Nick Hewlett, *Modern French Politics: analysing conflict and consensus since 1945*
     (Cambridge: Polity, 1998), 175.

2007.[93] And while not long ago the obituary columns were usually filled by people who reached adulthood by the time of the Second World War, it is no longer uncommon to find a baby-boomer in them. When noted 68 figures pass away, such as Benny Lévy in 2003 or Daniel Bensaïd in 2010, they are given extensive memorial treatment in the media.[94] Indeed, it may be speculated that one (largely unspoken) reason for the prominence of the 40th anniversary is that 68ers fear they will not be around for the 50th.[95] Nevertheless, similar fears were expressed at the time of the 40th anniversary of the end of the Second World War, which did not prevent large numbers of veterans going on to be healthy enough to mark the 50th and 60th anniversaries: and given the increased life expectancy of post-war generations, there is good reason to suppose the 68 memorial business has a long time to run yet. But there is something about a 40 year interval that lends itself to memorialisation: it was in the 1980s that the French debate about Vichy (1940–1944) became most heated, and in the late 1990s and early 2000s that the Algerian War (1954–1962) underwent a similar process. The age of retirement is a natural time to take stock and make sense of what people have achieved in their lives, and attempt to set the agenda

---

93   For example, Gérard Mauger, 'Des idées dans le mouvement: Pierre Bourdieu', *L'Humanité Hors-Série*, April 2008, 71; Etienne Balibar, 'A bientôt, Jacques Derrida', *L'Humanité*, 11 October 2004; Frédéric Martel, 'Jean Baudrillard: "A cette époque, le concept de révolution existait encore"', in *Les idées de mai 68*, *Le Magazine Littéraire Hors-série*, 13 (April–May 2008), 20–24; Jacques Julliard, 'Les passions d'Andre Gorz', and Jean Daniel, 'Partir avec elle', both in *Le Nouvel Observateur*, 27 September 2007.

94   Roger-Pol Droit 'Le trajet singulier de Benny Lévy du maoïsme à la tradition du judaïsme', *Le Monde*, 16 October 2003; Jean-Claude Miller, 'Benny Lévy faisait jaillir des lumières', *Libération*, 17 October 2003; 'Benny Lévy, le passeur', *L'Arche*, 549–550, November–December 2003, 40–61; the documentary *Benny Lévy, la révolution impossible* was released in May 2008; 'Daniel Bensaïd, philosophe, cofondateur de la Ligue communiste révolutionnaire', *Le Monde*, 13 January 2010; Laure Equy, 'Le théoricien de la LCR, Daniel Bensaïd, est mort', *Libération*, 13 January 2010; Arnaud Spire, 'Daniel Bensaïd, philosophe et militant, un intellectuel marxiste rare', *L'Humanité*, 13 January 2010.

95   I am grateful to Keith Reader for this point.

for posterity. Hence the increasing turn to autobiography: following the 2001 'revelation' about the Trotskyist past of the then prime minister and presidential candidate Lionel Jospin, there was a wave of publishing interest in the lost world of 1968-era leftism, notably autobiographies by militants such as Daniel Bensaïd and the historian Benjamin Stora, which do broach some of the more difficult issues around the heritage of 1968. More can be expected to follow.[96]

It would therefore appear that the 2008 anniversary, like 1968, looked both forward and back. A dominant 'official narrative' was certainly expressed with all due ceremony. Yet there are other versions of 68 that, if more marginal, have not been completely forgotten, and undergo processes of rediscovery and reformulation in different historical contexts. 1968 is both hard to transmit as heritage and hard to turn into an uncontested official memory precisely because it was a contestation that reached into so many areas of society, and continues to both inspire and irritate in the present. Certainly if the heirs of 68 continue to produce waves of protest in the present, the enemies of 68 are rather better at winning presidential elections. But the '68 years' contain too many elements that are uncomfortable for its friends, and too many that are uncomfortable for its enemies, for it to become just another page in the history books any time soon.

96   Benjamin Stora, *La dernière génération d'octobre* (Paris: Stock, 2003); Daniel
      Bensaïd, *Une lente impatience* (Paris: Stock, 2004); this material is discussed in
      Daniel Gordon 'From May to October: Reassessing the 1968 Generation', *Modern
      and Contemporary France*, 13, 2 (May 2005), 229–233, and Ian Birchall, *Historical
      Materialism*, 13, 4 (2005), 303–330; subsequent examples include Krivine, Ca te
      passera avec l'âge; (in English translation) Régis Debray, Praised Be Our Lords: the
      autobiography (London: Verso, 2007); Gilles de Staal, *Mamadou m'a dit: les luttes
      des foyers. Révolution Afrique, Africa fête …* (Paris: Syllepse, 2008).

WOLFGANG KRAUSHAAR

Hitler's Children? The German 1968 Movement in the Shadow of the Nazi Past[1]

Forty years after 1968, it is apparent that the controversies about historical assessments of the West German 1968 movement, which flare up at regular intervals, are far from over. Indeed, ongoing controversies on questions of memory have increased since the Berlin Wall came down and Germany was unified in 1989/1990. We can observe what the weekly newspaper *Die Zeit* has referred to as a veritable 'cultural struggle' in the field of memory. Indeed, the German 1968 rebellion has become an important terrain for battles over cultural memory. The debates involved offer a cacophony of voices, in which rather bizarre tones are at times most audible. Views on which perspective is most pertinent and productive seem to oscillate back and forth. Whereas early historical research focused almost exclusively on events in West Berlin and West Germany, scholars have now increasingly adopted multidimensional perspectives that consider international developments as well. However, this transition has been accompanied by a countertendency, in the shape of skeptical queries about whether such a broader focus might mean that the specific German context and its relevance for the development of the student movement are underestimated. Generally uncontested is the assessment that the West German 1968 movement constitutes a special case within the international spectrum of similar phenomena.

In West Germany, the conflicts of the 1960s about fundamental transformations of society and the political system were waged against

---

[1]   An abridged version of this chapter was published online as 'Hitlers Kinder? Eine Antwort auf Götz Aly' on 25 March 2009, http://www.perlentaucher.de/artikel/5353.html

the shadow of a Nazi past, with a bitterness that was unmatched in any other country, including the other two former major Axis powers with which Germany is frequently compared. Despite the history of Mussolini's fascism in Italy and imperialism in Japan, the histories of both these societies did not share a decisive dimension of Germany's past, namely, industrialised mass annihilation implemented by the state. Thus, although the 1968 movement in the Federal Republic of Germany shared numerous sociological and ideological traits with similar movements in other countries, it remains a unique phenomenon, and ultimately, the roots of this uniqueness must be sought in Germany's Nazi past, in World War II, and in the Holocaust, the annihilation of the European Jews. But the elementary geopolitical and hegemonic impacts of this most extreme occurrence in what Eric Hobsbawm has called 'the age of extremes' are also relevant: German partition, the East-West conflict, and the Cold War. It is anything but coincidental that the German 1968 movement came into being in the most extreme geopolitical setting that developed after 1945, in the wake of a destructive, murderous political system – in West Berlin, a city surrounded by East Germany, threatened by Soviet power interests, and controlled by the Western Allies.

Among the most prominent features of the era that saw the advent of the German student movement are thus the tensions between the Western powers and Soviet communism, with East Germany functioning as the Soviet Union's satellite and the *Sozialistische Einheitspartei Deutschlands* [SED, Socialist Unity Party of Germany] its instrument for securing political power. Aside from the border between the two Koreas, the confrontation between the two blocs was most heated and direct in Germany. Disputes about the advantages and disadvantages of capitalism and socialism were more than mere abstract debates; they addressed the core of political existence and, because of external factors and circumstances, were highly charged.

Those who lived in West Berlin at the time had to take sides; hardly anyone could afford to take an indecisive or evasive stand on these urgent issues. This fact was reflected in the special character of the *Freie Universität* [FU, Free University] in West Berlin, where the movement of 1968 had its origins. The FU was founded in 1948 as a result of conflicts at the Humboldt

University, which was situated in the Soviet-occupied sector. By its very name, the FU was labeled as an antithesis to the educational dictatorship of the socialist state and symbolised a worldview that called for practical consequences. As an academic institution, the FU uniquely embodied the values of the so-called 'free Western world'. Located in the idyllic, affluent neighbourhood of Dahlem, the university was in fact situated on the ideological frontlines of the Cold War.

It was thus by no means a coincidence that the unredeemed implications associated with the FU's programmatic mandate provoked heated reactions when the US government began waging an open war in Vietnam in 1965. The assertion that its military involvement in Vietnam (which ultimately lasted more than a decade) was unavoidable in the struggle to contain communism led to a severe loss of credibility for the USA. The former defender of Western freedom now appeared as an imperial power that did not hesitate to bomb a poor Southeast Asian people. Together with the older German generation's tendency to deny its Nazi past, the lack of a parliamentary opposition that came with the national grand coalition between Social Democrats and Christian Democrats, and fears about the advent of a new authoritarian state fostered by passage of the state of emergency act, this disillusionment with the USA fuelled fundamental doubts about the Western model of democracy.

A single spark was then all that was needed to set off the revolt. That spark was the death of Benno Ohnesorg, a student shot by a plainclothes policeman during a demonstration protesting against the visit of the Persian shah to West Berlin on 2 June 1967. Previous conflicts within the university had petered out within the academic institution, but the death of a fellow student not only set the Western sector of the divided city ablaze; it also quickly ignited similar fires at universities all over West Germany. The active motor of this non-parliamentary movement was the *Sozialistische Deutsche Studentenbund* (SDS, Socialist German Student Union), an organisation that, in 1968, had little more than 2,000 members in all of West Germany.

I

From the outset, there was no lack of distorted portrayals and at times far-fetched analogies and descriptions of the West German 1968 movement, which aimed chiefly to stigmatise what was perceived by the political mainstream as a new and rather baffling political opponent. The newspapers and magazines of the Springer Company, in particular, endeavored untiringly to unmask the leftist rebels at the FU as hooligans, rioters, and reincarnations of SA troopers. Politicians, among them many Social Democrats, cited Kurt Schumacher's warning about 'Nazis painted red' to articulate how similar, indeed, interchangeable those on the radical left and right in effect were.

There was also a chorus of critics accompanying these voices who ostensibly argued with the full weight of serious scholarship. Typical of a whole series of publications that were apparently intended to halt the advance of leftist theories was a volume edited by Cologne sociologist Erwin K. Scheuch, *Die Wiedertäufer der Wohlstandsgesellschaft*.[2] Scheuch drew parallels to the milleniarist Anabaptist movements that emerged in the sixteenth century to ostracise the student activists and their purported denial of reality and pursuit of spiritual awakening. In doing so, he adopted the phrase 'left people on the right', originally articulated by Otto-Ernst Schüddekopf, in an attempt to discredit the 'New Left'.[3] In Scheuch's opinion, the protagonists of the Außerparlamentarische Opposition (APO, extra-parliamentary opposition) were neither new nor left but rather totalitarian and dangerous like the political 'arsonists and murderers' of earlier decades of the twentieth century; they were, in his eyes, nothing more than 'ideological criminals'. Thus, Scheuch – who two years prior to this

---

2   Erwin K. Scheuch (ed.), *Die Wiedertäufer der Wohlstandsgesellschaft. Eine kritische Untersuchung der 'Neuen Linken' und ihrer Dogmen* (Köln: Markus Verlag 1968).

3   Otto-Ernst Schüddekopf, *Linke Leute von rechts. Die nationalrevolutionären Minderheiten und der Kommunismus in der Weimarer Republik* (Stuttgart: Kohlhammer 1960).

publication had gone on record as opposed to the state of emergency laws – was among the first to equate the rebels of 1968 with the propagandists of the annihilatory policies of previous totalitarian regimes.[4] And in another monograph that placed the New Left on the same level as the rightwing *Nationaldemokratische Partei Deutschlands* (NPD, German National Democratic Party), the notion of a direct progression of generations was suggested as an explanation, under the title 'The Sons of Hitler and Mao'.[5]

British author Jillian Becker followed this pattern with a book published at the height of the crisis set off by the terrorist attacks of the *Rote Armee Fraktion* (RAF, Red Army Faction) in the fall of 1977 with the provocative and succinct title *Hitler's Children*. However, Becker intended this label primarily as a characterisation of the RAF, one of the derivatives of the 1968 movement, and not of the movement itself.[6] Just how strong reservations about applying the interpretation suggested in the title even to one terrorist group initially were is apparent in the decision about the title of the German translation, which was published one year later. Fischer Verlag, which also later published Götz Aly's book *Unser Kampf*, was clearly so worried about offending readers that it added a question mark to the title of Becker's book.[7] This deference to possible sensibilities was perceived as inadequate by some. In a widely discussed review essay that appeared in the news magazine *Der Spiegel* upon publication of the British edition,

4   Various similar titles followed, such as a collected volume with a preface written by Helmut Schmidt, who later became West German chancellor: Kurt Sontheimer et. al, *Der Überdruß an der Demokratie. Neue Linke und alte Rechte – Unterschiede und Gemeinsamkeiten* (Köln: Markus Verlag 1970).

5   Giselher Schmidt, *Hitlers und Maos Söhne. NPD und Neue Linke* (Frankfurt am Main: Scheffler 1969).

6   Jillian Becker, *Hitler's Children. The Story of the Baader-Meinhof Gang* (New York: Lippincott 1977).

7   Jillian Becker, *Hitlers Kinder? Der Baader-Meinhof-Terrorismus* (Frankfurt am Main: Fischer 1978).

political scientist Martin Greiffenhagen referred to the title chosen by Becker as a 'disaster'.[8]

Becker retraced the emergence and development of what is referred to as the first generation of the RAF from its roots in the student movement in Berlin. Concentrating on the biographies of RAF founders Andreas Baader, Gudrun Ensslin, and Ulrike Meinhof, she linked their transformation to the personal histories of their parents and educators. Her conclusion was as follows, 'It was a youthful ambition to be heroic – to be the heroes their fathers had failed to be. At the same time there was another desire, to identify themselves with victims. Often in the late sixties students were heard to say, "We are the Jews of today." The recent victims had become hero-martyrs, and the children of the martyr-makers felt an envy of suffering – in German, more neatly, *Leidensneid*. This was not an assumption of guilt, but a repudiation of it.'[9] This evaluation in a sense reversed the reigning paradigm in German public discourse about the student movement.

A remark that was attributed to Gudrun Ensslin played a key role in this reversal. Ensslin, who later co-founded the RAF, attended a spontaneous meeting in the SDS main office on Kurfürstendamm in Berlin on 2 June 1967 after the death of Benno Ohnesorg and proclaimed in a highly agitated voice that 'It's the generation of Auschwitz – you can't debate with them!'[10] This phrase sounded like a political program and seemed to legitimate the use of violence; indeed, it resembled a call to arms. But there are serious doubts about the authenticity of the quote. Becker refers in her version to the account of eyewitness Tilman Fichter, at the time an SDS activist, who later became a social scientist. Fichter maintains that he can still recall the scene and utterance in question after four decades, despite doubts raised at various times. But in a conversation with the author of this contribution, he described the woman who spoke these words as dark-haired.[11] Photos from the period show, however, that Ensslin, who was

8   Martin Greiffenhagen, 'Hitlers Kinder? – Gewiß nicht', *Der Spiegel*, 31 October 1977, 55.
9   Jillian Becker, *Hitler's Children?* 69.
10   Ibid, 49.
11   Conversation between the author and Dr Tilman Fichter, 15 July 2004.

known only to insiders at the time, was in fact blond. The attribution of this key quotation to Ensslin, which has since found its way into numerous other accounts,[12] is perhaps the result of mistaken identity, if indeed these exact words were spoken at all.

Even in Becker's exclusive focus on the RAF, as an interpretive figure 'Hitler's Children' was an easy target for criticism. Critics perceived it as a pseudo-thesis that offered numerous options but actually had little explanatory power. They also held that explanations that referred back to the generation of Nazi perpetrators reduced complex developments to a question of family psychology. Such interpretations could also neutralise many of the positive stimuli that emanated from the student movement by equating the movement with the RAF. By framing the RAF as a direct descendant of Hitler, the student movement and its political activities were shifted into the shadow of Nazi mass annihilation and the categorically incomprehensible murder of the European Jews.

On the other hand, research by various scholars in recent years has confirmed that some prominent activists of 1968 indeed adhered to a number of the questionable ideological standpoints highlighted in Becker's book. Work by historians has demonstrated a problematic continuity with respect to anti-Zionist and anti-American attitudes frequently found in the older generation of Germans. These elements of continuity are most apparent when we recall two moments towards the beginning and the end of the West German 1968 movement that were marked by fundamental changes in the attitudes of its supporters.

Prior to June 1967, the pro-Israeli position of leftist student organisations led to extensive contacts and, in particular, to visits of student delegations and kibbutz stays; this was perceived by some in Germany and in Israel as a prelude to an official policy of reconciliation. In June 1967, just as the shots fired on Benno Ohnesorg triggered the formation of a nation-

12   One example is Stefan Aust's bestselling book, which has been published in several editions and also been the basis of a recent film: *Der Baader Meinhof Komplex* (Hamburg: Hoffmann und Campe 1985); expanded and updated editions: München 1997 and Hamburg 2008.

wide student movement, this position was replaced by a stance that was
not merely critical of Israel but often fundamentally hostile and increasingly linked to one-sided partisanship on behalf of the Palestinians.[13] The
Six-Day War in early June 1967 led to a dramatic change in the position of
the SDS towards Israel. Beginning in the early 1950s, when the SDS was
still the student branch of the *Sozialdemokratische Partei Deutschlands*
(SPD, Social Democratic Party of Germany), the organisation played a
pioneering role in advocating restitution for the Nazi crimes perpetrated
against the Jewish people and recognition of the independent state of
Israel; it continued to pursue these goals after being excluded from the
mother party in 1961. After the Six-Day War, the SDS assumed the role
of an avant-garde championing the cause of Palestinian independence.
Aggression and expansion were the labels now applied to characterise the
purported underlying motives of Israel's policies. Zionism was equated with
capitalism, colonialism, and imperialism, without regard for the historical
circumstances under which it emerged. This amounted to an unequivocal
declaration of hostility towards the state of Israel and its Jewish citizens.
Beginning in the summer of 1967, the SDS position in effect denied Israel's
right to exist as an independent state. That marked the first fissure. The
second began to emerge in the fall of 1969.

Especially among student activists in West Berlin, there were increasing signs in 1969 of militant anti-Zionism. Their slogan – 'strike the fascists
wherever you meet them' – seemed to be inspired by the famous call-to-
arms against the fascists first formulated by Hamburg communist Heinz
Neumann in 1929.[14] That was at least the slogan propagated in *Agit 883*,
with an average print run of 10,000 copies the most widely-read organ
of the student movement in West Berlin. In the course of that year, there

---

13   See Martin W. Kloke, *Israel und die deutsche Linke. Zur Geschichte eines schwierigen
     Verhältnisses* (Frankfurt am Main: Campus 1990); second expanded and updated
     edition Frankfurt am Main 1994.
14   Heinz Neumann, a communist from Hamburg, had called on contemporaries to
     attack the fascists in a text published in *Die Rote Fahne*, the central organ of the
     KPD on 5 November 1929; the phrase was a variation on a satirical slogan coined
     by writer Kurt Tucholsky 'Kiss the fascists wherever you meet them!'

were several smaller attacks on Jewish businesses. A bomb attack on the Jewish community center in Berlin, which fortunately failed, followed in the fall.[15] The device was placed inside the building on 9 November 1969 and set to explode at the very moment several hundred people gathered in the courtyard outside to commemorate those Jewish citizens who had been persecuted, humiliated, and murdered by the Nazis thirty-one years before.[16]

It was obvious that a group of activists from the disintegrating movement of 1968 had elected to test a new, violent strategy of escalation. By declaring that Jewish community centers were 'agencies of the Zionist state of Israel', this group redefined them as part of the 'battle zone' of the war in the Near East. Thus, in West Germany, the 'urban guerrilla' chapter in the history of the left movements, which had been opened with the creation of the RAF in spring 1969, was closely tied to an anti-Semitic attack.

By the time the first reflections on the fortieth anniversary of the death of Benno Ohnesorge appeared in the spring of 2007, intimations about anti-Semitic tendencies in the student movement of the 1960s had led to sustained unease in certain quarters. Journalist Jens Jessen was one of those who took up the issue and wrote in the national weekly *Die Zeit*, 'The most disturbing question that must be put to the activists of '68 is whether, ultimately, a clandestine loyalty to the Nazi worldview of their parents lurked behind their leftist rhetoric about new beginnings.'[17] In other words, the self-understanding of the student rebels as anti-fascists operating in a society that bore the mark of fascism – which had been cultivated

---

15   See Wolfgang Kraushaar, *Die Bombe im Jüdischen Gemeindehaus* (Hamburg, Hamburger Edition 2005).

16   The first to write in detail about the attack was Michael 'Bommi' Baumann, a former activist of the terrorist group *Bewegung 2. Juni*. 'There was a bomb in the Jewish community center,' Baumann wrote in his memoir published in 1975, 'appropriately enough it was found on the day of the Reichskristallnacht, it hadn't gone off. Actually everyone flipped out about it ... But the media had a field day, because stupidly enough, to top it off, it was exactly on Reichskristallnacht that the Germans were planting a bomb in a Jewish synagogue, there was no way you could explain that.' Michael Baumann, *Wie alles anfing* (München: Trikont Verlag 1975), 69.

17   Jens Jessen, Hitlers Kinder?, *Die Zeit*, 17 May 2007.

for decades – was based perhaps on a fallacy. In any event, the widespread anti-Zionism and Anti-Americanism in the ranks of student activists patently contradicted their anti-fascist image and fed the suspicion that a uniquely German kind of continuity was concealed behind this façade. Perhaps 'traditions' that were rejected on the surface were in fact being 'passed on unconsciously'. Thanks to these and other publications, Jillian Becker's questions once more entered the public spotlight.

II

A recent book published by Götz Aly (formerly a student activist and today a historian)[18] in 2008 has reignited debates about the continuity between the West German student movement and the Nazi era.[19] The title itself, *Unser Kampf* (Our Struggle), is a clear reference to Hitler's infamous

18   Aly gained a reputation as an unorthodox and controversial historian of Nazi Germany with the following publications: coauthored with Susanne Heim: *Vordenker der Vernichtung. Auschwitz und die deutschen Pläne für eine neue europäische Ordnung* (Frankfurt am Main: Hoffmann und Campe 1991); coauthored with Susanne Heim: *Das Zentrale Staatsarchiv in Moskau ('Sonderarchiv'). Rekonstruktion und Bestandsverzeichnis verschollen geglaubten Schriftguts aus der NS-Zeit* (Düsseldorf 1992); *'Endlösung'. Völkerverschiebung und der Mord an den europäischen Juden* (Frankfurt am Main: Fischer 1995); *Macht, Geist, Wahn. Kontinuitäten deutschen Denkens* (Frankfurt am Main: Argon 1997); *Rasse und Klasse. Nachforschungen zum deutschen Wesen* (Frankfurt am Main: Fischer 2003); coauthored with mit Christian Gerlach: *Das letzte Kapitel. Der Mord an den ungarischen Juden* (München: DVA 2004); *Im Tunnel. Das kurze Leben der Marion Samuel 1931–1943* (Frankfurt am Main: Fischer 2004); *Hitlers Volksstaat. Raub, Rassenkrieg und nationaler Sozialismus* (Frankfurt am Main: Fischer 2005); as editor: *Volkes Stimme. Skepsis und Führervertrauen im Nationalsozialismus* (Frankfurt am Main: Fischer 2006); coauthored with Michael Sontheimer: *Fromms – Wie der jüdische Kondomfabrikant Julius F. unter die deutschen Räuber fiel* (Frankfurt am Main: Fischer 2007).

19   Götz Aly, *Unser Kampf. 1968 – ein irritierter Blick zurück* (Frankfurt am Main: Fischer 2008).

autobiography and thus obviously intended to be a provocation. But this title is also presumptuous, since it reveals that the author feels qualified to speak in the first person plural (Unser or 'our') for an entire movement, for a collective context.

Examining the 1968 movement primarily in the context of the history of Nazi Germany, Aly suggests this is best understood as an offshoot of National Socialism. From the perspective of a generational construction, the generation of '1933' were the parents and the '1968ers' were their descendants – Hitler's children. In effect, Götz Aly's self-set assignment was to do what he could to portray the '1968ers' as dyed-in-the-wool '1933ers' and thus as the reincarnation of the most abominable proponents of totalitarianism. But as we have seen above, this approach, based on a monstrous equation, is neither new nor particularly original, but in fact follows in a long tradition of studies of the 1968 movement.

Presented as a mixture of historical research and autobiographical retrospection, the author attempts to draw conclusions about the entirety of developments based on his individual perspective. However, he cannot have firsthand knowledge of the core phase of the student movement: when he took up his studies at the Free University in the fall/winter semester of 1968–1969, the FU was no longer the lynchpin of the 1968 movement. Aly's role was thus that of a belated arrival on the radical leftist scene. As an activist at the FU's Otto Suhr Institute (the department of political science), he aimed in the early 1970s to promote the 'struggle in the universities' and supported the RAF within the context of the *Rote Hilfe* (Red Aid), which aided imprisoned members of the RAF and other organisations. Götz Aly elevates his view to the measure of all things. He extrapolates a part of the picture to create a panorama, from which he then boldly distills the essence of the history of the German student movement.

Aly brushes aside volumes on the movement published prior to his book as 'literature from veterans', asserting that these authors are incapable of taking note of anything other than the printed products produced by the movement itself during the period in question. He also claims to have been the first author to have utilised documents from the *Bundesamt für*

Verfassungsschutz, Germany's domestic intelligence agency.[20] His account also relies on studies about 'Students and Politics' commissioned by the German federal government and conducted by the Allensbach Institute for Demoscopic Research and on documents from professors like Ernst Fraenkel and Richard Löwenthal, who returned to Germany after being in exile during the Nazi era and subsequently found themselves embroiled in conflicts with their leftist students, including Rudi Dutschke, Bernd Rabehl, and other SDS spokespersons. The superficial impression that the sources used in writing *Unser Kampf* are quite balanced is, however, deceptive, since the author's personal experience as a student of political science at the Free University in Berlin remains the central resource. Due to its limited time frame and the obsessions associated with it, the study's empirical approach is skewed.

Aly is known for his opinionated attacks on fellow historians, who he labels as inept amateurs because of their alleged or real errors. For example, he has accused social historian Hans-Ulrich Wehler, considered by many to be the doyen of modern historiography in Germany, of failing to validate his work by consulting source materials, because he purportedly had no desire to dirty his hands in the archives.[21] In the face of this haughtiness it is all the more surprising that Aly's own book includes a number of errors. For example, the text asserts that the SDS was established in 1947 (40); elsewhere the author claims that the Green Party lost its seats in the *Bundestag* in the 1992 election because it was incapable of understanding developments in East Germany and the process of unification after 1989 (13). Both dates are incorrect. The first date should be 1946; the second is 1990. More serious is Aly's assertion that Karl-Heinz Kurras, the policeman who fired the shots that killed Benno Ohnesorg, was sentenced by an appeals court

20   There is ample proof that this is an incorrect statement; Bernd Rabehl, *Feindblick. Der SDS im Fadenkreuz des Kalten Krieges* (Berlin: Verlag Philosophischer Salon 2000) and Gerd Koenen *Das rote Jahrzehnt. Unsere kleine deutsche Kulturrevolution. 1967–1977* (Köln: Kiepenheuer und Witsch 2001) used documents from the intelligence agency in their accounts of the 1968 movement long before Aly did.

21   'I can only say: read Wehler! It's full of mistakes. Colleague Wehler doesn't dirty his hands in the archives!' in 'Der Streit-Historiker', *Die Zeit*, 19 May 2005.

to two years in prison and actually served four months in jail (27). This is a fabrication, since Kurras was in fact acquitted in all four trials (1967, 1970, 1971) on this charge and never served a prison sentence.[22] Moreover, the author's outraged accusation that the 1968 movement had paid no attention to the trials of Germans charged as perpetrators of mass crimes during the Nazi regime that took place that same year provoked vehement protest on the part of experts in the relevant fields of research.[23]

A further charge voiced by Aly with indignant conviction, namely that a speech made by Richard Löwenthal before 'students and the democratic public' in the main auditorium of the FU on 8 June 1967 was not to be found in 'any of the extensive collections of documents' (94), because these volumes edited by former leftist radicals 'produced nothing but biased self-legitimatinghistory', also proves indefensible on closer inspection. In fact, the bibliography of *Unser Kampf* lists a collection of FU documents edited by Siegward Lönnendonker, Tilman Fichter, and Jochen Staadt that includes the speech in question (241).[24] The decision of the *Bundeszentrale für politische Bildung* (German Federal Agency for Civic Education) to publish a special subsidised edition of Aly's book evoked incredulous reactions in the public arena.[25] But the book's main problem is not errors of fact. When and if such errors are recognised, they can easily be rectified.

22 This error angered one journalist so much that he wrote an entire article about it: Uwe Soukup, 'Für Überraschungen gut', *die tageszeitung*, 18 April 2008.

23 Werner Renz, 'Aly hat sich nicht kundig gemacht', *Frankfurter Rundschau*, 15 May 2008. Aly resolutely asserted that in 1968 'more Nazi trials were held' than in any other year. (151) Again, this was not true. The largest number of trials of suspected Nazi criminals took place between 1963 and 1966, in parallel to the Auschwitz trial in Frankfurt, which was a result of investigations initiated by Hessian attorney general Fritz Bauer.

24 Because of this error, the Fischer Verlag added an errata note to the book, in which the author apologised to the editors of the FU volume.

25 See Matthias Thieme, '68, ungenau', *Frankfurter Rundschau*, 6 May 2008; the editor of Aly's book, Walter Pehle, was asked by this journalist about the unusually large number of errors; Walter Pehle replied that books always had mistakes and that one could not check every detail.

What cannot be remedied is Aly's methodological approach, since it is the foundation upon which his entire account is based.

Aly's book begins with the claim that the 'German 1968ers were to a large extent driven by the pathologies of the twentieth century'. As a result, he argues, they resembled 'in a calamitous way' their parents, the generation of 1933 (7). This claim is supported with references to their disdain for pluralism, penchant for conflicts and activism, their delusions of grandeur, their ruthlessness, their pronounced inclination to foster personality cults and insistence on their right to self-empowerment, their at times manic urge to implement change, and, finally, an 'appetite for tabula rasa and violence'.

Aly suggests that the activists of the 1968 movement linked up with the 'heritage of the radical right student movement of the years 1926 to 1933' (10) and, after 1945, carried 'inside themselves the residual poison of the Nazis' (69). Based on this approach, Aly has no qualms when it comes to sketching purported parallels in the personalities and lives of Dutschke and Hitler or Dutschke and Goebbels. He claims, for example, that Goebbels, before he became Nazi propaganda minister, acted in a manner that resembled Dutschke decades later, when he called on his 'academic listeners to form revolutionary consciousness groups' (180).

Kurt-Georg Kiesinger, at the time West German federal chancellor, is cited as Aly's prime witness to support his assessment; however we should recall that Kiesinger had joined the Nazi Party in 1933 and advanced within the Foreign Office to become the deputy director of the radio propaganda department responsible for coordinating activities with the Reich Propaganda Ministry. Aly refers to the way Kiesinger dealt with the rebellious students as 'concerned and level-headed' (33–38). While this characterisation may be accurate, at least in part, it fails to reflect the fact that Kiesinger's reactions in this same period to accusations about his own activities under the Nazis were anything but 'concerned and level-headed'. In July 1968, Kiesinger was summoned as a witness before a Frankfurt district court in the trial of a former diplomat accused of participating in preparations to deport Jewish citizens. He testified that he had joined the NSDAP neither 'out of conviction', nor 'due to opportunism'. But the numerous journalists present to hear his testimony waited in vain to hear the more detailed explanation of his true motives that Kiesinger had announced would be forthcoming. Kiesinger never made good on this promise and, like many other politicians – among them then-Federal President Heinrich Lübke, accused of participating in building concentration camps – never supplied a credible explanation.

Aly argues emphatically that the 1968 movement was a 'very German, belated offshoot of totalitarianism' (8). Although he attempts to dispel an obvious suspicion by remarking that he does not aim to equate 'red and brown', he does imply that the student movement was to a high degree similar to the Nazi movement. The symptoms he lists are numerous and not to be dismissed lightly: both groups disregarded the institutions of a state governed by the rule of law, idealised their own members as a 'movement', developed a form of activism that was more radical than the usual forms of political praxis, adhered to an unchecked version of utopianism, and were inclined to anti-bourgeois attitudes and to unrelenting anti-liberalism.

While the totalitarian symptoms of both 'movements' are seemingly comparable, the question remains whether this argument is convincing as proof of the roots of the student movement in National Socialism. And is the decisive difference between the two indeed merely the fact that one emerged 'victorious' from its battle against the state, whereas the other lost?

III

Aly makes short shrift of his object of research and apparently does not care much about avoiding sweeping generalisations. And he seems to be a stranger to the notion that theoretical reflection must seek to analyse and understand developments. Instead, he is quick to simply articulate assumptions. The author's deficits are most apparent in those sections in which the purported correlation between the two generations should have been explicated. Yet Aly lacks the theoretical instruments that would allow him to mediate between the generation of Nazis he refers to as the '1933ers' and their children, the 'generation of 1968'.[26] Instead, he employs the trivial phrase cited above, the 'residual poison of the Nazis', that supposedly was passed on to the younger cohort from the older one. But what exactly is meant by this term; is he referring to totalitarian ideology, to a loss of values, a destructive and inhuman attitude or worldview? And if one of these diagnoses is indeed appropriate, how was this attitude passed on – by means of a social process, psychologically, or by some combination of the two? These questions remain unanswered.

Since Aly refrains from clarifying the generation concept used in his book, he lacks the decisive categorical foundations for addressing these issues. Under what social and historical conditions might it be useful to apply the generation concept? Where do its limitations lie? What factors contribute to configuring a historical type in a way that allows us to refer to a generation? And when is it more appropriate to instead call a group a generational cohort? In which cases is it completely inappropriate to employ this term, which has been misused so frequently in the past two decades in academic and popular discourse in Germany?

Readers will search in vain in *Unser Kampf* for distinctions between the concepts of movement and generation, between the 1968 movement and the post-1968 groups, between political sects and psycho-sects. Aly treats the phenomenon '1968' as an entity that remains for the most part static and unchanging. Without examining the decisive differences within the SDS between non-dogmatic and dogmatic Marxists, between anti-authoritarians and traditionalists, it is impossible to recognise internal developments, processes that lead to splits and faction-building, and outcomes that can be perceived as emancipatory or potentially totalitarian in nature.

---

26   There are, for example, no references to the influential use of the generation concept by Norbert Elias, the founder of the theory of civilisation: Norbert Elias, 'Der bundesdeutsche Terrorismus – Ausdruck eines sozialen Generationskonflikts', in Elias, *Studien über die Deutschen. Machtkämpfe und Habitusentwicklung im 19. und 20. Jahrhundert*, ed. Michael Schröter (Frankfurt am Main: Suhrkamp Verlag 1990), 300–389.

One must, however, credit Aly with including himself in some of his negative characterisations (and his book offers a whole series of them) and with being no less harsh in judging himself than others. The main objections to Aly's theses are as follows:

To a certain extent, Aly has reasserted a narrative first articulated in the late 1960s in the conservative press and the tabloids which claimed that 'red equals brown' and that the members of the SDS were behaving just like the SA. Aly has thus done the job of the most adamant and unrelenting opponents of the 1968 movement. Yet he has also played into the hands of the most undeviating supporters and glorifiers of the history of the 1968 movement in Germany, among whom there is now a rare consensus about the need to challenge Aly's assessments.

It was to be expected that the reactions to Aly's publication would be simplistic and one-dimensional.[27] The first critique of Aly's analogies, for example, was formulated by three university professors from the political left and was little more than an ideologically-motivated, across-the-board defense of the ideas of the student movement.[28] Aside from this kind of retrospective vindication, however, some commentators did offer more sophisticated arguments.[29]

27 Shortly before his book came onto the market, on the seventy-fifth anniversary of Hitler's accession to power, Aly published an article that was in effect a more adamant version of his penultimate, apparently programmatic chapter 'Thirty-threes and sixty-eights': Götz Aly, 'Die Väter der 68er. Vor 75 Jahren kam Hitlers Generationenprojekt an die Macht: die 33er', *Frankfurter Rundschau*, 30 January 2008.

28 Peter Grottian / Wolf-Dieter Narr / Roland Roth, '"Die Parallelisierung von 1933 und 1968 – Ein Binsenirrtum!" Eine Erwiderung auf Götz Alys Essay "Die Väter der 68er"', *Frankfurter Rundschau*, 9 February 2008.

29 Klaus Behnken, 'Blöde Lämmer, schwarze Schafe', *Jungle World*, 6 March 2008, 10–14; Clemens Heni, '1968=1933? Götz Alys Totalitarismusfiktion', *Blätter für deutsche und internationale Politik*, vol. 53, 4/2008, 47–58; Rüdiger Hentschel, 'Totalitäre Linke, antitotalitäre Linke', *Ästhetik & Kommunikation*, vol. 39, 140/141, 135–145.

IV

In contrast to Aly's account, in which many historical references are displaced, interrelationships misrepresented, and distinctions blurred, I would assert that the supporters of the West German 1968 movement did not constitute a generation. Instead, this was a protest movement with a relatively small number of supporters, which lasted only a short time, namely, from summer 1967 to fall 1969. Moreover, the rise of the movement paralleled the existence of the West German grand coalition of SPD and CDU,[30] as reflected in the label given the movement – the extra-parliamentary opposition or APO.

Such movements are unlikely to emerge unless the parliamentary system and the parties represented in that system lack the necessary capacity to integrate various political groups and currents. The formation of protest groups is always an indication that the political system is unable to address social disparity and the conflicts of interest that result and is therefore incapable of dealing with them within the framework of parliamentary disputes. This does not legitimise an anti-democratic ideological stance, but it does highlight the fact that neither positions that criticise the system, nor those that affirm it, appear out of the blue.

The APO of the late 1960s bore the mark of a fundamental ambiguity. Quite a few of the APO's activists vacillated between extra-parliamentary opposition and an anti-parliamentarian position, and groups that not only criticised but rejected the Federal Republic of Germany, the rule of law, and the institutions associated with it increasingly came to the fore. For many of these groups, an anti-statist stance was one of their most fundamental convictions. The distrust that fostered these ideas was in part fed by the suspicion that the West German state was permeated with former functionaries of the Nazi regime, right up to the highest levels of government. This mistrust was applied to various institutions and extended to the point where a generalised hostility towards institutions took hold. The slightest

---

30   See Wolfgang Kraushaar, *Achtundsechzig – Eine Bilanz* (Berlin: Propyläen 2008).

provocation sufficed to trigger the belief that the specter of a 'new fascism' had come into view. The refusal to accept the state monopoly on the use of force was a logical consequence of this seemingly hysterical attitude.

When a new coalition government was formed by the Social Democrats and Free Democrats as a result of the national elections in September 1969, it became apparent that the extra-parliamentary movement had failed more or less across the board, at least in an immediate political sense. Although the APO had played a role in keeping the right-wing NPD from being voted into the Bundestag, it had not realised any of its other goals. In the domestic sphere, the defeat of the opposition against the state of emergency laws was of decisive importance. Whereas in France, surprisingly, a united front of the workers and the student movement proved to be possible, at least for a time, in Germany this much-invoked union remained a mere chimera. Even before the emergency laws were approved by parliament on 30 May 1968, the APO had passed its zenith. The dominance of the Axel Springer publishing house was left untouched, university reforms proved to be disappointing, the Vietnam War went on unabated; in short, idealistic revolutionary expectations remained unfulfilled.

Within just a few months, the SDS, as the true driving force behind the APO's activities, practically fell apart. The dynamic currents within the movement, which considered themselves to be 'anti-authoritarian', seemed to be paralysed by the difficulties in mobilizing followers to rally in the streets and by the changed political realities of the new social-liberal coalition. With the advent of the new government under the leadership of SPD chancellor Willy Brandt, who promised to implement reforms, most of the preconditions for continuing the extra-parliamentary movement were swept away. Some of the APO's political demands, especially in the realm of education, were realised; others were modified or rejected outright. On the one hand, with the enactment of an amnesty for those convicted of crimes in connection with demonstrations, the federal government offered a gesture of reconciliation to those willing to be integrated into the system; this was followed, on the other hand, by a sign of deterrence with the enactment of the *Radikalenerlaß* (Anti-Radical Decree), which aimed to prevent opponents of the system from entering the civil service. Although the political potential of groups to the left of the SPD increased quantitatively, because this potential was quite diffuse it no longer constituted a united force and thus no longer represented a significance political challenge.

Radical-orthodox forces – neo-Leninists and Maoists – now set the tone. The majority of the former APO members were absorbed by the SPD and the newly established *Deutsche Kommunistische Partei* (DKP, German Communist Party). Other former members formed an entire spectrum of communist cadre organisations in various German cities. According to their self-understanding, these were the avant-garde of a virtually non-existent workers movement. The leading student activists of the APO summarily declared themselves to be the spearhead of the proletarian avant-garde and believed they could become the elite leadership of a working class that, in reality, had no great affinity with the notion of implementing radical change in the political system. When the SDS formally disbanded in March 1970, the stage had been set for the future course of the radical left in the 1970s.

Four basic political currents had emerged as successors of the former non-parliamentarian movement: one supported participation in parliamentary politics, one chose to make use of parliamentarianism for tactical reasons, and two harbored an extremely critical or hostile position towards parliamentarian democracy. The first was reformist in nature and had its strongest following in the SPD's youth organisation, the *Jungsozialisten*. The second was an orthodox communist group, which found its home in the DKP, after this communist organisation was declared legal, and followed the lead of the SED, the East German government, and the Soviet Union. The third was a Marxist-Leninist current that imitated the 'Proletkult' of the 1920s and established Maoist cadre organisations. The fourth and last can be characterised as non-dogmatic and neo-Marxist and formed the *Sozialistische Büro* (SB), as a kind of network coordinating office.

At the universities so-called *Rote Zellen* (Red Cells) increasingly emerged, but institutions of higher learning were no longer considered to be the centers from which political activism was to be organised. Conflicts instead crystallised outside the universities, in neighbourhoods and factories. The most radical of the leftist groups gave top priority to political work in the industrial sector, for they considered workers to be the only revolutionary subjects with sufficient potential. Supposedly, everything was merely a question of forming the right consciousness; the question was, more precisely, how workers' 'economistic' consciousness could be transformed as quickly as possible into a 'revolutionary class consciousness'. The fact that German steel workers went out on a wildcat strike in September 1969 was perceived by radical activists as a sign of the new self-awareness of the working class.

As a result of the fixation on the workers movement as the purported agent of revolution, numerous communist groups and pseudo-proletarian parties sprung up. The establishment in May 1970 of the terrorist *Rote Armee Fraktion* (RAF), whose members cynically referred to themselves as 'Leninists with a gun', emerged in this context. This armed cadre organisation, which poisoned the domestic climate in West Germany in the ensuing years in an unprecedented manner, claimed to be part of a larger whole, with that 'whole' a kind of proletarian struggle.

Most of these groups and movements were formed outside of the parliamentarian context; their relationship to parliamentary democracy was a tactical one at best. They were based on the rejection of the parliament and the multi-party state, although when spelled out this rejection took very different forms. A text on 'the transformation of democracy', written by Johannes Agnoli and published in the early days of the grand coalition, supplied the theoretical foundation for the repudiation of parliamentarianism.[31] This renunciation was so deep-seated that, in the eyes of the activists who had emerged from the APO, there was no need to examine it further; in effect, it was one of several basic convictions that were taken for granted. Although this alone did not constitute a totalitarian stance, from this point on, the transition to totalitarian formations proved to be fluid. Soon some political sects were beginning to celebrate bloody dictators like Stalin and Mao as heroes.

Generalisations are out of place when considering the APO and the 1968 movement and its impacts. There can be no doubt that this was a

---

31   Johannes Agnoli / Peter Brückner, *Die Transformation der Demokratie* (Frankfurt am Main: Suhrkamp 1968).

conglomerate of very different currents with highly heterogenic groups of actors and rather diffuse programmatic convictions. Thus, those who would attempt to reach universally applicable conclusions and postulate continuity between a 'movement of 1933' and the 1968 movement are skating on very thin ice.

At the same time, such objections should not be misunderstood as merely relativistic. The closer one scrutinises some of the groups and factions that emerged from the activist core of the 1968 movement, the more pronounced the proximity of some of their positions to totalitarian ideas become. In this movement, antiparliamentarianism, anti-Americanism, and a breed of anti-Semitism that was at times camouflaged as anti-Zionism clearly surfaced – and not only in the guise of radical slogans.

As defeat became apparent, the radical core of the 1968 movement attempted to compensate for its political weakness by adapting communist models and strategies. With elements taken from Leninism, Stalinism, and Maoism, these groups 'dressed up' in borrowed forms of identity. But what seemed to be revolutionary was in fact simply a version of totalitarian delusions of grandeur; it took a long time until this mistaken path was recognised for what it really was. These were individual political sects that emanated from the 1968 movement, but as mere 'decomposition products' of that phenomenon, they should not be taken *pars pro toto*.

With respect to these later offshoots, the charge that they were totalitarian was indeed justified. But Aly's claim that the 1968 movement as such was totalitarian and perpetuated the National Socialist ideology of the parents' generation does not stand up to careful scrutiny. Rather, it is the result of questionable arguments and methodologically untenable analogies. This charge instead betrays just how appalled a historian of Nazi Germany feels at having once belonged to a movement that became involved in totalitarian political patterns in the course of a process of radicalisation.

Götz Aly's book leaves the key question with respect to the historicisation of the German student movement unanswered: what was the relationship of the key actors of the 1968 movement to Germany's Nazi past?[32] Unfortunately, an opportunity to come closer to an answer to this question, four decades after the zenith of the West German student movement, would seem to be farther away than ever, thanks to Aly's polemical book and the media hype it unleashed.

32   On how the student movement confronted Germany's Nazi past see Christel Hopf, 'Das Faschismusthema in der Studentenbewegung und in der Soziologie', in: Heinz Bude/ Martin Kohli (eds), *Radikalisierte Aufklärung. Studentenbewegung und Soziologie in Berlin 1965 bis 1970* (Weinheim/München: Psychologie Verlags Union 1989), 71–86; Wolfgang Kraushaar, 'Von der Totalitarismustheorie zur Faschismustheorie – Zu einem Paradigmenwechsel in der bundesdeutschen Studentenbewegung', in: Alfons Söllner et. al. (ed.), *Totalitarismus: Eine Ideengeschichte des 20. Jahrhunderts* (Berlin: Akademie Verlag 1997), 267–283; Hans-Ulrich Thamer, 'Die NS-Vergangenheit im politischen Diskurs der 68er-Bewegung', in: Karl Teppe (ed.), *Westfälische Forschungen. Zeitschrift des Westfälischen Instituts für Regionalgeschichte des Landschaftsverbandes Westfalen-Lippe*, 48/1998, 39–53; Detlef Siegfried, 'Umgang mit der NS-Vergangenheit', in: Axel Schildt/Detlef Siegfried/Karl Christian Lammers (eds), *Dynamische Zeiten. Die 60er Jahre in den beiden deutschen Gesellschaften* (Hamburg: Christians 2000), 77–113; Bernd-A. Rusinek, 'Von der Entdeckung der NS-Vergangenheit zum generellen Faschismusverdacht – akademische Diskurse in der Bundesrepublik der 60er Jahre', in: Axel Schildt/Detlef Siegfried/Karl Christian Lammers (eds), *Dynamische Zeiten*, 114–147; Wilfried Mausbach, 'Wende um 360 Grad? Nationalsozialismus und Judenvernichtung in der "zweiten Gründungsphase" der Bundesrepublik', in: Christina von Hodenberg/ Detlef Siegfried (eds), *Wo 1968 liegt. Reform und Revolte in der Geschichte der Bundesrepublik* (Göttingen: Vandenhoeck&Ruprecht 2006).

JOHN FOOT

Looking back on Italy's 'Long "68"'. Public, Private and Divided Memories

To some, 1968 is a faded memory; to others, it is a gnawing guilt.

— ALESSANDRO PORTELLI[1]

Introduction. Italy's 1968

1968 produced a movement which lived for the present, and which (at least at first) exalted spontaneity. What was important was the moment itself, not the past and certainly not any legacy for future generations. As Portelli has written, 'the movement spoke to itself in countless meetings, great and small, and addressed the outside world mainly by means of the megaphone and the mimeograph ... their acts of speech were intended to be quick and ephemeral: a leaflet and a speech in a meeting are easily made, and easily discarded and forgotten. The movement's words were meant to be accessible now, not to last forever'.[2] Archives dedicated to material collected in 1968 and afterwards are small, incomplete and sparse.

Italy's 1968 was defeated, although many argue that it changed the world. Many protagonists saw themselves as veterans of a defeat, and this 'mourning' was difficult to cope with in subsequent years. Others took

1   'I'm Going to Say it Now. Interviewing the Movement' in Alessandro Portelli, *The Battle of Valle Giulia. Oral History and the Art of Dialogue* (Madison: The University of Wisconsin Press, 1997) 192.
2   'I'm Going to Say it Now', 183.

up the role of self-celebration, trotting out memoirs and studies for every year that ended with an eight. The dialectic between defeat and rose-tinted nostalgia produced a number of silences, especially about the more difficult aspects of those years. Moreover, 1968 also created a 'possessive memory', where those studying the past were above all those who had taken part in that past. In this sense, at least, 1968 was very similar to the anti-fascist armed resistance in Italy (1943–1945) in its creation of memories and myths, carried forward largely by veterans.[3]

When was Italy's '1968'? Some chronologies move the clock back, to the explosion in 1960 of anti-fascism and state repression or to 1962 and the Piazza Statuto riots in Turin (where young Southern immigrants clashed with police). Another study begins with a long account of the 1950s and the economic miracle.[4] Italian students began to occupy universities in the early-to-mid-1960s, usually over specific, 'corporate' issues. Thus the *practice* which would become commonplace in 1968 – *occupation* – was already well known (and almost well-worn) by that year. 1967 saw the real explosion of the movement, in the architecture faculties of Rome and Milan, in Trento, in Turin, at the Cattolica in Milan, in Pisa. 1968 in Italy had no one point of beginning, or end. Its multi-faceted, all-encompassing and pervasive nature was a strength, and perhaps also a weakness. Italy did not have a Paris-May explosion. It was an earthquake where the after-shocks went on for years. Passerini has referred to these occupations – in 1967–1968 – as 'the places where utopia seemed possible'.[5] Certainly, the occupations changed in a qualitative and quantitative way in that period, as compared to those of the mid-1960s.

3   P. Braunstein, 'Possessive Memory and the Sixties Generation', *Culturefront*, 1997, 66–69.

4   M. Flores, A. De Bernardi, *Il Sessantotto* (Bologna: Il Mulino, 2003). See also G. De Luna, *Le ragioni di un decennio. 1969–1979. Militanza, violenza, sconfitta, memoria* (Milan: Feltrinelli, 2009). For 1968 in a global context see G. Arrighi et al., *Antisystemic Movements* (London: Verso, 1989) and P. Ortoleva, *I movimenti del '68 in Europa e in America* (Riuniti: Rome, 1998).

5   'Il '68' in M. Isnenghi ed., *I luoghi della memoria. Personaggi e date dell'Italia unita* (Bari: Laterza, 1997), 380.

So we should certainly move the start of the movement back to 1967 at least. But when did 1968 *end*, if it has indeed ended? Some say that the 'real' movement was already over by 1968 or 1969, with the end of the first occupations and the move towards the working class. Others date the 'end' to the formation of organised political groups in the late 1960s and early 1970s. Some, alternatively, look for specific 'ends', the dissolution of the *Lotta Continua* political grouping in 1975 in Rimini after a split with the feminist movement, for example. 1977, with its new series of worker and student revolts, was a key moment, of continuity or separation depending on various points of view. The death of leading politician Aldo Moro at the hands of the Red Brigades left-terrorist group in 1978 – around the time of the 10th anniversary of May 1968 – also seemed to herald the end of a 'season' of struggle, and brought in what have become known by some as the 'years of silence' or the 'riflusso' (the ebbing).

Italy had a 'long May' (or a 'drawn-out May'), perhaps the 'Longest May' of all, with no one insurrectionary moment, but a prolonged series of struggles, debates and movements which lasted for over a decade. This length is an important factor in itself, and produced a high number of 'veterans'. How then should we refer to 1968? As '1968', perhaps? Or should we use '1968s'? These are not merely academic questions, as they impact onto crucial issues such as the continuity or otherwise with terrorism and political violence, the legacy of 1968 in terms of society, politics and institutions, and the ways in which '1968' has been remembered, represented and forgotten.

One of the key debates about 1968 is that linked to its 'turning-points', and this is also a question about when 1968 ended. On 12 December 1969 a bomb in a bank in Piazza Fontana in central Milan killed sixteen people, and injured nearly ninety. The device was placed by neo-fascists in alliance with sectors of Italy's secret services, but was officially blamed on the left. One innocent anarchist (Giuseppe Pinelli) died during interrogation after 'falling' from a fourth-floor police station window in Milan. Another innocent anarchist (Pietro Valpreda) spent three years in jail awaiting trial for having planted the bomb, and was only cleared in 1981. For many militants, Piazza Fontana represented a crossroads. This idea emerges clearly from historical analysis, studies of memory and interviews with generations linked to the 1960s and 1970s. Piazza Fontana has often been interpreted as a moment of 'loss of innocence'.[6]

After Piazza Fontana (and the 'Pinelli case'), the idea that violence was legitimate became far more widespread (in theory and in practice), political groups began to take control, and many were attracted to terrorism. There is no doubt that Piazza Fontana was and is a turning point in terms of the *memory* narratives elaborated by many militants. After 1969, the anniversary of Piazza Fontana became a moment of annual violent clashes with the state, which led to further deaths and more anniversaries. This was a date which the movement saw as its own and 'celebrated' through protest. 12 December 1969 thus constitutes – in terms of memory – a moment of transition, a date which marks a before, and an after.

Where was Italy's '1968'? This was a global movement, so much so that a *national* history of 68 is a misnomer. But 1968 was also intensely local, its patterns, rhythms and outcomes were deeply influenced by local contexts, histories and cultures. Geographically, Italy's '68 had no capital, no centre, no one dominant place, but many cores, and many of these local centres were peripheral to Italy itself. Trento – where a university had only been opened in 1962, was a town of just 60,000 people, geographically and politically marginal. By June 1967 the students there had already issued a manifesto for a 'negative university'. In Milan, the unexpected site of some of the first occupations was the most conservative institution of all, the private Catholic University. Architecture students in Rome and Milan were amongst the first to move. Pisa was another important site of protest. But the radical university occupations were also central and urban, in Turin, the Statale (State) University in Milan, the capital Rome with its 60,000 students. Much less important were those areas where the old left was already hegemonic – Bologna, for example – or those without universities. 1968 also transformed other places – where its history has barely been written – Lecce, Cagliari, Naples, Sassari, Pavia, Catania. Despite this absence of

6   See A. Sofri, *Memoria* (Palermo: Sellerio, 1990), 112–130, G. Boatti, *Piazza Fontana. 12 dicembre 1969: il giorno dell'innocenza perduta* (Milan: Feltrinelli, 1993), Einaudi, 1999, A. Bravo, *A colpi di cuore. Storie del sessantotto* (Bari: Laterza, 2008), 240–242.

a centre, research on 1968 has concentrated (with a few exceptions) on a few big urban centres – Turin but also Milan and Rome. The periphery has been neglected and yet the view from the edge can tell us a huge amount about what was going on in the supposed 'middle'.

For every participant in 1968, *their* local university or school tended to be the focus of their activity, *their* 'Paris'. 1968 also needs to be placed within the new social geography of post-boom Italy, an urbanising society that had experienced high levels of internal migration over two decades. Many of the protagonists of 1968 were migrants – Mario Capanna (a student leader in Milan) was from Umbria, for example, while Saverio Saltarelli, one of the movement's first martyrs, was from the South, from where he had migrated to Milan to study.

Within this wider geography, there were the specific local sites of protest, occupation and violence. Palazzo Campana in Turin, part of the university buildings occupied in November 1967, is perhaps the most important location in terms of written memory and historical analysis. Other crucial places included the university known as La Sapienza in Pisa, the Catholic University quadrangles in Largo Gemelli and the State University quadrangles in Via Larga in Milan, areas that would come under the (contested) cultural and political control of the student movement in the 1970s. Within these structures, the students took possession of huge classrooms and lecture theatres for the mass meetings (the *assemblea*) which became iconic to the image of 1968. Bars nearby became the bars 'of the movement', left-wing bookshops and stalls sprang up everywhere, occupied houses surrounded the university area, murals and graffiti covered the walls.

Meanwhile, other groups took control of *other* parts of the city. In Milan, young neo-fascists made Piazza San Babila into *their* zone, attacking or threatening those 'of the left' who passed through that area (which is very close to the university). There, the *sanbabilini* (as they became known) had their own bars and hangouts, and their own modes of dress and behaviour. In Rome, as well, the city by the 1970s had its left and right wing areas, and acts of violence against those who transgressed into the 'wrong' area were common. Each 'side' had its own 'look' – a uniform consisting of clothes and hairstyles which marked you out as on one side or the other.

Religious institutions played a role in the mapping of 1968. Parma's cathedral was occupied in September 1968 and Trento's Duomo was the site of a celebrated act of rebellion in the same year (at Easter). The peripheral Florentine neighbourhood of Isolotto saw a rebellion against the authority of the church, with mass being held in the street for years, or in non-religious places, after the decision to transfer a popular, radical, local priest. A tiny rural school in Tuscany became an unexpected site of political and religious pilgrimage, and produced probably the most important and original Italian text linked to the movement – *Letter to a schoolteacher* (1967).[7]

Specific places became part of '68 mythology. By the 1970s political violence was commonplace and (past and present) clashes with the police began to dominate both the practice *and* the memory of the movement. Valle Giulia in Rome remains the most important of these places in many ways, as the site of a powerful 'founding myth'.[8] However, Piazza Fontana was more central historically and politically, and in terms of memory. With the move towards an attempted alliance with the working class, especially but not only in the big cities, factory sites became the focus for the movement from 1969 onwards. The main FIAT factory (Mirafiori) gates in Turin remain the most celebrated of these sites, a place which reflected the history of the city in the 1960s and 1970s. In Milan, the focus spread to factories, with the huge Pirelli plant the most important centre of activity. Rome had no mass organised working class, and certain worker-protests there were magnified out of all proportion to their real significance. In every place links were made between the workers and the students who broke down symbolic walls which often separated cities from these factories. The student movement helped to make the working class *visible*, as workers came and spoke to huge student assemblies.

7   Scuola di Barbiana, *Lettera a una professoressa* (Florence: Libreria Editrice Fiorentina, 2006).

8   Portelli, 'I'm Going to Say it Now', 194.

Remembering Italy's 1968. *Private* memories

A myriad of private memories – those linked to individuals and groups which failed to find expression in public or permanent forms of memorialisation have marked Italy's post-1968 period. But many chose not to remember at all. Silences, gaps and omissions seem to mark private memories of 1968. There appears to be 'a vast area of words left unsaid, of forgetting, of confusion' (Passerini) as well as 'dogmatisms and ideological rigidities'.[9] Even a noisy discipline such as oral history, born out of 1968, has 'kept quiet' (Portelli).[10] But what do we mean by silences, and how can we analyse them? One problem with the idea of silences, or denial, is that its very existence is based upon assumptions about what *should* be talked about. It is impossible to prove that there have been silences, unless you allow for the obligatory presence of certain topics, areas or features. Silence is often in the ear of the interviewer, the historian, the journalist, and the link between forgetting and memory is not a zero-sum game (although it is often seen as such by those involved). There is a powerful rhetoric about silences, just as there is about forgetting.[11] Much of this is tied up with high *expectations* of memory, with political ideas about what should and should not be remembered, or forgotten. As John Dickie has put it, we also need to be aware of those 'horizons of expectations generated regionally, nationally and internationally about what local and urban identities, histories, places, memories, ought to be'. These expectations seem to be particularly high after wars, or when there are victims of civil or political violence involve, who often take on the role of martys.[12]

9   'Il 68', 379.
10 'I'm Going to Say it Now', 183–184.
11 For forgetting see P. Connerton, 'Seven types of forgetting', *Memory Studies*, 1, 1 (2008), 59–71.
12 There is very little work on 'expectations' of memory. For some important reflections regarding a post-earthquake city see J. Dickie, 'Messina: a city without memory?', unpublished conference paper (2006).

Given this important caveat, I have identified three forms of silence. Silences within *individual* narratives, *collective* silences and *historical* or *historiographical* silences. These three types of silences can overlap. Individual and collective silences often merge, and collective silences could be seen as a set or collection of individual silences. But collective silence is also often linked to particular organisations or groups – parties, classes, gender categories, generations. In the case of 1968, individual and collective silences are also confused with so-called historiographical silence, as so many of those who have written about 1968 in Italy were also participants in the events they have analysed as historians, sociologists or journalists.

In terms of individuals, ex-activists have claimed that a discussion of 1968 is, for them, an *impossibility*. This type of silence covers all three categories mentioned above, and is linked both to changes in individuals, and well as problems with language. Let us take the reflections of two important leaders from Italy's 1968 from the 1980s. For Luigi Bobbio, a leading member of the extra-parliamentary left group Lotta Continua, 'that period [1968] is unrecognisable, it has no meaning ... for me it is empty, an absence, something which is difficult to fill; we don't discuss it apart from through anecdotes. Its like saying "I don't recognise myself any more".'[13] And for Mauro Rostagno, student leader in Trento and Turin from the same organisation, 'those who could talk about that period, those who lived through it, because that was their life, don't do so (and not by chance) because we don't have the words, there aren't any words for that thing there'.[14]

For Bobbio, that figure from the past – *himself*, a long time ago – is no longer recognisable. It is something foreign, distant, painful. For Rostagno, it seems to be a question of a missing language to talk about that past. Anna Bravo has written of something more active in terms of omission, 'an almost physical resistance to any examination of the dark corners of the past'.[15]

---

13   Cited in Passerini, 'Il '68', 388.
14   1988, cited in D. Leoni, 'Testimonianza semiseria sul '68 a Trento' in A. Agosti et al (eds), *La cultura e i luoghi del '68* (Milan: FrancoAngeli, 1991), 175.
15   'Noi e la violenza, trent'anni per pensarci', *Genesis*, III, I (2004), 3.

To think about these issues further we need to go back to the question of the relationship between 1968 and the past, and the idea of 1968 as *in* the past, as part of history.

1968 *and* the past, 1968 *as* the past

How can we analyse the relationship between 1968 and the politics of memory? A crucial area was that linked to the relationship with anti-fascism and the resistance, and to the ways in which the myths linked to that recent past had been transmitted to the 1968 generation through their parents. Hilwig's important work has shown how many from the 1968 generation rejected the 'anti-fascism' of their parents. *That* anti-fascism was seen as conservative, as part of the status quo. This rejection was extremely painful for those from the resistance generation.[16] In some ways, it seems that the 1968 generation themselves are now making the same errors they had attributed to their elders.

A new '68 myth replaced the resistance myth, which pruned away the problematic aspects of its own history. As Bravo has written 'during my studies I have often come across written and oral testimonies of women from the Resistance, and I recognised that they were limited by their lack of discussion about partisan violence. I complained about it, I wasn't satisfied. And then I understood that I was doing the same thing with my own history and past'.[17]

The 1968 generation (or at least those on the left) were not opposed to the resistance in itself, but *to the way it was remembered*. This hostility

16 S.J. Hilwig, '"Are You Calling Me a Fascist?": A Contribution to the Oral History of the 1968 Italian Student Rebellion', *Journal of Contemporary History*, 36, 4 (2001), 581–597. See also S. Hilwig, Italy and 1968: Youthful Unrest and Democratic Culture (New York: Palgrave, 2009).

17 Cited in Simonetta Fiori, 'Noi donne e i silenzi sull' aborto', *La Repubblica*, 2.2.2005.

was thus largely to do with memory. As Passerini has written: 'I remember agreeing passionately with the *Quaderni Piacentini* (a left-wing journal): *NO NO NO. We do not want the Resistance dead to be "honoured" with monuments to those "who fell in every war" inaugurated by the local Bishop, the Prefect, a Judge, Police chiefs and Superintendents. Silence is better than this.*'[18]

As we shall see later, the 1968 movement also reproduced the language and form of resistance memorialisation in terms of its own 'martyrs'. While rejecting many of the official forms of anti-fascism, the movement also showed 'deep continuities' with 'the "military" reference-points of the Resistance'.[19] This contradictory and dynamic relationship with the past has yet to be analysed in detail by historians.[20]

In addition, the movement lived largely for the moment, it wanted to 'seize the day', it lived in an 'eternal present' and 'showed no interest in diachrony [in change coming over time], in its own past and its own future' (Poggio).[21] To cite Passerini again, 'the participants experienced a sense of beginning – of finding themselves situated at the beginning of time, a feeling expressed in the formula "being born again" used by various movements in various countries'.[22] Often this impatience towards the past took concrete forms, arguments with parents, elders, lecturers, teachers and politicians from that generation, or protests against traditional celebrations and anniversaries.

---

18   *Autoritratto di gruppo* (Florence: Giunti, 1988) 48, translated as *Autobiography of a Generation. Italy 1968* (Middletown: Wesleyan University Press, 1996).
19   G. De Luna, 'Aspetti del movimento del '68 a Torino' in *La cultura e i luoghi*, 195.
20   But see the important work of P. Cooke, 'The Resistance Continues: a social movement in the 1970s', *Modern Italy*, 5, 2 (2000), 161–73 and 'A (ri)conquistare la rossa primavera: the neo-Resistance in the 1970s' in A. Bull and A. Giorgio (eds), *Speaking out and silencing: culture, society and politics in Italy in the 1970s* (Leeds: Italian Perspectives, 2006), 172–184.
21   P.P. Poggio, 'Alcune considerazioni sui diversi modi di archiviare il Sessantotto' in Annali della Fondazione Luigi Micheletti. *Il Sessantotto, L'evento e la storia*, 4 (1988–1989), 105.
22   'Utopia and desire', *Thesis 11*, 68 (2002), 19.

Symbols and memory, however, were important in 1968, often as a *critique* of what had gone before. In Trento, the memory of World War One came under direct attack from the student movement, something which created further divisions between the city and the university. The blocking of the Italian president's entourage in that city on the 50th anniversary of the end of the war in 1968 was only one of the many contestations of previous memorial practices. At the same time, neo-fascist violence took on the Resistance myth, and public memory linked to that myth. In this chapter I understand *public* memory as all forms of memorialisation linked to public spaces, both in terms of structures and objects (monuments, plaques, gravestones) and activities around these areas (anniversaries, commemorations, interaction of other kinds). Plaques and resistance monuments were attacked and destroyed in the 1968–1969 period (and beyond). In part this was a provocative tactic, but it also showed how important public memory was in terms of the divisions, and of the political activity, of those years. It would not be an exaggeration to argue that 1968 and the 1970s saw yet another 'monument war' in Italy, after that of the *other biennio rosso* (2 red years) in 1919–1920.[23]

In April 1969 for example a partisan plaque was knocked down on the hills outside Brescia. The following month the same fate befell a plaque in Lodivecchio outside Milan. On 14 May 1969 the wreath hung beside the names of dead partisans in the centre of Milan was burnt. On 18 September a partisan plaque was smashed up in Como, and on 25 April 1970 similar events took place in Pavia. Memory was not forgotten in this period, it continued to be a political battlefield.

Silences have also been *historiographical*, above all with relation to the 'dark sides' of 1968. These barriers have recently begun to break down. For Bravo 'It wasn't all a golden age. It was also a period of pain and violence. And we need to take account of its darker sides'. This was exactly the type of reasoning which historians began to apply to the resistance itself in the

---

23   Archivio Italiano, *Rapporto sulla violenza fascista in Lombardia*, Cooperativa Scrittori, Rome, 1975. For a comparison of the two 'bienni' see *I due bienni rossi del Novecento 1919–1920 e 1968–1969. Studi e interpretazioni a confronto* (Roma: Ediesse, 2006).

1990s. These silences were not total. Looking back, even as early as 1988, many were critical of their own past selves. For one ex-militant at Trento, 'we spoke about the revolution as if it was imminent, and we looked on normal Trentini residents as if they were mad.'[24] Rostagno was more explicit about the leaders from 1968 – 'we acted like local dictators'.[25] Passerini's *Autobiography of a Generation* is a sustained critique of both the problems with the movement itself, and of the difficulties (personally and historiographically) of looking back on that movement.

Hilwig has argued that histories of 1968, with their concentration on *participants*, have 'glorified and glamorised' the movement.[26] There is certainly a type of approach which has masked criticisms of that past, avoiding discussions over the 'dark side' of the movement. There has been too little work on three key issues associated with 1968, violence, the question of democratic theory and practice, and the idea of difference, especially with regard to gender. Certainly there is also a problem with the same people being both the narrators *and* the analysts of this history, *and* of their own past.

Finally, we have the question of subjectivities and inter-subjectivities. Passerini has argued convincingly for an analysis of 1968 as the 'triumph of subjectivity', and she has also shown in her own work on 1968 that the importance of inter-subjectivity cannot be underestimated. In the 1970s many ex-participants in 1968 went into psycho-analysis, and this self-analysis contributed to an understanding of their own past. This process was generally kept silent, apart from in a few notable cases. Autobiographies of 1968ers have generally concentrated on the public aspects of that past (and of *their* past), not on the private side. In contradiction with one of the most famous slogans to emerge from 1968, the political had become separated from the personal.

The 1968ers – with the decline of the movement – took many different life paths. We might try and categorise post-1968 private memories

24   Cited in Leoni, *Testimonianza*, 187.
25   Ibid, 188.
26   Hilwig, 'Are You Calling Me a Fascist?', 581.

about 1968. One group could be called 'the deniers'. These people rejected their past, blaming the whole period for problems both at a personal and a public level. A second group might be called 'the claimers', those who stood up and commemorated 1968, who remained linked to and defenders of that past. Finally, the vast majority of people fell into a middle category, a grey zone of 'agnostics'. These people had changed over time; they still felt bound to that period, but in a variety of different ways, and they had often not actively thought about that past in subsequent years.

The history of '68' in Italy is often a self-referential history. Much of it has been written by those who participated directly in those events. They are (or were) *insiders*, depending on whether we think that a '68' community still exists (the 'sessantottini') or not. Many key players in 1968 went on to become historians of contemporary Italy, and many of these historians dealt (sooner or later) with '68' itself. Those who did not become academic historians often looked back on '68' as journalists, film-makers or novelists. There has been, at times, 'a "possessive" use of memory by a generation, with its access to the means of public communication, laid out the "facts" and – at the same time – created its own self-representation'. This has contributed to the creation of a 'sixty-eight mythology' (B. Armani).[27]

Various anniversaries have become a time for self-celebration and nostalgia. Plays, books and other forms of media presented an anesthetised version of 1968, stripped of any idea of self-criticism or even mild historical analysis. The banalisation of 1968 became more obvious with every anniversary. Emptied of all meaning, the revolution was re-evoked as a kind of good dream, with its own soundtrack, its familiar (if ageing) faces, its classic images (the Olympic clenched fist, pretty women on the shoulders of men, Jimi Hendrix, Janis Joplin). There was a tendency to forget, suppress and eliminate many of the aspects which made 1968 interesting, or worth studying, in particular its 'dark side'. Italian books or contributions to research on 1968 by 'outsiders' are rare. This tendency has had a number of effects.

---

27   'Italia anni settanta. Movimenti, violenza politica e lotta armata tra memoria e rappresentazione storiografica', *Storica*, 32 (2005), 43–45.

The first consequence of the way that the '68' story has been told and analysed is that many aspects of that history have been played down, and the role of the student militants, (and above all the *leaders*) and the revolutionary groups has been vastly exaggerated. Ordinary activists, or those whose lives were touched in some way by 1968, are conspicuous by their absence, especially if they happened to live in areas not seen as 'capitals' of '68 (Turin, Milan, Rome, Trento). At the same time, a number of other 'protagonists' have either seen their roles played down, or omitted entirely. This is true also for Catholics of all kinds (apart from a few important rebel priests).

Those not on the left are also omitted. *Comunione e Liberazione*, a Catholic social and political movement, was formed in 1969 (and in many ways 'against 1968'), but is barely mentioned in accounts of that period. Most versions also leave out those young people who identified with neo-fascists and far-right groups.[28] Other movements which had their origins specifically as organisations *opposed* to the left in 1968 are rarely mentioned, such as the 'silent majority' movement in Milan. Finally, the vast majority of young people – those who were part of '68', but not political militants – the 'non-participants' as Hilwig has called them – are simply not there. Neither is the next generation – the children of the flower children.[29]

---

28 But see the recent work by A. Bull, *Italian Fascism. The Strategy of Tension and the Politics of Nonreconciliation* (Oxford: Berghahn, 2007), A. Mammone, 'A Daily Revision of the Past: Fascism, Anti-Fascism, and Memory in Contemporary Italy', *Modern Italy*, 11, 2 (2006), 211–26, 'The Transnational Reaction to 1968: Neo-fascist Fronts and Political Cultures in France and Italy', *Contemporary European History*, 17, 2 (2008), 213–36.

29 But see the recent and important work of F. Colombo, *Boom. Storia di quelli che non hanno fatto il '68* (Milan: Rizzoli, 2008).

Monuments and public memory

1968 in Italy has led to very little public memory. I understand public memory as forms of commemoration which are intended for public spaces.[30] How has 1968 been remembered by the movement in terms of the creation of monuments and permanent forms of commemoration? What kind of memory practices are linked to 1968? How did these forms of memory differ from those already in place, such as memory linked to the Resistance or the Risorgimento?

Few of the key moments of 1968 itself are remembered publicly, through monuments, plaques or anniversaries, but the movement created public memory in one key area, for its *martyrs*. Those who died in clashes with the police, or in events linked to the bomb attacks of the 1960s and 1970s, were all remembered publicly, and at regular intervals, in the years which followed, and every city had its own martyrs. In Milan there were those who died in moments linked to the Piazza Fontana bomb of the 12 December 1969. The plaque dedicated to the anarchist Pinelli in 1977 in central Milan became one of the key sites of memory of the movement, something to defend as part of the movement's collective identity.[31]

Saltarelli was killed by a police tear gas canister, shot at close range, on the first anniversary of the Piazza Fontana bomb in December 1970. He died less than 100 metres from the bank itself, and his case attracted

---

30 For discussions of public memory see M. Rampazi and A.L. Tota, *La memoria pubblica. Trauma culturale, nuovi confini e identità nazionali* (Novara: UTET, 2007), A.L. Tota, ed., *La memoria contesa. Studi sociali sulla comunicazione del passato* (Milan: Franco Angeli, 2001) and A.L. Tota, *La città ferita. Memoria e comunicazione pubblica della strage di Bologna 2 agosto 1980* (Bologna: Il Mulino, 2003).

31 For Pinelli and Piazza Fontana see my 'The Massacre and the City, Milan and Piazza Fontana since 1969' in J. Dickie, J. Foot and F. Snowden (eds), *Disastro. Disasters in Italy since 1860: Culture, Politics, Society* (New York: Palgrave, 2002), 256–280 and 'The Death of Giuseppe Pinelli. Truth, Representation, Memory: 1969–2006', in S. Gundle and L. Rinaldi (eds), *Assassinations and Murder in Modern Italy. Transformations in Society and Culture* (New York: Palgrave, 2007), 59–72.

significant attention from the press and the movement.[32] It also created
a site of public memory, which is much less well known than the Pinelli
plaque (although older).

SAVERIO SALTARELLI
KILLED ON 12.12.1970
WHILE FIGHTING AGAINST FASCISM AND FOR SOCIALISM
HE WAS ONLY 23 YEARS OLD

In 1972, a young anarchist called Franco Serantini suffered a serious beating at the hands of police during a demonstration in Pisa. He was denied
proper medical care and died of his injuries in prison. A plaque was put up
on Serantini's house immediately after his death in May 1972 and a library
and study centre named after Serantini was opened in 1979. In 1982 (after
a long and failed battle for justice) a monument was put up in Pisa in a
piazza whose name is also dedicated to his memory. Over the years, and in
part thanks to the campaign, a number of books, films and songs centred
on the life of Serantini and his death. The failure of the campaigns for
justice and truth in terms of all of the 1968 martyrs only heightened the
importance of these memory sites.

Many of these 'martyr monuments' were created in order to inspire
further struggle, not just as places of commemoration. They were political
gestures of public memory – the memory of the *movement*. As such they
are different from many more sober resistance monuments from the war.
In Serantini's case the monument is made up of a large block of marble
with this inscription:

---

32   Saltarelli's death led to a campaigning book by C. Cederna, *Sparare a vista: come la*
     polizia del regime DC mantiene l'ordine pubblico (Milan, Feltrinelli, 1975) and was
     one of the issues dealt with in Dario Fo's more political theatre, such as *Pum Pum,*
     chi e? La polizia! (*Knock, Knock, Who's There? The Police*) (1972). He was also the
     subject of a song by Fo.

FRANCO
SERANTINI
1951 72
A TWENTY-YEAR OLD ANARCHIST BEATEN TO DEATH BY THE POLICE
WHILE PROTESTING AGAINST A FASCIST DEMONSTRATION[33]

1973 saw another death during a demonstration, this time in Milan close
to the Bocconi university, where student militant Roberto Franceschi was
shot dead by police in the street, from behind, in the head. As in the past,
a long legal and political struggle for justice came to nothing, but as with
other cases, a monument was created for Franceschi. The Franceschi monument is interesting because of the rich (and tortuous) debate which led up
to its creation, and the idea of this site as a 'non-monument'. These debates
were collected in a book, and involved artists, militants and the Franceschi
family. The monument replaced a plaque which had been destroyed (pre-
sumably by fascists) on numerous occasions.

A large metal structure, taken and adapted from a piece of factory
machinery, placed on the spot where Franceschi was shot, now stands in
his memory. It is both a work of art and a form of monument. Interestingly,
like many other such monuments (or non-monuments) of the 1970s, the
Franceschi site was dedicated not just to the victim himself, but also to 'all
those who, in the New Resistance, since 1945, have fallen during the struggle
to affirm that the means of production must belong to the proletariat'.[34]
In many of these cases – although not for Serantini, who was an orphan
– certain family members became part of the living memory of the past,

33   For the Serantini case and story see C. Stajano, *Il sovversivo. Vita e morte dell'anarchico
     Serantini* (Pisa: Biblioteca Franco Serantini 2002) (first published with Einaudi in
     1975). On the house where Serantini lived there is this plaque. A twenty-year-old
     comrade, who died at the hands, of bourgeois justice, lived in this house, which from
     now on the proletariat will re-name as, Piazza Franco Serantini.
34   *Che cos'è un monumento. Storia del monumento a Roberto Franceschi* (Milan: Mazzotta,
     1995). For the Franceschi case see the website of the association dedicated to his
     memory (http://www.fondfranceschi.it) and D. Bianchessi ed., *Roberto Franceschi.
     Processo di polizia* (Milan: Baldini & Castoldi, 2004).

carrying forward their campaigns against all the odds. This was true for a long time of Pinelli's wife, Licia Pinelli,[35] and of Franceschi's mother.

This language of these monuments has been analysed by Cooke, in his work on the idea of the 'new resistance' in the 1970s, and can be seen in even stronger terms in another part of Milan.[36] In 1975 two left activists died within two days of each other. The first – Claudio Varalli – was shot dead by a fascist in the centre of the city. The second – Giannino Zibecchi – was run over by a police vehicle during a demonstration in protest at Varalli's murder. Both 'martyrs' now have their own plaques close to where they were killed, and a collective monument near to the Universita Statale, the heart of Milan's student movement. This monument – like Franceschi's – is expressly political, violent (it calls for revenge) and collective. The use of first names only brings the victims closer to the interlocutor, humanising them (as do the faces on the statues):

16–17 APRIL 1975
CLAUDIO GIANNINO
PARTISANS WHO FELL AS PART OF THE NEW RESISTANCE
NO TO THE STATE OF VIOLENCE
YOU WILL PAY DEARLY, YOU WILL ALL PAY FOR THIS
NO TO FASCISM
NOW AND FOREVER, RESISTANCE

By the mid-1970s, the movement was aping, in terms of rhetoric and iconography, the resistance monuments they had rejected in 1968. But the new rhetoric also included the idea of revenge. There were even calls for these 'new partisans' to have their names added to the official lists of partisan martyrs from the war. The idea of a break with the resistance tradition, so strong in 1968, had been reversed, but the movement (by the mid-1970s)

---

35   P. Scaramucci, *Licia Pinelli. Una storia quasi soltanto mio* (Milan: Arnaldo Mondadori, 1982).

36   P. Cooke, 'The Resistance Continues: a social movement in the 1970s', *Modern Italy*, 2000, 5 (2), 161–173 and 'A (ri)conquistare la rossa primavera: the neo-Resistance in the 1970s', in A. Bull and A. Giorgio (eds), *Speaking out and silencing: culture, society and politics in Italy in the 1970s* (Leeds: Italian Perspectives, 2006), 172–184.

was interested above all in *specific* aspects of the resistance, in particular urban-based guerrilla warfare mixed with ideas about experiences in Latin America. A book about the experiences of a partisan with the resistance in Milan became a kind of bible for the movement.[37]

One of the features of all these objects of public memory is that they all deal with *negative* events – murders, deaths, killings. There is – as far as I know – no 'positive' public monument dedicated to 1968 in the whole of Italy (and not even a plaque). Italy's 1968 was difficult to remember. There had been too much violence, too many deaths, too much hatred. It produced collective silences. Another explanation lies in the sense of 1968 as a defeat. 1968 changed the world, but it didn't overthrow the system. After the excitement of the revolution and the hope of change, many participants were forced to deal with the harsh and mundane realities of everyday life.[38] This series of outcomes, the splintering of the movement, the creation of a diaspora and the extremely brief moments which made up the 'revolutionary' period of 1968 (as opposed to the 'long' moment of radicalisation) made public memory something which was almost impossible to construct.

Other memories and other martyrs

Martyrs were not only to be found on the left in the 1960s and 1970s. The right also had its own dead to mourn, avenge and remember. In this way, as well, a divided memory developed in many areas, with rival commemorations, legal battles and – occasionally – contestation of the 'other' memorial

---

37   G. Pesce, *Senza Tregua. La Guerra dei GAP* (Milan: Feltrinelli, 1995).
38   For these aspects see S. Serenelli, *1968 on the periphery. Family, Space and Memories of Daily life at Macerata, 1960–1980* (unpublished PhD thesis: UCL, 2008).

practices.[39] By divided memory, I mean the following: *the tendency for divergent or contradictory narratives to emerge from the same events, and to be elaborated and interpreted in private stories and in forms of public commemoration and ritual.* These memories are often incompatible with each other, but survive in parallel. Politics, historical interpretation and cultural change affect the ups and downs of the sides in conflict. Sometimes, conciliation takes place, and the memories 'merge'.

In the case of 1968 in Italy (and as with the silences we have discussed above) these divisions over the past are linked above all to the question of violence and terrorism. Parallel but competing narratives have drawn up different interpretations which are not simply about understanding the past, but about the facts themselves. Often, the type of dispute depends on who is doing the telling. Are the ex-protagonists, ex-non-protagonists, part of the 68 diaspora, or part of future generation? Who owns the memory of 68? Why are certain areas still taboo? Are the 'witnesses' still hegemonic? What role is played by political context, and by the supposed need to defend 68 from attack? So there are many issues which go beyond those of 'classic' divided memory – that seen in the Pinelli case, or the Ramelli case (see below). Memory is also divided within people's narratives, leading to silences, omissions and rhetoric. The idea of divided memory is useful for an understanding of the framework of 1968 narratives, but it is not enough. Many other areas need to be examined in order to get a full grasp of the various levels of memory and forgetting.

The police, and hence the state, which were increasingly in the middle between right and left (policemen were killed by both 'sides' in the 1960s and 1970s) also created memorials and commemoration. The extent of this depended to a great deal on individual cases. Many 'non-left' victims were denied memorials during the years dominated by political violence (the 1970s). Recently, this tendency has begun to change. A policeman called Luigi Calabresi, who was shot in May 1972 in Milan outside his house on his

---

39   For divided memory see my *Divided Nation. Memory and History in Twentieth Century Italy* (Palgrave, forthcoming) and G. Contini, *La memoria divisa* (Milan: Rizzoli, 1987).

way to work, had a statue put up to him *inside* the city's central police station in Milan in 1973. But it was not until 2006–2007 that official plaques and monuments were erected to his memory in the city itself.[40]

Right-wing martyrs have also had their sites of memory and anniversaries, such as those relating to the deaths of militants and others in Rome and Milan in the 1970s. These events have attracted considerable public attention in recent years, with books, memorials and, in some cases, the re-opening of judicial enquiries.[41] Some of these cases became extremely important in terms of neo-fascist memory. Mario Mattei was secretary of the local party section of the neo-fascist MSI party in Primavalle, on the edge of Rome. He had six children, and all eight members of his family were asleep when, during the night of 15 April 1973, a fire was deliberately started outside their house, with 5 litres of petrol. Six of the family managed to make it to the street, but the other two – Stefano (aged 8) and Virgilio (22) died in the flames. A terrifying photograph shows Virgilio enveloped by fire, on the balcony. It was the third time that this house had been attacked. A number of left militants were arrested and charged with the crime, while the left-press accused the police and the state of a conspiracy. 13 years later, in 1986, three ex-left-activists received 18 year sentences for murder and arson. Two of the men, who in the meantime had escaped abroad, confessed to the press that they had started the fire, but had not meant to kill anyone.

As with the left-wing martyrs, the far right kept the memory of Virgilio and Stefano alive through commemorations and a long battle for justice. For years, this memory was confined to neo-fascist groups, although in recent years this has begun to change, and the case has received recognition across political boundaries. This does not mean that the tensions which led to political violence in the 1970s have disappeared. The plaque (see the text below) put up in memory of the fire (where there is a *Parco Mattei*) was later smashed in half – and the family decided to leave it that way, as testimony to divided memories. On the 16 April anniversary there have

---

40   M. Calabresi, *Spingendo la notte piu in là* (Milan: Mondadori, 2007).
41   See L. Telese, *Cuori neri* (Milan: Sperling and Kupfer, 2006).

often been clashes between the extreme right and the extreme left. This
story has not yet reached a form of consensus.

Stefano and Virgilio Mattei
Martyrs for freedom
Thirty years on from their sacrifice
16 04 1973   16 04 2003

There have been numerous other controversies concerning the 'right-wing'
martyrs of the 1960s and 1970s. Here I would like to concentrate on one
other story, that of Sergio Ramelli.

On 13 March 1975 Ramelli was on his way home from school. He had
travelled by scooter, and was locking the vehicle up when he was attacked
with spanners by a group of young people. He died after being in a coma
for 48 days on 29 April of that year. He was 18 years old. Eye-witnesses
claimed that there had been about ten people in the group who assaulted
Ramelli, with two of them taking part in the physical side of the attack.
Ramelli was a neo-fascist militant, known for his political views at school
and in the neighbourhood. After a series of police and judicial enquiries
had come to nothing, the case was taken up by a magistrate called Guido
Salvini in the mid-1980s. A number of ex-medical students (most of whom
had since become doctors) – who had all been members of the far-left group
known as *Avanguardia Operaia* – were arrested. Ten people stood trial in
1987 and some of the accused confessed to the attack, claiming that had
not meant to kill Ramelli. In May 1987 seven of them received sentences
of between 10 and 15 years.

The Ramelli trial attracted a great deal of press coverage. Ramelli's
murder quickly became a highly emotive symbol for the far right, perhaps
the most important case of 'their' memory from the 1970s. In April 1976,
Enrico Pedenovi, local MSI councillor in Milan, was planning to attend a
commemoration for Ramelli. He was, instead, shot dead in his car close to
his house. In 1984 three members of the Prima Linea terrorist group were
found guilty of the murder. Pedenovi's death (like Saltarelli's for the left)
thus created a 'double anniversary'.

Since 1975, Ramelli has had plaques, streets and squares dedicated to his memory all over Italy, as well as songs, books, plays and other studies. Nonetheless, there was very little material about this case until very recently (apart from within neo-fascist circles). There are two plaques at Ramelli's house and where he was killed.

TO SERGIO RAMELLI
8   7   1956
29   4   1975
HE FELL FOR ITALY
HIS FASCIST COMRADES

29 APRIL 1975 – 29 APRIL 1985
SERGIO RAMELLI
Your struggle lives on with us

These plaques have been damaged on many occasions over the years. The commemorations for Ramelli and Pedenovi are often expressly political, marked by neo-fascist rhetoric. In this way, both the left wing and right-wing forms of public memory linked to the 1960s and 1970s have been unable to create new forms of memorialisation, and have instead preferred to rely on well-worn methods that draw on symbols and language from fascism, communism and the resistance. There is still some way to go before we can say that those years are 'closed', and that the events are no longer controversial, or divisive. Each side remembered its own dead, and kept a collective silence about those who died on the 'other side' of the political divide.

The memory of the 1960s and 1970s was and is a *divided memory*. Each side has its own martyrs, and the memories of the 'other side' are contested (sometimes violently) although there have been recent moves towards reconciliation and attempts to create shared narratives about the past. Each 'side' told its own story, removing the other side, or creating crude stereotypes. Moreover, these 'sides' were often divided over the facts themselves, not just on how and when to commemorate those 'facts'. There was much resistance on either side to the recognition of the other side's victims, and this resistance often took the form of silence over events, or the active covering up of political and personal responsibilities.

Gender and memory, gendered memory?

It is often argued that woman have 'disappeared' from memories of 1968 – a form of individual, collective *and* historiographical silence. This 'vanishing' is in part a result of the ways the 1968 story is told, as a series of battles (even though women participated in this violence), of big meetings, and/or through a succession of 'leaders' (very few of whom were women). But this disappearance also masks problems within the movement itself. As Passerini has written, 'the student movement supported the principle of direct democracy, criticizing the insufficiency of representative democracy: but in fact it practised forms of charismatic leadership'.[42] While 1968 preached equality for all, feminism built its strength around the recognition of *difference*, and these two ways of seeing the world inevitably clashed. Gender has also been excluded from *histories* of 1968, with a few notable exceptions, and moved forward into the 'feminist period'.

The reduction of 1968 to a few macho set piece violent clashes with the police, with their own rather pompous titles (the *battles* of Valle Giulia, Corso Traiano, etc etc) is one way of eliminating women from that same history. In those battles, women are invisible. This was a male war, fought (largely) by men. It also produced a conservative form of memory, around forms that might also have been used for conflicts from the Risorgimento, with visits to the 'battlefields' and anniversary celebrations. As both Pasolini and Debord claimed at the time, '1968' has now become firmly entrenched as part of the 'society of spectacle'.[43] The Battle of Valle Giulia created a founding myth, cemented through a song by the official singer of the movement, Paolo Pietrangeli. This myth has rarely been the subject of any historical analysis, but remains extremely powerful.

42   'Utopia and Desire', 24.
43   G. Debord, *The Society of the Spectacle* (New York: Zone Books 2008), P.P. Pasolini, 'Il PCI ai giovani!' in *Empirismo eretico* (Milan: Garzanti, 1977), 151, 'Contro i capelli lunghi', *Corriere della Sera*, 7.1.1973.

Many of the movements to which people switched after '1968' were
critical of 1968 itself, its methods, its practice, its theories. Feminism was the
most powerful of these critiques, and informed the practice and theory of
everything which came after 1968. Thus, the personal paths of many women
activists (and non-activists) went through stages which – in some cases –
were the negation of their own past. The feminism they adhered defined
itself against 1968, or what 1968 had become. This makes memory work –
and oral history – very complicated. To some extent, feminists themselves
played a part in their removal from 1968. And – in another direction – it
was interesting that many more women became important figures as terrorists than on the extra-parliamentary left, in the male-dominated 'groups'. It
is easy to think of three-to-four 'famous' female Italian terrorists. It is very
difficult to come up with any women who took on leadership roles within
the major extra-parliamentary groups.

History and historians

The anniversary of 1968 was more a burial service attended by the so-called veterans
than a moment of revival.

                                       — R. LUMLEY[44]

One of the difficulties in understanding 1968 was inherent to the movement itself – its almost schizophrenic attitude to itself, and to public institutions in general. Students were often ashamed of being students at all,
so they re-invented themselves as 'workers', or dropped out, or went into
politics full-time, or became real workers. People frequently refused to
accept their own identities, their own class, their own background, and
their own families. One of the famous slogans in Italy's 1968 was 'I want

44   *States of Emergency*, 329.

to be an orphan'. This radical self-re-invention made – and continues to make – the movement into a difficult category of analysis.

Perhaps one of the crucial legacies of 1968 was the way in which it renewed and revolutionised the study and teaching of history itself, and the interest in memory. Both Portelli and Passerini have provided a series of compelling reasons as to why oral history is particularly difficult with regard to 1968. For Portelli, there were questions of what to record, and why. Many oral historians who came from, and worked on the movement, recorded events, meetings, riots – not interviews. Such a format (individual, reflective) didn't seem appropriate at that time. In many ways, oral history was invented by 1968 itself. But this meant that, for Portelli, 'whenever oral historians tackle 1968 they are involved in something akin to autobiography – maybe not personally, but scientifically ... we are dealing with the roots of our scientific identity and method'. Thus, as Portelli states, 'by exploring 1968 I am exploring the legitimacy of my own work'.[45]

Did 1968 produce new ways of writing history? There is no doubt that 1968 and the 1970s revolutionised the practice of history. Cultural history, the history of everyday life, micro-history and oral history all exploded in the 1970s. Yet one of the paradoxes of this explosion – as we have already noted is the lack of application of these mew methodologies to the movement of 1968 itself, as well as what has been called the 'historiographical silence' about that period.

1968 failed in a number of ways.[46] But perhaps the most dramatic failure of all was where it had all started, in the universities. Many *sessanottini* became university professors, in the same halls and lecture theatres which they had once occupied. Yet, the power structures within these institutions (after a long period of apparent change) returned to the suffocating hierarchies which had been the source of the original protests. The university barons (*baroni*) restored their power, and exercised it as before, and many of

45 'I'm going to say it now', 190.
46 For a discussion of various outcomes from 1968 see P. Ginsborg, 'I due bienni rossi: 1919–1920 e 1968–1969' in *I due bienni rossi del Novecento*, 34–36 and 485–487 and see S. Tarrow, *Democracy and Disorder: Protest and Politics in Italy, 1965–75* (Oxford: Clarendon Press, 1989).

the systemic features which had made the students demand change remain – oral exams, the use of unpaid and dependent 'assistants', the arrogance of powerful professors, the institutionalised corruption of the *concorsi* system (the jobs competitions held for university posts, which are in theory open to all but in practice fixed for specific people).[47]

A final paradox, therefore, regards not just the methods used by historians, but ways of teaching and transmitting history. As we have seen, the structures of power and hierarchy (and corruption) in the university system have *not* been transformed – in the long run – by 1968. New methodologies have not revolutionised the structures of power, the departments or various disciplines.

---

47 R. Perotti, *L'università truccata* (Turin: Einaudi, 2008), D. Carlucci and A. Castaldo, *Un paese di baroni. Truffe, favori, abusi di potere. Logge segrete e criminalità organizzata. Come funziona l'università italiana* (Milan: chiarelettere, 2009).

TIMOTHY S. BROWN

United States of Amnesia? 1968 in the USA

'Americans,' writes David Farber, 'cannot seem to let the sixties go gently into the night.'[1] There are few national settings in which '1968' has been so heavily debated as in the United States of America. The sixties continue to haunt the American consciousness as (depending on the politics of the observer) unfulfilled dream or persistent nightmare. The reaction against the sixties continues to play a central role in American politics, the Vietnam War, especially, having become a sort of litmus test for political and cultural legitimacy. Yet if the war holds pride of place in the American politics of memory, focus on it has tended to obscure other important areas of contention. The broader emancipatory movement of the 1960s, even more than the war, has proven a fruitful ground for the emergence of stale tropes and flat stereotypes, in equal measure depoliticizing (the 'lost idealism' of the 'baby-boomers') and recuperative ('revolution' as sales tactic). Yet, while cultural reproductions of the war's legacy (e.g. films like *The Deer Hunter* and *Rambo*) and their instrumentalisation by the political right have been the object of significant scholarly study, rather less attention has been paid to the legacy of the radical democratic activism of the 1960s. To be sure, many scholars have emphasised the emancipatory aims and potential of the 1960s; but their conclusions have not played the main role in shaping public discourse on the decade.[2] Successfully positioned by the political right as

1   David Farber, 'Introduction,' in David Farber ed., *The Sixties. From Memory to History* (Chapel Hill & London: University of North Carolina Press, 1994), 1.

2   Important exceptions include the essays in David Farber and Beth Bailey (eds), *The Columbia Guide to America in the 1960s* (New York: Columbia University Press, 2001). See also Stephen Macedo ed., *Reassessing the Sixties* (Philadelphia: Temple University Press, 1996), and Jim Miller, *Democracy is in the Streets: From Port Huron to the Siege of Chicago* (New York: Simon and Schuster, 1987).

a short-lived generational revolt with an overwhelmingly negative legacy, the sixties have been lifted out of history in the United States, separated both from the preceding span of radical history and from the radical history that has followed. The title of this essay is thus misleading, for '1968' in the United States has not really been forgotten; on the contrary, memories of '1968' (defined in particular ways that we will examine) make up a critical component in Americans' understanding of themselves.

1. The disavowal narrative and the generational fallacy

At the most visible level, remembrances of '1968' in the United States have been played out in the public sphere as part of a hard-fought ideological battle. The battle is fought over one black and white proposition: the sixties were either a positive, life-affirming development, or a negative, destructive one.[3] Central to the latter position is a trope of moral decay and social decline, according to which the 1960s laid the ground work for all subsequent ills affecting society. Disseminated by well-paid and highly visible extreme-right commentators, it makes up a key element in a broad-based campaign at demonizing the 1960s.[4] This campaign, which

3   David Farber, 'The Sixties Legacy: "The Destructive Generation" or "Years of Hope"?', in David Farber and Beth Bailey (eds), *The Columbia Guide to America in the 1960s* (New York: Columbia University Press, 2001), 167–175.
4   See David Horowitz, *Radical Son: A Generational Odyssey* (New York: Touchstone, 1997); Peter Collier, *Second Thoughts: Former Radicals Look Back at the Sixties* (Lanham, MD: Madison Books, 1989); David Horowitz and Peter Collier, *Deconstructing the Left* (Los Angeles: Second Thought Books, 1991); Robert Bork, *Slouching Toward Gomorrah: Modern Liberalism and America's Decline* (New York: Regan Books, HarperCollins, 1996); Allen J. Matusow, *The Unraveling of America: A History of Liberalism in the 1960s* (New York: Harper and Row, 1984); Fred A. Wilcox, *Chasing Shadows: Memoirs of a Sixties Survivor* (Sag Harbor: Permanent Press, 1996); Ronald Radosh, *Commies: A Journey Through the Old left, the New Left, and the Leftover Left* (San Francisco: Encounter Books, 2001); Myron Magnet,

represents nothing less than an attempt to achieve a sort of Gramscian hegemony for the hard right in the United States, is inextricably linked to the rightward shift in American politics of the last several decades.[5] Notable for its vehemence, it is also recognisable for its intellectual dishonesty. 'Whether it be Nuremberg or Woodstock,' writes conservative critic Allan Bloom in a characteristic example of sixties-bashing hysteria, 'the principle is the same.'[6] The trope of moral decay and social decline is not just the province of conservative cultural critics like Bloom, but is pushed forward by former radicals who have made a career out of ritual self-abasement for their youthful sins. Two of the most famous of these second-thoughters are David Horowitz and Peter Collier. 'What we called politics in the sixties,' writes Collier, 'was exactly what ... many of our political leaders tried to say it was before we shouted them down – an Oedipal revolt on a grand scale.'[7]

The contention of Horowitz and others that whatever their good intentions, sixties radicals were naïve and foolish in their attempts to change society, is central to what the historian Geoff Ely has recently called the

---

The Dream and the Nightmare: The Sixties' Legacy to the Underclass (San Francisco: Encounter Books, 2000); President George W. Bush specifically referred to the latter as one of the most influential books on the development of his 'compassionate conservativism.'

5   On the influence of Gramsci's theory of cultural hegemony on the neo-conservative movement in the United States see Dave Brock, *The Republican Noise Machine: Right-Wing Media and How It Corrupts Democracy* (New York: Crown, 2004); Edward S. Herman and Noam Chomsky, *Manufacturing Consent. The Political Economy of the Mass Media* (New York: Pantheon, 1988); Thomas Frank, *What's the Matter With Kansas? How Conservatives Won the Heart of America* (New York: Metropolitan, 2004).

6   Allan Bloom, *The Closing of the American Mind: How Higher Education has Failed Democracy and Impoverished the Souls of Today's Student* (New York: Simon and Schuster, 1978), 314.

7   Peter Collier, 'Coming Home,' in Peter Collier and David Horowitz (eds), *Second Thoughts: Former Radicals Look Back at the Sixties* (Lanham, MD: Madison Books, 1989) 59–69.

'disavowal narrative.'[8] According to this narrative, the personal doubts of former radicals become the *sine qua non* of historical analysis. This locking together of large socio-cultural events with individual biographies becomes central to attempts at 'mastering' the American past.[9] The generational model – i.e. the idea of a 'sixties generation' that was responsible for '1968' – becomes a weapon of ideological quarantine, making rebellion a mere ephemeral product of birth cohort. Privileging the isolated voices of former radicals – making these voices stand in for a widely-based and multifaceted mass movement – makes it possible to keep the transformations of the sixties at a safe distance, reducing them, in Geoff Ely's wry phrase, to 'something that was not inhaled.'[10]

More interesting than the paranoid fantasies of conservative cultural critics and apostate former radicals are the ways in which 'common sense' ideas about the sixties – ideas that, to be sure, often resonate strongly with the talking points of the extreme right – permeate various facets of public discourse. It is well known that ideology disguises itself in 'conventional wisdom' and 'common sense,' and perhaps nowhere is this more the case than with 'the Sixties.' The very idea of 'the Sixties,' as Eleanor Townsley has pointed out, is a trope; that is, a 'figurative use of words, which organizes our understanding of contemporary US politics and society.'[11] Contained in the 'sixties' trope is the 'separateness' of the 1960s from other periods. Also present is the idea of the 1960s as being beyond human agency (e.g. a 'tectonic shift' or 'cultural big bang') and therefore, outside the realm of politics.[12] It is in the nature of tropes, as Townsley observes, that they

8   Geoff Eley, 'Telling Stories about Sixty-Eight: Troublemaking, Political Passions, and the Enabling of Democracy,' talk given at the annual meeting of the German Studies Association in St. Paul, Minnesota, October 4, 2008.
9   A point ably made for the French case by Kristin Ross; see Kristin Ross, *May '68 and Its Afterlives* (Chicago: University of Chicago Press, 2002).
10   Eley, 'Telling Stories about Sixty-Eight;' the reference is to former US president Bill Clinton's famous contention, in 1992, that although he had 'experimented with marijuana a time or two,' he 'didn't like it' and 'didn't inhale.'
11   Eleanor Townsley, 'The Sixties' Trope,' *Theory, Culture & Society* 2001 Vol. 18 (6): 99–123, 100.
12   Ibid.

mask their authors and hide the fact that they are tropes. The question thus becomes one of identifying the tropes and their authors. Operative in a number of spheres, ranging from official and semi-official punditry, through film and fiction, to television dramas and comedies, tropes related to the sixties make up part of the fabric of social consciousness in the US. It is to a significant handful of these tropes that we now turn.

2. 'Thank you for saving 1968.' The tropics of confusion

The term '1968' is frequently used as a shorthand – as in the title of this book – for a series of youth and student rebellions that took place around the world beginning in the mid-1960s and extending into the following decade. In the United States, where 'the sixties' is the shorthand term of choice for the broader rebellion, the term '1968' often has a slightly different inflection, being meant to suggest a series of political-social-cultural 'big events': the assassinations of Martin Luther King Jr and Robert F. Kennedy; the (police) riot at the Democratic National Convention in Chicago; the Tet Offensive in Vietnam; and (somewhat absurdly) the Apollo 8 moon mission that took the first photograph of the Earth from outer space on Christmas Eve 1968. '1968,' as the cover of the 40th Anniversary Special of *Time Magazine* put it, was the year of 'War Abroad, Riots at Home, Fallen Leaders and Lunar Dreams: The Year That Changed the World.'[13]

Considered together, these events tend to cancel each other out in a way that resists meaning. The juxtaposition of disparate, only marginally-related events gives rise to the idea of the sixties as a *confusing* time. Aside from representing a way of commenting on the 1960s without saying anything about them, the idea of the 1960s as 'confusing' is one of the key pillars of the forgetting of the sixties in the United States, which is also a part of their de-politicisation. For what was really confused in the 1960s

13   *Time Magazine*. 40th Anniversary Special. 2008.

was the narrative of the USA: a narrative of American exceptionalism and moral righteousness; a narrative enfolding the unproblematic use of American military power; a narrative of consensus in which 'politics' are a foreign import. Hence, the idea of confusion is bound up with the transparency of social and political relations. The November 2007 issue of *Newsweek* magazine proclaimed '1968' as 'The Year that Made us Who We Are.'[14] Complete with psychedelic cover by Peter Max (of Beatles fame) the magazine presents a typically content-free observation that begs a central question: 'Who are we?'

We know that the Sixties have arrived as a subject for popular consumption because Tom Brokaw – the newsman and historical mythologiser – has written a book and produced a TV documentary about it. Brokaw is the author of *The Greatest Generation*, a very popular book singing the praises of the WWII generation.[15] A key installment in the annals of what the cultural critic Tom Engelhardt has dubbed 'Victory Culture', the book celebrates, among other things, American martial prowess and the heroic mythology of the D-Day invasion of June 1944.[16] Brokaw's work on the WWII generation fits neatly under this 'Victory Culture' rubric, with its emphasis on the virtues – hard work, sobriety, probity – that supposedly characterised America during the years of the Great Depression and afterward. Brokaw's work on the sixties generation, which relies heavily on interviews with military and other establishment figures, also fits under this rubric.[17] The book's project of fitting the Sixties into the all-important heroic narrative comes out clearly. In a telling passage, Jim Lovell, William Anders, Frank Bormann are orbiting the moon in the Apollo 8 spacecraft. They are reading the bible, book of Genesis. Brokaw writes: 'When Bormann read the final passage – Genesis, chapter one, verse ten – the long, deeply painful, and disorienting year of 1968 and all those who went

14   *Newsweek*, 19 November 2007.
15   Tom Brokaw, *The Greatest Generation* (New York: Random House, 1998).
16   Tom Engelhardt, *The End of Victory Culture: Cold War America and the Disillusioning of a Generation* (Amherst, MA: University of Massachusetts Press, 2007).
17   Tom Brokaw, *Boom!: Voices of the Sixties: Personal Reflections on the '60s and Today* (New York, NY: Random House).

through it had an opportunity to stop and contemplate their place in the vast history of the universe. "And God called the dry land Earth; and the gathering of the waters he called Seas; and God saw that it was good.""[18] Lovell reported, continues Brokaw, that 'when Apollo 8 returned safely to Earth three days later, the crew was inundated with messages from people around the world saying, "Thank you for saving 1968."'

Here, in Brokaw's telling, American technological and moral triumphalism has the capacity to erase the 'pain and disorientation' of a year in which America's defining narratives have been challenged. This project is made explicit on the cover of the issue of *Newsweek* in which Brokaw's book is excerpted, which advertises the piece as the answer to the question of 'What the Sixties Mean.' There are a number of reasons why 'what the sixties mean' is important; but the most important is that the issues raised in the 1960s remain unresolved. Indeed, the cultural and political environment of the US over the last several decades would be unintelligible without reference to '1968.' Whether we speak of the so-called Reagan Revolution ('morning in America'); the efforts of the George Bush Sr to overcome the 'Vietnam War syndrome;' the taboo, under George Bush Jr, on failing to 'support the troops' (itself an implicit reference to Vietnam); all are implicitly or explicitly formulated in terms of the need to restore clarity to the vision of America.[19]

The confusion narrative is nothing new. Not only was it already around in the 1960s, but it permeated even sympathetic portrayals of the counterculture. In the 1969 movie *Alice's Restaurant*, based on the Arlo Guthrie song – billed as 'a pleasant, oddball, and highly diverting glimpse into one of the country's most confusing times' – young hippies lead a meandering, haphazard existence.[20] One dies from a drug overdose. Arlo and friends

---

18 Brokaw, *Boom!*.
19 On the relationship between the 'Vietnam Syndrome' and America's wars of the 1990s see Jerry Lembcke, *The Spitting Image: Myth, Memory, and the Legacy of Vietnam* (New York: NYU Press, 2000); see also Kevin Baker, 'Stabbed in the back! The Past and Future of a Right-Wing Myth,' *Harpers*, June 2006.
20 John J. Puccio, Review: Alice's Restaurant (1969). Special Edition DVD; http://www.dvdtown.com/reviewspec.asp?reviewid=604.

are arrested for illegally dumping trash, after which Arlo is rejected as unfit for military service because of his 'criminal record.' The hippie critique of authority in the film is made in a desultory, disconnected fashion. Inarticulate, incapable of articulating a coherent politics, Arlo and his friends enact a purely accidental rebellion. This depiction goes precisely against the actual project of the 1960s, which was an attempt by young people – halting, and with mixed results to be sure, but an attempt nonetheless – to affect a democratic renewal from below.[21] Against this historical reality, *Alice's Restaurant* stresses a depoliticizing generational model: 'Every generation,' promotional copy for the film reads, 'has a story to tell.' This reduction of the upheavals of the 1960s to a 'story' told by a 'generation,' neither any more or less important than any other, is part of a project of turning the sixties into an 'ideology free zone,' with the effect of protecting national consensus against the threat of national self-examination.

3. 'Headin' out to Eden': Hippie-crites and dangerous idealists

Depoliticizing depictions of the 1960s tend to revolve around the counterculture, and for good reason; in contrast to the political movement represented by Students for a Democratic Society (SDS) and the anti-war movement, with its well-articulated, ethical critique of official anti-Communism and imperial war-making, the counterculture – in particular, the 'back to the land' movement of the late 1960s and 1970s – represents a more inchoate form of politics, one more easily misrepresented. The movement and the counterculture were not of a piece, as a number of contemporaries

---

21   On the centrality of the rank and file democracy theme to the activism of the 1960s see Gerd-Rainer Horn, *The Spirit of '68. Rebellion in Western Europe and North America, 1956–1976* (Oxford: Oxford UP, 2006).

argued, and as much recent scholarship has demonstrated.[22] Yet, as a field for depoliticizing mythologies, the counterculture has several advantages. One of the most important of these is that it allows convenient forgetting of the Vietnam War, *the* key factor in synergizing protest in America during the 1960s. Focus on the counterculture, with its emphasis on play and lifestyle, also makes it easier to forget the central feature of the 1960s – a democratic engagement in government. Rife with stereotypes, the counterculture represents a potential source of embarrassment to former participants, the object of mirth for successive generations, and a boon for right-wing commentators seeking to delegitimise the sixties altogether.

Depictions of the sixties counterculture tend to fall into three areas. At its best, the counterculture is playful, creative, hopeful, joyous, if largely unpolitical.[23] The idea of the Sixties as a positive cultural revolution informs the great bulk of the memoir literature which, while positive in its evaluation of the sixties and their legacy, tends to downplay the political at the expense of the personal.[24] In the vast majority of fictional depictions,

22   For early, important, positive assessments of the counterculture see Theodore Roszak, *The Making of a Counterculture: Reflections on the Technocratic Society and Its Youthful Opposition* (Garden City, N.Y.: Anvhor/Doubleday, 1969); Charles A. Reich, *The Greening of America* (New York: Bantam, 1970). For more recent, less positive assessments of the impact of the counterculture see Todd Gitlin, *The Sixties. Years of Hope, Days of Rage* (New York: Bantam, 1987); Jim Miller, *Democracy is in the Streets: From Port Huron to the Siege of Chicago* (New York: Simon and Schuster, 1987). A very negative contemporary assessment is to be found in Gershon Legman, *The Fake Revolt* (New York: Breaking Point, 1967). The right-wing 'objectivist' philosopher also weighed in; see Ayn Rand, 'Apollo and Dionysus,' *The Objectivist* (Dec. 1969–Jan. 1970). Reprinted in Ayn Rand, *The New Left: The Anti-Industrial Revolution* (New York: Signet/New American Library, 1971).

23   See Iris Keltz, *Scrapbook of a Taos Hippie: Tribal Tales from the Heart of a Cultural Revolution* (El Paso, TX: Cincopuntos Press, 2006).

24   See Robert A. Roskind, *Memoirs of an Ex-Hippie: Seven Years in the Counterculture* (Blowing Rock, NC: One Love Press, 2001); Roberta Price, *Huerfano: A Memoir of Life in the Counterculture* (Amherst: UMASS Press, 2006); Farida Sharan, *Flower Child* (Aurora, CO: Wisdom Press, 2000); Margaret Hollenbach, *Lost and Found: My Life in a Group Marriage Commune* (Albuquerque, NM: University of New Mexico Press, 2004).

the counterculture is childish, irresponsible, and naïve; the butt of jokes. Represented visually by the ubiquitous tie-die and rainbows, the counterculture is personified in the 'airhead' of a hundred sitcom and movie characterisations. Finally, as we will see, the counterculture as a field for the activity of dangerously insane gurus and drifters informs a significant minority of popular portrayals.

One of the most salient elements in portrayals of the sixties counterculture is the theme of hypocrisy. The hippies, goes the message, were incapable of living up to their ideals, and frequently not really serious about them to begin with. Another key theme is the loss of innocence, both personal and national. Both appear prominently in T.C. Boyle's novel *Drop City* (2003), which depicts a hippie commune. After destroying the land at their first location in Northern California, and being kicked out for substandard living conditions, the communards relocate to Alaska. Against a backdrop of free love and drug use, the twin themes of hypocrisy and loss of innocence are played out. Women are coerced into being sexually 'free,' but reveal to each other (and to the reader) that they secretly don't like it. They do all of the cooking and cleaning in the commune; they are revealed as being the most naïve of the communards in their desire to escape lives back home that they found to be 'too much;' they are repeatedly 'too high;' they are childishly vegetarian while the men eat the meat they kill (until the women come to their senses and follow the male lead); and every female character ends up seeking the assistance (rescue) of a male counterpart.

At the same time, the largely lazy commune dwellers find themselves inadequate to the task of creating a new life in the wilds of Alaska. Once they get out of California, they cannot really handle living off the land and their situation deteriorates. One woman becomes a stripper and acquires a sexually transmitted disease; another leaves the commune to get married to a 'real' Alaska man. Star (the main lead) settles into her relationship with Marco (the only truly hard-working man in the commune, the lone exception to the lazy hippie stereotype represented by the others). All she really needed, goes the message, was a good man and a monogamous relationship.

Several of the men who were especially abusive toward women (including two that were involved in the rape of a 14 year old girl) die in a fiery blaze, literally. There is a real sense of Alaska presenting a 'truer' nature than other places and in doing so, revealing the naiveté of the hippies. There is little sense, in the book, of what Hippies might be trying to escape from, a shining example of historical amnesia.

At its worst, the counterculture is dangerous, a field for the murderous forays of misled idealists. Two key figures, in particular, have become important personifications of the counterculture in all its irresponsible and murderous excess: Timothy Leary and Charles Manson. Leary, as is well known, was a Harvard researcher who became an advocate for the importance of mind-expanding drugs. Arrested himself for drug possession in 1965 and 1966, Leary founded, in September 1966, a psychedelic religion: The League for Spiritual Discovery. Leary's mantra of 'Turn on, tune in, drop out' became one of the best-known slogans of the era. Charles Manson, a psychopathic hippie song-writer, led a commune of young men and women in a crime spree resulting in the murder of the pregnant actress Sharon Tate in August 1969 in the hopes of starting a race war Armageddon.

Even before the Manson murders, the 'hippie psychopath' in charge of naïve followers was finding expression in popular culture. The television science fiction series Star Trek, known generally for its optimistic, multicultural view of the future, explicitly took up the theme in a February 1969 episode entitled 'The Way to Eden.'[25] The episode dealt with the attempt of Captain Kirk and crew to (in the words of promotional copy for the episode) 'deal with the insane leader of a band of rebellious idealists who are searching for the fabled planet Eden.' The insane leader is Dr Sevrin, a famous scientist-turned-critic of society. A clear stand-in for Timothy Leary, Sevrin levels a withering critique against the 'artificial' society of his day, which he describes as 'poison.' Sevrin's followers behave like spoiled brats, scoffing at notions of duty and honor. Far from being drawn from the lower classes, they represent the best and the brightest – some are scientists, one is the son of an ambassador, another is a drop out from Star

25   Star Trek: Episode 75 (The Way To Eden): aired 21 February 1969.

Fleet Academy. Motivated by idealism, and under the spell of charismatic but dangerously-unhinged leaders, they stand in for a sixties generation in the thrall of misled idealism.

The hippies under the leadership of Dr Sevrin attempt to hijack the Starship Enterprise with the goal of arriving at the mythological planet 'Eden.' Using 'peace and love' as a stalling tactic, some of them put on a hippie jam session ('headin' out to Eden, yeah brother') while others try to take over the ship in secret. Dr Sevrin attempts to kill the crew of the Enterprise using deadly sonic frequencies as the hippies sing a song extolling the promised land of Eden they hope to visit. Stealing a shuttlecraft and landing on the planet Eden, the hippies discover that the local flora is filled with acid (pun intended!). The hippies burn their bare feet, and 'Adam,' a dedicated follower of Dr Sevrin, eats a poison apple and dies. Sevrin follows suit, demonstrating the self-destructive insanity that lies at the heart of his vision of utopia. To be sure, the show's treatment of the counterculture was not entirely unnuanced; some attempt was made to separate the aims of the counterculture more broadly from the aims of leaders like Sevrin/Leary. As the Vulcan science officer Mr Spock, the most rational member of the Enterprise's crew puts it: 'There is no insanity in what they seek.' Yet the message is clear that behind the idealism and fake-pacifism of the hippies – as personified, especially, by young members of the establishment gone wrong – lies a murderous danger.

4. 'The Manson moment':
The symbolic displacement of violence

An important theme in 'The Way to Eden' was that violence in society was being perpetrated not by the establishment, but *by* the counterculture *against* the establishment. This message – that violence came not from the forces of the state, but from the supposedly peace-loving hippies – came at a time when the American bombing campaign in Southeast Asia, which had been in the process of ravaging Vietnam with some 3 and ½ times the tonnage of bombs dropped by the United States in the Second World War, was being extended into Cambodia.[26] It also came just a few months after the Democratic National Convention in Chicago, at which demonstrators faced some 11,000 Chicago police, 6,000 National Guard, 7,500 U.S. army troops, and some 1,000 FBI, CIA & other agents. That the police assault on the demonstrators, broadcast on national television and beamed around the world, has gone down in the popular imagination as an example of violence on the part of the *demonstrators*, illustrates strikingly the sort of causal reversals, strategic elisions, and symbolic displacements that have characterised the handling of 1968 in the cultural memory of the United States.[27]

If it is true, as John Foot has argued, that violence represents one of the 'historiographic silences' of '1968' studies, the same cannot be said for

26   American B-52 Stratofortress bombers flew 19,500 missions over Southeast Asia in 1969, the year of the episode's airing, dropping some 27 tons of bombs per mission; 'B-52 Activity Statistics,' http://members.aol.com/warlibrary/vwb52.htm.

27   'Protestors target the Democratic National Convention in Chicago,' we read on the contents page of the anniversary issue of *Time Magazine*, 'and police fight back. Result: Bloodshed.' The implication, that it was the protestors who were responsible for the violence of the police, could not be more clear; 'Showdown in the Windy City,' *Time Magazine*. 40th Anniversary Special. 2008. On Chicago see David Farber, *Chicago '68* (Chicago and London: The University of Chicago Press, 1988). For a sense of how the theme of violence has been treated in the work of former militants see Susan Stern and Laura Browder, *With the Weathermen: The Personal Journey of a Revolutionary Woman* (Piscataway, NJ: Rutgers, 2007); Cathy Wilkerson, *Flying Close to the Sun: My Life and Times As a Weatherman* (New York: Seven Stories Press, 2007); David Gilbert, *No Surrender: Writings From An Anti-Imperialist Political Prisoner* (New York: Penguin, 2001); Assata Shakur, *Assata: An Autobiography* (Chicago: Lawrence Hill Books, 1987); Elaine Brown, *A Taste of Power: A Black Woman's Story* (New York: Anchor Press, 1987). For a scholarly treatment of the Weather Underground see Jeremy Varon, *Bringing the War Home. The Weather Underground, the Red Army Faction, and Revolutionary Violence in the Sixties and Seventies* (Berkeley: University of California Press, 2004).

the cultural memory of '1968' in the United States.[28] On the contrary, violence – of protestors against the state – is an ubiquitous theme, one that has penetrated far beyond the boundaries of right-wing polemics. The symbolic displacement of violence onto the left comes out clearly in Philip Roth's celebrated 1997 novel *American Pastoral*. In the novel, the life of the central character (deceased, his story told in flashback) is destroyed by his daughter's act of violence in 1968 against the Vietnam War. In this telling, as Laura Tanenbaum writes, '[v]iolence is seen as revealing the essence of the period's radicalism, negating its political claims, regardless of how atypical these acts may have been or the extent of the state violence to which they responded.'[29] Here, the sixties appear as 'trauma,' personal loss mirroring national loss. 'Roth's protagonist experiences this loss as violent,' writes Tanenbaum, 'and we thereby suspect that there are other reasons than the demands of the narrative that this novel – like so many recent novels and films about the period – revolves around the historically rare act of violence by the (white) radical left.'[30]

Another 'historically rare' act of violence – the murderous rampage by the followers of Charles Manson – has provided further material for the symbolic displacement of the state's violence onto opponents of that violence. The conflation of the counterculture and cult murder is a staple of mainstream treatments of the 1960s. The History Channel, a key site of dissemination for popular-historical interpretations in the United States – and therefore an excellent place to look for dominant narratives and semi-official ideology – displayed this dynamic in its recent documentary 'The Hippies.'[31] Although it features interviews with the editor of the National Review and a commentator from the right-wing Heritage Foundation, the

28   John Foot, *Looking back on Italy's 'Long "68"' Public, Private and Divided Memories*, chap. 2 in this volume.

29   Laura Tanenbaum, '"The Availing Stuff of our Experience": The Historical Novel and the American Sixties,' Working Papers on the Web, SUNY http://extra.shu. ac.uk/wpw/historicising/Tanenbaum.htm.

30   Ibid.

31   *The Hippies* (2007). Also available from the History Channel, tellingly, is *20th Century with Mike Wallace: Different Worlds: Hippies & Cults in America* (2006).

documentary nevertheless attempts a somewhat even-handed portrayal of the hippie phenomenon. Yet it also juxtaposes the so-called summer of love – itself far from representing the totality of the counterculture – with the Manson cult, making the not-so-subtle point that where the license of something like the counterculture appears, cult murder cannot be very far behind. Indeed, the visual maneuver at the heart of this narrative – quick cut from dancing hippies in the summer of love to a close-up of the face of Charles Manson, crazed eyes starring straight into the camera – makes a point impossible to miss. The juxtaposition of the racist Manson (who hoped the Tate-Bianca killings would spark a race war between whites and blacks) with a movement rooted in the cosmopolitanism of the beatniks and the civil rights movement of the early 1960s represents another one of the symbolic displacements by which the treatment of the sixties in the US is marked.

The trope of *misled* idealism embedded in the symbolic appropriation of figures like Timothy Leary and Charles Manson is intimately bound up with other, related tropes, notably those of lost idealism and hypocrisy. Typically, the loss of idealism is presented through the juxtaposition of two symbolic events; in this case, two rock festivals: Woodstock and Altamont. The former, which took place in Woodstock, New York in August 1969, is idealised as the high-point of the free-spirited counterculture; the latter, which took place outside Altamont, California in December 1969, is represented as the death of that counterculture. The killing of a concert-goer by Hells Angels hired to provide concert security symbolised, like the Manson killings, the essential hollowness of hippie ideals of peace and love.

Many of the portrayals of the counterculture – or those widely associated with the counterculture – such as Arthur Penn's *Bonnie and Clyde* (1967), and Dennis Hopper's *Easy Rider* (1969) – were steeped in violence. The latter, in particular, portrayed a nightmarish scenario of two worlds – one hippie, one straight – locked in murderous war with each other. Ending with the murder of its young rebel protagonists by enraged rednecks, the film signified both a growing disenchantment and a growing social paranoia on the part of the countercultural left. But filmic portrayals of the counterculture were by no means all steeped in negative imagery. The counterculture provoked widely differing assessments, both in the mainstream and on the left.[32] As Timothy Miller has pointed out, even the mainstream *Time Magazine* detected a core of ethical principles at the heart of the hippie movement.[33] More importantly, as the counterculture announced its disinclination to go away, and as the mainstream adopted more and more of the counterculture's style, slang and ideas, more positive evaluations of the counterculture became possible.

In the 1970 television movie *Tribes* (later released theatrically in Europe under the title *The Soldier Who Declared Peace*) Darrin McGavin stars as a Marine Drill Instructor charged with transforming a hippie into a Marine. The hippie, played by Jan Michael Vincent, refuses to suffer on command. Forced to hold buckets of sand with outstretched arms in the sun, Vincent's character finds inner peace, imagining himself romping in a field with his hippie girlfriend while Indian sitar music plays in the background. Questioned by a curious fellow recruit, he observes, 'maybe it's my karma to be here.' Refusing to play by the rules, he wins the grudging respect of his superior. 'No high school, no teams, no supervision,' observes Drill instructor McGavin, 'and yet you're in better condition than the rest of my recruits.' An advertisement poster for the film carries the legend: 'Wanted by the United States Marines, for A.W.O.L., insubordination, ... and doing his thing.'

This more positive take on the counterculture reflected, in part, the growing popularity of the anti-war movement. But it was also closely tied in with the recuperation of the counterculture by consumer capitalism.[34] This recuperative vision of the counterculture reached it apogee with the 'Caine' character played by David Carradine in the TV series Kung Fu, in which a wandering half-Chinese mystic is forced repeatedly to defend

32   See Michael Wm. Doyle, 'Debating the Counterculture: Ecstasy and Anxiety Over the Hip Alternative,' in David Farber and Beth Bailey (eds), *The Columbia Guide to America in the 1960s* (New York: Columbia University Press, 2001), 143–156.

33   Timothy Miller, *The Hippies and American Values* (Knoxville, Tennessee: University of Tennessee Press, 1991), 5.

34   For an early treatment of this theme see Daniel Bell, *The Cultural Contradictions of Capitalism* (New York: Basic, 1976).

himself against the predations of an assortment of old west rednecks.[35] It is not the image of the peace-loving seeker, however – let alone that of the principled rebel challenging the restrictive social mores and racism of the 1950s and 60s – but the stereotypical acid-casualty (who cannot 'remember' what happened in the sixties because of all the drugs he or she took) or the crazed Charles Manson (who reveals the dark madness behind all the talk of peace and love) that has come to predominate.[36] In the event-centric narrative of the United States, in which the burden of proof never lies with power, but always on the critics of power, the hippie as naïf, hypocrite, or murderer is an all-too-necessary figure.

5. Conclusion: 'A surfeit of democracy'?

At the heart of the cultural memory of '1968' in the USA lie two silences: One has to do with the looming specter of state violence represented by the Vietnam War. The other has to do with the rebellion (begun already in the 1950s, as Arthur Marwick has pointed out) against the socially restrictive conditions of daily life in Cold War America.[37] Both represented problems that demanded engagement from young people living in a democracy. But that is precisely the point and the problem – because for the well-funded

35 The series aired from 1972–1975.

36 'Most of us dropped too much acid to remember what went on back then anyway,' writes Gary Kamiya in his perceptive and critical review of Thomas Frank's book on consumer capitalism's co-optation of the counterculture (Frank argues that there wasn't anything much revolutionary there to co-opt to begin with). '[T]he relics of the counterculture,' he writes, summarizing what he sees as Frank's dismissive posture, 'reek of affectation and phoniness, the leisure-dreams of white suburban children like those who made up so much of the Grateful Dead's audience throughout the 1970s and 1980s;' Gary Kamiya, 'Were the '60s a Fraud?', http://www.salon.com/books/feature/1997/12/cov_22feature.html.

37 Arthur Marwick, *The Sixties. Cultural Revolution in Britain, France, Italy, and the United States c.1958–c.1974* (Oxford: Oxford UP, 1998).

ideological critics of the sixties, as well as for uncritical members of successive generations who repeat canards about the sixties out of ignorance or in
order to get ahead in a very different ideological climate, it is precisely the
example of democratic engagement represented by the sixties that needs
to be erased from memory. From the writers of the 1964 Port Huron statement, who called upon members of their generation to take democracy
seriously and to demand that the United States live up to the democratic
promises enshrined in its constitution; to the young people who sought
escape from the restrictive social and sexual mores of the parent generation; to the activists who pioneered the women's, gay and lesbian, African
American, Latino, American Indian, and Environmental movements; the
American '1968' represents a broad outpouring of democratic engagement.
Indeed, it was precisely this broad-based emancipatory-democratic push
that has prompted conservative fears about a 'surfeit of democracy' in
the United States.[38] To lift the sixties out of American history – a history
in which alternative lifestyles and living arrangements, as well as radical
populist moments, are a salient feature – is an act of historical myopia with
potentially dangerous consequences.[39]

The author wishes to thank Samantha Christiansen for assistance
with this article

38   Samuel Huntington et al, *The Crisis of Democracy: On the Governability of Democracies*
      (report of the Trilateral Commission, 1976).
39   Rosabeth Moss Kanter, *Commitment and Community. Communes and Utopias in*
      Sociological Perspective (Cambridge, Massachusetts, and London, England: Harvard
      University Press, 1972).

CLAIRE BREWSTER

Mexico 1968: A Crisis of National Identity

'The year that rocked the world'; 'the year of the barricades'; a 'magical year'; 'the year of revolt':[1] '1968' evokes a range of superlatives depicting the spirit of youthful protest that dominated political and social spheres across the world. Mexico was no exception. Yet any discussion of 'Mexico 1968' is inevitably dominated by two specific occurrences that shaped the course of the Mexican Student Movement. In October 1968 Mexico City hosted the Olympic Games. It was the first time that a Spanish speaking nation or a developing country had been given this honour. The second event is far less glorious: on 2 October, just ten days before the Olympic opening ceremony, after a planned demonstration in a plaza in the residential area of Tlatelolco, Mexico City, an armed confrontation led to the death, injury or imprisonment of hundreds of Mexican students and bystanders. This painful episode in Mexican history effectively ended the Student Movement and has dominated the way in which it has been remembered within the country.

Elsewhere coverage given to the Mexican students of 1968 has generally been scant. David Caute's somewhat ambitious attempt to discuss the tumultuous events of that year across the globe, dedicates just two pages to Mexico and merely repeats the vastly-underestimated government figures for those killed and injured during the Tlatelolco massacre.[2] The exception

---

1   Mark Kurlansky, *1968: The Year that Rocked the World* (London: Jonathan Cape, 2004); David Caute, *'68: The Year of the Barricades* (London: Paladin Books, 1988); Martin Klimke and Joachim Scharloth (eds), *1968 in Europe: A History of Protest and Activism, 1956–1977* (New York: Palgrave Macmillan, 2008), 2; http://www. guardian.co.uk/world/1968-the-year-of-revolt, Accessed 30 July 2009.

2   Caute, *'68: The Year of the Barricades*, 344–346. As discussed below, the official figures for this tragic event were immediately refuted by national and foreign eye-witnesses.

is Gerard de Groot's edited collection published on the thirtieth anniversary of '1968'. It includes chapters by the excellent scholars Eric Zolov and Donald Mabry that place the 1968 movement in a wider context of student protest and independent action.[3] More recent comparative studies, however, have returned the focus onto the Western World.[4] A series on BBC Radio Four, for example, featured day-to-day reports of the developing events from 1968 offering listeners a valuable glimpse of the underlying social, political, and generational tensions.[5] Yet the series included events only up until 31 August, and the Mexican Student Movement was not deemed sufficiently important to merit a mention. Perhaps because of the location of the 1968 Summer Olympics, Mark Kurlansky includes a chapter on Mexico in his study of 1968 and discusses the podium protest by US athletes John Carlos and Tommie Smith that took place following the men's 200 metre final. In an effort to enlighten his readers Kurlansky also sketches in 500 years of Mexican history. Unfortunately his chosen sources would surprise most Mexicanists, and the overall tone is that Mexico is and always has been a society based on violence.[6] Kurlansky's accounts of the Mexican Student Movement, however, and the twenty-fifth anniversary commemorations of the Tlatelolco massacre, are better researched, but the emphasis is on the government repression and on the massacre rather than the nature of the movement itself.[7]

While it is necessary to emphasise the violence employed by the Mexican authorities, there was more to 'Mexico '68' than state brutality. Following the work of Zolov and Mabry this chapter aims to help to rein-

---

3   Gerard DeGroot (ed.), *Student Protest: The Sixties and After* (London: Longman, 1998,) chapters 6 and 10.

4   See for example, Klimke and Scharloth (eds), *1968 in Europe*.

5   '1968: Myth or Reality', BBC Radio 4, producer Lucy Dichmont 1 March–31 August 2008. http://www.bbc.co.uk/radio4/1968/daybyday.shtml. Accessed 10 June 2009.

6   Kurlansky, *1968: The Year that Rocked the World*, 325. See in particular phrases such as 'there was a lot of killing going on in Mexico'; and his hypothesis: 'Some can be bought off and some have to be shot. That became the Mexican way.'

7   Ibid, 321–344.

state the Mexican Student Movement into accounts of '1968': to underline the hopes it generated as well as the aggression it provoked. Where it differs, is in considering the ways in which the students' supposed aims have been appropriated by different political actors during the last forty years. I also discuss the ways in which it has been commemorated within Mexico. Responses to cinematic representations of the massacre from the 1990s reveal the need for sensitivity in how this traumatic event is 'remembered'. I will first briefly outline some of the important events of the Student Movement itself to help provide the context.

Mexico '68: The student movement

Like their US and European counterparts, in July 1968 Mexican students took to the streets to voice their discontent with a system that no longer seemed to address their interests and concerns. It is remarkable that this happened on such a scale in Mexico as, since 1929, its political system had successfully controlled all opposition within the single-party State. Yet during the previous twenty-five years, stability and economic growth had improved the standard of living for many middle-class Mexicans; consequently, an unprecedented number of students were completing higher education. At the same time new cultural values were entering Mexico through radio, television, and via foreign tourists. The Mexican students knew about the Prague Spring, and were aware of student activities in places as far apart as Paris and Berkeley. There were a variety of reasons why they began to demonstrate in Mexico City: many harboured domestic grievances; some were protesting about global international affairs; and others no doubt were probably just caught up in the moment.

In comparison to the protests in Europe and the United States, the Mexican Student Movement was remarkably short. It broke out on 22 July 1968 following a clash between students from the National University and the Mexican Polytechnic.[8] Several students were injured and buildings were damaged. Political and social scientist, Judith Hellman, a student in Mexico in 1968 who attended the demonstrations and witnessed the Tlatelolco massacre, noted that riot police (*granaderos*) intervened and made several arrests, using such brutality that the student groups united and joined forces against the *granaderos*.[9] Four days later marches were organised to celebrate the anniversary of the Cuban Revolution. Further confrontations took place with the authorities as police denied access to the Zócalo, Mexico City's main square. The authorities raided the Mexican Communist Party headquarters, arresting several members. In response, a strike committee, El Consejo Nacional de Huelga (CNH), was established to emphasise six demands:

Repeal of Articles 145 and 145b of the Penal Code, which sanctioned the imprisonment of anyone attending meetings of three or more people that were deemed to threaten public order.

Abolition of the *granaderos*.

Freedom of political prisoners.

Compensation to those injured during disturbances.

Identification of officials responsible for bloodshed.

Dismissal of the chief of police, his deputy, and the commander of the *granaderos*.[10]

8   Although the affray is generally accepted to have been spontaneous, it was not unu-
     sual for Mexican students to express discontent. For an analysis of the tradition of
     student protests in the twentieth century see Keith Brewster and Claire Brewster,
     'The Mexican Student Movement of 1968: An Olympic Perspective', *International
     Journal of the History of Sport*, 26, 6 (2009).
9   Judith Adler Hellman, *Mexico in Crisis* (New York: Holmes and Meier, 1983), 174.
10   Reproduced in Elena Poniatowska, *La noche de Tlatelolco* (Mexico City: Era, 1971),
     69–70. Unless otherwise stated all translations are my own.

At the time, journalist Ricardo Garibay stressed that these were not revolutionary calls to change the political system; rather the students were appealing to the government to act within the bounds of the Constitution.[11]

By the end of July, military forces had attacked buildings in the University Campus; several students were injured and many were arrested. Secretary for Internal Affairs, Luis Echeverría Alvarez, explained that these measures had been taken to preserve university autonomy from anti-Mexican forces.[12] If his intention had been to curb the Student Movement, it failed: the army's violation of the university's autonomy strengthened it. The university rector, Javier Barros Sierra, and other teachers joined the students and on 13 August around 200,000 people, including members of independent unions and ordinary citizens, marched to the Zócalo. Emphasising their Mexican credentials, they called for the release of political prisoners, the fulfillment of the promises of the Revolution, and respect for the Constitution. Two weeks later, the crowd of protesters had grown to 300,000. With the situation unresolved, the university rector, Javier Barros Sierra, called for students to return to their classes, but the students rejected this and on 13 September thousands marched in silence through the streets of Mexico City. Many had their mouths taped over; placards and a single loudspeaker transmitted the message that their silence was a protest against the lack of public dialogue, and to show the students' discipline in contrast to the violence used against them.[13] The government's response was to order the army to occupy part of the University Campus. On 23 September Barros Sierra resigned in protest, but by 30 September the situation had eased. The army left the campus and Barros Sierra returned to his post.

Given the improvement in the situation between the students and government forces, the extreme violence of 2 October was unexpected and why it happened will probably never be uncovered. Mexican officials have

---

11 Ricardo Garibay, 'La hora cero', *Excélsior*, 27 September 1968, 7.
12 Luis Echeverría, quoted in Poniatowska, *La noche*, 277.
13 Leobardo López Arretche, *El grito, México 1968* (Mexico City: Filmoteca de la UNAM, 1968).

insisted that the students fired first and that government forces responded
in self-defence. Survivors claim that government agents, wearing white
gloves, entered the surrounding buildings and infiltrated the crowd. Tanks
blocked all exits to the square; a helicopter shone lights onto the crowd;
the army then opened fire. The terrified students ran for cover. Some tried
to enter a colonial church that borders the plaza, but the doors remained
closed. The priests inside did not open them.[14] There are also wide dispari-
ties in the casualty numbers: official figures eventually stated there had
been forty-three deaths, with eight soldiers injured. Yet most Mexicans
believe that between 300 and 500 people were killed that night. Of the
estimated 2,000 people imprisoned, over seventy remained in jail five
years later.[15]

The massacre left a generation devastated by death, imprisonment, and
terror. This use of force against Mexican citizens, the majority of whom were
young students from middle-class backgrounds, has proved to be a defining moment in recent Mexican history. The way in which the movement
is remembered is profoundly affected by the fact that the government at
first tried to disguise the casualty numbers, and because it has consistently
insisted that the students fired on the army. The Mexican press followed
government guidelines in concealing the extent of the tragedy. As I have

14   Poniatowska, La noche, 166–171; Fernando Benítez, 'Los días de la ignominia', La
     Cultura en México, 23 October 1968, ii. For a vivid eye-witness account in English
     see, John Rodda, 'Trapped at Gunpoint in the Middle of Fighting', The Guardian, 4
     October 1968, 1, 2. For a discussion of the action of the priests see, Elena Poniatowska,
     'Con Méndez Arceo', Siempre, 7 January 1970, 34.
15   Elena Poniatowska, 'Massacre in Mexico', in W. Dirk Raat and William Beezley
     (eds), Twentieth-Century Mexico (Lincoln: University of Nebraska Press, 1986),
     257; Michael Meyer and William Sherman, The Course of Mexican History (New
     York: Oxford University Press, 1987), 670; Octavio Paz, Posdata (Mexico City: Siglo
     Veintiuno, 1970), 38: Poniatowska, La noche, 170; Rodda, 'Trapped at Gunpoint',
     1, 2; John Rodda, 'After the Games are Over', The Guardian, 1 November 1968, 10;
     Francisco Ortiz Pinchetti, 'Políticamente, el movimiento triunfó', Proceso, 2 October
     1978, 11.

argued elsewhere,[16] the government's attitude did not prevent Mexicans from obtaining a more realistic sense of the massacre, but it did succeed in severely restricting public acknowledgement of what had happened and, for many years, it impeded any attempt to commemorate those who had died.

Similarly, the Mexican government's denial of any wrong-doing against the students, and the eagerness of politicians elsewhere in the world to ensure that the Olympic Games went ahead as scheduled, have led to a general attitude of 'forgetting' the Mexican students. This has made it all the more important for those who had been involved in the movement to ensure that the transformation of Mexican society during the summer of 1968 is remembered. This sense of amnesia also applies to other student groups at the time. While individuals may have been aware of what had happened, the repression used against the Mexican students tended not to feature in written accounts of the time.[17] This is despite powerful eye-witness newspaper reports by foreign journalists such as John Rodda. Rodda, who had been trapped by gunfire for several hours on a balcony overlooking the Tlatelolco plaza, was among a small number of people who called for the Olympic Games to be cancelled. His vivid portrayals of his horrific ordeal and the aftermath were published on the front pages of *The Guardian* newspaper.[18]

After the massacre Mexican politicians, like members of the armed forces, strictly adhered to the official line that the students had attacked

16   Claire Brewster, 'The Student Movement of 1968 and the Mexican Press', *Bulletin of Latin American Studies*, 21, 2 (2002), 171–190.

17   See for example, Tariq Ali, *1968 and After: Inside the Revolution* (London: Blond and Biggs, 1978); Tariq Ali, *Street Fighting Years* (London: William Collins and Sons, 1987).

18   See John Rodda, 'Olympic Games to go Ahead in Spite of Mexico Rioting', *The Guardian*, 4 October 1968, 1; Rodda, 'Trapped at Gunpoint', 1, 2; John Rodda, 'Olympic Games Organisers Taking a Grave Risk', *The Guardian*, 5 October 1968, 1; John Rodda, 'Dum Dum Bullets were Used', *The Guardian*, 5 October 1968, 1; Rodda, 'After the Games', 10. For his recollections forty years later, see John Rodda, '"Prensa, Prensa!": A Journalist's Reflections on Mexico '68', ed. Keith Brewster, *Reflections on Mexico '68* (Oxford: Wiley/Blackwell, 2010).

first. The notable exception was the poet Octavio Paz, who was then ambassador to India. Paz had been closely following events in Mexico and had
suggested ways of resolving the conflict. He later explained, 'I did not
agree with all of [the students'] demands, but I argued that peaceful means
should be used [to resolve the protests]'.[19] Interviewed in November 1968,
Paz described the massacre as 'an act of terrorism by the [Mexican] State'.[20]
Paz also withdrew from the Cultural Olympics: he had previously agreed
to submit a poem to an international reunion of poets. Instead, he wrote
and distributed 'México: Olimpiada de 1968' (Mexico: Olympiad of 1968)
to the national and international press. Dated 3 October 1968, the poem
voices Paz's anger and disgust.[21]

   Paz's stance was very much appreciated by the students and their supporters.[22] In 1970 a group of youths nominated Paz the 'padrino' (godfa-
ther) of their generation. Mexican university students traditionally elect
'padrinos' in different disciplines, but the significance is far greater than the
translation suggests. A padrino is a substitute father, a spiritual guide, and
a friend. Paz's work had been important to the students. They had carried
banners bearing quotations from his poems during their marches and, as
the writer and political prisoner José Revueltas reveals, in 1969 Paz was an
inspiration to the inmates of Lecumberri Prison, including Martín Dozal
who was then on hunger strike. In an open letter Revueltas stated: 'Here
in prison we all think about Octavio Paz. [...] Martín Dozal reads Octavio
Paz in prison. You have to realise the great importance of this, what a pro-

19   Octavio Paz, quoted in Roderic Camp, *Intellectuals and the State in Twentieth Century
      Mexico* (Austin: University of Texas Press, 1985), 211–212.
20   Jean Wetz, 'Entrevista con Octavio Paz', *Le Monde*, 14 November 1968, reproduced in
      Rafael Rodríguez Castañeda, 'Octavio Paz a *Le Monde* en 1968', *Proceso*, 25 September
      1995, 16, 18.
21   Octavio Paz, 'México: Olimpiada de 1968', *La Cultura en México*, 30 October 1968,
      iii. For a more detailed discussion of this poem see Irene Fenoglio Limón's chapter
      in this book.
22   For messages of support see *Siempre*, 16 October 1968, 12–14 and *La Cultura en
      México*, 23 October 1968, vii–ix.

found hope there is in this simple act. [...] This teaching awakens us.'[23] A generation of educated Mexicans was no longer accepting the dictates of the single-party State, but was instead seeking more relevant instructors.

The memory

In the words of the political author and journalist, Elena Poniatowska, who had followed the Mexican Student Movement with much sympathy: 'In 1968 Mexico was young, and it made everyone young. [...] It was the most intense period in many years, and once things calmed down, many came to appreciate that it was the most intense period of their lives. Something was irredeemably lost in 1968, [...] but something was won.'[24] Poniatowska is perhaps the most widely known of the writers and intellectuals who have worked to keep the Student Movement in the Mexican public conscious-ness. Her book, *La noche de Tlatelolco* (*The Night of Tlatelolco – Massacre in Mexico* in its English version), a chronology of the movement through the words of those who participated in it, was published in 1971. It was an instant best-seller. In 1991 it was in its fiftieth edition; 250,000 copies had been sold in Mexico and it has been translated into several languages.[25] In re-telling this story at a time when most of those who had taken part were dead, in prison, or were living in hiding, Poniatowska was taking a great personal risk – she was kept under surveillance and her publishing house

23   José Revueltas, 'Aquí, un mensaje a Octavio Paz', *La Cultura en México*, 22 October 1969, xi.

24   Elena Poniatowska, 'The Student Movement of 1968', in Gilbert Joseph and Timothy Henderson (eds), *The Mexico Reader* (Durham, N.C.: Duke University Press, 2002), 556.

25   Patricia Vega, 'Celebra 20 años la primera edición de *La noche de Tlatelolco*', *La Jornada*, 27 August 1991, 40. The average number of copies sold in Mexico at that time was around 1,000. The English version appeared in 1975. Elena Poniatowska (trans. Helen Lane), *Massacre in Mexico* (New York: Viking, 1975).

received bomb threats. She nonetheless 'remembered' the movement using a style that since then has become very much her own: she visited those in prison and wrote down their testimonies; remarkably, and at their insistence, quoting many of their names alongside their words.[26]

The book is probably the most influential study of the Student Movement and was a deliberate attempt to represent the movement as a whole. It opens with a thirty-page section of photographs that chart the jubilation and solidarity of its early days. This is overtaken by the escalation of violence: soldiers; tanks; youths behind prison bars; a scene from a mortuary; and finally a vigil that was held on 2 November 1968, during which relatives defied an armed presence by going to the plaza where they placed flowers and lit candles to their dead or missing children.[27] The text of *Massacre in Mexico* is divided into two sections. The first details reasons for joining the Student Movement, and portrays the marches, the camaraderie, the chants, and expectations. The second part describes the night of 2 October through the eyes of the students and inhabitants of Tlatelolco; it also includes press cuttings and the comments of soldiers, foreign visitors and journalists. By providing details of her informants, Poniatowska shows how various sectors of society were caught up in the movement and its brutal suppression: students, teachers, parents, neighbours, newspaper reporters and photographers were all affected by the events of that tragic evening.

In the 1990s, the cultural critic and long time supporter of the Student Movement, Carlos Monsiváis, stressed the impact of *Massacre in Mexico*: 'It changed the perception of the Student Movement.'[28] Through Poniatowska's work, generations of Mexicans would come to understand the wide range of individual and collective motives that had led to the mass protests. Her book documents the measures taken against the students

26 Marco Antonio Campos, 'Elena Poniatowska: No olvidar a los olvidados', *La Cultura en México*, 2 February 1994, 48.
27 2 November is Mexico's Day of the Dead, a pre-Columbian festival in commemoration of the lives of the ancestors.
28 Claire Brewster, Unpublished interview with Carlos Monsiváis, 1996.

by the authorities, as well as the personal tragedies behind the distorted government statistics of the casualties.

Other publications were less well received. Octavio Paz was among those who immediately sought to explain the wider significance of the Student Movement.[29] His short book, *Posdata (Post-script)*, presents a disparaging study of the nature and structure of Mexican politics, and places the Mexican Student Movement in a global context. Paz notes that although the protests were part of a world-wide phenomenon, the students were also acting spontaneously; each country had its own specific causes and characteristics. He depicts the Mexican students as 'reformist and democratic', adding that their demands were 'really moderate'.[30] The more contentious part of Paz's analysis is his emphasis on the fact that the carnage took place at a pre-Columbian temple. Paz links the massacre with the Aztecs' mass sacrifices and states: 'The killing at Tlatelolco shows us that a past we thought was buried is alive.'[31] He proposes a complete revision of Mexican history; a critical review. By learning the lessons of its past, he suggests, Mexico could understand its present and shape a better future.

In *Posdata*, Paz is intensely critical of the Mexican political regime, describing it as 'lacking in internal democracy and dominated by a hierarchy that pays blind obedience to each president',[32] and it is not surprising that the book was publicly denounced by President Díaz Ordaz. Yet other critics viewed the links that Paz had made to Mexico's past as somehow justifying the massacre. In 1978 Antonio Deltoro inaccurately maintained that Paz was suggesting that the Aztec war god was responsible for the massacre rather than President Díaz Ordaz, and he accused Paz of not understanding Mexican problems.[33] Reviewing *Posdata* in 1973, author

---

29   Among the others are Carlos Monsiváis, *Días de guardar*; (Mexico City: Ediciones Era, 1970); Carlos Fuentes, *Tiempo mexicano* (Joaquín Mortiz, 1971); Luis González de Alba, *Los días y los años* (Mexico City: Ediciones Era, 1971).

30   Paz, *Posdata*, 21–40. Quotes taken from 35.

31   Ibid, 40.

32   Ibid, 51.

33   Antonio Deltoro, 'Las responsabilidades de Huitzilopochtli', *Nexos*, September 1978, 23.

Carlos Fuentes explained that Paz's book, although a best-seller,[34] had been the object of criticism from both sides of the political spectrum. Those on the Right denounced it as 'an anti-Mexican tract'; 'the radical Left and the liberals were scandalised by Paz's psychological and anthropological analysis of the deep-lying myths of the Mexican conscience'. Fuentes describes *Posdata* as 'an uncomfortable book' of which 'few literate Mexicans have actually approved'. It made Mexicans uneasy, Fuentes explains, because Paz challenged Mexico to 'take a good look at itself, at its cultural and mythical past. The ghosts of our history will only be buried [...] if we critically examine their reality'. Fuentes underlines that critics of the Left were misconstruing Paz's objectives: 'They were demanding that he cease to be what he is, a writer, and become what he was not and did not want to be: an avenging demagogue, an active political leader.'[35] Paz's position was made more difficult in that he had been the only government official to resign following the massacre, and his poem 'México: Olimpiada de 1968' was deemed to have been a timely and appropriate reaction. This had led to increased expectations placed upon him by certain sectors of society; yet Paz did not have a radical political agenda, he was simply following his conscience. In 1993 Paz acknowledged the fierce criticism of *Posdata*, but stood by his findings, stating that his interpretation had neither been insensitive nor unfounded; it was merely his perception of the massacre.[36] Yet for Paz's critics, 1970 was simply too soon to apply an academic treatment onto a still-raw wound. His analysis sharply contrasts to other early academic interpretations of 'Mexico 1968'.[37]

---

34   In 1993 *Posdata* had reached twenty editions and had been translated into English, French, and German.

35   Carlos Fuentes, 'Mexico and its Demons', *New York Review of Books*, 20 September 1973, 16, 19.

36   Julio Scherer, 'Salinas, modernización, TLC, democracia, el 68, el poder', *Proceso*, 18 October 1993, 8.

37   See for example, Monsiváis, *Días de guardar*; Fuentes, *Tiempo mexicano*; Hellman, *Mexico in Crisis*, first published 1978, all of which adopt a more straightforward narrative and analysis.

As Irene Fenoglio Limón illustrates in her chapter of this book, in time the Student Movement would stimulate a wealth of literature. Those most deeply affected by it were educated and articulate, and often well-connected members of society. Consequently plays, poems, novels, films, and documentaries have been written and performed about the Student Movement. Yet, as Dolly Young pointed out in 1985, it is inevitably referred to as 'Tlatelolco literature' due to its focus on the events of that tragic night.[38] Despite considerable efforts taken by Mexican writers such as Poniatowska and Carlos Monsiváis to resurrect the entire experience of the Student Movement, it has been a difficult task to prevent the violence used against the students dominating the collective memory to such an extent that the hope the students inspired was obscured. Eric Zolov's excellent study of youth culture in Mexico notwithstanding,[39] the massacre has nonetheless overshadowed the movement. For as long as the Mexican government refused to acknowledge the extent of the bloodshed on 2 October, 'Tlatelolco' has dominated the way in which 1968 has been remembered in Mexico and beyond. Rosario Castellanos underlines this imperative in her poem, 'Memorial de Tlatelolco' ('Memorial of Tlatelolco'): 'I remember, we remember/ That's our way of helping [...]/ I remember, let us remember,/ Until we feel that justice is among us.'[40]

Remembering the Mexican Student Movement, then, has above all meant combating a general sense of 'forgetting': overcoming the government's denial of any wrong doing against its own citizens, and ensuring that the spirit of participation generated by the thousands of young people who

38 Dolly Young, 'Literary Responses to Tlatelolco 1968', *Latin American Research Review*, 20, 22 (1985), 76–85. In this early study of the 'Tlatelolco literature' Young states that works on Tlatelolco were already 'too numerous to list'. She nonetheless provides a comprehensive summary of those that had been produced at that time. Ibid, 83–85. See also Guest Editor, Victoria Carpenter, 'Tlatelolco 1968 in Contemporary Mexican Literature', *Bulletin of Latin American Research*, 24, 4 (2005); ed. Keith Brewster, *Reflections on Mexico '68* (Oxford: Wiley/Blackwell, 2010). See chapters by Chris Harris, Ryan Long and Hazel Marsh.

39 Eric Zolov, *Refried Elvis: The Rise of Mexican Counterculture* (Berkeley: University of California, 1999).

40 Rosario Castellanos, 'Memorial de Tlatelolco', in Poniatowska, *La noche*, 163–164.

took to the streets was not lost in the process. As Monsiváis had written in September 1968,[41] 'Mexico has been transformed. [...] A generation has decided not to follow the dismal conformist example of its predecessors.' He expressed hopes that as a consequence of the Student Movement universities would become the site of 'the permanent fight to democratise the country'. Monsiváis emphasised that the movement's major victory had been 'the creation of a true national conscience'. He underlined the 'academic responsibility' to fight for the freedom of those imprisoned for their part in the movement and to present an objective analysis of what was happening in Mexican society.[42]

Throughout the duration of the Student Movement, Monsiváis worked intensively as a magazine editor and radio broadcaster to ensure that its progress was reported in the national news. His book, *Días de guardar* (*Days to Preserve*), a collection of articles written from 1966 to 1970, was published in 1970. As one who had closely followed the course of the movement, Monsiváis was ideally placed to write about it, yet although the Student Movement is the focal point of his book, he concentrates on specific incidents rather than its entire course. He describes in detail the demonstration of 1 August in which Rector Barros Sierra and several lecturers joined the students. He also discusses the 'Silent March' of 13 September, in which the students revealed themselves to be orderly and disciplined.[43] Monsiváis does not dwell on the events of 2 October; he notes that the massacre was a decisive moment that revealed the true nature of the country. He underlines that beneath a facade of stability and progress the Mexican political system had turned against its citizens: behind the democratic rhetoric lay economic chaos and corruption; peasants were living in misery, there was mass unemployment, the electoral system was

---

41   The undated article was published in the 9 October edition of *La Cultura en México*, but was probably written towards the end of September. The magazine went to press at least two weeks in advance of its publication date. The articles discussing the Tlatelolco massacre, for example, appear in the 23 October issue.

42   Carlos Monsiváis, 'Puntos de vista sobre el Movimiento Estudiantil: Las exigencias del retorno', *La Cultura en México*, 9 October 1968, xvi.

43   Monsiváis, *Días de guardar*, see in particular 214–253; 258–275.

a shambles, and people were being imprisoned for their political beliefs while assassins went unpunished. In considering the massacre, Monsiváis instead reflects on 2 November, Mexico's Day of the Dead on which relatives and friends paid tribute to those who had died and disappeared one month earlier. Monsiváis provides a factual reconstruction of the events of 2 October interspersed with the messages left in November: 'We won't forget you'; 'History will judge you'.[44] Reviewing *Días de guardar*, critic and author José Emilio Pacheco noted the intense sorrow within its pages; it marked the end of an era. He pointed out that the 'days to preserve' were strictly limited; the Student Movement had lasted just sixty-nine days. Pacheco underlined, 'we're in an era that's very difficult to write about': difficult because the brutality of the movement's sudden end was 'an open wound',[45] but also difficult because those who dared to write about political issues at that time became targets for reprisals.

Commemorations 1977–1992

Although perceptions of the Student Movement may have changed through the work of Poniatowska and others, more overt manifestations of commemoration were initially confined to literary circles or conversations within the home. It would take nine years before the movement was 'remembered' in the mass demonstrations that had so emphatically defined it. In April 1977 the former students took to the streets once again; this time to voice their fury when the man who had been president in 1968, Gustavo Díaz Ordaz, was appointed ambassador to Spain. Díaz Ordaz was largely held to blame for the massacre. Indeed, he had publicly claimed responsibility for it in his September 1969 address to the nation, during which he

44   Ibid, 304.
45   José Emilio Pacheco, 'Monsimarx, Monsimailer, Monsimad', *La Cultura en México*, 17 March 1971, xiii.

spoke with pride of having saved the country from 'anti-Mexican forces'.[46] In response to his appointment around 10,000 people marched through the streets of Mexico City.[47] They were led by many former students of 1968; Elena Poniatowska was among them. Such was the strength of feeling shown against Díaz Ordaz that, in contrast to the iron hand with which he had controlled the country during his presidency, he was forced to resign within two weeks of taking up his appointment. The official rationale given was that a detached retina made it impossible for him to carry out his duties.

This 'victory' perhaps gave the former students the confidence to make their presence felt once more. It also coincided with a government promise for political reform: opposition parties were allowed to hold up to 25 per cent of the seats in Mexico's National Congress. And on 2 October 1978, the tenth anniversary of the Tlatelolco massacre, a public commemoration took place. There had been no such gatherings in previous years because government forces had severely restricted access to Tlatelolco. In 1978 the event took place despite a huge military presence. Monsiváis depicted the scene as 'one of the great images of contemporary Mexico'.[48] In one of the first public statements extending the political aims of the movement, he noted that the students of 1968 had 'taken the first steps towards demanding full democracy'.[49] He emphasised that many of the surviving former student leaders were becoming an increasingly effective political opposition.

Again in contrast to ten years earlier, these demonstrations were given much publicity. The Mexican press had recently undergone a considerable opening. The draconian measures employed by President Echeverría in July 1976 to censor Mexico's most critical daily newspaper, *Excélsior*, had backfired and would result in the birth of several new newspapers

46   'Texto integro del Informe Presidencial', *Excélsior*, 2 September 1969, 12, 13, 27–30.
47   Elena Poniatowska, 'El movimiento estudiantil de 1968', *Vuelta*, June 1977, 26.
48   Carlos Monsiváis, 'Si una nación entera se avergüenza ...', *Proceso*, 9 October 1978, 20.
49   Ibid, 20.

and magazines.[50] Two of these, *Nexos* and *Proceso*, dedicated the majority of their September and October 1978 editions to the reflections, views and comments of those who had been involved in the student protests. *Nexos* included a full chronology of the movement and *Proceso* published a list of the prisoners who, in November 1970, had been sentenced from between three to seventeen years in jail. Most of them had been released as a 'goodwill' gesture by President Echeverría in 1971; information that *Proceso* did not supply.[51] Poniatowska wrote a chronicle of the 1978 commemorative march in which she noted how the lives of the former students had irretrievably changed as a result of 'Mexico 1968'. She applauded the wisdom of the rector and the teachers who had supported the students ten years earlier; she heralded the student leaders as 'pure and invincible', and claimed that the movement had been 'the greatest independent mobilisation in the history in contemporary Mexico: the most extraordinary movement since the Revolution'. Moreover, as she noted, many of the former students were continuing the struggle by working within oppositional political parties. 'Their revolutionary effort hasn't diminished', she underlined, 'it's grown'.[52]

Ten years later, in the presidential election of 1988, the extent of this opposition could be measured. In a bitterly contested election, politicians and their supporters of both the Left and Right used the twentieth

50 For further details of the '*Excélsior* Coup' see, Kenneth Johnson, *Mexican Democracy: A Critical View* (New York: Praeger Publishers, 1978), 60–61; Enrique Krauze (trans. Hank Heifetz), *Mexico, Biography of Power* (New York: Harper Collins, 1997), 750–751; Elena Poniatowska, 'Otra vez frente al papel desnudo: No podemos ...', *Siempre*, 28 July 1976, 24–27; Vicente Leñero, *Los periodistas* (Mexico City: Joaquín Mortiz, 1978); Héctor Aguilar Camín and Lorenzo Meyer, *In the Shadow of the Mexican Revolution: Contemporary Mexican History 1910–1989* (Austin: University of Texas Press, 1993), 208–209; Claire Brewster, *Responding to Crisis in Contemporary Mexico* (Tucson: University of Arizona Press, 2005), 88–92.

51 See *Nexos*, September 1978, 2–11, 14–15, 17, 19, 21–25; *Proceso*, 2 October 1978, 6–23; *Proceso*, 9 October 1978, 18–22; *Proceso*, 16 October 1978, 6–10; 23 October 1978, 20–23; *Proceso*, 30 October 1978, 6–14.

52 Elena Poniatowska, 'Diez años después: El rumor de las manifestaciones', *Proceso*, 2 October 1978, 19–22. Quotes on 19, 22.

anniversary of the Student Movement to support the validity of their own campaigns. The main opposition, which had much support, was a coalition of left-wing groups led by Cuauhtémoc Cárdenas and Heberto Castillo. Cárdenas was the son of Mexico's most popular post-revolutionary president (Lázaro Cárdenas 1934–1940). Castillo, a former teacher, had been a member of the Student Movement: in August 1968 he had been hospitalised following a clash with government forces; he was among those who were rounded up after the massacre, and was imprisoned for several years. After his release he established a workers' political party. In January 1988, Castillo stated that he viewed the forthcoming election as the culmination of his political struggle; one that would fulfil the hopes and expectations of the Student Movement.[53]

Yet Octavio Paz, who supported the ruling party candidate Carlos Salinas, also made the bold, and to many observers surprising, stance of linking Salinas's presidential campaign to the Student Movement. For many, Salinas merely provided a new face to the same ruling party of 1968. Yet in an interview published in the then leading Mexican daily newspaper of the Left, *La Jornada*, Paz stated: 'I believe that there has been an immense, gradual evolution in the Mexican political system, which began [...] with the rebellion of the middle-class students, [...] and that has now taken this [Salinas's candidacy] much more important step towards democracy.'[54] Hence both political parties were appropriating the students' professed aims at a highly symbolic time: twenty years later, when a new generation of voters had grown up under the shadow of the Tlatelolco massacre.

The election brought a highly controversial win for Salinas. Four days after the ballot, and with the opposition coalition in the lead, the computing system 'crashed'. Three days later, it was announced that Salinas had won by a narrow margin. This result, and the nature in which it had come about, brought mass demonstrations again to the streets of Mexico City.

53   Víctor Avilés, 'Para sobrevivir: Entrevista con Heberto Castillo', *Nexos*, January 1988, 84.
54   Braulio Peralta, 'Gradual e irreversible el camino a la democracia', *La Jornada*, 7 July 1988, 20.

Paz continued to underline the links between the students' ambitions in 1968 and Salinas's plans for the future. He wrote, 'the [Student] Movement ended in a pool of blood. [...] Now it has been born again'. He pointed out that in 1968 Mexico had faced a dilemma: '[Then] the youths, [...] sustained that the only answer [...] was violent revolutionary change. They were [not] democratic.'[55] Yet in *Posdata* Paz had specifically described members of the Student Movement as, 'reformist and democratic'.[56] Furthermore, in an interview back in 1970 Paz had emphasised: 'What the students asked for was democracy.'[57] This was a quite a contradiction. In remembering the Student Movement at this crucial time, Paz was distorting his memories of the students' aims and contesting his own analysis.

Carlos Monsiváis, who wholeheartedly wrote in support of the opposition coalition, also linked the 1988 demonstrations to those of twenty years earlier. He drew an ominous parallel: 'As in 1968 the strategy of dispelling reality simply by not admitting it on TV has continued.'[58] Monsiváis underlined that the mere suspicion of a defeat for the governing party should give hope to all those who had previously been excluded from political participation. For him, the 1988 election marked the Student Movement's physical and psychological coming of age.[59] Agreeing with Monsiváis, in an open letter to Octavio Paz, former student leader Adolfo Gilly stated that all votes for the opposition party candidate were the culmination of a long political struggle.[60]

So in 1988, the Student Movement was appropriated by actors from across the political spectrum for very different ends. The governing party won the day and President Salinas was inaugurated in December. But once

---

55   Octavio Paz, 'Historias de ayer', *La Jornada*, 10 August 1988, 10.
56   Paz, *Posdata*, 35.
57   Mercedes Valdivieso, 'Entre el tlatoani y el caudillo', *La Cultura en México*, 8 April 1970, ii.
58   Carlos Monsiváis, 'Notas sobre la campaña de 1988/II', *La Jornada*, 13 July 1988, 17.
59   Carlos Monsiváis, 'Notas sobre la campaña de 1988/III', *La Jornada*, 14 July 1988, 6.
60   Adolfo Gilly, 'Carta a Octavio Paz', *La Jornada*, 22 August 1988, 12.

168 CLAIRE BREWSTER

in office, Salinas did make some concessions and gave government positions to members of the 'generation of 1968' who were willing to take them. In 1992 Gilberto Guevara, who had spent over two and a half years in prison for his part in the Student Movement, became Secretary for Education. Among his duties was to update Mexican history books: for the first time the Student Movement was included in school textbooks. No blame was apportioned, but the entry states that the government took a hard line against the students, and that the army broke up a meeting at Tlatelolco on 2 October at which there were many deaths.[61]

The details may have been scant, but this was a major breakthrough in officially recording the Student Movement. The publication of 'unofficial' literature about the Student Movement had continued throughout this period. Under Salinas it expanded as the president sought to distance his administration from that of Díaz Ordaz in the 1960s. The receptions of two fictional versions of the Tlatelolco massacre that appeared during Salinas's presidency are particularly worthy of discussion: *Rojo amanecer* (*Red Dawn*), and *Regina: Dos de octubre no se olvida* (*Regina: 2 October is not forgotten*).

In 1989 Jorge Fons's film, *Red Dawn*, a dramatic reconstruction of the massacre was released. It is set inside one of the apartments overlooking Tlatelolco plaza and gives an account of the events of 2 October 1968 through the eyes of the 'typical' middle-class Mexican family living there: an elderly man, a veteran of the 1910 Revolution; his daughter, a housewife; her government bureaucrat husband; and their four children, two youths who are politically active students, a girl aged around thirteen years, and a boy of nine. Tensions between the generations are clearly shown as the children listen to popular music, question their parents, and show an awareness of political issues. Their parents and grandfather act as voices of reason, demanding respect for authority. The father leaves for work, the two youngest children go to school and, disobeying orders to stay at home, the two youths go out to meet their friends. A sense of foreboding

<hr>

61   Sonia Morales, 'Incluir a Salinas en los libros de texto fue una imprudencia', *Proceso*, 17 April 1995, 40–41.

increases throughout the day as soldiers are positioned within the residential building, the electricity supply and telephone lines are cut, making it impossible for the bureaucrat father to warn his family that something is about to happen.

Four members of the family are caught in the shooting: the girl, on her way home after doing homework at a friend's house; her grandfather, who went out to find her; and the two youths who were at the fateful meeting. All manage to return home safely: the youths have been slightly injured and are in the company of a group of other students thrown together while sheltering from the gunfire – none of whom know each other. One of them is seriously injured; his sister, who had been with him at the meeting, had been killed. The family is shown to stick together in the face of adversity: the father returns from work horrified at what he has seen in the plaza. Soldiers come to the apartment looking for fugitives, but the grandfather draws on his revolutionary pedigree and underlines that he is a military man, like them, and that they are on the same side. Some time later, a second group of militia demand entrance. They are more aggressive: they ridicule the grandfather's revolutionary record, and ignore the father's position as a government employee. They force their way into the apartment, discover the fugitives and slaughter everyone they find. There is a sole survivor: the youngest child who, following his grandfather's advice, had remained in a secure hiding place throughout the ordeal.

This dramatisation, the first of its kind concerning the massacre at Tlatelolco, was a box-office success. Although presented as fiction, many of the events were in accordance with eyewitness accounts. The passing of time throughout that fateful day is clearly marked. The lights that were shone just before the shooting began can be seen from inside the apartment and the crowd is shown to have been infiltrated with men wearing white gloves. The total disintegration of the social order within the space of a few hours is depicted in the grandfather's loss of his status as a former revolutionary soldier, and the father's lack of influence as a government employee: past and present deeds can not save the family. There is perhaps a tiny glimmer of hope in that the youngest child obeyed his grandfather and was spared, thus implying that the revolutionary legacy is still valid, as are family values. But the child has a horrific awakening as he finds his entire family dead, and he walks hesitantly barefoot and alone into a bloody dawn. The film ends as he steps into Tlatelolco plaza, picking his way through the bodies as council employees hastily try to clean away the evidence.

Antonio Velasco Piña's novel, *Regina*, was less well-received. *Regina* is the fictionalised story of one of the victims at Tlatelolco, Ana María Regina Teuscher. Velasco Piña's *Regina* has been educated in Tibet and is transformed into a Messiah, a leader, a saint, and guru; a chosen queen who died during a predestined massacre.[62] One important difference is that whereas *Rojo Amanecer* tells the story of a fictional family as if it were a documentary, *Regina* romanticises the all-too-real death of a nineteen-year-old medical student. Ana María Regina Teuscher was one of the few victims to have been named by the Mexican authorities. Her death was announced in the national press.[63] A photograph of the young woman's body was published in *Siempre* magazine and Velasco Piña is said to have become so 'obsessed' with her sad fate that he based his novel around her.[64] In 1987 the Teuscher family objected to the use of Regina's photograph in the first edition of the book, but their complaint had no further repercussions.[65] Six years later a polemic occurred in the Mexican press when plans were proposed to make the novel into a film. In February 1993 Elena Poniatowska published her concerns. She recalled what she had found out about Teuscher when compiling *Massacre in Mexico*: members of her family had declined to be interviewed as they were too upset; no-one had mentioned her as one of the student leaders. Poniatowska underlined: '[Regina] has been converted by Velasco Piña into a mythical being. [...] Unlike Velasco Piña, I can't believe that Regina Teuscher's destiny was to die at Tlatelolco, it's simply too cruel'.[66] Poniatowska also voiced her concern that this reconstruction of Tlatelolco did not address the issue of responsibility. Velasco Piña, she stated,

62   Antonio Velasco Piña, *Regina* (Mexico City, Jus, 1987).

63   *Excélsior*, 4 October 1968, 18. No details are given of how she died.

64   Elena Poniatowska, 'Regina', *La Jornada*, 11 February 1993, 1, 24.

65   Luis Enrique Ramírez, 'A debate, *Regina*, de Velasco Piña; ¿mito o realidad del movimiento de 68?', *La Jornada*, 5 February 1993, 23.

66   Elena Poniatowska, 'Las fuerzas ocultas del 68', *La Jornada*, 5 February 1993, 23.

exonerates those who were declared to have been to blame. [...] Was the collective assassination written beforehand? [...] Did Díaz Ordaz fulfil a heavenly order? Were those who fired from the roof tops archangels? [...] Was the green flare really a radiant star? [...] Did those who ran to save themselves commit a sin because their mission was to die and was that why the priests didn't open the church doors?[67]

Poniatowska made similar comments during a presentation of Velasco Piña's book in February 1993. At this event, a woman continually sought permission to speak. She was eventually permitted to introduce herself as María Luisa Teuscher de Vomend, Regina's sister. She asked Velasco Piña what right he had to use her sister's memory to propagate lies and to make money. She applauded Poniatowska for providing a rational voice and left, giving Poniatowska her telephone number.[68] María Luisa Teuscher's trust in Poniatowska was not misplaced. Faced with the Teuscher family's distress, Poniatowska abandoned her current work; she visited María Luisa Teuscher the following day and composed the family's version of Regina's story.[69]

This account, including photographs of Regina as a child, was published in *La Jornada*.[70] Poniatowska explains that Regina Teuscher had been at Tlatelolco on 2 October with her friend Guillermina. The two were separated in the chaos following the shooting; Guillermina was injured and taken to a first aid post from which she informed Regina's family what had happened. The family then undertook a 'hellish expedition' in search of Regina that ended in a mortuary. Regina Teuscher had been shot six times in her back as she tried to run away from the soldiers.[71] Poniatowska ends by describing the reactions to this story of the reporter

---

67   Ibid, 24.
68   Ramírez, 'A debate, *Regina*', 23.
69   Carlos Puig, 'Defiende Alfonso Arau Regina, otra visión del 68', *Proceso*, 8 March 1993, 50. Puig affirms that Poniatowska wrote this article the day after she met María Luisa Teuscher.
70   Poniatowska, 'Regina', 1, 24.
71   Ibid, 24. Her body had been taken to the mortuary rather than 'disappeared', as did so many others, because the private secretary of the then Secretary for Internal Affairs, Luis Echeverría, was a friend of Regina's father.

Luis Enrique Ramírez, who was accompanying her, and of María Luisa
Teuscher's daughter, Marion:

> Almost 25 years after the massacre, I see horror in the young face of Luis Enrique, a
> horror that he had never experienced before. It shook him. He, who was always so
> cheerful, was disconsolate. [...] Marion was equally affected: to these two 21-year-
> olds what had happened was incomprehensible. A quarter of a century has been
> insufficient time to wash away the blood that was shed. It still remains. Luis Enrique
> asks, incredulously, [...] the great unanswerable question: Why?[72]

In this passage Poniatowska is underlining the impact of the details of
Regina's fate on two young people, and directs her readers to share their
indignation. She is not writing for sensationalist reasons, but to emphasise the reality for victims such as Regina and her family. In doing so,
Poniatowska bridges the previous twenty-five years: the washing away of
the blood is a direct reference to Octavio Paz's poem, 'México: Olimpiada
de 1968' and to Rosario Castellanos's 'Memorial de Tlatelolco', both of
which mention the efforts to clean the plaza after the massacre, and to the
government's efforts to conceal the tragic event. Luis Enrique's great question 'why' is unanswerable because there has never been an enquiry into
what happened. It also recalls cartoonist Abel Quesada's powerful image
that was published in *Excélsior* on 3 October 1968. Instead of his usual
cartoon, Quesada submitted a rectangle that was filled with black ink. It
bore the simple accusing caption: '¿Por que?' (Why?).[73] In a minimum of
space, Poniatowska brings the past into the present. She includes cultural
signposts for those old enough to remember the massacre, and incorporates
younger readers by describing the strong reactions of two people who had
been born after 1968.

Stepping into the debate, the man who would have edited the film,
Alfonso Arau, explained that *Regina* does not try to exonerate President
Díaz Ordaz; nor did he believe that it was important that details of Regina's
life had been invented. For Arau, a main concern was that through the novel

---

72   Ibid, 24.
73   Abel Quesada, '¿Por Qué?', *Excélsior*, 3 October 1968, 7.

Regina now existed in people's minds. He added that Carlos Monsiváis had praised the book as 'a magnificent chronicle of 1968' although he did not agree with its magical realism.[74] Here, perhaps, lies the key to the issue: precisely how should the massacre be documented? Over twenty years earlier Octavio Paz had made an academic analysis in *Posdata*, rooting it in the Aztec past. His critics felt that this was not an appropriate way of recording what had happened as it diminished the present government's responsibility. In *Regina*, Velasco Piña was making an even more extreme analysis. This was accepted as an author's right of freedom of speech until it was apparent that it caused deep offence and further injury to the family of one of the victims. There have been many ways of remembering the Mexican Student Movement and the Tlatelolco massacre in particular but, as Poniatowska revealed, the limits of acceptability were strictly defined.

Mexico 1993: A memorial and a promise

In September 1993, former student leader Luis González de Alba noted the changes that the students of 1968 had brought to Mexican society:

> We've modified the country, created political parties, unions, publications, laws, social and political changes. Mexico has become something else ... the watershed ... the epic of 68 ... the tragedy. We couldn't raise a monument to the victims, but we have raised ourselves: we've never given way, we were the image of chastity and purity; juvenile honesty against the dismal depravity of the government.[75]

González de Alba underlines how the spirit of participation had not been swept away, and he recalls the 'epic' as well as the 'tragedy'. The purity of those who took part in the Student Movement, he underlines, can be seen

---

74 Puig, 'Defiende Alfonso Arau Regina', 50.
75 Luis González de Alba, '1968: La fiesta y la tragedia', *Nexos*, September 1993, 24.

in the recent improvements in Mexican political life. Moreover, they had
done so by remaining true to the spirit of 'Mexico '68'.

On 2 October 1993, formal recognition was finally given to the victims
of Tlatelolco. On the twenty-fifth anniversary of the massacre, amid strict
security, a monument was unveiled at Tlatelolco bearing the names of those
known to have died there, and a section of Rosario Castellanos's poem that
had been written for Poniatowska's *Massacre in Mexico*.[76] Official recognition was a major step forward, but in July 1993 Monsiváis had called for
an inquiry to discover who had been behind the killing and who had concealed the number of deaths.[77] Two months later, Monsiváis was invited by
the former student leaders to join a Truth Commission. The commission
asked to consult the archives of newspapers and television stations; and
called for information from several former Mexican politicians, and the
former US ambassador.[78] Its task was to establish what had happened, not
to apportion blame. Not one of those contacted replied.[79]

President Salinas's apparent openness proved to be a superficial gesture:
a paragraph in a history school text-book was one thing; an inquiry into the
massacre was quite another. Instead, he announced that the archives would
be opened in 1998, in accordance with international law. 3,000 boxes of
papers were duly released and in September 1999 they could be consulted
in Mexico's National Archive. It was a daunting task as the papers were in
random order and related to national security investigations throughout
the twentieth century. Even if access were made more easily available, it
would be unlikely to reveal the full picture, as in 1968 the director of the

76   Alberto Aguirre, 'En las marchas conmemorativas del 68', *Proceso* 11 October 1993,
     15.
77   Carlos Monsiváis, 'Mitificación y desmitificación y nueva mitificación del 68', *Proceso*,
     26 July 1993, 36.
78   Morales *et al*, 'Protagonistas del 68', *Proceso*, 11 October 1993, 8–11.
79   Mireya Cuéllar, 'Facilitará Estados Unidos información acerca del 68', *La Jornada*,
     3 October 1993, 3.

University archive had been ordered to destroy everything to do with the Student Movement.[80]

Yet investigations have continued. In 1998, Sergio Aguayo Quezada's book, *1968: Los archivos de la violencia (1968: The Archives of Violence)* was published. It concluded that controlled repression had turned into chaos following a lack of communication.[81] This is perhaps the most comfortable explanation. The following year Carlos Monsiváis and Julio Scherer shed new light on the massacre in their book, *Parte de guerra (War Dispatch)*. The political journalist Scherer had relentlessly pursued the personal archive of the former Mexican Secretary of Defence, and eventually obtained it from his grandson. The documents reveal that ten armed officers were placed in buildings around Tlatelolco square with orders to shoot on the crowd.[82]

Each year 2 October is remembered. On the thirtieth anniversary of the massacre, the spokesperson of the Zapatista rebels, Subcomandante Marcos, issued a communiqué on behalf of the Zapatista Liberation Army, in which he called for the Student Movement as a whole to be remembered and not just its brutal end:

> [1968] is also, and above all, the Silent March, [...] the meetings, the graffiti on the walls, the brigades, [...] the subversive street dressed in the new clothing of dignity. It is the street as a territory for another politics, the politics of below, a new one, one that struggles, the rebel one. It is the street talking, discussing, displacing cars and traffic lights, asking, reclaiming, demanding a place in history.
>
> 68 is a window to peer through, and learn from the open confrontation between various forms of making politics, between different forms of being human.

80 Sonia Morales, 'Informes de 37 dependencias de la UNAM', *Proceso*, 11 October 1993, 14–15. Access to the 1968 files in Mexico's National Defence archive, if they exist, was not possible in 1998 and 1999. The personal files of members of the armed forces show a remarkable lack of activity of any nature between 1966 and 1970.
81 Sergio Aguayo Quezada, *1968: Los archivos de la violencia* (Mexico City: Reforma, 1998).
82 Julio Scherer García and Carlos Monsiváis, *Parte de guerra Tlatelolco 1968* (Mexico City: Nuevo Siglo Aguilar, 1999), 39–44, 53–54; Pascal Beltrán del Río, 'Informes del Pentágono apuntaban ya la responsabilidad de Gutiérrez Oropeza', *Proceso* 27 June 1999, 11–12.

As the Zapatistas underline, the Student Movement was more than the violent suppression of Mexican youths by government forces. It is, of course, important to keep this tragic affair in the public memory, but restricting commemorations exclusively to the massacre negates the important path that the students had been trying to create. The Student Movement was more than 'Tlatelolco', just as Tlatelolco the place is not merely synonymous with the massacre of students. Concentrating solely on the force used against the students is ironically helping to give the perpetrators of the violence a 'victory' by overshadowing the students' efforts. And in keeping with the practice of imposing aspirations onto the students, the Zapatista communiqué continues: 'The Mexico of 68 is the Mexico of those who live and breathe rebellion and the struggle for justice in the only way possible to them – as a lifetime struggle. The Mexico of those who keep demanding, struggling, organising, resisting.'[83]

As part of their education, groups of Mexican school children are taken to Tlatelolco plaza throughout the year; they are shown the monument, and the bullet holes that still mark the ground and the walls around the church doors. After formal recognition had been granted to the victims in 1993 it was easier to acknowledge what had happened. The end of the ruling party's seventy-one years in power in the July 2000 election has made it easier still, and the hundreds of documents in the National Archive may yet be catalogued. In the meantime, scholars persist in their search for answers. Although it is unlikely that the 'truth' of what happened to end the Student Movement will ever be fully clarified, for better or worse the 'Tlatelolco literature' has kept the Student Movement alive in the public consciousness.

83   Subcomandante Insurgente Marcos, 'Tlatelolco: Thirty Years later the Struggle Continues', in Juana Ponce de León, ed., *Our Word is Our Weapon: Selected Writings of Subcomandante Marcos* (London: Serpent's Tail, 2001), 143–146.

Post-script

It was not until 2007, thirty-six years after the publication of Poniatowska's *Massacre in Mexico*, and nine years after the Zapatistas' renewed plea to remember the movement as a whole, that there was a more complete testimony to the Student Movement. In November 2006, Mexico's National University acquired the former headquarters of the Department of Exterior Relations, which overlooks Tlatelolco plaza, and converted it into a Cultural Centre. A large section of it now houses a permanent exhibition, Memorial del 68, which opened in October 2007. After consulting what was left in the National and University archives, gathering evidence from public and private collections, and conducting interviews with those who had taken part in the movement in 2006 and 2007, it provides a vivid recreation of the Mexican Student Movement as a whole. The exhibition traces the changes in culture during the 1950s and 60s. In doing so it underlines that the movement should not be seen in isolation, but within the context of worldwide pressure for more political freedom. After providing the setting, the course of the movement is shown, day-by-day, through brief explanations illustrated with colourful displays of hand-made banners, leaflets and newspaper cuttings. Several of the protestors were art students and they used their talents to ridicule leading government officials in drawings and cartoons. The Tlatelolco massacre is an important part of the exhibition, of course: one room has clothes, shoes and bags strewn on the floor illustrating the desperate flight of the students. There are newspaper reports of the tragic affair, and large reproductions of Abel Quesada's blank 'cartoon', and Rosario Castellanos's 'Memorial of Tlatelolco'. Octavio Paz's 'México: Olimpiada de 1968' is etched onto a glass window that overlooks the preColumbian ruins among which the students tried to avoid the gunfire. At times sombre but at others expressing hope and jubilation, the movement is commemorated. In the words of one of the participants: 'It was like taking a two-month long intensive course in citizenship.'[84] After thirty-nine years, the Student Movement, in its entirety, is gaining a more secure place in the collective memory. In the words of Elena Poniatowska, who opened this latest exhibition: 'no homage to that great moment in our history is excessive'.[85]

The consequences, then, of the Mexican Student Movement of 1968 are multiple and varied. It has been used by a variety of people for different political ends, but in being used, abused and distorted, it has nonetheless survived. 1968 has subsequently become a watershed in Mexican history, marking the point after which the Mexican state could no longer purport to be the guardian of Mexican democracy and the protector of its people. Nothing can compensate for the tragic deaths of so many young people, but their hopes of wider participation in political life have lived on.

84   Quoted as part of the National University's Memorial del 68, Centro Cultural Universitario, Tlatelolco, Mexico City.
85   Poniatowska, 'The Student Movement', 556.

PART 2

Personal Testimonies

DANIEL BENSAÏD

1968 in France: An Unclassified Affair

In 1968, Daniel Bensaïd was a 22-year-old student of philosophy at the Nanterre campus outside Paris and it was here that student protest first erupted before spreading to the Latin Quarter and the Sorbonne in central Paris. Already an activist within the Trotskyist grouping, the JCR (Communist Revolutionary Youth) and a member of the IVth International, Bensaïd was not new to revolutionary politics, but he would go on to become one of the leading figures of the French student movement of 1968. On 22 March, Bensaïd was one of a group of 142 students who occupied a room (the Council of University Professors) in the administrative block in Nanterre, in protest against the arrest, the previous day, of a group of students who had been taking part in an anti-Vietnam War demonstration in central Paris. This action has been described as the 'founding event'[1] of the May '68 events in France: the students would go on to produce a political tract and declare themselves a new protest movement (the March 22 Movement). In the summer of 1968, Bensaïd wrote a book with his fellow Trotskyist Henri Weber in which they analysed the political significance of the May 1968 events. This book was completed in hiding, when both authors had taken refuge in the home of the novelist Marguerite Duras, following the French government's prohibition of the leftist political groupings to which they belonged. In this work,[2] Bensaïd and Weber argued that the student movement had acted as an 'avant-garde' for a broad class struggle which, in the absence of a true revolutionary party, was unable to reach its proper conclusion. 1968 was therefore a 'dress rehearsal' for the true revolution which was still to come.

1   Bernard Brillant, *Les Clercs de 68* (Paris: Presses Universitaires de France, 2003), 162.

2   Daniel Bensaïd and Henri Weber, *Mai 1968: une répétition générale* (Paris: Maspero, 1968).

The authors sought to examine the strategies to be followed by the students which might allow them to achieve a genuine socialist revolution.

Until his recent death, Daniel Bensaïd was recognised, like few other activists of May 1968, as an authentic voice and as a spokesperson for the May events in France. Yet, what distinguished Bensaïd from many other ex-student activists was that he remained staunchly faithful to the revolutionary impetus of 1968 and to its leftist legacy. Drawing on the title of one his own books, Bensaïd was one of a handful of 'rebelles' after 1968, refusing to abandon their leftist ideals at a time when the majority of former activists had become 'repentis', shunning the 'excesses' of their youth and pursuing a more moderate socialist or even right-wing line.³ Bensaïd's own trajectory was that of an activist and intellectual who remained intransigent in his political views, his commitment to class struggle and to revolutionary social change. When the JCR was dissolved in June 1968, Bensaïd, along with Alain Krivine and Henri Weber, helped to found the Communist League in 1969 and he became a member of its political bureau. This was dissolved again in 1973, becoming the Communist Revolutionary Front, before changing its name to Communist Revolutionary League in 1975. Bensaïd gained recognition outside France as a leading activist and theorist of the international Trotskyist movement with close links to the IVth International. In February 2009, he helped to launch the New Anticapitalist Party (Nouveau Parti Anticapitaliste) under the leadership of Olivier Besancenot, which claimed to bring together all those forces in society which sought to 'break with capitalism'. In the words of one commentator, Bensaïd positioned himself throughout his political career 'clearly and firmly on the side of those who seek to make revolution possible.'⁴

As a professor of philosophy at the University of Paris VIII and as the author of over thirty books, Bensaïd was also recognised as a leading figure within the French intellectual Left and was particularly renowned for his work on Karl Marx and Walter Benjamin. At the time of the 40th anniversary commemorations in France, Bensaïd participated actively in public

---

3   Daniel Bensaïd and Alain Krivine, *Mai Si! 1968–1988: Rebelles et repentis* (Paris: La Brèche, 1988)

4   *L'Humanité*, Editorial article, 2 February 2008.

debates about 1968. He sought through his books, press articles, public state-
ments and speeches to reaffirm the continued significance of 1968 for political
activism and for working-class mobilisation today. Where other commenta-
tors emphasised the political failings of 1968 or saw it as the beginning of a
descent into individualism, Bensaïd reaffirmed the importance of May as
a precursor to today's social movements, from the 'big strikes' of 1995 to the
2006 wave of protest against the right-wing government's youth employment
bill. Bensaïd also vehemently criticised those former activists who, in his
view, undermined the political significance of 1968 (Daniel Cohn-Bendit) or
politicians who, like Nicolas Sarkozy, attacked its legacy in France today. In
this essay, Daniel Bensaïd reflects on the political and social meaning of 1968
in France and in the world today. He writes from the perspective of someone
who was directly involved in the events he describes and whose own political
trajectory was shaped by them, but also as someone who remained true to the
revolutionary impetus of May 1968 and who refused to abandon its leftist
ideals. His paper provides an important example of 'living memory', writ-
ten from the perspective of someone who participated in and influenced the
1968 events and whose narrative often challenged the official public memory
of what occurred.

'When one becomes reconciled with an event, she said, it is because one
no longer understands anything about it (...) Whoever speaks of reconciliation in an historical sense, she said, also means pacification and
mummification'[5]

Is May 1968 now finished with? In a certain sense of course it is finished
with and has been finished for quite some time. Perhaps since Charles de
Gaulle's radio broadcast and the demonstration on the Champs-Elysée
of 30 May 1968 or maybe even since the election at the end of June of
that year of a right-wing majority. Or since the signing in June 1972 of a
Common Programme for the Left. Or even since the defeat of that same
Left in the 1978 general elections which followed the suppression of the

5   Charles Péguy, *Clio* (Paris: Gallimard, 1942), 257.

Portuguese revolution in 1975, the transition to monarchy in Spain in 1976 and the historic compromise on austerity in Italy. Or even, more recently, since the victory of François Mitterrand in France in 1981 or the liberal turn of 1983.

The 'end of 1968' was not broadcast for the first time during the commemorations for the 40th anniversary. This is not today's news or even yesterday's. To a certain extent and from a certain perspective, 1968 is well and truly over and yet, from another perspective and to a different extent it is not. It is unfinished in the sense that this is still a contentious event, one that makes waves, an unclassified affair over which there is no easy agreement. Yet if we were to become reconciled and to make our peace, as Charles Péguy said once about another famous affair,[6] it would mean that we would no longer draw any inspiration from it. It would mean that living memory would become ossified within a history of archives and monuments.

If any proof was necessary that this is unfinished business, that its spectre still haunts us today, it is enough to consider the reactionary fury of Nicolas Sarkozy's speech at Bercy on 29 April 2007: 'In this election, we must decide if the legacy of May '68 should be perpetuated or if it should be liquidated once and for all. I want to turn the page on 68.' Forty years on! What a curious determination of purpose and what a strange recriminatory discourse. In 1871, the victorious government troops made the Sacré-Coeur the monument symbolising all the crimes attributed to the Paris Commune. During the Second World War, the Vichy government transformed 'Work-Family-Homeland' into a sacred ideal, a means to atone for the sins of the Popular Front, held responsible for the defeat of 1940. Is it now a question of atoning for the excesses of a '68 generation held responsible for the decadence and decline of French society?

For the new generation of activists, those of the anti-globalisation movement or of protest against the Iraq war, those of the 2006 demonstrations

---

6   In *Clio*, Charles Péguy reflects on the Dreyfus Affair (1894–1906) during which he, along with other intellectuals in France at that time, had mobilised in support of Dreyfus and in opposition to what they saw as a miscarriage of justice.

against the French government's youth employment bill[7] or the liberal reform of universities, 1968 seems very distant indeed. Forty years is further in the past than the Popular Front was for us during the 1968 events. Has 1968 become a sanitised event, a conference theme, primary matter for a positive historical knowledge? Of the Dreyfus affair, Péguy's Clio said: '[History] is just there, it is just on the far horizon and it seems to be still there, still a text and matter for recollection and for memory, to be evoked by the memorialist or chronicler. As it is near, close at hand, it does not seem to have become historic. Let us not worry, my children (it's still Clio speaking), and let us mourn for it: it is as dead as it could be, it will no longer divide us'. And yet, like the French Revolution and the Dreyfus Affair, 1968 continues to divide us and we still haven't become reconciled with these events or been able 'to lose prematurely and artificially the meaning of this event, its intelligence, its inner meaning, its secret and literally the memory of this event'. All this even though 'the tactic of politicians has been precisely and exactly to transform us prematurely and artificially into historians',[8] and to transform us from activists into historians of the May events.

Memory still haunts history's sleep. Because 'if there is a sense of the real, and nobody would doubt that it has a right to exist, then there should also be something which might be called a sense of the possible'.[9] What is still interesting is not the ashes of May '68 but its embers, the resurgence of defeated and repressed possibilities. Forty years is not enough to make us bow down and lower our heads before this *fait accompli*.[10] And we don't

7　In Spring 2006, France was hit by a wave of social protest in opposition to the right-wing government's youth employment bill (Contrat première embauche), which at the height of the movement mobilised 800,000 demonstrators. This protest resulted in the government's decision to withdraw the proposed bill.
8　All quotations are from Péguy, *Clio*, 1942.
9　's'il y a un sens du réel, et personne ne doutera qu'il ait son droit l'existence, il doit bien y avoir quelque chose qu'on pourrait appeler le sens du virtuel' Robert Musil, *L'Homme sans qualités* Tome 1 (Paris: Editions de Poche).
10　See Friedrich Nietzsche, *Seconde considération intempestive* (Paris: Garnier-Flammarion), 147.

have bruised knees from a continued genuflection before the fleeting verdicts of a ventriloquist history. As Louis Auguste Blanqui insisted during the bitter aftermath of the Commune, 'the parting of ways stills holds the promise of hope'.[11]

Already forty years, four decades and four anniversaries. A commemorative procession and a permanent revision. In May 1978, the impetus of the events was reaching exhaustion. In France, a divided Left had just lost an election which had seemed a certain victory and the oil crisis and recession had brought an end to the 'Thirty Glorious Years'. The dominant classes in Portugal and Spain had succeeded in bringing an end to dictatorship. The commemoration of 1968 was therefore caught between a nostalgic farewell to the youth culture and a sense of retrospective maturity. In May 1988, François Mitterrand had just won his second presidential election and Rocard's government was implementing its socio-liberal agenda. Having become the 'Mitterrand generation', the 68ers gloried in their own social success and in their conversion to realism. In May 1998, the Berlin wall came down and the Soviet Union ceased to exist. With this, the brief history of the twentieth century was over. Remaining on the other side of the wall, 1968 seemed to have been consigned to prehistory. All that was left was a trail of 'societal reforms' put in place throughout Europe which had no longer required, in order to be implemented, the force of a general strike or the erection of barricades.

2008 is then the general liquidation promised by Nicolas Sarkozy, the time for repentance and penance. In his encyclical of July 2007, *Faith and Reason*, Pope Benedict XVI set the tone, describing 1968 as a period of 'crisis in western culture' and condemning 'the intellectual and moral relativism of May 1968'. Sarkozy's speech at Bercy directly echoes this papal appeal for a new civilisational crusade.

On the one hand, 1968 was an event in which the national and international dimensions were almost inseparable. Behind the French May, we find the Vietnam War, the Prague Spring, the development of the Palestinian

---

11   Louis Auguste Blanqui, 'L'Eternité sous les astres' in *Maintenant il faut des armes!* (Paris: La Fabrique, 2007).

national movement after the Six Day War, the rebellion led by Polish students and an almost planetary mobilisation by young people. In February 1968, there was just a handful of us on the Esplanade des Invalides chanting 'Free Modzelewski and Kurón'.[12] A few weeks later, there were tens of thousands of us chanting 'Rome, Berlin, Warsaw, Paris!' to celebrate what we saw as a convergence of protest against capitalist exploitation, colonial oppression and bureaucratic despotism.

On the other hand, this was an event in which the social and cultural aspects were inextricably linked. An unprecedented general strike in France, equivalent to 150 million days lost in strike activity (compared with 37 million for the Italian movement of 1969 and 14 million for the 1974 miners' strikes in Britain). Yet, at the same time, this was a cultural awakening in cinema and music, with, for instance, the Rolling Stones' *Street Fighting Man* and James Brown's *I'm Black and I'm proud* or even Jimmy Hendrix' take on the American national anthem. Not to mention a growing critique of daily life and of consumer society which prefigured the social movements of the 1970s. Everything was possible or so we believed, using a slogan first proclaimed by Marceau Pivert during the Popular Front. A whole field of possibilities seemed to open up to us, but one which was not without its limits. It is this which differentiates determined and concrete possibility from undetermined and abstract possibility which is simply the opposite of the impossible.

1968 was the culmination of a quarter of a century of economic reconstruction and growth. The Fifth Plan elaborated for the period from 1966 to 1970 by the Planning Commission,[13] set a maximum threshold for unemployment at 2.5% of the population and it was agreed that to reach a

12 Karol Modzelewski and Jacek Kurón were student figures at the centre of the Polish protest movement at the University of Warsaw and had mobilised against the Communist Party, criticising bureaucratic despotism and calling for an 'antibureaucratic revolution'. The were both incarcerated in 1965 and later released in 1967. Now deceased, Kurón was later a minister under the presidency of Lech Walsea and Modzelewski is today a researcher in medieval history.

13 Economic growth between the late 1940s and 1973 was state-planned and based around a series of economic plans put in place by the national Planning Commission.

level of 500,000 of unemployed would trigger a revolutionary explosion. Trade union demands were mainly concerned with an adjustment of wage rates and a better distribution of 'the fruits of growth'. This explains why there was a return to work without significant protest, even though the gains made, although significant (principally a 37% salary increase overall and new trade union rights in the workplace), fell well short of what might be expected of an unprecedented movement and had far less symbolic importance than the paid holidays obtained in 1936 or social welfare in 1945. There were few examples of workers' autonomy and the trade unions maintained control of negotiations.

Today we also recognise the exclusively masculine composition of the movement's leadership and the strongly masculine nature of the demonstrations. The new feminist movement started after the events, on 20 August 1970, when a wreath was placed at the Arc de Triomphe at the tomb of the unknown solider in honour of 'the wife of the unknown solider'.[14] Similarly, there was hardly any mobilisation amongst conscripts within army barracks. The movement of soldiers' committees only really took off in the period from 1973 to 1974 culminating in the protests on rue de Draguignan and rue de Karlsruhe. Finally, if there were a dozen deaths during the events (including the Maoist secondary school pupil, Gilles Tautin and two Peugeot workers at Sochaux) and if there was some shocking violence, this was also relatively well controlled and limited by both sides. All the signs tell us that if the nature of power was well and truly called into question during the week of 24 to 30 May, the conditions to bring this revolutionary situation to fruition were not there.

The retrospective reduction of the May movement to a moment of anti-authoritarian liberation or an attempt to modernise moral values, creates a depoliticised and depoliticising interpretation, one that is clearly assumed in an article by Manuel Castells: 'Because ultimately, the May '68 revolution was cultural and not political. It was not concerned with

---

14   It was as a result of this action carried out by a handful of women that the French media began to speak of the 'Mouvement de Libération des femmes' which became the driving force in French feminism during the 1970s.

power, but sought to dissolve this.'[15] Having earlier proclaimed somewhat injudiciously that 'everything is political', he now declared conversely that nothing was. Whether 1968 was simply a revolution or rather a cultural reform, a modernisation of ways of living, or even a magical and imagined dissolution of power, we must now apparently forget about it rather than dare to contemplate its reality. Daniel Cohn-Bendit has also declared that the game is over: 'May is finished, finished just like the French Revolution is finished.'[16] This urge to proclaim the end of the French Revolution in order to exorcise its spectre is not new and François Furet was a master at this over twenty years ago. From the point of view of its actors, the Revolution was, however, 'frozen' (in the words of Saint-Just) from the winter of 1793 onwards and was finished as an event from the period of the Thermidor at least. Yet it was far from having exhausted its effects and its resurgences. For Cohn-Bendit, 1968 is finished because 'what defined the revolt no longer exists [...]. We didn't understand at the time what the Grenelle negotiations signified in terms of a break with conservative political thought. We have the proof today with the Grenelle of the Environment: we can see that this reference has ended up becoming a positive historical symbol.'[17] By a rhetorical magic trick, the Grenelle agreements, the terms of which were massively rejected by the assembled workforce of Renault-Billancourt

15   Manuel Castells in *Courrier International*, 20 December 2007. A young Spanish refugee and an assistant to Henri Lefebvre in the sociology department in Nanterre, Manuel Castells had gone to Berlin in February 1968 to take part in a demonstration against the Vietnam War and had travelleled in one of the coaches chartered by the Communist Revolutionary Youth, which he then supported.

16   Daniel Cohn Bendit, *Forget 68* (Paris: Broché, 2008).

17   Daniel Cohn Bendit, *Politis*, 26 July 2007. The Grenelle agreements were negotiated between representatives of Pompidou's government and the leaders of the main trade unions and employers unions on the 25th and 26th of May 1968 at the Ministry of Work on rue de Grenelle in Paris and offered concessions to workers (wage increases and workers representation) in a bid to bring the strike movement to an end, but these were rejected by French workers and the strike continued. The term Grenelle has been revived in recent years and used to describe major public negotiations such as the 2007 agreements on environmental protection (the Grenelle de l'Environnement).

and which have since been understood as a concerted attempt to stifle the movement, have become today the jewel in the crown, the very symbol, the positive legacy of 1968. This was little other than the belated tribute of a rabble-rouser reconciled with the wisdom of communist party strategists whom he accused at the time of bureaucratic 'senility'.[18]

Grenelle, or how to stop a strike in order to suppress a movement. In the end, Cohn-Bendit, Castells and many others, have abandoned the idea that 1968 was about 'changing the world without taking power', slowly, surreptitiously and at a snail's pace. But the world changes all by itself and it doesn't wait for us or even need us to do so. It is changing continuously with the speed of an all-consuming circulation of goods, with the spatial bulimia of capital, with a headlong rush towards strategies of domination. Globalisation is exactly the kind of chaos and permanent upheaval that was so lucidly predicted over one hundred and fifty years ago: 'The bourgeoisie cannot exist without constantly revolutionising the instruments of production, and thereby the conditions of production, and with them the whole relations of society. This constant revolutionising of production, this continuous upheaval of the whole social system and this perpetual instability is what distinguishes the bourgeois epoch from all earlier ones. All traditional and fixed social relationships with their train of ancient and venerable prejudices and opinions are swept away, all newly-formed ones become antiquated before they can ossify. All that is solid melts into the air, all that is holy is profaned and man is at last compelled to face his real conditions of life, and his relations with his kind.'[19]

The world is changing but it is changing for the worse as well as for the better. We must therefore ask ourselves what kind of society we want to live in and what type of humanity we do not wish to become, since we do not have a clear conception of what we would like to become. And the answer to this question lies, whether we like it or not, in class relationships and

18   Daniel Cohn-Bendit, *Le gauchisme, remède à la maladie sénile du communisme* (Paris: Seuil, 1968).

19   Karl Marx and Friedrich Engels, *Manifesto of the Communist Party* (1848) in T. Roberts and A. Hite (eds), *From Modernization to Globalization* (Oxford: Blackwell Publishing, 2000), 29.

power struggles. This is what centuries of bitter class struggle have taught us and it is a lesson which we would be unwise to forget. To recast Grenelle as a legacy of 1968 and to present the Grenelle of the Environment as a model of peaceful 'social dialogue' is precisely to erase the class struggle. It is to sweep away all wrong-doing, all contention, all conflict in favour of a consensus between a State, recognised as legitimate, and a 'civil society' in which workers and bosses, the exploited and the exploiters, the wealthy and the dispossessed, all sit down together at the same table.

The context for the revolt no longer exists, affirms Danny the Green.[20] Yet this has not disappeared but simply changed and become more urgent, more desperate even, in the face of growing injustices and inequalities. 'We want everything!' some proclaimed following the May events, to which others added 'Everything immediately'. This was the romantic illusion of a society without unemployment, which believed that material wealth was within reach and which had faith in the great march of progress. 'It's getting better' Paul McCartney sang back then, 'getting so much better all the time'. Forty years on, faced with the social and ecological disasters of a savage capitalism, a majority of the population is convinced that future generations will live worse than earlier ones. Is it getting worse? Another reason to remain faithful to the event and not to let the door close on possibilities for the future.

Nicolas Sarkozy's speech of 28 April 2007 at Bercy had a tone of social revenge: 'May 1968 imposed intellectual and moral relativism (...) The cult of the money king and of short-term profit was carried by the values of May 1968. I call on the French people to break definitively with the spirit, the behaviour and the ideas of May 1968. I call on them to break definitively with the cynicism of May 1968. I call on them to reconnect politics with morality, authority, work and the nation.' Work–family–homeland: the very essence of the Vichy trilogy. With this funeral oration to the spirit of May, the circle of historic revisionism is complete. In 1978, it was already the farewell ceremony: order had been re-established in Portugal and the divided

---

20   The author is referring to Daniel Cohn Bendit, a European deputy for the Green Party.

Left had lost the general elections. In 1988, as a prelude to the depoliticised pomp and ceremony of the bicentenary, it was Mitterrand's rewriting of May 1968 as the backdrop for modernisation and as the springboard for a new hedonistic generation. One year before the fortieth anniversary, Sarkozy with his strange rhetorical vanishing trick makes the largest general strike in history disappear from view and turns May 1968 into the scapegoat for the faults of the liberal counter-reform! The misdeeds which he attributes to 1968 – the worship of money, the pursuit of profit, generalised competition – are not, as he claims, delayed effects of 1968, but the results of the decline which followed it. In *The New Spirit of Capitalism*, Luc Boltanski and Eve Chiapello highlight the distinction between the 'social critique' (of inequality and injustice) and the 'artistic critique' of alienation in the workplace and in daily life. This separation is not inevitable.[21] In 1968, the desire for more individual freedom, for more liberal values, for sexual revolution combined perfectly well with the aspiration towards social revolution. And the affirmation of the individual was in no way opposed to collective solidarities and societal emancipation.

The irony of history is that the accession of the respectable Left to the business world, a distant echo of 1968, was in fact its very negation. Those were the Tapie years, the Séguéla years, the Lang years, a time of privatisations and money-making, of bread (a little) and games (a lot)[22] and of spectacular monuments (the Louvre pyramid and the Arche de la Défense). As forty-somethings, the 68 generation having become the 'Mitterrand generation' celebrated its own social promotion: perform your daily devotions before the Paris Stock Exchange and get rich through share options. Even more stupefying than the multiplication of bread was that of money making more money.

Why, despite everything, does May 1968 retain such an important symbolic resonance today, across the world even more so than in France?

---

21   Luc Boltanski and Eve Chiapello *The New Spirit of Capitalism* (Verso, 2007).
22   'Bread and games' or 'bread and circuses' (from Latin: panem et circenses) is a metaphor for handouts and petty amusements that politicians use to gain popular support, instead of gaining it through sound policy.

1. If it had simply been a question of a youth revolt, we could speak
    about it in the same way as the anti-Vietnam War protest is spoken
    about on American campuses or the revolt by the Provos on the
    streets of Amsterdam. In most advanced capitalist countries, moral
    values have evolved, individualism has been affirmed, the right to
    abortion has been gained and these changes happened anyway
    without having required the longest and greatest general strike
    in the history of France. Was this movement comparable to the
    great workers' struggles of the 19th and 20th centuries? The last
    battle of the anti-Dreyfusard intellectuals, of the Popular Front
    or the Liberation? Or did 1968 symbolise a new strike for the
    21st century, in a country with an urban majority, where wage-
    earners constituted over 80% of the active population, where the
    peasantry, young people of school age, a minority of technicians
    and white-collar workers all shared the same hegemony of work-
    ing life and where football teams claimed the status of workers'
    cooperatives.[23] Perhaps the truth lies somewhere in between. This
    strike was a watershed that stood between 'no longer' and 'not
    yet', between that which gently fades away and that which has
    not yet taken place.

2. May 1968 is not an event limited to metropolitan France or even
    to the Francophone world but this was a global event. We might
    speak about it differently, if it didn't signify communist occu-
    pied factories, the Tet offensive of February 1968 in Vietnam,
    the Prague Spring, the agitation by Polish students, the revolt by
    Pakistani youth, the anti-war movement in America, the embers
    of the Cultural Revolution in China, the massacre in Ttatelolco
    Square and the raised gloved fists on the Olympic podium in
    Mexico. 1968 is therefore the symbolic date of a defining moment,
    when the despotic apparatus of Stalinism began to show its cracks,
    when the anti-bureaucratic struggles in the East, the independence

---

23   In 1968, a number of French football teams fired their managers and declared a status
     of self-management as workers' cooperatives.

movements in Algeria, Vietnam, Palestine and the Portuguese colonies seemed to become interconnected with workers protest in France and Italy. The turning away of the 1970s opened the way for the counter-attack of the Thatcher/Reagan years. The spectre of social and mass revolution had retreated. Then came the time of religious revolution, and Michel Foucault looking at Iran was the first to understand how the times had changed.[24]

Instead of giving in to a fatalistic vision of history and to a paradoxical determinism, we might remember that something else was possible on the threshold of the 1970s which might have prevented some of the deep-seated tensions that exist today. The protagonists of the 1960s were called Patrice Lumumba, Malcom X, Che Guevara, Ben Barka, Frantz Fanon, Miguel Enriquez, Amilcar Cabral, all of whom were assassinated or died at a young age. This was a different story to that of Ben Laden and Mullah Omar today. This was one of the rare moments where history can follow two different paths. In a chapter from *Vol de la mésange* ('Flight of the blue tit') entitled 'Farewell', François Maspero speaks about a separation from a loved one, against the backdrop of a manhunt in Bolivia that was being reported on the radio. Without ever mentioning the name of the man being pursued, the chapter closes with the following lines: 'In the morning the fog had returned, the beams of the headlights were dimmed by it, the fog-horn sounded loudly. It was 9 October 1967 and the radio declared that the day before, Bolivian special forces had at last shot dead, in a distant valley in the Andes, this man whose memory would stay with them forever.'[25] During those days of October 1967 when we refused to believe it, when we took comfort in imagining some kind of media conspiracy, we shared this sense of irreparable loss, without understanding what this would come to

24 In 1979 Michel Foucault made two tours of Iran and published a series of essays in the Italian newspaper *Corriere della Sera* which only appeared in French in 1994 and in English in 2005. These essays caused controversy with some commentators who argued that he was insufficiently critical of the new Iranian regime.

25 François Maspero, *Le Vol de la mésange* (Paris: Nouvelles, 2006).

signify. Seeing the confusion that reigns today, we understand better the meaning and relevance of that loss.

'Many will die, victims of their errors' Che had predicted in his message to the Tricontinental.[26] Perhaps the revolutionaries of this lost generation were victims of their errors. But let us attribute blame where it is due. They were primarily victims of an implacable enemy, one which orchestrated the military landing at the Bay of Pigs, which supported military dictatorships, which drew up the Condor plan in Chile, which launched Operation Djakarta, and which, during the same period, bombed the Vietnamese people with napalm. They were also victims of those who refused to make, as Guevara insisted, Vietnam and Indochina an inviolable territory and who instead engaged in a disastrous and merciless war. They were also victims of their own errors to a certain extent which needs to be acknowledged. Because if it is relatively easy to admit having been wrong and if it is even easier to claim against all the evidence that one was never wrong, what is difficult is to recognise that one was wrong without those errors having been in vain, because they were partly right even if history seems to deny this. Undoubtedly they committed errors, those defeated ones, errors of strategy, of tactics, of organisation and so did all of us. At least they didn't mistake their enemy. And it is in this that their defeat is not a disaster or a humiliation, but rather could still become a 'victorious defeat' depending on whether we are capable of continuing the struggle.

A rational revolutionary, Che Guevara condemned 'an illogical moment in the history of humanity' in which it was urgent to act without any certainty of success. This sense of urgency, this impatience seems all the more justified today when we consider the price paid for the missed opportunities and betrayed revolutions of the twentieth century: Georges Bush's war without limits, uncontrolled violence, the rise of inequalities, the explosion of shanty-towns. And more generally the social revenge of the wealthy and dominant, their arrogance, the macabre dance of capital on the bodies of the defeated. What we might justifiably ask is whether in

---

26   Che Guevara's 'Message to the Tricontinental' was sent to the Tricontinental solidarity organisation in Havana in the spring of 1967.

1967 and 1968, there was still time or if it was already too late to revive the communist ideal buried under the crimes of Stalinism. At least Che Guevara and those like him tried and at least they dared – as Rosa Luxembourg said about the Bolsheviks before allowing herself to criticise them. And like her, when we speak about the errors of this revolutionary generation, we should begin by doing them the justice of acknowledging that they dared. Dared to challenge the unbearable order of the world. They failed and we failed with them, but this failure obliges us to maintain a critical loyalty.

Certainly the 1960s were also years full of illusions. Those of unlimited growth, of a wealth that was within reach, illusions that shaped the demands for 'everything immediately' and that of 'live fully and enjoy without restrictions'. It would be longer and more difficult than we could have imagined, but the appeal to 'change the world' is no less important and no less urgent today than forty years ago.

Translated with introduction and additional notes by Sarah Waters

PART 3

Marginal Voices

SUSANNE RINNER

Transnational Memories: 1968 in Recent German Fiction

Whilst 1968 symbolises the height of the student movement in West Germany, this movement was not restricted to the West and it did not occur in isolation. Rather, it interacted with other protest movements around the world, transforming the West-German student movement into an international event. These movements ultimately transcended national boundaries and conventional East–West and North–South divisions and formed a transnational sphere. This transnational sphere continues to shape the cultural memory of these events that emerges in the 1990s.

Some recent historiographical research examines the international and transnational dimensions of 1968 and its memory. Gerard J. DeGroot provides a comparative overview of the international student movement of this period which highlights similarities in goals, themes, and methods without disregarding the national distinctions.[1] As Martin Klimke and Joachim Scharloth emphasise, the transnational dimension of the 1960s protest was already perceived by its contemporaries and it was one of its crucial motors.[2] These comparative studies fill important gaps in the flourishing field of 1960s studies.

However, in literary criticism, book-length studies on the fictional representation of 1968 and its international and transnational aspects are still missing, even though in the last two decades literary texts, especially

---

1   Gerard J. DeGroot (ed.), *Student Protest. The Sixties and After* (London and New York: Longman, 1998), and Gerard J. DeGroot, *The Sixties Unplugged. A Kaleidoscopic History of a Disorderly Decade* (Cambridge: Harvard University Press, 2008).

2   Martin Klimke and Joachim Scharloth (eds), *1968 in Europe. A History of Protest and Activism, 1956–1977* (New York: Palgrave Macmillan, 2008).

novels, increasingly participated in the 'memory contest'[3] of the 1960s. In addition to texts that are 'national' (i.e. written in German by Germans), and 'international', (i.e. written in other languages about the German movement), authors with a migration background who write in German contribute to the retrospective treatment of the student movement. In this chapter, I argue that these texts make innovative contributions to the construction of a cultural memory of 1968 in recent German fiction. They broaden our understanding of the representation of the 1960s as an international and global event, emphasise its transnational aspects, and reflect contemporary developments within an ever more globalised world.

The concept of cultural memory gained importance in particular after 1989, a turning point when the need to write a history of and for the newly unified Germany emerged. Many of these attempts positioned 1968 as a central event to mark the arrival of the Federal Republic in the West, a move that seemed to be confirmed by the end of the GDR.[4] Furthermore, the fall of the Berlin Wall enabled access to the Stasi-files, which had a profound impact on the re-writing of history. In addition, the connections between West-German terrorism and the GDR became apparent, initiating new controversies about the influence the state in the East had exercised over internal affairs in the West. Former terrorists who were granted exile in the GDR and had lived there under false names lost their cover and had to stand trial after 1989.

The victory of a red-green coalition in the federal election in Germany in 1998 coincided with the thirtieth anniversary of 1968. Whilst the student movement had been commemorated in the old Federal Republic right from the start, marked by speeches, conferences, and book publications,

---

3   Anne Fuchs, *Phantoms of War in Contemporary German Literature, Film and Discourse: The Politics of Memory* (New York: Palgrave Macmillan, 2008), 3.

4   Compare Geoff Eley, 'Telling Stories about Sixty-Eight: Troublemaking, Political Passions, and Enabling Democracy', *German Studies Association Newsletter* XXXIII.2. (2008/09), 39–50. Eley provides a detailed account of the diverging positions regarding 1968. Whilst many historians acknowledge the centrality of 1968, others express ambivalent, if not negative assessments of its legacy in order to downplay its significance.

this election provided a new opportunity to emphasise the significance of 1968. The new German parliament and government included many former activists and participants. Thus, interest in the 1960s student movement surged.[5] Attempts to denounce the student movement as a violent and in its core anti-democratic movement left their mark on academic research. Currently, little attention is paid to the student movement in the 1960s and the development of very diverse groups in its aftermath, whilst much attention is focused on terrorism and the question of violence and its precursors.[6] This focus on violence was fuelled by the 2001 terrorist attacks in the United States, which caused German commentators to compare and contrast terrorism in Germany in the 1970s and terrorism in the new century.[7]

Whilst 1998 seemed to mark the ambivalently received zenith of power for the former 1968ers, in 2008, the year of the fortieth anniversary, we observe the aging of the student movement. The participants in the events in the 1960s and 1970s are actively shaping their legacy. They collect, analyse, and publish their recollections and convert their memories into fiction and history in order to maintain the significance of 1968 for the future.[8] This

5 Whilst those on the left in particular felt as if their former comrades had sold out, those critical of the movement and its 'long march through the institutions' scrutinised former deeds and misdeeds of the newly elected officials. This interest even led to a plenary session which investigated the conduct of then foreign minister Joschka Fischer during the 1970s in Frankfurt/Main, where he had participated in street protests that included violent clashes with the police. Compare the transcript of the session of the German parliament on 17 January 2001 which includes a discussion of the possible meeting between Joschka Fischer and the terrorist Carlos (Ilich Ramirez Sanchez) (Plenarprotokoll 14/142).

6 Within the field of literary criticism, Ingo Cornils is the notable and important exception to this trend that seems to support attempts to silence, and at times even criminalise, the German student movement at all levels, e.g. Ingo Cornils, 'Long Memories: The German Student Movement in Recent Fiction', *German Life and Letters* 56 (2003), 89–101.

7 Compare Peter Schneider, 'Rächer wollen sie sein', *Die Zeit* 11 (8 March 2007), 11.

8 E.g. the most recent autobiographical accounts by Peter Schneider, *Rebellion und Wahn. Mein '68* (Köln: Kiepenheuer & Witsch, 2008), and Götz Aly, *Unser Kampf. 1968 – ein irritierter Blick zurück* (Frankfurt a.M.: S. Fischer, 2008).

process transforms personal experiences of the 1960s and 1970s, and their
memories thereof, into a generational experience that is broad enough and
thus worthy to shape the unified historiography of the new German state
and to emphasise its place within a globalised world.

Monika Shafi's assessment that there is a 'relative lack of 1968 novels'[9]
is contradicted by the ongoing literary interest in the 1960s and 1970s. The
sheer number of literary representations of the German student movement,
their comparability in content and form, and the intensity of the debates
in the 1990s enables us to speak about an emerging genre of novels about
the generation of 1968.[10] Authors, narrators, and literary figures engage in
the poetic labour of remembering and forgetting and of telling, writing,
and performing biographies, autobiographies, stories, and history. Whilst
historians like Konrad Jarausch suggest that 1968 resists most attempts of
narrativisation, I argue that literary texts are uniquely suited to represent
one of the most transformative periods in Germany, Europe, and the world
because they share similarities in their narrative form and make important
contributions to the discourse on cultural memory.[11] Therefore, the interpretation of these fictional narratives provides fruitful insights into the
interrelatedness of German literature and the public discourse in Germany

9   Monika Shafi, 'Talkin' 'Bout My Generation: Memories of 1968 in Recent German
     Novels', *German Life and Letters* 59 (2006), 201–216, 213.
10   Among them: Bernd Cailloux, *Das Geschäftsjahr 1968/69* (2005), Sophie Dannenberg,
     Das bleiche Herz der Revolution (2004), Friedrich Christian Delius, *Amerikahaus
     und der Tanz um die Frauen* (1997), Ulrike Kolb, *Frühstück mit Max* (2000), Klaus
     Modick, *Der Flügel* (1994), Sten Nadolny, *Selim oder die Gabe der Rede* (1990),
     Emine Sevgi Özdamar, *Seltsame Sterne starren zur Erde: Wedding-Pankow 1976/77*
     (2003), Robert Schindel, *Gebürtig* (1992), Bernhard Schlink, *Der Vorleser* (1995),
     Elke Schmitter, *Leichte Verfehlungen* (2002), Peter Schneider, *Skylla* (2005), Leander
     Scholz, *Rosenfest* (2000), Franz Maria Sonner, *Als die Beatles Rudi Dutschke erschos-
     sen* (1996), Franz Maria Sonner, *Die Bibliothek des Attentäters* (2001), Ingrid Strobl,
     Ende der Nacht (2005), Uwe Timm, *Der Freund und der Fremde* (2005), Heipe
     Weiss, *Fuchstanz* (1999), Ulrich Woelk, *Rückspiel* (1993) and *Die letzte Vorstellung*
     (2002).
11   Compare Konrad H. Jarausch and Michael Geyer, *Shattered Past. Reconstructing
     German Histories* (Princeton: Princeton University Press, 2003).

and highlights the significance of ensuing memory contests after the fall of the Berlin Wall.

In this context, the creative participation in the discourse on 1968 by novels written in German by Turkish-German writers has been mostly overlooked so far. I argue that these texts create a transnational moment of cultural memory in Germany. This transnational memory advances our understanding of the 1960s and addresses theoretical and methodological challenges within the discourse on 1968 as well as within the discourse on German-Turkish literature.

My reading of Emine Sevgi Özdamar's *Seltsame Sterne starren zur Erde* (2003, *Strange Stars Stare at Earth*) is guided by two considerations: the importance of transnationalism for our understanding of 1968 and the significance of the construction of a cultural memory for the future of unified Germany within Europe and the world. Thus, I would like to introduce the term transnational memories as a chronotope in order to explore the 'intrinsic connectedness of temporal and spatial relationships that are artistically expressed in literature.'[12]

The concept of transnationalism encourages us to think of the migration and exchange of people, texts, and ideas as the norm rather than the exception in the twentieth and twenty-first centuries, yet a norm that inherently defies our understanding of norms as exclusionary, hierarchical, fixed, with homogenous boundaries. In the twentieth century, literary history, at times grudgingly, acknowledged experiences of forced migration. Studies of immigrant and exile experiences and their aesthetic manifestations were undertaken. Yet, traditionally, German literary criticism found it exceedingly difficult to study literary texts, authors, and movements that could not be analysed strictly within national parameters and its linguistic manifestations. Recently, however, literary and cultural studies have placed an emphasis on migration studies and experiences of various diasporas. With the fall of the Berlin Wall in the 1990s, it became clear that it is not

---

12   M.M. Bakhtin, 'Forms of Time and of the Chronotope in the Novel. Notes toward a Historical Poetics', *The Dialogic Imagination*, ed. Michael Holquist, transl. Caryl Emerson and Michael Holquist (Austin: University of Texas Press, 1981).

German identity that is at stake when talking about migration, but rather
it is a question of redefining this identity in order to account for a population in Germany that is more diverse than ever.[13]

The history of German-Turkish literature and its reception within
scholarly debates are particularly perplexing issues. German-Turkish literature emerged in the 1960s, yet it was not recognised as such, but categorised as *Gastarbeiterliteratur* (guest worker literature), as literature
written by and about guest workers between the 1960s and 1980s. In the
late 1980s this term was replaced by other equally misleading terms, among
them *Ausländer- und Fremdenliteratur* (foreigner literature), *Literatur der
MigrantInnen* (migrant literature), and *interkulturelle Literatur* (intercultural literature). Literature written by non German-German authors
continues to be placed in a separate category. This is manifest in the yearly
award of the Chamisso Prize, a literature prize that has been awarded annu-
ally in Munich since 1985 to authors whose mother tongue and cultural
background are non-German and whose works make an important contribution to German literature. In addition to being awarded the Chamisso
Prize in 1990, Özdamar also received the Bachmann Prize in 1991. This

13   Compare research conducted by Leslie Adelson (*The Turkish Turn in Contemporary
      German Literature: Toward a New Critical Grammar of Migration* [New York:
      Palgrave Macmillan, 2005]), Jeffrey Peck (*Being Jewish in the New Germany* [New
      Brunswick, N.J.: Rutgers University Press, 2006]), and Azade Seyhan (*Writing
      Outside the Nation* [Princeton: Princeton University Press, 2001]), to name just
      three of the most prolific literary critics and theorists who emphasise the new,
      much more diverse, and, as a result, much more complex situation that emerges
      in Germany at the turn of the new millennium. This trend is mirrored in histo-
      riographical and sociological studies and oral history projects, e.g. in the work by
      Karin Hunn (*'Nächstes Jahr kehren wir zurück ...': Die Geschichte der türkischen
      'Gastarbeiter' in der Bundesrepublik* [Göttingen: Wallstein, 2005]), Eva Kolinsky
      ('Migration Experiences and the Construction of Identity among Turks Living in
      Germany', *Recasting German Identity. Culture, Politics, and Literature in the Berlin
      Republic*, eds. Stuart Taberner and Frank Finlay [Rochester: Camden House, 2002],
      205–218), Ayhan Kaya ('German-Turkish Transnational Space: A Separate Space
      of Their Own', *German Studies Review* 30 [2007], 483–502), and Viola B. Georgi
      (*Entliehene Erinnerung. Geschichtsbilder junger Migranten in Deutschland* [Hamburg:
      Hamburger Edition, 2003]).

triggered an intense debate in the media and in academia since this was perceived as crossing deeply engrained borders that separate the German and the non-German literary space.

In the twenty-first century, fiction by migrant authors has moved away from the margins and has become a focal point in the study of German literature. In this process, the definition of German literature is slowly changing. In his monograph *Cosmopolitical Claims. Turkish-German Literatures from Nadolny to Pamuk*, B. Venkat Mani aims to demonstrate 'that recent German and Turkish novels upset normative perceptions of dominant cultural production in a nation, its language, and its literature through new forms of imaginative expressions.'[14] In *Novels of Turkish German Settlement. Cosmopolite Fictions*, Tom Cheesman argues that Turkish-German writers have become integral to the German literary scene. They include bestselling novelists Renan Demirkan and Akif Pirinçci, prestigious literary prize-winners Emine Sevgi Özdamar and Feridun Zaimoğlu, and the critically acclaimed Aras Ören and Zafer Şenocak. Tom Cheesman focuses on these and other writers' perspectives on cosmopolitan ideals and aspirations, ranging from glib affirmation to cynical transgression and melancholy nihilism. What Cheesman calls their 'literature of settlement'[15] is paradigmatic for European cultures adapting to diversity and negotiating new identities. Sten Nadolny's bestseller *Selim oder Die Gabe der Rede* (1990, *Selim or the Talent of Speaking*) is one of the most prominent examples of this transnational engagement.[16] Leslie Adelson argues that 'Nadolny's work does not rely on direct intertextual allusions to an earlier phase of postwar German literature but probes instead the epistemological shortcomings

14 Venkat B. Mani, *Cosmopolitical Claims. Turkish-German Literatures from Nadolny to Pamuk* (Iowa City: University of Iowa Press, 2007), 7.

15 Tom Cheesman, *Novels of Turkish German Settlement: Cosmopolite Fictions* (Rochester, NY: Camden House, 2007), 12.

16 For the authors' comments on this process see Sten Nadonly, 'Wir und Die – Erzählen über Fremde', *Schreiben zwischen den Kulturen: Beiträge zur deutschsprachigen Gegenwartsliteratur*, ed. Paul Michael Lützeler (Frankfurt a.M.: Fischer, 1996), 65–74.

of an altogether nonliterary form of German opposition to fascism: the student movement of the late 1960s and early 1970s.'[17]

The 1960s and 1970s lend themselves in particular to the kind of explorations that led to the collapse of essentialist and exclusive notions of Germanness. In Germany, the student movement was marked by an engagement with the legacy of the Third Reich, a burden and responsibility young people in other countries did not face. At the same time, the German movement connected with the uprisings around the world in their joint concern over continued oppression in the so-called free Western world and around the globe. Thus, to authors with a hyphenated identity who were eager to be taken seriously within the German literary market and who at the same time were transforming it, the 1960s and 1970s offered a unique opportunity to enter a restricted national space, the discourse on the legacy of the Third Reich, and simultaneously emphasise the international and transnational aspects of the movement and its concern over oppression in capitalist societies.

In a similar vein, Sabine von Dirke claims that the issue of minority discourses is closely connected to the broader transformation of the cultural paradigm in the 1990s. Thus, she links the emergence of transnational fiction written in German directly to processes that began with the student movement and found new literary forms in the late 1970s and early 1980s. Resentment or distrust regarding monocultural and totalizing paradigms as well as an enthusiastic celebration of heterogeneity and plurality by postmodern theorists characterise the political, discursive, and aesthetic landscape of this fiction.[18]

Nadolny's novel also triggered a methodological debate that foreshadowed and advanced the notion that literature by bilingual and bicultural authors should be recognised as full contributions to discourses within Germany. Already in 1994, Leslie Adelson emphasised the need 'to chal-

---

17   Leslie A. Adelson, 'Opposing Turkish-German Questions in Contemporary German Studies', *German Studies Review* 17 (1994), 305–330, 312.

18   Sabine von Dirke, 'West Meets East: Narrative Construction of the Foreigner and Postmodern Orientalism in Sten Nadolny's *Selim oder Die Gabe der Rede*', *The Germanic Review* 60 (1994), 61–69.

lenge such Turkish-German oppositions and to ask what methodological alternatives a multiculturally oriented German Studies has to offer.'[19] Ülker Gökberk, however, sharply criticises Adelson's reading of the novel and instead analyses Nadolny's novel in light of the tension between different theoretical and methodological models that emerged in the late 1980s and 1990s, mainly *interkulturelle Germanistik* (intercultural Germanistics) and a cultural studies paradigm that emerged in the US.[20]

The Turkish-German author Emine Sevgi Özdamar has attracted interest from literary and cultural critics, yet little has been written about the connection between her texts and the discourse on 1968 – Elizabeth Boa and Monika Shafi are notable exceptions. Özdamar is one of the most prominent contemporary authors in Germany and has received many prizes for her work including the Kleist Prize (2004). Özdamar was born in Turkey in 1946 and came to Germany as a young adult in 1965, where she worked in a factory in Berlin and lived in a hostel with other workers. She started to learn German and became interested in theatre and subsequently studied acting in Istanbul. After her return to Germany in 1976, she worked with Bertolt Brecht's pupil Benno Besson at the *Volksbühne* in East Berlin and later in France. After the publication of a collection of stories called *Mutterzunge* (1990, *Mother Tongue*) Özdamar published her first novel, *Das Leben ist eine Karawanserei – hat zwei Türen – aus einer kam ich rein – aus der anderen ging ich raus* (2000, *Life is a Caravanserai – Has Two Doors – I Came in One – I Went Out the Other*). This novel and the two following two works *Die Brücke vom Goldenen Horn* (1998, *The Bridge of the Golden Horn*) and *Seltsame Sterne starren zur Erde* form a trilogy.[21] The trilogy reflects on the 1960s and 1970s in both Turkey and Germany and contains autobiographical elements.

19   Adelson (1994), 306.

20   Ülker Gökberk, 'Culture Studies und die Türken: Sten Nadolnys *Selim oder Die Gabe der Rede* im Lichte einer Methodendiskussion', *The German Quarterly* 70 (1997), 97–122. See Leslie Adelson's response to Ülker Gökberk in *The German Quarterly* 70 (1997), 277–282.

21   Emine S. Özdamar, *Die Brücke vom Goldenen Horn* (Köln: Kiepenheuer & Witsch, 1998), *Das Leben ist eine Karawanserei hat zwei Türen aus einer kam ich rein aus der*

Monika Shafi focuses on the second part of Özdamar's trilogy and
asks to what extent the concept of generation is useful in analysing West
Germany's 1968 and its legacy as represented in Uwe Timm's novel *Rot*,
Günter Grass' narrative *Mein Jahrhundert*, and Özdamar's *Die Brücke vom
Goldenen Horn*. She grants Özdamar's novel a special status by arguing that
the text unsettles the dichotomy between the German mainstream and a
multicultural niche-discourse and overcomes the restrictions of placing
1968 solely in the context of a German cultural memory.

Whilst Shafi's interpretation provides valuable insights, I am propos-
ing to shift the overall argument to a different ground and read the trilogy
and in particular *Seltsame Sterne starren zur Erde*, the least studied text of
the trilogy so far, in response to Leslie Adelson's study *The Turkish Turn
in Contemporary German Literature: Toward a New Critical Grammar of
Migration*.

Adelson argues that prevailing analytical paradigms are inadequate
to grasp the social dimensions inherent in the literature of migration. She
seeks 'a new critical grammar for understanding the configuration of cultural contact and Turkish presence in contemporary German literature.'[22]
Therefore, Adelson introduces 'the concept of touching tales as an alternative organizing principle for considering Turkish lines of thought.'[23] She
understands Turkish lines of thought 'not in terms of identity politics,
ethnic difference, or national mentalities, but as figurative story lines reshaping key points of reference and orientation in German and transnational
cultures through the looking glass of Turkish migration.'[24]

In line with Adelson's argument, I am not reading Özdamar's text as
a phenomenon of the diaspora or as an expression of the theme of transnational migration. Rather, I choose to read *Seltsame Sterne starren zur
Erde* as one contribution to the discourse on 1968 by a Turkish-German
author without which this discourse would remain incomplete. Thus, its

---

anderen ging ich raus (Köln: Kiepenheuer & Witsch, 1992), and *Seltsame Sterne
starren zur Erde* (Köln: Kiepenheuer & Witsch, 2003).

22   Adelson (2005), 5.
23   Adelson (2005), 20.
24   Adelson (2005), 21f.

particular significance for this discourse needs to be analysed, since it is inseparable from the project of the discursive envisioning of 1968. Adelson ascribes this 'labor of imagination'[25] to literary strategies of transformation, strategies that can be observed in Özdamar's text.

With Adelson, I am not asking what the text says about the figure of the Turk but I am asking what the text narrated by the figure of the Turk says about East and West Berlin and about the time period of the 1970s in the aftermath of the student movement and during the *Deutscher Herbst* (German Autumn), the height of West-German terrorism in the fall of 1977. I am focusing on the concept of transnational memory that allows us to understand how time and space make use of national boundaries and histories in order to transcend them.

Elizabeth Boa discusses Özdamar's novels *Das Leben ist eine Karawanserei* and *Die Brücke vom Goldenen Horn* as hybrids in terms of genre, perspective, and language use: 'In conveying a complex sense of transformative interchange between culturally heterogeneous countries under the impact of social and political change, both novels combat fixed national or cultural stereotypes.'[26] I would like to go one step further and suggest that these texts also manifest the transnational nature of writings by migrant authors who insert themselves in the national discourse by writing in German. These authors also emphasise the transnational nature of the student movement of 1968 that transcends the national boundaries.

Özdamar's first novel, *Das Leben ist eine Karawanserei* chronicles the childhood and adolescence of a girl born at the end of World War II in the Anatolian city of Malatya. As Turkey modernises, her father's repeated unemployment drives the family to Istanbul, Bursa, and Ankara. Her family's uprootedness and the increasing influence of American culture, in particular via American movies, lead the protagonist to refuse gendered expectations connected with Muslim values. She earns money for the family as an actress; however, due to the increasing difficulty of earning a living in

25 Adelson (2005), 14.
26 Elizabeth Boa, 'Özdamar's Autobiographical Fictions: Trans-National Identity and Literary Form', *German Life and Letters* 59 (2006), 526–539, 526.

Turkey the young woman decides to sign on with the Turkish government
in order to migrate to Germany as a so-called guest worker. By the close of
the novel she is on a train heading for Germany, sharing a compartment
with a prostitute and a lesbian couple.

Whilst this novel takes place in Turkey it foreshadows themes that gain
importance throughout the 1960s and throughout the world: the quest
for personal liberation, often inspired by American cultural influences and
sometimes forced by economic necessity is accompanied by the decreased
importance of class and class consciousness. In the 1960s the emerging
New Left, currently often described as a social movement, borrowed from
a variety of theoretical sources both Marxist and non-Marxist in order to
call for a different kind of revolution that focuses on the (emotional) needs
of the individual. The young girl lives in a predominantly local agrarian
society, yet the numerous attempts by her father to achieve and maintain
his middle class status dislocate her into urban and increasingly cosmopolitan environments. Her quest for knowledge and education, combined
with the intent to become an artist, seems to fail as her escape coincides
with the loss of social standing. She leaves her home by joining the working class. As she boards the train to Germany the idea of the New Left is
foreshadowed. Personal liberation is not solely based on solidarity among
the working class, but extends to numerous individuals with a variety of
backgrounds and experiences. As she shares her compartment with men
and women, workers and non-workers, a prostitute and a lesbian couple, it
is apparent that all migrants are unified by the quest for personal liberation
and by the lack of work that forces them to migrate to Germany.

This first novel of Özdamar's trilogy could be described as a
Bildungsroman of the making of a female guest worker from Turkey. Pushing
past the boundaries of the realistic narrative in the *Bildungsroman*, Özdamar
also includes elements of a magic-realist style in the tradition of Jorge Luis
Borges, Günter Grass, and Irmtraud Morgner. The narrator combines information and observations with accounts of dreamlike, mythic, and fairy-tale
occurrences in order to confront the legacy of colonialism, the two world
wars, the Armenian genocide, the Holocaust, and fascism. This dual focus
of *Das Leben ist eine Karawanserei* on personal liberation and the critical engagement with the past and historical oppression also foreshadows

the 1960s. The struggle to verbalise and to fight for one's own rights was motivated by the critical engagement with the past, e.g. in Germany with the history of the Third Reich. At the same time the youthful rebellion against restrictions imposed by parents and society as represented in schools, universities, and houses of worship led to an increased interest in this past in the first place since the legacy of the Third Reich could be utilised as a strong weapon against the parents' generation and their (hidden and repressed) feelings of guilt and shame.

The second part of the trilogy, *Die Brücke vom Goldenen Horn* begins in 1966 and tells the story of the struggles of the newly arrived Turkish workers in Berlin. The narrator is a young adult now and reflects her adolescence, in particular the constant struggle with her parents who discouraged her from becoming an actress. This desire drove her to neglect her school-work in favour of attending the theatre, acting, and learning her roles. Her parents also disagree with her decision to work in a factory in Germany, since they have the aspiration that at least their children will escape the fate of a working class existence. These reflections are interspersed with accounts of the narrator's new life in Berlin. Escaping the confinement of both home and work the narrator discovers the German theatre and the student scene in Berlin.

Boa also reads the second part of the trilogy, *Die Brücke vom Goldenen Horn* in the context of the German student movement and the political situation in Turkey:

> *Die Brücke vom Goldenen Horn*, while telling a highly specific story, also conveys representative experiences common to a generation of young, educated people from many countries in the late 1960s who learned languages, traveled, read Marx, protested against Western imperialism, sought sexual liberation, but who would also begin in the early 1970s to question the power relations between the sexes. In Berlin and Istanbul the protagonist becomes a female apprentice, a Wilhelmine Meister with a theatrical vocation, visiting the Berliner Ensemble in Berlin and attending acting school in Istanbul where she also mixes, as the only woman, among the intellectuals who meet in the Captain's Café.[27]

27   Boa, 536.

The novel is written in an innovative and highly individualised language consisting of an amalgam of Turkish and German. This language manifests itself in the text in particular via the spelling of German words based on their pronunciation and the oral comprehension of the Turkish narrator. On this level, form and content converge. The novel is written in an invented language that some have characterised as a hybrid language exemplifying the situation of Turkish migrants in Germany. This invites the analysis of language and its use by the narrator and the characters in the novel. The narrator and the other guest workers who live together in a hostel attempt to learn German. Soon, the possibilities and impossibilities of translation appear. Whilst the Turks learn enough German to be able to function at work, their understanding is shaped by their first language.

One of the hostel's supervisors, a Turkish communist, attempts to educate the women. He aims to increase their knowledge of German as well as to raise their class consciousness. However, his teaching produces mixed results. Most women are content to be able to perform their work and to participate in the West-German consumer society. They defy any attempt to further their education, let alone to raise their political awareness with humour. They communicate by using an amalgamated language and different translators and construct a social community within the hostel that coexists with the dominant German society. This community rests on the cultural foundation of the Turkey they left, their home they long for.

The protagonist rebels against her teacher for a different reason. His language, the language of the Old Left, is insufficient to quench her thirst for authentic and aesthetic experiences, namely to lose her virginity and to become an actress. She enjoys living in the hybrid linguistic space that is marked by language games that defy analysis and clear meanings and that privilege the play with the mother tongue within the German space and the predominantly Turkish space within the hostel.

Her love for literature and in particular the dramatic arts bring the protagonist in touch with another linguistic space, the language of German theatre. This language allows her to bridge the abyss between her native tongue and the language of the host country. It emphasises the creative use of language, thus allowing for personal expression within a highly mediated performative and aesthetic setting. Furthermore, exploring the students' nightlife in Berlin, she soon realises that the students offer a different language than her teacher at the hostel. It is the subculture of the 1960s that invites a language that reflects on language use and its limitations, and that ultimately, if only for a short time, declares the supremacy of the experience over the word.

This theme is closely tied to the literary discourse about the 1960s in Germany.[28] The 1960s were marked by an attempt to find an adequate language for the students' discontent and experiences. Thus, the experiences in a hybrid linguistic space, such as the ones the narrator recounts, are particularly well suited in order to explore the various underlying issues of the 1960s. In their quest for liberation, the students were also searching for a new language.[29] The shared knowledge base that informed this new social movement did not so much rest on the writings of the Old Left but on an unruly mix of texts by members of the Frankfurt School, Herbert Marcuse, Sigmund Freud, and Wilhelm Reich. These texts, in conjunction with global influences, e.g. the American Civil Rights movement and the post- and anti-colonial writings from South America, encouraged the students to distrust language and its claim to power. The students emphasised immediate experiences over language and preferred language that invites self-exploration and self-discovery.

As important as finding a new language as a motivating factor for their activities was the students' distrust of language. The students considered language to be a tool in the hands of those in power who used this tool to silence and to keep silent rather than to liberate. These issues are skilfully addressed in *Die Brücke vom Goldenen Horn* where the Turkish migrants soon rely on the narrator who turns into a translator. Due to her role as a translator between German and Turkish, the narrator is soon

---

28   Sean McCann, 'Do You Believe in Magic? Literary Thinking after the New Left', *Yale Journal of Criticism: Interpretation in the Humanities* 18.2 (2005), 435–468, and Gerhard Hoffmann, 'The Sixties and the Advent of Postmodernism', *The Sixties Revisited: Culture-Society-Politics*, eds. Jürgen Heideking, Jörg Helbig, and Anke Ortlepp (Heidelberg: Universitätsverlag Winter; 2001), 191–235.

29   Compare Roman Luckscheiter, *Der postmoderne Impuls. Die Krise in der Literatur um 1968 und ihre Überwindung* (Berlin: Duncker & Humblot, 2001).

called upon even to mediate in arguments that take place in Turkish, which further increases her influence. Within the student movement, the focus lies on a language that would enable the students to speak about and for the oppressed. The students overlook the fact that language also enables communication with the oppressed. However, this dialogue did not occur in the 1960s, a failure that is demonstrated by the students' problematic self-representations in the so-called *Väterliteratur* (literature of the fathers) of the 1970s.[30]

In the end, the narrator returns home. Inspired by the student protests in Berlin she intends to work on political change in Istanbul. However, the political situation there is significantly different and the narrator is confronted with a brutal regime and the remainders of Kurdish persecution as represented in the desolate landscape she experiences on a journey to Eastern Anatolia.

Ten years later, she returns to Berlin. This homecoming is remembered in the third part of the trilogy, *Seltsame Sterne starren zur Erde*. This last text most clearly invites an autobiographical reading, as it is told from the perspective of a first-person narrator. In addition, *Seltsame Sterne starren zur Erde* takes the form of a diary, a literary genre that creates the impression of authenticity and seems to grant access to real life experiences. Within the highly mediated frame of aesthetic expression, this literary strategy connects Özdamar's trilogy to other fictional texts written by German-German authors about the 1960s after 1989. Writers such as Peter Schneider and Uwe Timm shift from a third person perspective deployed in novels published in the 1970s to the first person perspective. This shift reveals the emphasis that all three authors place on a reflective mode of narrating, one that stresses personal remembering as an important process for the construction of a cultural memory of 1968. The construction of this kind of cultural memory serves the dual purpose of constructing

---

30 Compare Susan G. Figge, 'Fathers, Daughters, and the Nazi Past: Father Literature and Its (Resisting) Readers', *Gender, Patriarchy, and Fascism in the Third Reich: The Response of Women Writers*, ed. Elaine Martin (Detroit: Wayne State University Press, 1993), 274–302.

a coherent narrative that is at the same time much less homogenous than the term cultural memory suggests. This narrative is shaped by numerous and at times conflicting voices and by contrastive memories of experiences and their critical reflection.

In *Seltsame Sterne starren zur Erde*, the narrator is not only distinguished by her Turkish background, but it is the German past and present that shape the narrator's work and life. Their poetic transformation as a 'labor of imagination' performed by the narrator turns this hybrid text into an important contribution to the discourse on 1968. The text is not only informed by the Turkish-German background but also by the attempt to contribute to the reworking of cultural matter that shapes the future of German history. Therefore, instead of assuming that a text by a Turkish-German author creates a kind of a parallel world or occupies a niche in an otherwise German context, I am interested in the ways these Turkish-German texts participate in the numerous debates about the German past and its function and place in Germany's future, debates that marked the 1990s in Germany.

'In Deutschland zu leben, ist ein Beruf' ('To live in Germany is a profession.') the narrator observes on a cold and overcast day in East Berlin.[31] In response, she pursues a career as a writer, actress, and theatre director. These creative professions allow her to work with personal and historical experiences and to turn them into poetic expressions. *Seltsame Sterne starren zur Erde* chronicles and reflects these first beginnings of the narrator's professional life.

The text encompasses the time between fall 1976 and January 1978. References to chronology and history in the first part of the book are presented as quotes from newspaper headlines and movie announcements. The second part of the book takes the form of a diary. The narrator leaves her hometown Istanbul, her family, and her husband and moves to West Berlin in order to begin an internship at the *Volksbühne* in East Berlin. Whilst the political events of the *Deutscher Herbst* serve as the backdrop for the narrator's experiences in the communal post-1968 living project in

---

31   Özdamar (2003), 213.

Wedding, the Berlin Wall seems to be a true *Schutzwall* (protective bar-
rier) for the narrator insofar as it allows her to begin her theatre career with
some of the most famous representatives of the East-German theatre scene
and to create a poetic existence for herself during her stay in East Berlin.
Her depiction of the Berlin Wall as a protection is one of the moments
that most clearly demonstrate how the German mainstream discourse is
interrupted and unsettled by a voice that interprets German history in the
twentieth century and its physical manifestation, the Berlin Wall, in a very
different light. Taking the unusual step of working in the East, the narrator documents the rehearsals at the *Volksbühne*, analyses her experiences
in East and West Berlin, and creates close textual connections between the
urban spaces Berlin and Istanbul.

And whilst Istanbul as a city between Europe and Asia, between West
and East is of course the literary topos per se for discussing transience as
well as the chronotopes of historical developments and political alliances,
the literary convergences of the two cities that Özdamar creates seem to
foreshadow the wars that are marking the twenty-first century – fuelled
by religious and ethnic struggles and seemingly insurmountable cultural
differences between the West and the rest of the world.

Seltsame Sterne starren zur Erde is less concerned with the dangers
of forgetting the past than it is with creating and contributing to the new
conditions for remembering twentieth-century Germany in a present situation that a multitude of people, more diverse than ever, share: children
and grandchildren of victims, perpetrators, and bystanders, former East
and West Germans, the 'real' Germans and those of a non-German heritage
and tradition. And it is no coincidence that the project of approaching the
past and the 'work' of engaging with the past in the 1990s is conducted by
a Turkish-German author since many German-German authors are more
interested in normalcy, in appeasing unsettling memories, and in creating
their own legacy.

The narrator in the text writes a personal account that takes on the
hybrid form of autobiography and diary and includes notes and drawings
from her work at the *Volksbühne* in East Berlin. She inserts quotes and references that indicate her familiarity with German literary and intellectual
history and emphasise her self-understanding of belonging in this context.

This intertextuality suggests that attempts to categorise this literature as Turkish-German and in-between are obsolete. Already the title – a quote taken from Else Lasker-Schüler's poem *Sterne des Fatum* – indicates that the kind of imaginative labour the narrator undertakes makes connections instead of creating borders and thus challenges the notion of fixed identities, be they personal or national. Rather than adhering to the notion of the autonomous subject placed in between the Turkish and the German worlds or experiencing the diaspora, the narrator contributes to the rewriting of German history for the twenty-first century. Furthermore, since the narrator as an artist works with a variety of media – writing, drawing, and performing/directing – the artist is not defined by the genre that she is working in but claims a poetic existence and creates her own life as an expression of this poetic work. Thus, the narrator is able to transform the notion that 'In Deutschland zu leben, ist ein Beruf' whereby she characterises 'Beruf' here as a burden, a meaningless occupation, an alienating job, or a form of exploitation within the capitalist system. Instead, the narrator turns work into a productive, poetic, transforming, and transformative labour of the imagination that takes on a meaning beyond the personal.

Despite all the literary repercussions in Özdamar's text, the narrator maintains her independence and takes control of the narrative by making her voice heard. Yet it is not a voice that makes or refutes claims, it is not a voice that attempts to be heard within multicultural identity politics. It is a voice that is radically individualised without obscuring her various alliances: Turkish-German migrant, holder of an East-German visa, illegal resident in West Berlin, member of a West-Berlin commune, artist, student, woman, granddaughter, daughter, sister, wife, lover, friend.

Özdamar's text documents the estrangement from the German New Left. Even though the narrator clearly sympathises with the New Left she also distances herself: she asserts that they speak a different language – too theoretical, too political, and too abstract. She exposes the self-indulgence of members of the New Left in both East and West, especially in comparison with the political situation of the Left in Turkey. In her role as narrator, director, and visual artist, the narrator is the observer and chronicler of historical developments in East and West. This status guarantees narrative control and shapes her unique insights and perspectives with respect to events in Germany. Two examples highlight this strategy:

In the West, sitting around the dinner table with the members of the communal living project, the narrator records the conversation as if it were a play. The conversation is triggered by the word 'deprimierend'[32] (depressing) which sets the stage for each of the participants-turned-actors to recite predictable lines about specific German *Befindlichkeiten* (mental states) either popular among the students of the 1970s or among those criticizing the rebellious youth: 'Die junge Generation, die nach Westberlin abgehauen ist, kann sich nicht mit dem Kalten Krieg identifizieren. ... Hier sind die jungen Leute entweder links oder in Psychobewegungen. ... Wir wollen eins zu eins leben. Wir haben keine Karriereabsichten. Wir wollen experimentell leben.'[33] In the vein of a Socratic dialogue in which each rhetorical move is pre-determined and predictable, the narrator assigns each of her friends a specific role as she listens to and records their conversation. In an ironic twist, the narrator in the meantime washes the dishes. This scene unmasks the members of the New Left as stuck in a theoretical and mainly rhetorical posturing at the expense of meaningful or sometimes just necessary productivity – like washing the dishes!

In the East, the narrator is able to share her love for the theatre and to start a career as a German-speaking actress and director. Yet she remains an observer, and she takes on the role of the student which further complicates the gender dynamic in the text. All of her role models and teachers are male, and whilst the narrator is wondering why she does not have sex with them or anyone else in the East for that matter, she seems to be content to play the role of the exotic and female other in need of an education. Most importantly, even though she meets many of the political dissidents in East-Germany she is not really interested in their political lives. Political

---

32   Özdamar (2003), 51.

33   'The young generation, that fled to West-Berlin [after WWII], does not identify with the Cold War ... Here, young people belong either to the Left or to consciousness raising groups ... We want to live an authentic life. We do not have any career goals. We want to explore and experiment.' [My translation] *Seltsame Sterne starren zur Erde*, 52.

events and debates in East Berlin serve as the background for the narrator's personal and professional development. Whilst this could be read as naiveté on part of the narrator, I propose to read this as a strategy to de-centre and refashion events from the perspective of a Turkish-German voice.

Shafi comments on this narrative strategy in *Die Brücke vom Goldenen Horn* and takes the narrator's ironic distancing as an indication that she is outside of the political movement on the left in Germany in the 1960s and 1970s. However, I read the narrator's position in *Seltsame Sterne starren zur Erde* as both outside and inside. She is not outside because of her origin yet she is outside because she maintains her own self. She is inside because she is able to add another perspective to the experiences of 1968. This insight creates a transnational moment of cultural memories: the narrator with a Turkish background appropriates and reflects the German experiences in the twentieth century. They are not foreign experiences but rather they are the experiences as they become available to her in her unique position as someone who is an illegal resident in West Berlin, a legal visitor in East Berlin, and a Turkish citizen unwilling to live in Istanbul. The creative appropriation of the German past, the Third Reich, the GRD and the old FRG, and the Cold War through the lens of the events of 1968 turns *Seltsame Sterne starren zur Erde* into a novel that belongs to the genre of 1968 novels whilst at the same time emphasizing the importance of transnational exchange.

Encompassing and expanding the concept of identity, transnationalism points to the importance of border-crossing and across-the-border interaction whilst questioning the narrative of the nation-state. Reading *Seltsame Sterne starren zur Erde* proffers an insight into the convergence of the concept of transnationalism with the discourse on 1968. The text subverts the idea of the nation state by adding another voice and other experiences that challenge the dominant narrative of the German past, e.g. how the narrator understands and experiences the Berlin Wall, the German 1960s and 1970s, and the numerous attempts to come to terms with the Nazi past. The text adds another important aspect to this narrative by pointing to 1968 as a central experience for the narrator.

My understanding of cultural memory adds a spatial dimension to the chronological one. By analysing the importance of origins, locations,

and destinations, of border crossing and travel, 'situations' intersect with
the 'moment' of 1968 – a narrative move that is reflected not only in the
countries represented in *Seltsame Sterne starren zur Erde* (most importantly Turkey, France, West Germany, and the GDR) but also in the form
this text takes as a hybrid genre. It is here where one needs to account for
both the space and the passing time. Whereas the space alludes to the difference of experiences, the impossibility of understanding, and the need
for dialogue across the spatial divide, the passing of time historicises this
experience, emphasizing change and the possibility for understanding. The
hybrid genre responds to these complex demands by allowing the narrator
to create her poetic existence within the literary traditions.

Narratives within the genre of 1968 novels provide insight into the
relationship between fiction and the public discourse in Germany and
thus connect literary studies to other disciplines. I argue that albeit a small
group, Turkish-German authors make an important contribution to the
discourse on 1968 in the 1990s. I read them as examples of a transnational
moment of cultural memory rather than as diasporic texts by authors with
hyphenated identities. These novels simultaneously shape and reflect the
discourse on 1968 in Germany. Whilst the protagonist's wanderings from
Istanbul to West and East Berlin provide a first layer of transnationalism,
the perception of someone who is everything but the typical West-Berlin
'1968er' narrating her experiences of that time, and the subsequent challenge
to the predominant view on the German past, e.g. Özdamar's Berlin Wall
vs. how East or West Germans see it, adds the second layer. The third layer
turns 1968 into an important event of the German past in itself by being a
central experience of the protagonist's German existence. Complementing
these layers of transnationalism is the notion of cultural memory, which I
understand both chronologically and spatially. Whilst space can separate,
the need for dialogue to facilitate understanding beyond this spatial divide
historicises the experience and thus opens up the possibility of understanding and literal and figurative border-crossing.

STUART J. HILWIG

An Oral History of Memories of 1968 in Italy

The global student revolt of 1968 rocked cities from Tokyo to Turin and shook the lives of activists and ordinary citizens everywhere. Immediately following that eventful year, scholars, journalists, and activists took up the pen and produced an unabated stream of memoirs, retrospectives, and scholarly volumes. Most of these works have sought to answer the fundamental question of why the energies of the young coalesced in an eruption of anti-authoritarian protest in the year 1968.[1] On the twentieth anniversary of 1968, the Marxist scholar, Paul Piccone published an article entitled, 'Reinterpreting 1968: Mythology on the Make,' in which he noted that with each passing decade, a new round of books appears on the student revolt that essentially affirms and mythologises the views of former activists. Piccone argued that scholars must 'unmask' some of the myths of '68 in order to reveal the more nuanced dimensions of that key year.

Despite Piccone's implication that a 'true 1968' must lie beneath the mythology created by former activists, this study shows that the 'other side' has also engaged in a process of myth making. An inquiry into the views of non-students who remember the events of the late 1960s reveals that their memories of this momentous period are similarly strewn with mythic narratives and tropes that continue to evolve with each passing year. This chapter's goals are twofold: the first is to listen to the voices of those on the other side of the barricades, the non-students, who observed and

---

1 P. Piccone, 'Reinterpreting 1968: Mythology on the Make', *Telos* 77 (1988), 7–43. The editors of a recent collection of interviews by non-activists have also noted the overwhelming influence of former student leaders upon the literature of the *Sessantotto*; see Circolo Gianni Bosio, eds. *Un anno durato decenni. Vite di persone communi prima, durante e dopo il '68* (Roma: Odradek, 2006).

interacted with the student movement in a variety of ways; the second is to analyse the ways that non-students have remembered the events of '68 about thirty years after the student upheavals.[2] Moving beyond much of the literature that focuses upon the activists and homogenises non-students as 'The Establishment,' we shall discover that the non-students' memories of the 1968 protests were even more varied than those of the activists.[3] Drawing upon the oral testimony of university professors, school teachers, police, lawyers, journalists, and workers, we shall see that those who had direct dealings with student activists ultimately interacted with the student rebels in a multitude of different ways. By analysing the ways that ordinary citizens have remembered Italy's student revolt, what emerges is a more complex picture of the 1960s that blurs previous dichotomies between the students and non- students. Further complicating this study of the larger society's response to protest is the fact that memory is inconstant, inconsistent and inescapably influenced by the passage of time, the media, the rhetoric of public figures, and the normal cognitive processes of forgetting.

The study of memory is an elusive undertaking that has yet to yield any major consensus in the field. As Bill Niven noted, scholars continue to propose new words that are essentially reiterations of previous terms and concepts.[4] Furthermore, memory studies encompass the work of historians, sociologists, psychologists, anthropologists, linguists, literary theorists, and ethnologists who bring a variety of methodological tools to the field and often find it difficult to address the concerns of those outside

2   The majority of the oral interviews used in this study were conducted in 1997 and some were conducted in 2002.
3   For a similar example see A. Confino's critique of Y. Zerubavel's *Recovered Roots: Collective Memory and the Making of Israeli National Tradition* in which Confino charges Zerubavel with mistakenly presenting Jewish society as a 'monolith' and therefore, 'bereft of its sociology and its politics.' 'AHR Forum: Collective Memory and Cultural History: Problems of Method', *American Historical Review* (December 1997), 1397.
4   B. Niven, 'Review Article: On the Use of "Collective Memory"', *German History* 26(3) (2006), 335–336.

their discipline. This study does not seek to engage the methodological debates concerning memory but rather will make use of some terms from memory studies. Two key terms and their definitions are as follows.

Personal memory meaning those reflections that the interviewee self-consciously offers from first hand experience and are denoted by phrases such as 'I remember that ...' These types of memories are the subject of frequent debate between sociologists and psychologists so rather than engaging in the debate over the nature of personal memory, we can acknowledge the role that both social and cognitive factors have in the process of shaping, reshaping, and forgetting past events.[5] This study puts the ball in the respondent's court by accepting as *personal memories* those recollections that the interviewee claims as unique to their own experiences or in which they participated.

Collective memory signifying those memories created when a group experiences a set of events. For example, a former professor who recalls the time a group of his colleagues met to decide what to do about the occupation of university classrooms. *Collective memory* can also be the memory of significant events shared by separate individuals such as recollections of the day that Martin Luther King was assassinated. In both cases, collective memories are common experiences that have left a mark upon groups as small as a handful of university professors or as large as an entire generation.[6] Furthermore, as Maurice Halbwachs noted, individuals may be members of different groups simultaneously.[7] Similar to personal memory, collective memory may be subject to revision, contamination, forgetting

5   An excellent psychological study comparing individual or personal memory with collective memory may be found in: M. Weldon and K. Bellinger, 'Collective Memory: Collaborative and Individual Processes in Remembering', *Journal of Experimental Psychology* 23(5) (1997), 1160–1175.

6   For a concise overview of 'collective memory', see: W. Kansteiner, 'Finding Meaning in Memory: A Methodological Critique of Collective Memory Studies', *History and Theory* 41 (May 2002), 188–189; and S. Crane, 'AHR Forum: Writing the Individual Back into Collective Memory', *American Historical Review* (December 1997), 1376–1377.

7   M. Halbwachs, *On Collective Memory*, 53.

and homogenisation over time. These memories can be acted upon by texts, television, radio, and the stories told by 'those who were there.' Pierre Nora elaborated on the idea of collective memory by noting that collective memories become 'historical memories' by rooting them to places or sites in an attempt to solidify their existence for long periods of time.[8] Again, as with personal memory, collective memory fuses with other types of memory continually recreating itself. Oral recollections of past events offer an excellent example of this fusion as the respondent often draws from pieces of personal, collective, and historical memory in describing an event.

The oral testimonies in this essay came from a series of twenty-four interviews conducted in 1997 and 2002. The goal was to understand the Italian '68 from the perspective of teachers, professors, police, workers, the clergy, journalists, and workers. Each interviewee answered a series of five questions about different aspects of the *Sessantotto*. In total, nine of the respondents were female and fifteen were male, their ages in 1968 ranged from their early 20s to 58 years old.[9] As such, this chapter makes no claims to be a quantitative analysis of non-students' memories of student activism but rather offers qualitative evidence supporting a richer and more nuanced understanding of the interaction between student activists and non-students.[10] Also the temporal distance of three or more decades

---

8   See P. Nora, 'Between History and Memory: Les Lieux de Mémoire', *Representations* 26 (Spring 1989), 7–25.

9   The five questions sought to elicit a larger dialogue:
1. 'What were you doing in 1968? What was your occupation? Could you describe your family at that time.'
2. 'Which aspect of the student movement do you believe struck the Italians the most?'
3. 'In your opinion, what was the relationship between the students and the press?'
4. 'In your opinion, did the student protests provoke a new discussion of fascism in Italy and the political past? Why or why not?'
5. 'Which specific event of the student movement do you remember best? Why?'

10   For a comprehensive study of the non-student response to the Italian student movement of the late 1960s, see: S.J. Hilwig, *Italy and 1968: Youthful Unrest and Democratic Culture* (Basingstoke, UK: Palgrave Macmillan, 2009).

from the time of the student revolt to the date of the interviews enables us to study the ways in which the semantics and place of the *Sessantotto* has shifted in the popular memory of the Italians.

In analysing the ways that people responded to student protest, we must first look at the ways that memory and history interact in oral history. The methods of oral history cause respondents to draw not only from their personal and collective memories but also compel them to historicise the events knowing that the interviewer will ultimately use and record their memories in a printed text. Oral historians are often struck by the bewildering array of factual discrepancies and emotional conflicts that arise when their subjects recall personal and collective memories.[11] Luisa Passerini's *Autobiography of a Generation* highlights the dilemma of writing an oral history of a contemporary subject based upon a multiplicity of personal narratives. Indeed, Passerini concludes with the admonition that there are as many stories about the sixties as there are eyewitnesses and that memories left by those years are not uniform or predictable.[12] These often dissonant memories are defined in Alessandro Portelli's recent work, *The Order Has Been Carried Out*, which introduces us to the concept of 'divided memory' whereby not only do different people remember an event differently, but 'memory divides, more painfully and dramatically, also *within* persons ...'[13] The emotional pain that is often relived by the respondent is best described by Victoria Langland who has characterised the difficult recollections as

11   See C. Dejung, 'Oral History und Kollektives Gedächtnis: Für eine Sozialhistorische Erweiterung der Errinerungsgeschichte', *Geschichte und Gesellschaft* 34(1) (2008), 96–115; M. Kurkowska, 'Archiwa Pamieci: "Oral History"', *Historyka: Studia Metodologiczne* 28 (1998), 67–76; and D. James, 'AHR Forum: Meatpackers, Peronists, and Collective Memory: A View from the South', *American Historical Review* (December 1997), 1404–1412.

12   L. Passerini, *Autobiography of a Generation*, trans. Lisa Erdberg (Hanover, NH: University Press of New England, 1996), 152.

13   A. Portelli, *The Order Has Been Carried Out: History, Memory, and the Meaning of a Nazi Massacre in Rome* (New York: Palgrave Macmillan, 2003), 206.

traumatic 'memory knots' that lie close to contemporary consciousness and may flare up to disquiet the psyche when past events are recalled.[14]

One useful tool in identifying these painful and 'divided memories' as well as fluctuations between personal and collective memory, is to listen to changes in narrative voice by the respondent. In an earlier essay on the parents of student activists, I noted that interviewees often alternated between personal narratives using 'I' or 'we' and impersonal or detached narratives using a variety of constructions with third person delineators such as 'they/them', 'the students', 'you (plural)', and 'one can see …' in their recollections of the *Sessantotto*. Such shifting between personal and impersonal voices enabled the respondents to praise the individual actions of their protesting children while offering critical and even negative generalisations about the student movement as a whole.[15] One would expect that the parents of activists might remember the actions of their children favorably but a similar phenomenon is also found among non-students who did not have any familial connection to the protesters.

An excellent example of these divided memories among non-students comes from an ex-captain of the municipal police. A former police officer in Turin's mobile police unit, Armando Altomare, speaking in a justificatory tone offered this personal memory,

> My duty was to keep public order and preserve civil liberties. We only entered the Palazzo Campana at the request of Rector Allara, and the majority of the students left peacefully – only a few had to be carried out …

14   V. Langland, comments at 'Memories of 1968: International Perspectives', University of Leeds, 16–18 April 2008.

15   S.J. Hilwig, 'Are you calling me a fascist? A Contribution to the Oral History of the 1968 Italian Student Rebellion', *Journal of Contemporary History* 36(4), 581–597. Another scholar who has observed changes in voice between men and women is Isabelle Bertaux-Wiame who found that French men tended to use I and women more often employed we when speaking about migrating from the countryside to the city. See P. Thompson, *The Voice of the Past: Oral History, Third Edition* (Oxford, UK: Oxford University Press, 2000), 179.

Switching to a more judicious, impersonal voice, the officer offered a retrospective summation when he recalled,

> For the most part, the majority of the students were passive, well-behaved but then, of course, you had a few of these extremists.

Altomare's detached tone then changed abruptly as he recalled his initial reaction to what he saw inside the university buildings during the evacuation of the student occupants. Returning to personal narrative and a collective memory he may have shared with his fellow policemen, he said:

> When we entered the Palazzo Campana ... The halls, they were filled with broken chairs and litter, and the restrooms were covered with filth and used prophylactics – really, a total mess (*cazzino*).[16]

In negotiating his own memory of the *Sessantotto*, Altomare conceded the relatively non-violent character of the student movement. He did, however, repeat the collective mantra among many of the police that there were always a minority of extremists, '*instigatori, barboni* (bums) or *delinquenti.*'[17] It seems that the traumatic shock of entering the Palazzo Campana after the student occupation continued to fill him with disgust. Such recollections show that memory can be a storehouse of measured, thoughtful reflections and intense emotionally charged images that seem to resist the ameliorative effects of time.

Another example of these divided memories comes from Norberto Bobbio, a noted professor of law at the University of Turin and father of student activist, Luigi Bobbio. Alternating between personal and impersonal narratives, Professor Bobbio offered these recollections:

16   Armando Altomare, former *Maresciallo di Polizia*. Interviewed by the author. Turin: 3 July 1997.
17   At an interview of a younger police officer from Rome, Piero Giacobelli, a pair of older police officers frequently interrupted the interview calling the student activists, 'instigatori, barboni, and delinquenti.' Giacobelli interviewed by the author. Turin: 18 June 2002.

On most things, they (students) were right – the university needed reform and a better relationship between the students and faculty ... My faculty tried to find an accord with the students, BUT the assembly of the students was NOT A DEMOCRATIC assembly. The leaders were always the *contestatori* – they did not have secret ballots and only the elite spoke! The leaders, you understand, were all from the bourgeoisie but they wanted to ally with the workers.[18]

Offering a personal anecdote and continuing to speak of the activists as a unified group, Professor Bobbio further recalled an incident in his own classroom when he felt intimidated:

One time, I remember, I entered my lecture hall for a class on jurisprudence and a group of *agitatori* walked right up to my lectern. I tried to speak with them, to reason with them, but as I spoke, the students in their seats became rowdy, whistling and yelling, so I became a bit intimidated and sensed the whole thing was useless and I left.[19]

These two memories both speak of the student movement in critical terms and include words such as '*contestatori*' and '*agitatori*' that may also be found among the collective memories of non-students. When asked about his relationship with this son, one of the '*contestatori*', Bobbio's tone softened perceptibly and he offered this personal recollection:

My relationship with Luigi remained good because he was reasonable ... I did not fear for Luigi because the student marches and demonstrations were all non-violent. There was some verbal violence, but no physical violence.[20]

Bobbio smiled and even recalled a humorous incident that belied Luigi's paradoxical position as a bourgeois leader of a proletarian revolution:

18   Norberto Bobbio interviewed by the author. Turin: 23 April 1997. Words capitalised
      to denotes speaker's emphasis.
19   Ibid.
20   Ibid.

> I remember one time, my wife wanted to take Luigi and the others to go buy shoes. Luigi refused to get new shoes. He said that he wanted to live and dress as a worker and that he would not buy new shoes. Yes, a revolutionary moment![21]

In these few sentences, Bobbio has expressed a variety of memories characterizing the student movement in general as an initially well-intentioned search for reform but in practice, an undemocratic and even threatening phenomenon. His son's involvement, on the other hand, is portrayed as 'reasonable,' 'non-violent' and evoking a happy moment of nostalgia.

These frequently contradictory accounts certainly attest to the contentious nature of the *Sessantotto* and may be an attempt by the respondent to cope with their own cognitive dissonance regarding the turbulent years of student unrest. Alternating between first and third person voices enables a respondent to combine a personal anecdote from the late 1960s with the collective memories of the era expressed in the third person. As such, personal anecdotes provide a good sense of the respondent's emotions at the time when they interacted with student activists and the collective memories provide an excellent window into the changing politics of memory that surround the *Sessantotto*. Thus, the seemingly incongruous mixing of oppositional personal and collective memories enables someone to combine a series of extremely critical personal experiences with student activists with a *post facto* collective memory of the 1968 student movement as a social phenomenon that led to positive changes for Italy. Gianni Alasia, a former labor leader in Turin during the late 1960s offered many critical assessments of the student revolutionaries:

> Let me tell you, when I was at the CGIL (*Confederazione Generale Italiana del Lavoro*) in the 1960s, I had contact with thirteen different groups in the schools – socialists, communists, Marxists – my goodness, there were three different Chinese (Maoist) groups alone! – These student Chinese – with all due respect to China – a great country whose revolution changed the world – but these Chinese in Rome and Turin, they weren't so serious.[22]

21   Ibid.
22   Giovanni Alasia interviewed by he author. Turin: 24 April 1997.

Throughout the interview, Alasia, a former Anti-Fascist Resistance fighter and member of the Socialist party since the 1940s, frequently disparaged the student New Left referring to the activists as 'infantile extremists' and even argued that the New Left embarrassed former Partisans by their excessive idolisation of the militant anti-Fascist Resistance. Despite his criticisms of the student movement in general, he spoke very highly of student rebel Luigi Bobbio, whom he described as 'a good boy, respectful and well-spoken who knew and understood many things.' Alasia not only spoke highly of Luigi Bobbio, but matched his words with action in 1968 by appearing as a defense witness at the trial of Luigi Bobbio and his fiancée, Laura DeRossi.[23] By the end of the interview, Alasia returned to a detached impersonal voice. Historicizing a collective memory, he noted that, 'Yes, the *movimento studentesco* was extremist and infantile, but it was a great push for democracy in Italy – and rightfully so!'[24] Blurring the distinction between collective and personal memory, Alasia clearly offers a negative sentiment that he would have shared with many of his colleagues but then passes a historical judgment on the student movement that carries a positive political lesson for the future.

The process of historicizing the Italian student revolt of 1968 began before the barricades had even been cleared from the streets and similarly, the memories of what happened quickly became politicised with the appearance of stories in the press and television footage. These media outlets began a process of solidifying the collective memories of the 1960s by inscribing descriptions and explanations of the events in the semi-permanent media of newsprint and celluloid film. Furthermore, prominent politicians and public figures went 'on record' by issuing statements that were recorded in the press. Given the variety of media outlets and their ownership, several competing records of the *Sessantotto* emerged as leaders of the Italian Communist Party etched a very different record of the *Sessantotto* than

23   Ibid.
24   Ibid.

their Christian Democratic colleagues.[25] Though personal memories have retained a great deal of variety and viewpoints, the media representations of events have continued to shape the nature and telling of these personal recollections.

Generally, those who were Communists or Socialists prior to 1968 maintained positive views of the student movement and those on the Right prior to 1968 have tended to retain negative opinions of the student revolt. For example, Ilario and Paola Falcioni, two retired schoolteachers from rural Umbria had very different memories of the *Sessantotto*. Ilario, a moderately conservative member of the Christian Democrat party remembered the *Sessantotto* in the following personal memory:

> I taught middle school in 1968 in a small town near Spoleto. All of my students were the children of farmers and the school reform law that made it obligatory to attend school to fourteen years of age was relatively new – there was not a lot of intellectual activity there. We knew very little of the student movement, only what some might have seen on television. Paola, she taught elementary school at that time, so neither of us were much affected by the university unrest ... I remember seeing the demonstrations and parades on TV and later the Battle of the Valle Giulia and the furious battles with police and then the whole thing became a political question ... when a movement gets so large, there is always someone who will try to profit from the confusion.[26]

Ilario's testimony shows the importance that the media, particularly images from television, have had on historicizing and politicizing the collective memory of the student movement in the minds of non-students. Scholars Raphael Samuel and Daniel Sherman both attest to the overwhelming importance of visual imagery in the creation of memories. Sherman argues that seeing images like those shown on television allows the viewer to participate vicariously in a collective memory even though they were not

25   For a discussion of the differences between 'official' and 'vernacular' or personal memories, see: J. Bodnar, *Remaking America: Public Memory, Commemoration, and Patriotism in the Twentieth Century* (Princeton, NJ: 1992), 13–14, 245, 247.
26   Ilario Falcioni interviewed by the author. Perugia: 26 March 1997.

there.[27] Paola, on the other hand, sympathised with the Left and her recollections are shaped more by her emotional and familial connection to
the *Sessantotto*. She responded to the interview questions in the following
way:

> It is true what my husband said that we lived far from the protests, but for women,
> the *Sessantotto* became a dividing point because before that, women's problems were
> personal, not to be shared, but after the *Sessantotto*, women felt they could share their
> problems with each other and we were no longer alone in our troubles.[28]

Paola then offered a personal anecdote that revealed her pro-student
sympathies:

> At that time, my brother was enrolled in the Faculty of Engineering at the University
> of Bologna and they had this project to tear down and rebuild a building in the old
> part of the city; so my brother and these engineering students who were also activists
> made a plan to reconstruct the area but keep intact the life of the community there
> and they even made a film, very well done I might add, about the whole thing and
> presented it to their professors. The professors, instead, refused to consider all their
> hard work as the equivalent of an exam. Those professors just would not change
> with the times![29]

Clearly the differences in Ilario and Paola's memories of 1968 stem from
more than just differing political views. Ilario was and has remained outside
of the events of the *Sessantotto* opting to recall images from the media and
interpreting the period as one that was unconnected with his own life. Paola,
on the other hand, has come to interpret the period as one that affected
her personally and she has taken possession of a collective memory of the
student revolt both as a woman and in her memories of her brother who
was a participant. For her, memories of the Italian '68 have been mediated
by gender and family relationships in ways that have trumped the iconic

---

27   See R. Samuel, *Theatres of Memory, Volume I: Past and Present in Contemporary
     Culture* (London: Verso, 1994), viii; and D. Sherman, *The Construction of Memory
     in Interwar France* (Chicago: University of Chicago Press, 1999), 14.
28   Paola Falcioni interviewed by the author. Perugia: 26 March 1997.
29   Ibid.

images from television and the press. The Falcionis' memories, like those of Norberto Bobbio and Gianni Alasia, seem to suggest that despite critical assessments of the student movement as a whole, those who had personal contact with individual activists often recall very different memories of the *Sessantotto*.

In critically analysing these personal and collective memories of the non-students' *Sessantotto*, we can observe some important patterns. The personal recollections, often spoken in first person, offer the broadest range of experiences and the greatest level of candor. In general, these personal memories paint the years of student revolt as ones that provoked powerful emotions among the respondents. Ethnohistorians have long noted the influence of emotions upon memory. Michael Harkin writes,

> Memory is especially charged with emotion, since we remember people who are dead, possibilities that are closed off, a world of childhood that, as Proust described it, is magical but unattainable.[30]

When non-students are asked to recall personal memories from the late 1960s, the student movement's goals, politics, and theories take a back seat to vivid, sometimes tragic images of isolated moments from the time.

The following examples of personal memory show the primacy of emotions and reveal the principal trigger for these emotions may be the traumatic sense that the sacred had been profaned. For example, Giorgina Levi, a schoolteacher and Communist Deputy during the late 1960s, remembered visiting the University of Turin's Palazzo Campana during the first student occupation in November 1967. Her personal memory of the visit is marked by the potent image of 'professors crying because they had lost their power.'[31] In another example of personal memories that have been marked by a profaning of the sacred came from Professor Norberto Bobbio. He recalled being profoundly shaken by the police evacuation of student occupants from the Palazzo Campana in December 1967:

---

30   M. Harkin, 'Feeling and Thinking in Memory and Forgetting: Toward an Ethnohistory of the Emotions', *Ethnohistory* 50(2) (Spring 2003), 268.
31   Giorgina Levi interviewed by the author. Turin: 14 April 1997.

What really struck me, the big turning point, was when the police entered the university to evacuate the students – this had never happened before, not even under the Fascists – it was like entering a church.[32]

Like Levi, Bobbio's experience is a personal and visceral one as he clearly equates the sanctity of university space with the Church's ancient right of sanctuary. For many professors, the police invasion of university buildings in the 1960s not only disturbed the Italian universities' long standing tradition of autonomy, but also seemed to be an act of sacrilege. Similar to police captain Altomare's shock at discovering used contraceptives scattered on the floors of the university, Bobbio's recollection stands out as a traumatic jolt to his moral beliefs.[33] Such personal memories differ greatly from the collective memories of crowded university classrooms, political debates, and teach-ins. The clarity and specificity that characterise these personal memories suggest that they may have changed less with the passage of time than collective memories of 1968. Despite the general view that personal memory is flawed and historically inaccurate, clinical research has demonstrated that,

after a relatively brief period of time (only a few days) during which the individual retains a very detailed picture of the event experienced, recollection then enters a process of selection and organisation, before being stamped almost indelibly on the memory.[34]

Furthermore, as we shall see, these personal accounts often prove to be the most problematic for historians and social scientists because they do not fit well with the more homogenised collective memories of the 1960s.

Turning to the collective memories of the *Sessantotto*, one finds recurrent patterns among our twenty-four respondents. The collective memories of both those who were intimately connected with the students and those who only read and heard about student protests from the media tended

32   Norberto Bobbio interviewed by the author. Turin: 23 April 1997.
33   See note 13 in this chapter.
34   N. Wachtel, 'Memory and History; an Introduction', *History and Anthropology* 2 (1986), 209.

to lump all student activists into a monolithic *movimento studentesco* and dichotomised the *Sessantotto* as either 'good' or 'bad' for Italy. Consistently expressed in past tense and often in third person, these collective memories evince a feigned detachment and seeming objectivity. In fact, the creation of many of these collective memories can be traced to stories published in the press during the late 1960s. As scholars have noted, the conservative and centrist presses constructed an image of the New Left students that was typically negative, portraying students as either objects of ridicule or serious threats to public order. The left-leaning presses, on the other hand, countered this vilification of the students with a diametrically opposed vision of the students as real reformers dedicated to non-violence.[35] The oral testimony of non-students is often interspersed with subconscious references to these press-created images. Oral historian and cultural anthropologist, Ruth Finnegan has observed the ways that myths constructed by the media circulate within a particular culture, becoming part of the oral recollections of family and personal histories. She argues that, 'Myths and images current in particular epochs or in particular cultures themselves affect family and individual memories, and shape the ways they represent the past, even their own experiences.'[36]

Though there are several collective memories and a wide range of images that appear among the interviewees' recollections of the *Sessantotto*, we shall examine six of these memories that recur among the non-students' oral testimony. First and foremost of these collective memories is the notion that the student activists were *figli di papà* ('daddy's kids' or spoiled

---

35   For the press's depiction of the New Left student activists see: T. Gitlin, *The Whole World is Watching: Mass Media in the Making and Unmaking of the New Left* (Berkeley: University of California Press, 1980); M. Brasted, 'Framing Protest: *The Chicago Tribune* and the *New York Times* during the 1968 Democratic Convention', *Atlantic Journal of Communication* 13 (January 2005), 1–25; K. Fahlenbrach, *Protest-Inszenierungen* (Wiesbaden: Westdeutscher Verlag, 2002); and S.J. Hilwig, 'The Revolt Against the Establishment: Students Versus the Press in West Germany and Italy', in C. Fink, P. Gassert, and D. Junker, eds. *1968: The World Transformed* (Cambridge: Cambridge University Press, 1998), 321–349.

36   R. Finnegan, 'Family Myths, Memories and Interviewing', in R. Perks and A. Thomson, eds. *The Oral History Reader, Second Edition* (London: Routledge, 2006), 179.

children). The idea of the student activists as the privileged offspring of elite citizens was popularised by the poem, 'The Communist Party to the Young!' written by the writer Pier Paolo Pasolini in April 1968. In the poem, Pasolini blamed the New Left students whom he calls *figli di papà* for the violence that occurred during the Battle of the Valle Giulia. He further sympathised with the police whom he claimed were the 'children of the poor.'[37] Variations of this collective memory ubiquitously emerge in the recollections of non-students and particularly among police and industrial workers.

The agents of public order whom Pasolini praised in his poem frequently used the term '*figli di papà*' in their oral testimonies. Angelo Gentile was born in 1925 near Reggio Calabria and had moved north to Turin after the Second World War. In the late 1960s, he worked in the radio and telecommunications section of the *Polizia di Stato*. Gentile remembers one incident in particular during the *Sessantotto*:

> I remember one Saturday afternoon, a group of about twenty hotheads attempted to blockade and terrorise the center of Turin, and in Via Po in a bar a youth was also killed. In the Piazza Castello at the headquarters of the Prefect there were a hundred protectors of order who could have easily stopped and dispersed the *contestatori* but they had the order to not intervene, to ignore them. The police begged, pawed the ground, but the orders to take action did not arrive, even when the local authorities repeatedly asked Rome for permission to intervene and disperse the *contestatori*. A mystery. It was known then that some of the heads of the contestation were *figli di papà* who stood on high, in high political spheres, reached not by merit, but with scams that abused honest citizens and whose children with their contestation, sought to imitate their fathers.[38]

Although Gentile did not specifically mention Pasolini's poem, his sentiments mirror the contempt Pasolini had for the radical students. In a similar interview with Giuseppe Patero, another former police officer born in

---

37   Pasolini quoted in: *Heretical Empiricism*, ed. L.K. Barnett, trans. B. Lawton and L.K. Barnett (Bloomington, IN: Indiana University Press, 1988), 150. Originally appeared in *L'Espresso*, 16 April 1968, *Nuovi Argomenti* 10 (April–June 1968), and *Il Corriere della Sera*, 12 June 1968, 3.

38   Angelo Gentile interviewed by the author. Turin: 11 June 1997.

southern Italy in the 1920s, the term *figli di papà* was used interchangeably with the term *Sessantotini*.[39]

The industrial workers, even those who participated in joint student-worker associations such as *Lotta Continua* and *Potere Operaio*, held similar collective notions about the student activists' bourgeois origins. Vittorio Rieser, a former graduate student and leading figure in the student-worker association *Potere Operaio* remembered that the trade unions not only were diffident toward student offers of help in the workers' struggles but even posted bulletins in the factories referring to the student protesters as *figli di papà*.[40] Francesco Albergoni, a young Communist worker at FIAT's Rivalta factory eagerly joined the radical student-worker association, *Lotta Continua* in the late 1960s and attended many of the student rallies and occupations. Though he enjoyed a good relationship with many of the student leaders, he conceded that class played a role in the unfolding of the *Sessantotto*:

> Yes, we had a lawyer of our own, Bianca Guidetti-Sera, 'our mama' in those days. She defended all the activists, but you know, most of those students did not get big fines or jail terms because they came from elite, bourgeois families. The workers, that was another story entirely, in the Hot Autumn, we paid the price for our strikes and union activities.[41]

In 1968, the PCI's press organ made their pro-student line explicit when *l'Unità* published an article entitled, 'A Communication from the Direction of the PCI – The Communists support a renewed and democratic University.'[42] However, even some journalists who worked for the newspaper were critical of the bourgeois backgrounds of the leadings student activists. Andrea Liberatori, one such journalist, commented:

---

39   Giuseppe Patero was born in Sicily in 1926. Interviewed by the author. Turin: 18 June 2002.

40   Similarly, the French trade unions sought to obstruct the formation of a student-worker alliance in May 1968. Vittorio Rieser interviewed by the author. Turin: 2 June 1997.

41   Francesco Albergoni interviewed by the author. Turin: 23 May 2002.

42   *L'Unità*, 28 February 1968, 2.

I must say something, the ones who participated in this movement, they were not the masses, they were the elite, the vanguard – because, after all, not many families could afford to keep their children in the university for eight to ten years. These are the facts.[43]

A second powerful collective memory that is invoked by the mention of the term *Sessantotto* is the potentially violent image of students marching in the streets carrying flags, shouting slogans, and waving fists. For those who were not personally acquainted with the protesters or living far from major universities, such a collective memory represented the most typical and easily recalled image from that year. Again, the press with the greatest circulation, the conservative and centrist dailies, succeeded in producing a frightening image and rhetoric for the *Sessantotto* that is indelibly imprinted upon the memories of non-students. The inflammatory news photographs and headlines have remained etched in the collective memories of the Italian people because they provoked powerful emotional responses in the reader and offered forms and faces to those who had never witnessed a student demonstration. A former Christian Democratic Deputy, Piero Melograni ran a small business in Rome during the late 1960s and remembered the imagery of the *Sessantotto*:

INTERVIEWER: Which aspect of the student movement do you believe struck the Italians the most?

MELOGRANI: The episodes of violence! The strikes, the occupations, the battles with police! Everybody saw them on TV and in the newspapers – they struck everyone.

INTERVIEWER: In your opinion, what was the relationship between the students and the press?

MELOGRANI: They (students) did not think to create an official relationship with the press, instead it was all spontaneous. I think it was done badly by the students due to their battles with journalists, however, the journalists were very interested in the students because they made news.[44]

---

43   Andrea Liberatori interviewed by the author. Turin: 28 May 1997.
44   Piero Melograni interviewed by the author. Rome: 30 April 1997.

Later in the interview, Melograni mentioned that he lived near the Valle Giulia but did not know any of the students personally. His remarks are typical of those who had little personal contact with student activists and are similar to Ilario Falcioni's recollections of watching the movement on television.[45]

In both Melograni and Ilario Falcioni's memories, it is the photojournalists' images of protest that are most readily recalled in oral testimony. Using images as placeholders to recall events has been well-documented throughout history. Cultural historian Peter Burke's observations on the transmission of social memory during the Early Modern period also makes sense for the twentieth century: 'Images, pictorial or photographic, still or moving. Practitioners of the so-called "art of memory" from classical antiquity to the Renaissance emphasised the value of associating whatever one wanted to remember with striking images.'[46] Historian of contemporary Italy, John Foot has also noted that the frequent reprinting of dramatic photographs of the 'Battles of '68' during the various anniversaries of the events has helped to solidify these public memories in the Italian collective conscience.[47]

The presses' striking imagery that has left such an indelible impression upon those who lived through the 1960s, also leads to our third form of collective memory that emerges in the oral testimony of non-students. Most of the respondents tended to divide the *Sessantotto* into an initial 'good' and peaceful phase followed by a violent and 'radical' phase. Following Nora's notion that collective memory passes on to historical memory by materializing and rooting an event in a specific place (the park surrounding the University of Rome's School of Architecture) and time (March 1, 1968),[48]

45 For Ilario Falcioni's recollections see pages 12–13.
46 P. Burke, 'History as Social Memory', in: T. Butler, ed. *Memory: History, Culture and the Mind* (Oxford, UK: Basil Blackwell, 1989), 101.
47 J. Foot, keynote address, 'Looking Back on the "Long '68" in Italy: Public, Private, and Divided Memories,' at 'Memories of '68: International Perspectives,' University of Leeds, 16–18 April 2008.
48 P. Hutton, *History as an Art of Memory* (Hanover, NH: University Press of New England, 1993), 150–153.

the Battle of the Valle Giulia has become a historical memory because it
has since been interpreted as a caesura in the course of the history of the
student movement. The oral testimony of non-students from a wide variety of backgrounds often utilises this segmented sense of the course of the
student movement. Andrea Liberatori a journalist for *l'Unità* recalled,

> In the first phase of the student movement, most workers, people in the street, and
> *l'Unità* was favorable; but in the second phase – with the violence, with the Battle
> of the Valle Giulia, people began to side with Pasolini ... In the second phase also
> emerged the personalities of the movement, the so-called *Sessantottini* who wore
> blue jeans, Eskimo parkas, and had beards![49]

Ironically, Liberatori worked for the one major daily that maintained
a pro-student line even after the Battle of the Valle Giulia and did not
publish Pasolini's remarks because of his critical stance toward the PCI.
Nevertheless, Liberatori accepts and continues to recall the years of protest based upon a chronology constructed by the centrist and conservative
presses. The radical phase may also be denoted in the memories of onlook-
ers by the changing fashions and facial hair of the activists. Returning to
Ruth Finnegan's ideas of the ways that printed myth and imagery interact
with collective memories, she warns us that, '... our memories are built up
through myth and images, by the conventions and ideologies around us.
In a way our narrative models, drawn from the culture we live in, shape
even our own first-hand experience and expression.'[50] The shift toward
violence in the spring of 1968, frozen in the news photographs of the press
and versified by Pier Paolo Pasolini, have become crystallised in the collective memory of many Italians. Scholars have also noted this change in the
movimento studentesco, what political scientist Marco Revelli dubbed the
beginning of the 'guerilla phase' as activists moved their protests beyond
the universities and into the streets in the spring of 1968.[51]

---

49   Andrea Liberatori interviewed by the author. Turin: 28 May 1997.
50   R. Finnegan, 'Family Myths, Memories and Interviewing', 180.
51   M. Revelli, 'Il '68 a Torino. Gli Esordi' (1991), 240–244; P. Ginsborg notes, 'Valle
      Giulia was a critical step because up until that moment the student movement had
      been relatively pacific.' *A History of Contemporary Italy: Society and Politics, 1943–1988*

The fourth collective memory that can be found in the oral history of the Italian sixties is the association of those years with traumatic events from Italy's past. In particular, oral testimony from many of the respondents included references to the early years of Fascism and the Resistance of 1943–1945. These types of backward looking comparisons are quite common in collective memory due to the fact that myths or stereotypes about past individuals or groups are in constant oral circulation within the collective memory of a people. The psychologist N.N. Korzh has documented the role of historical knowledge in shaping collective memories about current events. He writes, 'But perception and evaluation of the present in many respects depends on knowledge of the past. We can say that the present exists in the context of the past.'[52] When a new individual or group, in this case student protesters, comes along that seems to 'fit,' even superficially, these stereotypes, the psychological processes of 'leveling' and 'sharpening' work to place this new experience more firmly within the mold of the previous myth or stereotype.[53] This process of leveling is evident in an angry reader's letter to the editors of *La Stampa* recalling the years of Fascism and connecting the Left-wing occupants of the Palazzo Campana to Mussolini's *squadristi*. The author identified himself as 'an indignant ex-partisan,' who '[did] not, in fact, believe that there is a big difference between the March on Rome and the occupation of the University. The weapons remain the same: intimidation and contempt for democratic laws.'[54] The conservative former policeman, Angelo Gentile, echoed similar words, though with a very different meaning, when asked if the students had provoked a new discussion of Fascism and the Italian past:

(London: Palgrave Macmillan, 2003), 304. See also G. Galli, 'The Student Movement in Italy', 501; and C. Oliva and A. Rendi, *Il Movimento Studentesco e le sue lotte* (Milan: Feltrinelli, 1969), 21–22.

52   N.N. Korzh, 'Representation of Historical Knowledge in Collective Memory', trans. M.E. Sharpe, *Journal of Russian and East European Psychology* 39(3) (2001), 70.

53   P. Burke, 'History as Social Memory', 104.

54   *La Stampa*, 'Specchio dei tempi', 5 December 1967, 2.

Yes, the student manifestations provoked nostalgia for Fascism and the political past because the citizens felt abandoned by the state that did not defend them from the hoodlums that blocked all of the activity in the center of the city. They were the absolute *padroni* (bosses) and no one could react for fear of succumbing to those hotheads who as individuals were rabbits but in mass became lions capable of destroying and harming everything.[55]

On the other side of the barricades, Serena Nozzoli, a former student protester at the State University of Milan, recalled twenty years after,

I had already seen terrorism in 1968 … the feet on the professor's desk, bringing up Che Guevara as a topic for the economics exam, with this insolent pretense, this arrogance provided by numbers … things slightly reminiscent of Mussolini's thugs that, however, all seemed like revolutionary demonstrations, while I saw in them a type of violence … taking advantage of the mob to do things they wouldn't have done themselves …[56]

Though the New Left students of the 1960s had little in common with the early Fascist mobs of the 1920s, the initiation of a more violent phase in the students' confrontations with police in the spring of 1968 helped to foster this comparison.

Conversely those sympathetic to the student protesters and members of the Italian left have collective memories that associated the students with the Anti-Fascist Resistance. Former Partisan of the *Resistenza* and father of a student activist, Benevenuto Revelli, interpreted the *movimento studentesco* as a continuation of the struggle to fight the remaining vestiges of fascism in Italian life. Revelli recalled,

For Marco, who grew-up in our house, it was a climate of anti-Fascism, of the Resistance … *Lotta Continua*, which was founded in part by my son, was originally called *Nuova Resistenza*, and I and some other ex-partisans even met with Marco's group several times. We had a common bond in the continuous rejection of fascism and neo-fascism, and these students, they had an important role in confronting the neo-fascists, the *Missini*.[57]

---

55   Angelo Gentile interviewed by the author. Turin: 11 June 1997.
56   L. Passerini, *Autobiography of a Generation*, 147–148.
57   Benevenuto Revelli interviewed by the author. Cuneo: 11 April 1997.

Revelli's notion that the left-wing students had an 'important role in confronting the neo-fascists' conjures up memories of the political street fighting of the 1920s. Again the press helped to construct a linkage between the student New Left and the anti-fascism of the Old Left. On January 21, 1968, the PCI's *l'Unità* printed a full-page pictorial article entitled, 'From the Resistance to today.' Placing a photo of student anti-Vietnam demonstrations next to pictures of the famed anti-Fascist protests in Genoa in 1960 and the marches for land reform in southern Italy during the late 1940s, *l'Unità* implied that the student demonstrations fell within the continuum of the Communists' historic and continual struggle against the residues of Fascism in the postwar era.[58] The students, most of whom had been born after the war, understood the Fascist period and the Resistance only through a few fragmented collective memories. The majority of Italians who had lived through the era preferred to forget, as in the phrase, 'I wasn't there, and if I was, I was sleeping.'[59] The principal attorney for the student activists in Turin and a former Resistance member herself, Bianca Guidetti Serra recalled the students challenge to the older generation's collective memories of Fascism and anti-Fascism:

> In the 1950s and early 60s, the discussion of Fascism was minimal, practically nothing, there was an attempt to forget, but in the late 1960s there was a resurgence of talk about Fascism and the Resistance. In 1968 there was a discussion not only about the dictatorship, but also present authoritarianism. This was, you see, because after the war, many Fascists returned to politics ... there was authoritarianism in the 'high offices' of government.[60]

Historian Nicola Tranfaglia had been an editor of the journal *Resistenza* in the late 1960s and later took a position as professor at the University of Turin in 1969. He offered remarks that further elaborated on Guidetti Serra's recollections:

58 *L'Unità*, 21 January 1968, 10.
59 'Non c'ero, e se c'ero, dormivo' in R. Ben-Ghiat, 'Fascism, Writing, and Memory: The Realist Aesthetic in Italy, 1930–1950', *The Journal of Modern History* 67 (September 1995), 660.
60 Bianca Guidetti Serra interviewed by the author. Turin: 10 June 1997.

These students wanted to understand more about fascism and at the same time, they were influenced a lot by anti-fascism. In fact, they began to talk about an existential anti-fascism in the form of a distinct rebellion against Italian democracy in which the power always lies in the center-right, with the left always in opposition – so some students actually believed that fascism had won because the right continued to rule twenty years after the war was over![61]

Both the activists and many former anti-fascist Partisans shared the sense that their efforts during the *Sessantotto* represented another manifestation of the Resistance stretching back for half a century.

A fifth collective memory that figured prominently among non-student observers of the movement, whether they were on the left or right, is their recollection of the student activists' overwhelming idealism. Maria Valabrega, the key journalist who covered the student protests for the conservative *La Stampa* recalled in almost Romantic tones,

> They were beautiful and terrible years, beautiful because there was a movement of strong ideals, sometimes it went well and sometimes it erred, it was however a very strong movement, made of values in which the kids indisputably believed to the death, they were all in good faith.[62]

Valabrega identified herself as being a member of the non-communist left and noted that she frequently disagreed with her editors who wrote negative headlines and bylines for her stories of the student movement. Law professor and father of a student activist, Norberto Bobbio borrowed a slogan from the French '68 when he remarked on the idealism of the students,

> *L'imagination prend le pouvoir!* The youth always dreams of a better world. Fascism was also a dream of a better world for young Italians after the First World War; a reaction against the society and politics in which they found themselves. The *Sessantottini* wanted a better world fortunately we did not have the same consequences.[63]

---

61 Nicola Tranfaglia interviewed by the author. Turin: 20 June 2002.
62 Maria Valabrega interviewed by the author. Turin: 6 June 1997.
63 'The imagination takes power!' was a slogan of the French May of 1968. Norberto Bobbio interviewed by the author. Turin: 23 April 1997.

Such retrospective attention to the earnestness and sincerity with which the students pursued their goals may be partially explained by the idea that the *Sessantotto* represents an abrupt caesura in the modern history of the Italian university. Twentieth-century Italy had experienced eruptions of public protest on the part of industrial workers and farmers, but the universities, traditionally the preserve of the wealthy elite, had been relatively quiet throughout most of the century until 1968 when large numbers of students allied themselves with the left for the first time.[64] Many ordinary citizens recalled the surprise they experienced when the normally complacent university students marched in the streets with the righteous indignation that had been more typical of the working classes.

Lastly, the collective memories of non-students often contain a synthetic sense of retrospective summation. The oral testimonies of those who recall the student revolt of 1968 frequently contain a 'final verdict' on the era. Though few of these verdicts are truly final, they do provide a window into the status of the *Sessantotto* within the historical consciousness of the Italian people at the time of the interview. In 1997 and 2002 when these interviews were conducted, the overall assessments of the student movement were positive as many different respondents mentioned the *Sessantotto* as a 'global movement' that ended with positive gains for Italians. Don Giuseppe Tuninetti, a priest and archivist at Turin's archdiocese who had been a student in the Faculty of Letters at the university in 1968 remarked, 'The *Sessantotto* was a global contestation, a just revolution.'[65] Giuseppe Patero, a former policeman from Turin said, 'It (the student movement) was a positive phenomenon of global character from which Italy also benefitted because of the formation of new elites.'[66] Nicola Tranfaglia who became a history professor at the University of Turin in 1969 commented, 'Some say that fascism ended in the 1960s.'[67] In particular many respondents mentioned a sense that democratic processes

---

64   P. Ginsborg, *A History of Contemporary Italy*, 308.
65   Don Giuseppe Tuninetti interviewed by the author. Turin: 5 May 1997.
66   Giuseppe Patero interviewed by the author. Turin: 18 June 2002.
67   Nicola Tranfaglia interviewed by the author. Turin: 20 June 2002.

had been reinvigorated, that the nascent feminist movement would later secure greater civil equality for women, and that a serious discussion of fascism had been renewed by the students. Clearly these collective memories have been reshaped *post facto*, becoming historicised due to changing politics and media representations of the student movement. Just as collectors acquire new items and discard older or less valuable ones, so does collective memory selectively pick up and expunge older memories. Part eyewitness account, part shared memory, part retrospective analysis and part media collage; collective memory updates or revises all forms of memory with each passing year.

The fact that our diverse group of interviewees held similar collective recollections suggests a few possibilities. The passage of time, in this case about thirty years, has perhaps softened the negative memories of the student movement among some of the non-students who realised that though much seemed to be changing at the time of the marches and occupations, much remained safely the same. Furthermore, psychologist Elizabeth Loftus has argued that memories are more likely to change or become distorted with the passage of time. Loftus further has shown the ease with which people's memories can be altered by offering new information after an event.[68] This changing position of the *Sessantotto* in the Italian people's memories may bolster Piccone's notion that former activists have propagated a mythic and celebratory 1968 that reappears in the popular and academic media on every tenth anniversary year of the *Sessantotto*. These somewhat apocryphal images of the 'year that rocked the world'[69] may have worked their ameliorative magic on the collective memories of those who witnessed the student revolt. That many Italians spoke of positive outcomes from the *Sessantotto*, despite the conservative press's propagation of extremely negative images and ideas about the student movement in 1968, suggests that the formerly anti-student media has altered its characterisations of student activism.

---

68   E.F. Loftus, 'When a Lie Becomes Memory's Truth: Memory Distortion After Exposure to Misinformation', *Current Directions in Psychological Science* 1 (1992), 121–123.

69   Term from M. Kurlansky, *1968: The Year that Rocked the World* (New York: Random House, 2004).

Undoubtedly, the media has continued to feed and reshape the collective memory of the *Sessantotto* over the years. For example a colorful article on the *Sessantotto* that appeared in *Specchio della Stampa* on 22 February 1997 offered a more benevolent or ambiguous image of the era than any of *La Stampa*'s articles from 1967 and 1968. Titled, "68 the year that upset the world,' the article declares in retrospect, 'The demonstrations against Vietnam, the occupations of the schools, the assemblies in the factories: in that fatal year the youth dreamed of bringing the imagination to power. They did not succeed, but their utopia profoundly modified society ...'[70] Furthermore, many of those interviewed noted that the press was notorious for sensationalism and have continued to privilege their own personal experiences over the provocative headlines and photographs that have shaped the collective memories of the period.

In conclusion the ever growing literature on the 1968 student movements will be greatly enriched by the voices of those who were there but did not march. Oral history and memory studies offer powerful tools to help scholars listen to and understand these previously silent participants in the *Sessantotto*. In analysing the oral recollections of non-students about thirty years after the student uprising, a number of patterns emerge from their diverse personal histories. Those who had actual contact with student activists offer a wide range of personal memories characterised by powerful emotions, both positive and negative. Frequently these memories are recounted in first person voice and are markedly different, even oppositional, to their more detached collective memories expressed in a third person narrative. Furthermore, witnesses of the student movement often relate positive impressions of activists they knew personally while demonizing an amorphous mass of 'student radicals.' The clarity and emotional astonishment expressed in the personal memories of these eyewitnesses shows that, like the activists, those watching from the other side of the barricades also felt that nothing would ever be the same.

70 "68 l'anno che sconvolse il mondo' *Specchio della Stampa* 57 (22 febbraio 1997), 82–100.

STUART J. HILWIG

The collective memories, on the other hand, tend to feature recurring tropes and images. This chapter has analysed six of these collective memories that occurred frequently among the oral testimonies of non-students: the notion of the student activists as *figli di papà* or spoiled children; the dramatic image of students marching in the streets; the bifurcated sense of the movement as having a distinct peaceful phase followed by a violent phase; the equating of the student New Left of the 1960s with either the Fascists or the anti-Fascists of Italy's past; the recollection of the students' romanticised idealism; and the retrospective summations that have been heavily influenced by the changing perception of the *Sessantotto* over time. Though these collective memories are necessarily shaped by the respondent's gender, class, occupation, and politics, the ubiquity with which these collective memories emerged across demographic lines suggests that over time, the memory of the Italian *Sessantotto* has been subjected to the incursion of myths from the period. The iconic images from the Italian press and television; sound bytes from politicians, then and now; and the growing corpus of former activists' memoirs and writings have left most eyewitnesses with a handful of fragmented collective memories. Despite the passing of these collective memories into historical memory, personal memories still arise vivid and fresh with emotional intensity. Some recall a profaning of the sacred, others remember the undeniable idealism of the students, and still others retell stories filled with intimate personal memories such as a son's refusal to shop for shoes as a gesture of solidarity with the working class. Shaped by humor, pathos, and irony, these personal memories are true artifacts as they are less affected by the passage of time and their recovery through the use of oral history is indispensable for an understanding of the year that rocked the world.

LAN YANG

Memory and Revisionism: The Chinese Cultural Revolution on the Internet

Two years before 1968, China launched the Great Proletarian Cultural Revolution ('Cultural Revolution' or 'CR' for short), which both inside and outside China has been known as the most sensational political movement in contemporary China under the People's Republic. The Cultural Revolution can be divided into two phases: the first phase was from May 1966 to April 1969, and the second from May 1969 to October 1976. The most radical campaigns and events of the Cultural Revolution took place in the first phase.[1] Unlike the Western 1968 movements, which mobilised protest outside established institutions, the Chinese Cultural Revolution was initiated and supported by the supreme authorities of the Chinese Communist Party (CCP) headed by Mao Zedong. Moreover, although the movement assumed the name of a cultural revolution, its primary impact on China was in the domains of ideology and politics, whereas the influence and legacy of the Western 1968 campaigns were as much in politics as they were in culture. In spite of differences, however, the Chinese Cultural Revolution played a significant role in the worldwide 1968 movements, and thus the Cultural Revolution and its memory can be regarded as an important facet of the year 1968. Nevertheless, in the context of memory and legacy of the worldwide 1968 movements, scholars have generally neglected the Chinese Cultural Revolution, although the movement has

---

1   Many scholars prefer to date the movement from 1966 to 1969, but the post-CR Chinese government dates it from 1966 to 1976, and other scholars have also adopted the latter definition. See Lowell Dittmer, *China's Continuous Revolution: The Post-Liberation Epoch 1949–1981* (Berkeley: Centre for Chinese Studies, University of California, 1987), 77–78.

interested many scholars in the study of China.[2] Similarly, many scholars in China studying the Chinese Cultural Revolution are ignorant of the Western 1968 campaigns.

In China, after the death of Mao, the post-Cultural Revolution authorities launched a subversive attack against the movement.[3] A series of resolutions were made by the CCP Central Committee to criticise the Cultural Revolution and its theory and practice.[4] Since the late 1970s, the mainstream framework of the collective memory has been established, according to which the movement was deemed a national catastrophe, marked by social upheaval and cultural destruction. The mainstream memory can be conventionally divided into public memory and personal memory.[5] The public memory is primarily formed by the official media, historiography, literature and the arts. The personal memory is mainly based on individual

2   For instance, Mark Kurlansky's *1968* covers the campaigns of many areas such as Poland, France, Germany, the United States and Mexico, but it does not include the Cultural Revolution of China.

3   Before his death in 1976, Mao claimed that the Cultural Revolution was his most important undertaking under the PRC, and was worried about the counterattack by the opposition factions after his death. See Xiao Shanmu, 'Introduction to Ma Bin's New Book *Remember Mao Zedong*' [Ma Bin Tongzhi xin shu *Jinian Mao Zedong dao du*] (2007), http://www.wengewang.org/htm_data/38/0711/10360.html.

4   Among the resolutions, 'The CCP Central Committee's Resolution on Certain Issues in the Party's History since the Founding of the People's Republic of China' [Zhongguo Gongchandang Zhongyang Weiyuanhui guanyu jianguo yilai Dang de ruogan lishi wenti de jueyi] (Jun. 1981) is the most important. See the Documentary Institute of the CCP Central Committee [Zhonggong Zhongyang Wenxian Yanjiushi], *A Collection of Important Documents of National Congresses and Plenary Sessions since the Third Plenary Session of the Eleventh National Congress* [Shiyi Jie San Zhong Quanhui yilai Dang de lici quanguo daibiao dahui Zhongyang quanhui zhongyao wenjian xuan bian] (Beijing: Zhongyang Wenxian Chubanshe, 1977), 157–217.

5   See Andreas Huyssen, *Present Pasts: Urban Palimpsests and the Politics of Memory* (Stanford: Stanford University Press, 2003), 8.

discourses expressing authors' encountered persecution, trauma and/or contrition. There appeared a large number of memoirs and reports.[6]

Mainstream scholastic historical study and representations of the Cultural Revolution in China have been in accord with the governmental stand and the depiction of the movement was generally characterised negatively.

The Cultural Revolution has attracted the attention of Western scholarship in Chinese studies almost since its commencement. The scholarship has also established its own dominant accounts against the movement, which generally concur with the above Chinese mainstream perspective.

It is evident that historical accounts are sometimes hard to be separated from memory discourses. On the one hand, many historical accounts are based on memory discourses, and on the other hand, some memory discourses also include historical accounts.

The primary content covered in the dominant accounts of the Cultural Revolution includes the following features: the causes, purposes, objectives, methods, consequences and influence of the movement. With regard to the causes, purposes and objectives, for instance, most representative accounts maintain that the Cultural Revolution was in nature mainly about personal struggles within the Party. As for the methods of the movement, the leading accounts present them as a mixture of brain-washing and a personality cult. The consequences and influence of the Cultural Revolution have been portrayed as a great setback to the national economy and culture.

Many other political, cultural and military events or campaigns in history have been criticised in the world, and have formed a negative public memory. However, the nature of the Chinese Cultural Revolution only becomes controversial from the 1990s, when the mainstream negative memory of the movement is challenged by a non-mainstream memory.

---

6   The two best-known personal memoirs are *Contrition* [Suixiang lu] (Beijing: Zuojia Chubanshe, 1987) by Ba Jin, the late chairman of the National Association of Chinese Writers, and *Reminiscences in Cowsheds* [Niupeng zaji] (Beijing: Waiyu Jiaoxue Yu Yanjiu Chubanshe, 2009) by Ji Xianlin, the late head of the Institute of South Asian Studies of Beijing University. Both of the two works criticise the Cultural Revolution severely.

Unofficial and/or semi-official discourses and studies have started to break through the authorities' prohibition and show the writers' positive attitude towards the Cultural Revolution.

The accounts based on people's positive memory of the CR movement had hardly been in evidence in China before 1989 when the government suppressed the students' hunger strike at the Tiananmen Square. After the Tiananmen incident, a number of Party officials and independent intellectuals began to rethink and reappraise the Cultural Revolution, and dissenting voices emerged showing sympathy and an effort to justify the CR movement. However, these dissenting voices went unheard by the general public because under governmental censorship, they could not readily be published. Since the turn of the century, however, and coinciding with the rapid development of information systems in China, these dissenting voices have turned to the internet as a site for publication. Ranging from veiled and moderate tones to more open and forceful viewpoints, they have been gaining considerable momentum, rigorously challenging the mainstream collective memory of the movement. Governmental censors initially attempted to close down these websites, but with the emergence of increasing numbers of pro-CR websites and writings, alongside public pressure for increased freedom of speech, recent clampdowns have been less energetic.[7]

The internet writings comprise a variety of styles such as historical narratives, political and cultural analyses, personal memoirs and admiring poems. Many of them are serious argumentative articles which cover explorations on the above-noted facets: the movement's ideological foundation, cultural context, social background, practical process, consequential influence, etc. According to Andreas Huyssen, 'the act of remembering is always in and of the present, while its referent is of the past and thus

---

7   The main argument for the pro-CR websites and writings is that since the post-CR government has claimed to develop democracy and speech freedom, people should have the right not only to criticise the Cultural Revolution in accordance with the official resolutions, but also to affirm the movement according to their own views.

absent.'[8] In the internet pro-CR writings, the positive memory of the Cultural Revolution has normally been presented in a comparative perspective with the social and cultural changes and reality of the post-CR period. It is probably due to their non-official publication or unorthodox nature that the internet-based pro-CR writings have not received much mainstream scholarly attention. This article focuses on the pro-CR writings on the internet, and through analysing the internet writers' reflection on and rethinking of the Cultural Revolution, aims to provide a comparative perspective for scholars to study the CR movement and its memory as regards its objectives, significance and impacts.

This study draws on about fifty publicly-accessible websites on the Cultural Revolution in the Chinese language. These websites can be categorised into three groups: First, the websites dedicated to the Cultural Revolution. They carry only CR related writings and documents. The established dedicated websites include The Study of Chinese Cultural Revolution [Zhongguo Wenge yanjiu wang],[9] The Great Proletarian Cultural Revolution [Wuchanjieji Wenhua Da Geming],[10] and The Cultural Revolution Rebels [Wuchanjieji Wenhua Da Geming zaofanpai].[11]

---

8   See Andreas Huyssen, *Present Pasts: Urban Palimpsests and the Politics of Memory*, 3–4.

9   The site is http://www.wengewang.org/, which includes such thematic threads as Research on the CR, Memoirs of the CR, Debates of the Current Events Related to the CR, Documents of the CR and Reviews on the CR Literature and the Arts. Until the end of October 2008, there were 26,379 pieces of writings published/reproduced on this site.

10   Its site is http://hgy818.phpbbweb.com/hgy818.html. In addition to similar threads to those on The Study of Chinese Cultural Revolution, it includes other threads such as People of the Cultural Revolution (mainly the leaders of the Cultural Revolution), Rebels Are Fighting, Reviews on the Cultural Revolution, and Capitalist-Roaders Are Still Going Ahead.

11   It includes two sub-sites: 'Historical Exploration' [Lishi ban] (http://hgy818.phpbbweb.com/hgy818.html), which mainly discusses the CR theory and practice and has special accounts of the Red Guards' rebelling activities during the Cultural Revolution and their persecuted experience after the movement, and 'Contemporary Exploration' [Xianshi ban] (http://www.freepowerboards.com/hgy818/index.php), which focuses on the current ideological situation and social reality and the proposed

The second group are the websites on Mao Zedong, on which the writings about the Cultural Revolution are prominent because of its central position in Mao's later political career. Among them Mao Zedong[12] and The Flag of Mao Zedong [Mao Zedong qizhi wang][13] are most influential. Finally, apart from the above two directly-named categories of pro-CR websites, there are quite a number of other websites with a strong ideological orientation carrying pro-CR writings. Most of the websites are identifiable since their names are drawn from the period of the CR or from its principles and concepts.[14]

As for pro-CR writers on the internet, whilst it is impossible to ascertain the identity of all the contributors to these websites, some have been publicised and they include the following professional groups: retired CCP cadres, including high ranking officials; professional intellectuals including writers, scholars, journalists and teachers; college students including graduates and those still undertaking their studies; and workers, peasants and soldiers, many of whom are retired.

---

new Cultural Revolution in the future (there is a special thread The Second Cultural Revolution in this site).

12   The site is http://www.mao1893.net/, of which the threads such as Reviews on Mao and Reappraisal of Mao are specifically related to the Cultural Revolution.

13   This site (http://mao9.70.7871.com/) has become so big that it has over 100,000 documents available. Due to its open and firm position of praising the Cultural Revolution, this site was closed down for a period by the governmental censorship, although it continued to run later.

14   For instance, the website Utopian Village [Wuyou zhi xiang] (http://www.wyzxsx. com/Article/Index.html/) is known for carrying pro-CR writings, of which the metaphorical name indicates the ideal world of communism. Another example is Voice of Workers and Peasants [Gongnong zhi sheng] (http://www.gnzs.cn/). According to the ideological principles of the Cultural Revolution, workers and peasants played the central role in the proletarian revolution. The above three categories of websites originate in China and there are few websites produced in other languages. Apart from these categorised websites which are specially related to the Cultural Revolution, many other Chinese websites also carry pro-CR writings. Nevertheless, the basic stance of these websites may be neutral in ideology or against the CR culture. These websites are mostly based overseas.

In terms of their ideological stance, the writers generally claim to uphold Marxism and Maoism, but they have had different experiences in their ideological career and personal life. A number of them were in power in both Mao and post-Mao times, many of them being promoted to even higher rankings in the post-Mao period. Of them the best-known include Li Erzhong, Wei Wei, Ma Bin, Zheng Tianxiang, Li Chengrui, Han Xiya and Wu Lengxi who are representative of old communist officials and intellectuals.[15]

Among the old and well-known writers, some suffered mistreatment and came under persecution during the Cultural Revolution, but were later rehabilitated and promoted after the movement. Ma Bin is one such example. He had been vice-minister of the Ministry of Metallurgy before the Cultural Revolution, but was put into prison for six years during the CR period. Soon after the Cultural Revolution, he was reinstated and was later promoted. However, he has firmly upheld Mao's thought on the Cultural Revolution and become one of the leading writers defending the movement.

Although quite a number of elderly high-ranking officials and intellectuals can be seen debating online, the most active group of writers are middle-aged intellectuals, including scholars, critics, journalists, artists, and

---

15   Among them, for instance, Li Erzhong, over ninety years old, joined the CCP in the 1930s. He had studied sociology and economics in Japan in his early years. He successively held the posts of provincial Party secretary in Guangdong, Shanxi and Hebei. After retirement, he has held a number of honorary professional positions, including council member of the Association of Poetry of China, council member of the Association of Calligraphy of China, and professor of Wuhan University. His publications on politics, economics and literature come to over 10 million Chinese characters. Wei Wei, who died in 2008, was one of the best-known contemporary Chinese writers. He joined the CCP in Yan'an in 1938 and held a number of high-ranking posts, including minister of the Ministry of Culture in the post-CR time. He initially supported the post-CR government in criticizing the Cultural Revolution, but like many other old communist officials and intellectuals, he later changed his views and promoted re-evaluation of the Cultural Revolution and rethinking of the post-CR policies of the CCP.

teachers influenced by Marxism and Maoism.[16] They generally participated in the CR movement as Red Guards, and they were familiar with the theory and practice of the movement. Some of them suffered persecution in the post-CR period, but most of them have lived ordinary lives. A number of well-known middle-aged writers are professors of prestigious universities.[17] They have published widely in journal articles and monographs, although due to the relatively free environment of speech on the internet, their internet publications can be more straightforward or radical with regard to the presentation of their pro-CR views.

In spite of being in a minority, young writers also participate in discussions on the internet and they are normally university graduates. They grew up in the post-CR era, and the current mainstream politics is thought to have imbued their thinking with a brand of anti-CR ideology. However, deviating from this official ideology, they are taking a stand in favour of the Cultural Revolution.[18]

On websites based outside China, more and more pro-CR writers have given voice to their viewpoints in recent years. They might oppose the CCP government, but they disagree with the stance which denies the Cultural Revolution wholly.[19]

16   For a number of well-known writers, people can know their age through their identification such as autography, biography and media introduction. For anonymous writers, based on their personal experience and memory, many writings indicated the range of the authors' age.

17   Quite a long list of the well-known pro-CR writers or 'leftist scholars' can be found in http://www.wengewang.org/read.php?tid=14600.

18   More and more young people are joining the pro-CR debate on the internet. See Yongzh, 'From Worshiping Foreign Countries to Worshiping Mao – My Road to Understand Mao' [Cong chong-yang-zhe dao chong-Mao-zhe – Wo dui Mao Zedong de renshi zhi lu] (2009), http://www.wengewang.org/read.php?tid=16515&fpage=4, and Yue Jin, 'A Defending Debate of an Informative Student in a Classroom' [Yi ge fan-zhidaofenzi de ketang lunbian] (2009), http://www.maoflag.net/Forum_ShowNote.asp?board_id=1-1&id=514527.

19   Wang Xizhe and Wu Zhenrong are well-known examples. Wang lived in Guangdong before he left for America. He joined the Red Guards movement but was later put into prison during the Cultural Revolution. Wu Zhenrong currently lives in Korea. He

The main purpose of the pro-CR writings on the internet is to challenge official resolutions or propaganda and the mainstream scholastic documents and personal historiography, which are all opposed to the Cultural Revolution. The following themes about the Cultural Revolution figure prominently in these writings: ideological foundation, leaders, democracy, economy, social welfare development, literature and the arts, and the second Cultural Revolution.

1. Ideological and theoretical foundation of the Cultural Revolution

The general definition of the Cultural Revolution's ideological or theoretical foundation is 'continuous revolution under the dictatorship of the proletariat'. Following the Soviet Union's example, after the foundation of socialist China in 1949, the top CCP leaders had shared a view that the main concern of the socialist system was development of production instead of class struggle. However, since the late 1950s, Mao and a number of party leaders started to have different views, according to which, in spite of the socialist public ownership, a variety of inequalities occurred and were developing throughout society in relation to people's income, living standard, medical insurance, educational opportunity, etc. These inequalities were likely to give rise to privileged strata in society. Before the Cultural Revolution, the authorities headed by Mao formulated an ideological perspective which determined that there still existed class opposition and the danger of capitalist restoration in the socialist system. In particular,

---

was born and grew up in Shaanxi and participated in the movement in his hometown. They have connection with overseas Chinese anti-CCP organisations. Nevertheless, unlike many other overseas anti-CR democratic activists, they hold that the Cultural Revolution cannot be dismissed completely and try to understand it from a perspective of democracy movements.

some Party officials were seen to be in favour of representing the interests of the bourgeoisie. These officials were labelled capitalist-roaders in the Party. It was alleged that without a continuous revolution against them, these capitalist-roaders would take the lead in a capitalist restoration and a dictatorship of the bourgeoisie. This ideological reasoning of continuous revolution was the theoretical foundation of the Cultural Revolution.[20]

After the Cultural Revolution, the denunciation of the movement initially focused on this ideological and theoretical foundation because it was directly related to the causes, purposes and objectives of the movement. According to the post-CR authorities, the CR authorities headed by Mao overestimated the class opposition in socialist China and the corruption of the CCP. They claimed that the theory of continuous revolution was unsupported in Marxist doctrines, and that public ownership and the ideology of collectivism had wiped out the propertied classes and the foundation of opposition between the proletariat and the bourgeoisie. They thus attributed the Cultural Revolution and its ideological and theoretical foundation to the CR leaders' (mainly Mao's) political mistakes.[21]

Western scholarship has generally laid stress on the process and methods of the movement rather than on its ideological and theoretical foundation. We have not found substantial accounts either justifying or criticising the theory of continuous revolution. Similar to anti-CR writers in China, many Western scholars thought that the CR movement was primarily related to the CR authorities' personal interest.

However, a large quantity of internet writing discusses the ideological concept of continuous revolution and argues for its legitimacy and significance. Many of them put the theory into the perspective of the communist movement and claim it as being a further development of Marxism. According to them, Marx only discussed the proletarian revolution to

20   A detailed official explanation of the expression can be seen in 'The Political Report of the 9th CCP National Congress', http://www.marxists.org/chinese/24/marxist. org-chinese-linbiao-19690401.htm.

21   See the Documentary Institute of the CCP Central Committee, *A Collection of Important Documents of National Congresses and Plenary Sessions since the Third Plenary Session of the Eleventh National Congress*, 179–89.

establish socialism, but not revolution to consolidate socialism. The internet writers state that the target of Marx's proletarian revolution therefore is the bourgeoisie, which exists outside the communist party. The objective of the proletarian revolution is to impose proletarian government and public ownership, i.e. socialism. However, the establishment of socialism cannot ensure it will not change its colour. Nevertheless, Mao's continuous revolution is a socialist revolution and its objective is to consolidate the proletarian government with public ownership. The targets of the revolution are the people in power taking the capitalist road within the communist party.[22]

Some other internet writings question the reasonability of the theory of continuous revolution from the point of view of Marxism and the idea that the superstructure should be appropriate to the economic base. According to the writers, the revolution in the realm of superstructure, which is related to a society's history, culture and ideology, is much more complex than that in the society's economic base which can be established through political revolution. Before the Cultural Revolution, in spite of the socialist economic base (i.e. the public ownership established through the CCP's proletarian revolution), the superstructure was to some extent still associated with traditional culture and ideology based on feudalism and capitalism. For instance, privileged classes or strata and their privileged positions were perfectly justified in traditional Chinese culture, and the centre of Confucianism was the social order of hierarchy. This traditional culture was at odds with the CCP's claimed political principles of collectivism and egalitarianism. However, it turned out that the communist principles were hard to embed in people's self-consciousness. Many people had the intention to develop their own privileges in socialist China, and a number of Party officials were themselves becoming a privileged stratum by means

22 Although similar reasoning and sayings appeared in official documents of the Cultural Revolution, the internet writings highlighted them through analysis in depth. See Weidongderen, 'The Thought of Continuous Revolution under the Proletarian Dictatorship Is not Allowed to Be Denied' [Wuchanjieji zhuanzheng xia jixu geming de xueshuo bu rong fouding] (2008), http://www.wengewang.org/htm_data/38/0804/13263.html.

of their power. All these trends could be traced to traditional culture and ideology that promoted hierarchical prerogatives and individual privileges. Mao thus stated in the Cultural Revolution that the bourgeoisie was inside the Communist Party. Thus, the Cultural Revolution, as its name indicated, was firstly a campaign against old culture, old convention and old ideology, and was intended to develop the superstructure so it would be suited to the established socialist economic base.[23] This could also explain the special campaign against Confucianism in the Cultural Revolution, which was claimed to exterminate the 'root' of revisionism for the capitalist road.

Moreover, putting it in a sociological perspective, many internet writers argue for the theory of continuous revolution by analysing the social reality during the post-CR period. In his article 'Long Live the Theory of Continuous Revolution under the Dictatorship of the Proletariat', Qian Fu defends the CR's theoretical foundation by means of a detailed account of the social changes after the movement. According to him, post-CR China has been following a path different to socialism under Mao, by promoting private ownership and exacerbating the gap between rich and poor. The result is that the majority of public-owned enterprises have been privatised and millions of workers have become unemployed. The gap between the rich and the poor has become so huge that the official statistics indicate that zero point four per cent of the population now own seventy per cent of the wealth of the country.[24] Moreover, during the Cultural Revolution the prevailing communist ideology meant that honour, selflessness and altruism were promoted, but in the post-CR period, personal gain has become a popular social virtue. A variety of renounced social phenomena such as gambling, mafia, swindling, drugs, prostitution and robbery, which had been widespread in the long history of China, were generally

23   See The Central Committee of the CCP, 'The Decision on the Great Proletarian Cultural Revolution (8 August 1966)' [Guanyu Wuchanjieji Wenhua Da Geming de jueding (1966 nian 8 yue 8 ri tongguo)], http://www.wyzxsx.com/Article/Class10/200803/34610.html.

24   See Chunqiuxing, 'Who Are Making Troubles, and Who Are Suffering from the Troubles?' [Shui zai zheteng? Zheteng le shui?] (2008), http://economy.guoxue.com/article.php/18684.

wiped out from the country under Mao's communist party, but they have again become unchecked during the post-CR period. Furthermore, the corruption of current party officials has run rampant and the Chinese wealthiest class (millionaires and billionaires) are mainly found amongst party officials and their relatives.

There is no doubt that this social reality has aroused aversion and indignation of not only the pro-CR internet writers but also some anti-CR personnel. For instance, Liu Yuan, a high-ranking Party official whose father Liu Shaoqi was labelled the 'No. 1 Capitalist Roader' and was severely persecuted during the Cultural Revolution states:

> For about thirty years, the Chinese economy has been developing rapidly, a number of people have become rich, and people's living standards have increased. However, at the same time, the polarisation between the poor and the rich has emerged, the whole nation is overflowing with the desire for wealth, the corruption and degeneration of officials is running wild, criminal offences are on a rampage, egoism becomes fashionable, people have lost ideological conviction ... In brief, it is certain that the capitalist restoration which Mao Zedong tried to avoid has appeared in this country, and many of his foreseen negative factors have now become reality.[25]

The writers thus warn that China is taking the road of bureaucratic capitalism, and all the social phenomena are within Mao's prediction on which the continuous revolution theory was based. They conclude that the current social reality has borne out the significance of the ideological and theoretical foundation of the movement.[26]

In fact, more and more data has now emerged indicating that the post-CR authorities did intend to develop capitalism in China, something which the Cultural Revolution aimed to prevent. For instance, it has been revealed that Zhao Ziyang, the CCP general secretary between 1987 and 1989, believed that China had to take the capitalist road before its develop-

25   See Liu Yuan, 'It Is Extremely Wise to Discuss the Golden Mean of Confucianism' [Ji gaoming er dao Zhongyong] (2008), http://luoyuan.blshe.com/post/637/291111.
26   See Qian Fu, 'Long Live the Theory of Continuous Revolution under the Dictatorship of the Proletariat' [Wuchanjieji zhuanzheng xia jixu geming lilun wansui] (2008), http://www.wengewang.org/htm_data/38/0809/14887.html.

ment into socialism.[27] Moreover, the post-CR authorities have named the
new line of privatisation and market economy 'particular Chinese socialism'
or 'the primary stage of socialism'. Xin Ziling, a leading anti-CR scholar of
politics, admitted that the 'primary stage of socialism' was actually capitalism.[28] His claims and explanations have encountered severe criticism
online and the related data are widely quoted in the pro-CR writings to
justify the theory of continuous revolution and the CR movement.

Finally, it is evident that by defending the theory of continuous revolution, the above internet accounts about the theoretical foundation of the
Cultural Revolution have directly touched upon the controversial questions of the causes, purposes and objectives of the movement. They have
refuted the dominant argument by scholars that the Cultural Revolution
was mainly related to Mao Zedong's personal character and his belief in
perpetual conflict and struggle,[29] and in particular the claim that Mao
initiated the CR movement in order to deal with Liu Shaoqi, the then
Number 2 leader of the CCP, and to reinforce his prestige and power.[30]

27   Zhao's idea represented many people's understanding of socialism, which was claimed
      to be based on Marx's exposition about social development from feudalism to capital-
      ism and then to socialism/communism. Similar to the Soviet Union, China's socialism
      was directly established from the CCP's democratic revolution against feudalism,
      which leaped over capitalism in development. Zhao had an advisory board in poli-
      tics and economy, whose members advocated making up the stage of capitalism. See
      Li Bisheng, 'Seven Questions People Should Give and Answer' [Renren dou ying
      tiwen he huida de qi ge wenti] (2008), http://www.reviewing.cn/article/2008/1005/
      article_2848.html.
28   Xin Ziling, 'The Starting Point of Political Reform' [Zhengzhi gaige de tupokou]
      (2008), http://blog.tianya.cn/blogger/post_show.asp?idWriter=0&Key=0&Blog
      ID=319888&PostID=13721480.
29   According to some observers, Mao personally preferred conflict and struggle to col-
      lective harmony, propriety and benevolence, and the major strain of Mao's thought
      was his emphasis on class struggle, on military virtue and the employment of the
      language of war and conflict. See A. James Gregor and Maria Hsia Chang, 'Anti-
      Confucianism: Mao's Last Campaign', in Gregor Benton (ed.), *Mao Zedong and the
      Chinese Revolution* (London: Routledge, 2008), vol. II, 250–270.
30   According to the publications, due to the setbacks of a series of the Party's policies
      and campaigns between the late 1950s and early 1960s, such as the people's commune

According to the theoretical foundation of continuous revolution, however, dealing with a group of leaders within the highest authorities could neither be the sole nor the most important goal of the movement. The opposition between Mao and Liu may be less a personal disagreement than an ideological conflict. In their book *Liu Shaoqi Whom You Have Not Known*, Liu Yuan (Liu's son) and Wang Guangmei (Liu's wife) claimed that Liu had held different views on the direction of China since the early 1950s and that Liu and Deng Xiaoping had tried to pursue a different political line which placed emphasis on the economy rather than on ideology. Mao's line emphasised class struggle according to which ideological orientation had more decisive significance.[31]

Furthermore, as indicated by many internet writers, the interpretation of the Cultural Revolution based on Mao's personal interest and character can neither explain fully the theoretical foundation of continuous revolution under discussion nor the practical aspects of the movement. For example, from the point of view of the leaders, if the national movement had been only based on a personal opposition between Mao and Liu, why was it necessary for Mao to usher the movement into a nationwide campaign? Moreover, from the point of view of the common people, if the movement had been only for Mao's personal agenda against his colleagues, it would be inconceivable that the broad masses from all over the country actively and passionately participated in the movement.

---

system and the Great Leap Forward, Mao's power and prestige within the Party was damaged, and Mao strove for winning back his power and prestige by launching the Cultural Revolution. Mao was determined to purge Liu Shaoqi and a number of other high-ranking officials. See Jonathan D. Spence, *The Search for Modern China* (New York: W.W. Norton & Company, 1991), 590–609, and John K. Fairbank and Edwin O. Reischauer, *China: Tradition and Transformation* (Sydney: George Allen & Unwin, 1984), 504–14.

31 Quoted in Xiao Shanmu, 'Introduction to Ma Bin's New Book *Remember Mao Zedong*', http://www.wengewang.org/htm_data/38/0711/10360.html.

2. Mao and other CR leaders

Since Mao's leading position in the CCP was established in 1935, his authority had never been officially questioned during his lifetime, and his prestige in the nation reached its peak during the CR period. During the post-CR period, however, in view of the official denunciation of the Cultural Revolution, Mao's role was re-appraised. According to official discourse, Mao's political trajectory before the late 1950s was admirable and he made a great contribution to the country, but his career during the Cultural Revolution was erroneous, leading the country to a national catastrophe.

However, on the internet we can see a very different perspective which defends and glorifies Mao. Since the official criticism mainly focuses on Mao's theory and practice during the Cultural Revolution, the internet writers' argument is primarily focused on Mao's thinking and action during the movement. The writers argue it was the Cultural Revolution that represented the most brilliant milestone of Mao's revolutionary career. In his *Mao Zedong's Everest*, Mei Qiao states, 'The theory of continuous revolution under the proletarian dictatorship and the practice of the Cultural Revolution was the Everest of Mao's whole life course in following Marxism and Leninism.'[32]

The internet pro-CR debate also covers the results of a number of public opinion polls held by semi-official or official newspapers and journals, which unanimously showed that Mao was regarded as the greatest national hero.[33] The pro-CR writers argue that Mao has been dead for over thirty years, that he has been criticised by the mainstream propaganda since the 1980s, and that people cannot benefit from glorifying Mao today, but according to the polls he is still held in esteem by the people. This indirectly

32   See Ma Li, 'The Blackened History Is More Brilliant – The Reading Notes on Mei Qiao's *Mao Zedong's Everest*' [Bei mo hei de lishi geng huihuang – Mei Qiao *Mao Zedong de Zhufeng* du hou] (2007), http://www.wengewang.org/htm_data/38/0706/6807. html.

33   See Xiangchunshu, 'Why Is Mao the Heroic Idol of the Current Young Generation?' [Weihe nianqing yidai de xinmu zhong de yingxiong ouxiang hai shi Mao Zedong] (2008), http://bbs3.creaders.net/forums/general/messages/652129.html.

indicates the present attitude of the broad masses of the people towards the Cultural Revolution.

As for other top leaders who actively conducted or promoted the CR campaign, such as the well-known Gang of Four, they were persecuted by the post-CR government. Great quantities of official and unofficial publications were produced to attack them. Initially, there were few writings online commenting on these persecuted CR leaders. However, in recent years, along with the development of pro-CR writings on the internet in quantity and in depth, more and more writers have started to reappraise them. Special websites are emerging which defend, praise and commemorate them and their action, and in which, in addition to the writers' articles, the CR leaders' photos, speeches and writings can also be seen. According to these writings, firstly, similar to Mao, in view of the justified revolutionary nature of the movement, the radical CR leaders should not be seen as political criminals but as heroes and martyrs of the proletarian revolution. Secondly, more and more documents including official archives and the personal reminiscences of those involved suggest that the charges of counterrevolution and conspiracy to subvert the government against them are basically groundless frame-ups. Finally, some speeches and writings by the radical CR leaders are reviewed and acclaimed by the internet writers. For example, Zhang Chunqiao's views on capitalist restoration and proletarian dictatorship are widely quoted to criticise the post-CR social reality, and Jiang Qing's statements about the modern theatre are commended while the writers condemn the decadent and pornographic trends of the contemporary arts in China.

3. Democracy of the Cultural Revolution

It is known that many Western scholars and overseas Chinese activists for democratic campaigns have always emphasised that the Cultural Revolution was based on obscurantist and autocratic policy, and that the masses were mobilised to participate in the movement through the authorities' brain-washing policy and political persecution. This criticism was echoed in the official post-CR resolutions, propaganda and historiography. According to them, the CR movement promoted the cult of personality and asceticism, and there emerged an anti-democratic trend both inside and outside the Party during the period. This trend was thought to have been rooted in traditional feudalist culture and ideology endorsing hierarchy and submission to sovereigns.[34]

However, the internet writers challenge the mainstream criticisms by arguing that the Cultural Revolution represents the most democratic practice in Chinese history. According to the writers, the most prominent slogan for socialism and communism upheld by the CCP before the post-CR period was opposing privilege and promoting equality. Based on the CR theory of permanent revolution, the movement was launched to overthrow the privileged stratum within the Party, i.e. the people in power taking the capitalist road. In methodology, the CR government adopted the well-known Four-Great-Ways policy: speaking out freely, airing views fully, holding great debates and writing great-character posters, which were officially acclaimed as the great democracy of the proletariat in the CR movement and incorporated into the Constitution of the PRC. The common people, especially the mass of student youth, were encouraged to rebel against their superiors, to attack the existing rules and regulations, and to break with the established traditional conventions.

Nevertheless, the post-CR authorities abolished the Four-Great-Ways policy soon after they gained government control. In Feilongzaitian's article 'Great Democracy versus Small Democracy', the author claims that although the elite have more freedom of speech in the post-CR period, the common people, especially labouring masses, have generally lost the right to challenge their superiors or employers. In other words, the post-CR period has

---

34   See the Documentary Institute of the CCP Central Committee, *A Collection of Important Documents of National Congresses and Plenary Sessions since the Third Plenary Session of the Eleventh National Congress*, pp. 188–189.

more democracy for the minority of the elite but the CR period had more democracy for the majority of the common people.[35]

A group of overseas Chinese writers such as Wang Xizhe and Liu Guokai proposed two concepts to define the nature of the Cultural Revolution: 'the authorities' Cultural Revolution' [guanfang Wenge] and 'the people's Cultural Revolution' [renmin Wenge]. The former refers to the CR authorities' political persecution in the name of 'proletarian dictatorship', and the latter to the common people's campaign for anti-bureaucracy under the CR slogan 'It is right to rebel'. Although they oppose the CR movement in general, they agree that 'the people's Cultural Revolution' contained the spirit of democracy.[36]

More and more writings based on the CR participants' memory and reflection can now be seen on the internet to discuss democracy during this period. For example, Wu Zhenrong, a well-known overseas Chinese internet writer as mentioned above, was a 17 year-old high school student in 1966 when the Cultural Revolution started. He has published a large quantity of memory writings online to discuss the claimed democratic nature of the Cultural Revolution. His memoirs and recollections are widely quoted or reprinted on different websites and other outlets. In his article 'On 1966' [Lun 1966 nian],[37] for instance, he recalls and analyses his experience of rebelling and other people's enthusiasm in the movement. According to him, people had never gained the right or power to challenge their leading organisations, superiors, rules and conventions and that they had used to hold them in awe, veneration or even hatred; this explains how excited and enthusiastic the common people became in the movement:

35 See Feilongzaitian, 'Great Democracy versus Small Democracy' [Da minzhu yu xiao minzhu] (2007), http://www.wengewang.org/htm_data/38/0709/8440.html.

36 See Liu Guokai, 'On the People's Cultural Revolution – writing for the Fortieth Anniversary of the Cultural Revolution' [Lun renmin Wenge – wei Wenge sishi zhounian er zuo] (2005), http://www.boxun.com/hero/liugk/155_1.shtml.

37 1966 was the first year of the Chinese Cultural Revolution. Wu's article 'On 1966' was written in 2008 and can be seen in http://www.wengewang.org/htm_data/38/0809/14966.html.

As a former participant of the great movement, I have made a list of the leading organisations which we rebelled against. It includes eight levels of CCP leadership: the Party Branch of Yuxian High School, the Party Branch of Xiaonan Village, the Party Committee of Zhangdian Commune, the Education Bureau of Xingping County, the Party Committee of Xingping County, the Party Committee of Xianyang Prefecture, the Party Committee of Shaanxi Province, and the Party Committee of Northern China.[38]

According to him, some of these organisations had been beyond reach in the past, but now the grass-roots young people could challenge and criticise them with confidence. This might to some extent explain the Red Guards' fanaticism and radicalism in their rebellious actions and also the unprecedented personality cult of Mao during the Cultural Revolution, that is, all the 'liberated' people cherished great gratitude and reverence to Mao who offered them the 'great democracy and freedom'; gratitude and reverence became a factor in the foundation of the cult of the highest CR leader.[39]

Wu Zhengrong concludes that people will never find another government in Chinese history to launch a nationwide campaign and mobilise the broad mass of the people to attack its established bureaucratic order and system. They will also never find another party leader which can organise the non-party masses to challenge the party's authority by rebelling against its officialdom and leadership. From this point of view, the Cultural Revolution was the most prominent movement for democracy and freedom in Chinese history.

38   Ibid.
39   Ibid.

4. Economy of the Cultural Revolution

The Chinese economic situation during the Cultural Revolution has not attracted much attention of Western scholarship, but it has been one of the most common objects of denunciation made by the post-CR authorities and propaganda, according to which the national economy of China suffered catastrophic loss and came to the edge of collapse in the ten years of the CR.[40] Often, the supply of means of subsistence fell short of demand in the CR period.

However, the internet writers argue that the CR national economy developed well from an overall point of view if people take the following factors into account: First, the proportion of the planned national economy during the CR period had laid stress on the country's capital construction and means of production instead of means of subsistence. Second, China in the Cultural Revolution relied on itself in developing its independent economy, but in post-CR China, a great deal of investment came from abroad, in other words, the prosperity of the post-CR economy is greatly based on foreign economies. Third, the CR government emphasised communist internationalism and offered much financial, industrial and military support to small countries of the Third World.

According to Shuangye, an active pro-CR writer, Mao set a general line for the national economy when the Cultural Revolution was launched, that is, 'Grasp revolution, promote production', which later became one of the best-known political slogans of the CR movement. Shuangye provides a detailed account of the economic development of the CR period. In comparison between 1965, the last year of the pre-CR period, and 1976, the last year of the CR era, there was a series of facts indicating the rapid

---

40 See Ye Jianying, 'Talk at the Celebration Meeting of the Thirtieth Anniversary of the PRC' [Zai qingzhu Zhonghua Renmin Gongheguo chengli sanshi zhounian dahui shang de jianghua] (Sept. 1979), in the Documentary Institute of the CCP Central Committee, *A Collection of Important Documents of National Congresses and Plenary Sessions since the Third Plenary Session of the Eleventh National Congress*, 84.

development of the national economy during the CR years. For instance, the increase of grain yield was 91.2 billion kilograms, crude oil increased 6.7 times, and the industrial production in general registered an average increase of ten per cent for the ten years of the CR.[41]

In an article entitled 'The Achievements of the Ten CR Years Were Innumerable, Miraculous and Undeniable', the author (his/her penname is qwqwqw_1963) compares the national economy of the CR years with that of the post-CR period and concludes that in terms of GDP, the development after the Cultural Revolution was to some extent faster than that of the CR period. Nevertheless, there exist essential differences in nature between the two periods: the development of the post-CR period has been based on immediate interests, laying stress on means of subsistence, ignoring environmental protection and selling national and collective enterprises. The development of the CR years emphasised long-term interests, giving priority to heavy industry, capital construction, means of production and environmental protection. Moreover, it was the economic development during the pre-CR and CR period that offered a solid foundation for the economic development of the post-CR period.[42]

5. Social welfare development in the Cultural Revolution

On the pro-CR websites, many articles compare the social welfare development between the CR and post-CR periods. Equality was a key concern of the CR movement, and the CR authorities initiated a large number

41   See Shuangye, 'On Several Issues of the Cultural Revolution' [Guanyu Wenhua Da Geming jige wenti de cuqian kanfa] (2007), http://www.wengewang.org/htm_data/38/0707/7107.html.
42   See qwqwqw_1963, 'The Achievements of the Ten CR Years Were Innumerable, Miraculous and Undeniable' [Wenhua Da Geming shi nian shuoguo leilei, chengji huihuang, kan cheng qiji, wu fa fouding] (2007), http://www.wengewang.org/htm_data/38/0712/10888.html.

of new policies aimed at reducing the distinction between social strata, professions and localities including town and country. Two policies were vital for the CR government to carry this out. The first was universal education. In general, primary and secondary schooling became compulsory and free of charge; higher and tertiary level education was selective, but it was free and the students even had stipends to cover living expenses. The second important policy was a public health service. Most notably, the cooperative medical service was established in the countryside, ensuring that the farmers could have their free medical treatment in their villages and communes.

In the post-CR period, however, and under the flag of the market economy, the government carried out a radical policy by which national education and health were regarded as enterprises, the development of which was to be based on market principles. Thus, not only universities and colleges but also primary and secondary schools started to charge school fees and the fees increased rapidly. The medical service system became so profiteering that the hospitals took profit as their target and charged patients unfairly. Although the current government has started to adjust these policies in response to people's discontent, the market trend of education and medication has not been substantially checked.

In his 'Education in China: Reform or Retrogression?' Jiang Weigang gives a detailed account of Chinese educational history under the CCP. According to him, the general direction of the CR national education was the general people's education, but in the post-CR period it has become 'elite and aristocrat education'. The hierarchy of educational institutes has become so prominent that all the schools, colleges and universities are officially categorised according to their teachers, facilities, locations and results of examinations and the charges are different according to the categorised rankings. Since the high-ranking schools and universities charge more than low-ranking institutes, a large number of students prefer the latter to the former because their parents cannot afford to pay the higher fees. Due to financial difficulties, the suicide of parents and students and the prostitution of students have increased year on year. Moreover, the schools and universities are authorised to set additional charges for failed students in entrance examination. Thus, for wealthy students, even if their examination marks are lower than fixed standard, they may still go to higher-ranking institutes when they pay the additional fee.[43]

As regards national health, by exploring people's average life-span, Yundanshuinuan, a known internet writer, puts the national medical service under the CCP into a historical perspective. He quotes official statistics, according to which the average life-span of the whole people increased from thirty-five to sixty-eight during the pre-CR and CR period (1949 and 1978), of which the difference is thirty-three, but it has increased from sixty-eight to seventy-one during the post-CR period, of which the difference is only three.[44]

Another writer, Yao Li, investigates the development of health services in the countryside, which shows the greater achievements of the national medical service during the Cultural Revolution as opposed to after the movement.[45]

In brief, through their comparative studies, the internet writers conclude that in terms of social welfare the CR movement was not a catastrophe as alleged by the post-CR propaganda but an era promoting welfare services for the people.[46]

43   See Jiang Weigang, 'Education in China: Reform or Retrogression?' [Zhongguo jiaoyu: gaige haishi daotui] (2004), http://www.boxun.com/hero/2007/voacnn/47_1. shtml.

44   Yundanshuinuan, 'Great Medical Reform (1949–1978): The Average Life-Span from 35 to 68' [Weida de yi gai (1949–1978): Ren jun yuqi shouming cong 35 sui dao 68 sui] (2007), http://www.wengewang.org/htm_data/38/0708/7933.html.

45   See Yao Li, '"In Medical and Health Work, Put the Stress on Rural Areas": A Historical Perspective on Mao's 26 June Instruction' ['Ba yiliao weisheng gongzuo de zhong-dian fang dao nongcun qu' – Mao Zedong 'liu er liu' zhishi de lishi kaocha] (2004), http://www.chinese-thought.org/shgc/005968.htm.

46   It is noticeable that since the official denial of the Cultural Revolution in the post-CR period, we have seen huge numbers of official criticisms against the CR movement and its various policies, but we have not seen serious denigration of the new CR welfare systems, although they were abolished by the post-CR authorities.

6. Literature and the arts of the Cultural Revolution

It is known that during the Cultural Revolution, literature and the arts were one of the most prominent fields under the control of the radical CR authorities. According to the post-CR authorities, the literature and the arts of the Cultural Revolution had three key negative features: insufficiency in quantity, ideological orientation in content and artistic simplicity in quality.

However, the internet writers disagree with the above criticism. According to them, the production of literary and artistic works in the CR years was not more than that in the post-CR period but not less than that in the pre-CR time. Especially, since the CR literary and artistic authorities emphasised the direction towards representing and serving the common people (workers, peasants and soldiers), the folk forms and styles based on local areas were flourishing. Wuxianglang states, 'If we take the variety of local forms and styles into consideration and if we take all the masses' writings and performances into account, the literary and artistic production of the Cultural Revolution might be more than that of the post CR period.'[47]

As for the content, the internet writers challenge the mainstream criticism and claim that the post-CR authorities and critics mainly review the CR products from the perspective of vulgar sociology and overemphasise negative aspects of their ideological orientation. The writers allege that the ideological orientation is by no means inferior to the amount of crimes, sex, murder, etc., which is prevalent in post-CR literary and artistic works. While discussing the model theatrical works, which were the most important during the Cultural Revolution, Guo Songmin, a well-known media commentator in China, argues that post-CR critics denounce the model theatrical works as being packed with ideological messages rather than

47   See Wuxianglang, 'Why Were the Literature and the Arts so Prosperous during the Cultural Revolution?' [Wenge shiqi de wenxue yishu weishenme neng baihuaqifang da fanrong] (2008), http://www.wengewang.org/htm_data/38/0802/12065.html.

human feelings such as familial love, but they are full of greater love, the love for the whole proletariat instead of only one's immediate family.[48]

Moreover, in terms of artistic quality, the internet writers argue that the standard of the CR model theatrical works is substantially higher than that of the post-CR works, but that it has been underestimated by the post-CR propaganda. According to the writers, the ideological orientation of the model theatrical works was prominent, which might be regarded as a weak point beyond the CR context, but their artistic quality is also prominent. If the literary and artistic reviews on the CR literature and the arts left behind their ideological factors but focused on their artistic characteristics, the conclusion would be very different, namely that the CR literature and the arts were artistically sophisticated and significant.[49]

7. Calling for the second Cultural Revolution

Based on the above arguments for the rationality and importance of the Cultural Revolution, many internet writings call for a second Cultural Revolution. Although a number of writers disapprove, most internet writers admit that the first Cultural Revolution failed. However, the writers insist that in spite of the failure, the spirit and principles of the movement will be carried forward. Thus the discussion of the necessity, possibility and process of the second Cultural Revolution becomes one of the most popular topics in internet writings.

48   See Guo Songmin, 'A Letter to a Friend regarding the Human Nature of the Model Theatrical Works' [Guanyu 'Yangbanxi' de 'renxing' wenti zhi youren de yi feng xin] (2008), http://www.hongqiwang.com/read.php?tid=2016.
49   See Banyuexing, 'On the Model Theatrical Works' [Tan Geming Yangbanxi] (2008), http://www.wengewang.org/htm_data/38/0802/12059.html; Guo Songmin, 'The Model Theatrical Works Are Artistic Summit of Beijing Operas' [Yangbanxi shi zhongguo jingju yishu de dianfeng zhi zuo] (2008), http://bbs1.people.com.cn/postDetail.do?view=2&pageNo=1&treeView=1&id=85221504&boardId=2.

According to the writers, since China is now taking the capitalist road, which the first Cultural Revolution aimed to prevent but failed to do so, it is necessary for China to have a second Cultural Revolution. They think that the post-CR social reality has given rise to extensive discontent, which is the social foundation for the broad masses of the people to support and participate in the second Cultural Revolution. Moreover, the first Cultural Revolution was the precedent, and, drawing lessons from it, people can do better when carrying the second Cultural Revolution through to fruition.

In his 'On the Cultural Revolution', Ma Bin describes the proposed second Cultural Revolution in great detail. Quoting Mao's statement that the first Cultural Revolution could not solve all the problems and that there should be more Cultural Revolutions in the future, Ma claims that the second Cultural Revolution will be the continuation of the first Cultural Revolution, of which the main mission is to attack bureaucracy, corruption and revisionism within the CCP and to re-establish the proletarian dictatorship and socialist system. As for the methodology and practice, he outlines a set of principles for the second Cultural Revolution. For instance, 'It will be a movement of study and a movement of the masses for self-education. It will not allow any beating, swearing, arrests or insults, but will promote criticism and self-criticism in the manner of "a gentle breeze and a mild rain".'[50]

In view of increasing responses to support the proposed second Cultural Revolution, Ma Bin suggests that the party and the people should start to make preparations for the second Cultural Revolution now. The preparation would include the following aspects: to establish well-organised leadership, to conduct socialist education, to mobilise the masses, to study Marxism and Mao's Thought, to sum up the successful experience and draw lessons from the first Cultural Revolution, and to establish a series of special newspapers and journals.[51]

---

50   See Ma Bin, 'On the Cultural Revolution' [Lun Wenhua Da Geming] (2006), http://
     www.wengewang.org/htm_data/38/0709/9041.html.
51   Ibid.

This study focuses on the internet pro-CR debate based on memory rather than on the CR movement itself, but these two subjects are related to each other because the theme of the debate is around the movement. The debate offers new evidence and new perspectives for the study of the movement. Although a number of the internet writings are ideologically radical and/or biased in views and presentation, most of them represent serious research written in an academic style. It is likely that the current debate is developing into a grand campaign to challenge the official denunciation of the movement. Moreover, unlike some anti-CR writers' suggestion that it might have official backing, the pro-CR campaign is not part of any official mobilisation because it challenges the post-CR governmental resolutions and policies.

It is well known that at the initial stage of the post-CR period the official or mainstream renunciation of the Cultural Revolution was in general hailed by the nation's citizens. The people's support was the social foundation of the post-CR governmental policies and resolutions to denounce the movement without any reservation. Nevertheless, after about thirty years, why have huge numbers of people started to defy the official or mainstream representation and argue in favour of the Cultural Revolution?

In view of this fact, are there any significant aspects of the CR movement which have been misrepresented or misconceived by the post-CR government and its leaders? For instance, as regards the general theory of continuous revolution, according to the official post-CR resolutions, the CR movement was mainly based on Mao's misjudgement of the danger of the capitalist direction of the CCP. However, the internet writers who experienced the Cultural Revolution admit that in the late period of the movement they felt tired of the seemingly endless 'continuous revolution' and started to doubt Mao's statement that there existed the danger of capitalist restoration in socialist China. This was the basis on which they initially agreed with the post-CR resolutions and propaganda that Mao's judgement for the theory of the Cultural Revolution was wrong. Nevertheless, when they later realised to their surprise that in the name of 'socialism with Chinese characteristics', the post-CR government was really taking the capitalist road, and in possession of the main body of national wealth, with a domineering bureaucrat-capitalist stratum emerging in

China, they started to rethink and appreciate Mao's prediction and decision, and have thus joined the pro-CR internet debate.

Moreover, according to the post-CR mainstream reviews, the Cultural Revolution had nothing to do with democracy and freedom due to the centralised power of the CR authorities. However, according to the internet writers, during the Cultural Revolution, although the persecuted people who accounted for a minority of the nation were deprived of their freedom, the majority of people, including those participating in the rebellion, got a variety of freedoms under the Four-Great-Ways policy. These included freedom of speech (countless oral and written speeches attacking the Party's authorities at all levels), freedom of association (thousands upon thousands of associations under the flag of rebellion emerged in the country), freedom of assembly, freedom of demonstration, freedom of strike (including students' strike), and freedom of publication (referring to the Red Guards' newspapers and journals). Furthermore, it was the highest authority of the Party that called the broad masses to rebel against the Party's own established leading and administrative order. This was unique in Chinese history. Compared to the post-CR period in which all the above freedoms have been banned, the Cultural Revolution emerges as an unusual period with democracy and freedom, although the nature and significance of the democracy and freedom needs further definition and exploration in a study of contemporary China and the Cultural Revolution.

Capitalism and socialism continue to represent the two key opposite ideological lines in Chinese politics, with socialism claimed as the fundamental purpose of the CCP. It is for this reason that, although the economic base or means of production has been changing towards capitalist patterns, the official political banner of the post-CR China is still socialist and the authorities maintain that they are learning about capitalism to improve socialism. It is evident that the CCP and its government have now reached a crossroads: a further development of capitalism, including political reform, or a steadfast development of socialism. In general, the capitalist road is welcomed by propertied strata including wealthy Party officials, but the socialist road is supported by the people. Since the Cultural Revolution was claimed to consolidate socialism and to prevent capitalism in both theory and practice, it is getting hard for the current CCP authorities not

to rethink the movement while facing the demand of the masses for rehabilitating the movement. The study of the Cultural Revolution has been
under the control of the government in China since the late 1970s, and all
the official speeches and discourses about the movement have been channelled into the narrative of 'national catastrophe' as defined in the post-CR
Party resolutions. The internet is playing an increasingly significant role
in encouraging and helping people to express their own views on the CR
movement. Many internet writers have gone so far as to suggest that the
second Cultural Revolution of the future should be directly carried out
on the internet, making the internet the battleground of rebels against
the capitalist-roaders.⁵² The current Chinese government is facing a difficult choice: the simplistic and complete renunciation of the Cultural
Revolution made by the former post-CR governments is encountering
subversive challenge, but approval of the challenge will lead to denial of
the post-CR reform while suppression or denial of the challenge will lose
the support of the people. In view of their developing influence, therefore,
the dissenting voices based on people's memory of the Cultural Revolution
cannot be neglected by either government or scholars.

52   See Li Yang, 'The Cultural Revolution in the Past versus the Internet at Present'
      [Dangnian de Wenge, jintian de hulianwang] (2008), http://www.wehoo.net/
      dispbbs.asp?boardID=21&ID=4216&page=1; Anonymous, 'If China Has the
      Second Cultural Revolution Now' [Jiaru jintian Zhongguo baofa di'er ci Wenhua
      Da Geming] (2008), http://www.reviewing.cn/wangyou/2008/1024/article_2493.
      html.

PART 4

Fictional Imaginaries

INGO CORNILS

Utopian Moments: Memory Culture and Cultural Memory of the German Student Movement

Introduction

For the historian Jay Winter, '1968' represents a key moment in the twentieth century when what he terms 'minor utopians' 'succeeded in putting the notion of liberation of many different kinds in the minds of millions of their contemporaries'.[1] Whilst conceding that their immediate achievements were meager or nonexistent, he argues that their visions of an alternative reality precipitated 'a series of moments of possibility, of openings, of hopes and dreams rarely realized, but rarely forgotten as well'.[2]

Judging from recent publications, the German Student Movement continues to represent 'unfinished business', precisely because the utopian moment, in a very German and Faustian sense, did not last. At the Leipzig book fair in the spring of 2008, the theme of '1968' dominated the headlines. Every publisher, large or small, had at least one book in their catalogue[3]

---

1 Jay Winter, *Dreams of Peace and Freedom. Utopian Moments in the 20th Century* (New Haven: Yale University Press 2006), 151.

2 J. Winter, 2.

3 Most notable: Norbert Frei, *1968. Jugendrevolte und globaler Protest* (München: dtv 2008); Reinhard Mohr, *Der diskrete Charme der Rebellion. Ein Leben mit den 68ern* (Berlin: WJS-Verlag 2008); Götz Aly, *Unser Kampf. 1968 – ein irritierter Blick zurück* (Frankfurt: Fischer 2008); Albrecht von Lucke, *68 oder neues Biedermeier. Der Kampf um die Deutungsmacht* (Berlin: Wagenbach 2008); Daniel Cohn-Bendit / Rüdiger Dammann (eds), *1968. Die Revolte* (Frankfurt: Fischer 2007); Gerd Koenen / Andres Veiel, *1968. Bildspur eines Jahres* (Köln: Fackelträger Verlag 2008); Peter Schneider, *Rebellion und Wahn. Mein '68. Eine autobiographische Erzählung* (Köln:

about the 'year that changed everything'.[4] Compared to the 30th anniversary, though, the delicate consensus that '1968' in Germany represented a 'successful failure'[5] was challenged both by former activists and historians. While the majority were at pains to explain the wider context to actions which, post 9/11, are regarded as much less of a misdemeanor than before, a minority openly attacked the 'myth of 68' which had been created, in their view, to guarantee the 68ers a political and cultural hegemony way past their sell-by-date.

There are two obvious ways to explain the continued interest in the German Student Movement, four decades on. The first is the fact that the 68er generation will be well into their 70s when the 50th anniversary comes around. They are therefore keen to influence the way their defining moment is recorded in the history books. The second is the demise of the red-green coalition in 2005 when chancellor Gerhard Schröder and foreign secretary Joschka Fischer lost their majority in an early general election and were replaced by Angela Merkel who, as leader of the conservative opposition, had challenged the generation of 68 to explain what they had ever done for Germany in a heated parliamentary debate in 2001 following Fischer's 'outing' as a former street fighter.[6] This very visible loss of power and influence in 2005 of the generation that had gone on the 'long march through the institutions' in 1968 and had only belatedly come to power in 1998 meant that they had become vulnerable to revisionist interpretations.

A third, more complex reason for the longevity of the topic in Germany has generally been ignored in the struggle for interpretation

Kiepenheuer & Witsch 2008); Wolfgang Kraushaar, *Achtundsechzig. Eine Bilanz* (Berlin: Propyläen 2008). See also Axel Schildt, 'Eine schöne, wilde Zeit', in: *Die Zeit*, 14 March 2008, 44; and, hiding behind a study of German Romanticism: Rüdiger Safranski, *Romantik. Eine deutsche Affaire* (München: Hanser Verlag 2007).

4   Wolfgang Kraushaar, *1968. Das Jahr, das alles verändert hat* (München: Piper 1998).

5   See my 'Successful Failure? The Impact of the German Student Movement on the Federal Republic of Germany', in: Stuart Taberner / Frank Finlay (eds), *Recasting German Identity. Culture, Politics and Literature in the Berlin Republic* (Rochester: Camden House 2002), 105–122.

6   'Successful Failure?', 120–122.

between the poles of historicisation and memorialisation of the German Student Movement.[7] This chapter will explore the romantic, nostalgic, almost palpable sense of loss that many former participants feel for those 'magic moments' when 'the private was political', when, in the 'unity of thought, feeling and action' experienced in collective acts of protest and self-emancipation, they briefly glimpsed that they could 'make history' and change society in the utopian direction that their ideological leaders and intellectual fathers had described.[8]

The sense of loss that permeates the consciousness of the 68ers not only relates to the 'magic moments' that would sporadically return in later decades during protests against nuclear energy, Cruise Missiles, or the war in Iraq. It relates directly to the traumatic experience of a dream cut short by the bullets of a policeman and a would-be assassin who took out the heart of an idealistic and optimistic movement and, in some extreme cases, turned it into the mindset of terrorists.[9]

It is no accident that German writers continue to return to these moments – to many intellectuals, they represent a watershed in West Germany's short history.[10] But it was only recently that the victims on both sides came to be seen as individuals, real people as opposed to pawns in the ideological struggle between protesters and the state. Given that the 'subjective' memorialisation of former activists lacks the general applicability and simplicity that would make it useful in any ideological debate, recent memory texts like Uwe Timm's *Der Freund und der Fremde* (The Friend and the Stranger, 2005), Daniel de Roulet's *Ein Sonntag in den*

---

7   For a broader discussion of these terms see the introduction to this volume.
8   See my 'Romantic Relapse? The Literary Representation of the German Student Movement', in: Chris Hall / David Rock (eds), *German Studies Towards the Millenium* (Bern/Frankfurt/New York: Peter Lang, 2000), 107–123.
9   See my 'Joined at the Hip? The Representation of the German Student Movement and Left-Wing German Terrorism in recent Literature', in: Gerrit-Jan Berendse / Ingo Cornils (eds), *Baader-Meinhof Returns. History and Cultural Memory of German Left-Wing Terrorism* (Amsterdam / New York: Rodopi 2008), 137–155.
10   See my 'Folgenschwere Schüsse. Die Kugeln auf Benno Ohnesorg und Rudi Dutschke im Spiegel der deutschen Literatur', in: *Jahrbuch für Internationale Germanistik*, Vol. 2 (2003), 55–73

Bergen (A Sunday in the Mountains, 2006) and Peter Schneider's *Rebellion und Wahn* (Rebellion and Delusion, 2008) fly under the radar of the continuing debate about the historical achievements (or otherwise) of the 68ers. At the same time, as will be shown, these texts provide an essential 'human factor' to the inexorable pull of historicisation and add a hitherto unacknowledged element to the production of the cultural memory of the German Student Movement.

The friend and the stranger

The first of the tragic events that transformed the nature of the German Student Movement was the death of the student Benno Ohnesorg, an innocent bystander who was shot dead by a plain-clothes policeman during a demonstration against the state visit of the Shah of Persia in West Berlin on 2 June 1967. This event lifted the German Student Movement onto a different level. It galvanised, politicised and mobilised thousands and made them fear that what had happened to Benno Ohnesorg could happen to any of them. The fact that state authorities and the tabloid press owned by newspaper tycoon Axel Springer blamed the students and that the policeman who killed Ohnesorg got off scot-free while student demonstrators were put in jail proved to many observers that the young West-German democracy was but a thin veneer and that the authoritarian structures of Germany's past had not yet been overcome.

In his autobiographical text *Der Freund und der Fremde* (2005),[11] German writer Uwe Timm examines his own memories of Benno Ohnesorg. Both had met at the *Braunschweig Kolleg* in 1961, a college that allowed gifted mature students to gain their entrance qualifications for university. Uwe Timm, today one of the foremost writers of his generation, has repeat-

11   Uwe Timm, *Der Freund und der Fremde* (Köln: Kiepenheuer und Witsch, 2005). Hereafter: FF. All translations my own.

edly written about the German '1968' – the novels *Heißer Sommer* (Hot Summer, 1974) and *Rot* (Red, 2001) are considered key texts about the era[12] – yet never disclosed that he had been a close friend of Ohnesorg. Following on from his previous 'memory project', the celebrated *Am Beispiel meines Bruders* (2003, Engl. transl. *In my brother's shadow*, 2005), Timm finally found a suitable form that allowed him not only to compose a requiem for his friend but to rediscover and confront his own former self which was profoundly affected by his friend's death.[13]

The narrative – part autobiography and part documentary – starts with an image that casts Benno Ohnesorg in the pose of the medieval German poet Walter von der Vogelweide.[14] Timm's first memory of meeting the stranger, sitting on a wall by a river, writing poems, is obviously stylised, and mainly serves to underline their mutual love for literature and a desire, on Timm's part, to flesh out Ohnesorg's somewhat two-dimensional personality. Timm recalls how they read to each other their first literary efforts, and how, six years later, when he heard of Ohnesorg's death on the radio in Paris, he abandoned his PhD project to join the revolt, thus turning the personal into the political.

The events are mediated through remembered telephone conversations and photographs, especially the picture that would become a representation of one of the key moments of the year.[15] Timm reminds the reader of the details of the image, while reconstructing his own reactions:

12 See my 'Long Memories. The German Student Movement in Recent Fiction', in: *German Life and Letters*, Issue 56:1, January 2003, 89–101; and 'Uwe Timm, der heilige St. Georg und die Entsorgung der Theorie', in: Frank Finlay / Ingo Cornils (eds), *(Un-)erfüllte Wirklichkeit. Neue Studien zu Uwe Timm* (Würzburg: Königshausen 2006), 55–71.

13 See Gerrit Bartels, 'Spürbares Bewegtsein', in: *die tageszeitung*, 17 September 2005.

14 Walter von der Vogelweide famously pondered the ethical/political question 'wie man zer welte solte leben' (how one should live in this world) in his *Reichston* (1198–1201).

15 The image, according to German news magazine *Der Spiegel*, has become 'an icon of the student protest'. It is part of the permanent exhibition in the German Historical Museum in Berlin.

A few days later I saw his picture in a magazine, and seeing him again like this came as a shock. He is lying on the street, his face, his hair, his hands, his long, thin arms and legs immediately recognisable. He is lying on the asphalt, dressed in khaki trousers, a long-sleeved shirt, his arm outstretched, his hand open and relaxed, his eyes closed, as if he was sleeping. Next to him kneels a young woman in a black dress or cape. The woman might have come from the opera, was my thought, perhaps a doctor. She looks up, as if she wants to ask something or give an instruction, and supports, in a gentle gesture, his head by the back of his neck. One can clearly see the blood on his head and on the ground. In this black-and-white it could have been a frame from the film *Orphee* by Cocteau, that was my first thought when I looked at the photograph, this transformation. It was one of his favourite films. (FF, 11/12)

Timm wanted to write about his friend at the time, but felt unable in his shock and anger to find the right words, with every sentence 'acquiring an aggressive, abstract tone – a tone that had never been his' (FF, 11). Almost forty years later, Timm has found that personal voice which reflects his friend's gentle personality and outlook:

> We, reading Jean-Paul Sartre in those days, were convinced that one – as paradoxi-cal as that may sound – is damned to be free, and yet this very freedom offered the choice to turn into someone different from what one had been turned into, and what one had made oneself into. (FF, 56)

The focus of their intense discussions about aesthetics, art, literature and a new way of thinking was Albert Camus's *L'Etranger*, which promoted an attitude that they vowed to adopt in their own lives: to shun conventions, and always to maintain an inner distance. However, it is exactly this pose of existentialist 'distance' which turned Timm into a stranger to his friend and prompted him not to go to University in West-Berlin with him but move to Munich and establish himself on his own. Forty years on, he realises that he may have made a mistake when he cut himself free of the friendship with Ohnesorg: '*The dead remind us of the things we failed to do, our mistakes, our wrongdoings. They are our ghosts.*' (FF, 78 italics in original)

This is not to say that Timm has become one of the many former activists who today distance themselves from their utopian ideals. In fact, he still maintains the necessity of the protest. But the movement, Timm suggests, didn't start as a collective uprising – it was based on the emotional response of individuals to events, on their aesthetic and moral revolt against the establishment. Following his personal *Erinnerungspfad* (memory path), Timm visits the woman on the picture, the *Engelsgestalt* (figure of an angel; FF, 119) who herself has become part of history. It was her act of kindness and solidarity, her human response to the inhuman act, that 'saved' the moment from turning into the ugly murder that it represented at face value. By giving the dying Ohnesorg his dignity, easing his parting, this woman has become an essential element of the moment.

Inevitably, the book turns into an essay on the significance and power of myths: of the ancient Orpheus myth or the modern myth of the 68ers, of which Timm's friend has become a significant part. For the death of Benno Ohnesorg has become a 'moment' in time: one that is invested with a special significance. For a minority it provided the excuse to form terrorist groups (e.g. *Bewegung 2. Juni*, or the Red Army Faction). For many it has become a key date to be commemorated. It is endlessly revisited by historians and novelists, and used by the media as shorthand for a generational narrative and experience. And yet, while Timm accords himself the role of Orpheus who can bring back the dead, he not only augments the myth, but also deconstructs it, reminding his readers that Benno Ohnesorg was a real person who became the unlikely hero in a struggle for a better world with better beings in it. By recalling the aesthetic aspirations and moral foundations of the movement, Timm recaptures its essence, and provides a corrective to its cultural memory.

A Sunday in the mountains

If Benno Ohnesorg's tragic death was the catalyst for the 'hot' phase of the German Student Movement, the attempted assassination of its ideological leader and figurehead Rudi Dutschke on 11 April 1968 marked the second tragic event of the German Student Movement, after which it lost its innocence and eventually collapsed. Violent protests followed

during the Easter weekend when tens of thousands of protesters in West
Germany congregated around the Springer publishing houses in West
Berlin, Hamburg and Munich, with thousands more protesting in every
major Western capital. The East-German songwriter Wolf Biermann put
it succinctly in his *Drei Kugeln auf Rudi Dutschke*: 'we know exactly who
pulled the trigger'.[16]

For months, Rudi Dutschke had been branded as 'Public Enemy No.1'
in the Springer Press. As with the assassination of Martin Luther King a
week before, there was a widespread feeling that the student leader had taken
the three bullets to the head on behalf of the whole movement. While he
struggled to regain his health and speech, the movement never recovered
from losing its charismatic spokesperson. He characteristically tried to
befriend his assassin, a dim-witted painter with nationalistic background
who had read too many sensationalist headlines. Rudi Dutschke died on
Christmas Eve 1979 as a direct consequence of the assassination attempt.
On the day of his funeral, Axel Springer's son committed suicide.[17]

Daniel de Roulet's autobiographical text *Ein Sonntag in den Bergen*[18]
carries a seemingly gentle dedication 'In memory of a woman I loved in
my youth (1948–2005)', but it turns out that this youthful lover provided
the motivation for a crime:

> On a beautiful Sunday during the Cold War, high up on a Swiss mountain, I set fire
> to Axel Caesar Springer's chalet. (SB 7)

De Roulet, a Swiss author who argues that 'the 60s never happened in
Switzerland' and who is well-known for his critical stance (his most out-
spoken text *Double* describes the perfidious Swiss 'Fichen' system of state

---

16   See my '"The Struggle Continues". Rudi Dutschke's Long March', in: Gerard J.
      DeGroot (ed.), *Student Protest. The Sixties and After* (London and New York:
      Longman, 1998), 100–114.
17   Gretchen Dutschke, *Wir hatten ein barbarisches, schönes Leben* (Köln: Kiepenheuer
      & Witsch 1996), 483.
18   Daniel de Roulet, *Ein Sonntag in den Bergen* (Zürich: Limnat Verlag 2006). Hereafter:
      SB. All translations my own.

surveillance), sets out to explain why he set fire to the chalet in January 1975, and what made him decide to confess his crime.

The trigger for his decision, according to de Roulet, was a throw-away comment by German chancellor Gerhard Schröder during a state visit to Switzerland in 2003, when he observed: 'I don't know if you experience this as well – every day I find myself fighting the very things that I supported as a young person.' (SB 7) As if sensing that such an admission of his generation's lack of integrity will not convince his readers, de Roulet supplies a second, personal reason for coming clean: his girlfriend and accomplice at the time recently died of cancer, and he now feels able to admit his responsibility and his mistake, for it is his realisation that he had been wrong about Springer which is the third reason for his confession. De Roulet believed, like so many young people outraged by the assassination attempt on Rudi Dutschke, that Axel Springer was ultimately responsible. He also (erroneously, he admits) believed that Springer was a Nazi, and that former Nazis and the rich should not be allowed to find refuge in his native country.

Rudi Dutschke, to the politically engaged intellectuals in Switzerland at the time, presented an exciting alternative to the conservative status quo: 'We liked what he wrote, his incisive analyses, and his promise of a different world' (SB 32). More importantly, his girlfriend declares: 'Yes, I like Rudi. Springer has really done him over badly' (SB, 32). This, apparently, was enough reason for de Roulet to set his plan into action. One Sunday morning, after a night of passionate sex at the Palace Hotel in Gstaad, they climb the mountain where Springer's chalet is situated and set fire to the empty property.

For years to come, the Swiss police would suspect the West-German Red Army Faction. De Roulet claims that their action was a matter of principle: 'We wanted to keep our country pure and white, wanted to sweep clean the mountains, so that the brown plague and foreign dictators would not be able to build their nests here.' (SB, 69) He argues that Springer had a choice; that he could have tried to understand the student revolt instead of leading the fight against them in his newspapers: 'You [Springer] could have prevented the assassination attempt on Dutschke.' (SB, 85)

There is little further justification for the arson attack, yet the action itself is given a kitschy literary glow: 'I was about to break the law, but the landscape spent itself in aloof splendour' (SB, 96); 'Taking action is not a simple thing. Then I thought about Rudi Dutschke and the bullet that threatened his life. Yes, I had a bone to pick with him over who was responsible for so many printed lies.' (SB, 99); 'all that was left of the snobbish building was a small heap of ash' (SB, 109); 'for two days and two nights, helicopters danced around the magic mountain' (SB, 110).

De Roulet does not explain what made him change his mind about Axel Springer – it may have been one of the recent biographies that re-evaluate the tycoon's policies in the light of the collapse of Communism and the fall of the Wall, or the realisation that instead of the Cold War, we now find ourselves in a very different kind of war which does not care about the enmities of the past. Nor did his 'labour of love' have a long-term impact: he and his girlfriend split up soon after that Sunday in the mountains. He leaves the reader speculating: why did Axel Springer's son commit suicide on the day of Rudi Dutschke's funeral? Did he want to atone for the deeds of his father or was he simply suffering from depression? Once again, de Roulet, the 'weekend terrorist', depends on hearsay.

Unsurprisingly, *Ein Sonntag in den Bergen* was strongly criticised for its 'vanity' and 'naivety',[19] but in the context of cultural memory production it is interesting to note that, just like Uwe Timm in France, Daniel de Roulet felt instinctively 'connected' to the tragic event happening elsewhere. His description of the ascent, the exhilaration felt during the anticipation and execution of the plan, his awareness of the mutually heightened sexual attraction, the experience of the unity of thought, action and feeling, all amount to a 'magic moment', something that a more gifted writer would not have needed to signpost with a reference to Thomas Mann's Swiss-set novel *Der Zauberberg* (The Magic Mountain, 1928).

19   Cp. WOZ No.10, 9 March 2006.

Rebellion and delusion

Peter Schneider, a well-known author, screenwriter and political essayist in the Berlin Republic, was a significant figure in the German Student Movement. Following an impressive showing with his rousing *Wir haben Fehler gemacht* (Yes, we made mistakes) speech on 5 May 1967 during a teach-in at the Audimax of the Free University of Berlin[20] and the production of a satirical 'Wanted for murder' poster on the occasion of the Shah of Persia's state visit to West-Berlin in June 1967, the young writer was chosen by none other than Rudi Dutschke himself to prepare the Anti-Springer campaign which included a country-wide debate[21] and was to culminate in a 'tribunal' in February 1968. The tribunal was a disaster, mainly because militant groups had attacked Springer outlets which meant that sympathetic liberals and intellectuals refused to support it. With the international Vietnam Conference taking place the same month, the activists had clearly reached their limits. Lovesick, disillusioned with sectarian infighting and shocked by the attempted assassination of Dutschke on 11 April, Schneider left West-Berlin that summer to go to Italy, first to stay with the recovering Dutschke, and then with rebellious students in Trento. His short narrative *Lenz* (1973), modelled on Georg Büchner's *Lenz*, is considered *the* iconic text of the German Student Movement. Focusing on the despair and confusion of a young activist following the disorientation and fragmentation of the movement into communist splinter groups, the book rang in a phase of introspection in German literature that became known as *Neue Innerlichkeit*.

Like Uwe Timm in *Rot* (2001), Schneider continues to reflect on the significance and long-term consequences of the German Student Movement in many of his works. Both are concerned that, after the collapse of Communism and post 9/11, the movement will go down in history mainly as the catalyst for the terrorism of the Red Army Faction – an

---

20   http://www.glasnost.de/hist/apo/fehler.html [accessed 11 November 2008]
21   Peter Schneider, 'Bild macht dumm', in: *Konkret* No.3, March 1968, 14–17.

interpretation suggested by Gerd Koenen's semi-autobiographical *Das rote Jahrzehnt* (2001) – and that its essence will be forgotten. As public figures, they are well aware that they are key players in Germany's continuing debate about who gets to interpret the era before it congeals into cultural memory.

With *Skylla* (2005), Schneider published a novel that showed a former 68er turned successful lawyer confronted with his past and the fatal consequences of his fiery speeches.[22] His 'autobiographical narrative' *Rebellion und Wahn* (2008)[23] sheds further light on his role in the movement, focussing on his life as writer, activist, and lover of a woman simply referred to as 'L.' who occupied his every thought and who eventually (though briefly) joined the terrorist organisation *Bewegung 2. Juni*. While one needs to remember that Schneider will be economical with the truth, one senses that he tries to be as open as possible, without giving in to the sensationalist press and neo-conservatives who are gleefully waiting for another former activist to renounce his former beliefs. Schneider doesn't go that far, at least at the start of *Rebellion und Wahn*, when he romanticises the 'historic moment':

> [...] I would not be fair to us and the general mood at the time in Berlin were I not to speak about the euphoria that, like an intoxicating wind, was blowing through the streets of Berlin in those months. Then everything seemed possible, especially the impossible – and we, carried by this wind, felt as if history itself had chosen us to build a new society according to new rules. It was an intoxication without drugs, an intoxication of a 'historically necessary' and 'scientifically founded' utopia which had taken control over our hearts and minds. (RW 11)

Like Timm, he remains adamant about the necessity of the movement at the time:

---

22   See my 'Literary Reflections on '68', in: Stuart Taberner (ed.), *Contemporary German Fiction. Writing in the Berlin Republic* (Cambridge: Cambridge University Press, 2007), 91–107.

23   Peter Schneider, *Rebellion und Wahn. Mein 68* (Köln: Kiepenheuer und Witsch, 2008). hereafter: RW. All translations my own.

> The most important achievement of the 68er movement in Germany remains that it broke the culture of obedience – massively, and perhaps forever. (RW 278)

And yet, by reading through his diaries of the time, Schneider can't help but feel a deep gulf opening up between his former self and his current self:

> The young man who talks to me through the diaries of those years is close to me and at the same time frighteningly strange. The political convictions of this stranger often seem ridiculous or forced; his intimate confessions [...] make me impatient. (RW 13/14)

Schneider admits that he was deluded, part of 'the specifically German delusion of a global revolution' (RW 278), which advocated violence to achieve its ends. In hindsight, and in striking similarity to Daniel de Roulet, he realises that he had turned himself into 'a frightening revolutionary' to impress his then girlfriend L. (RW 280/281). By turning the private into the political, his former self was following in an emotional mindset that had taken hold of many of the 68er generation.

What if?

It is understandable that writers like Timm, de Roulet and Schneider mourn the passing of their formative years and dreams, even if, in hindsight, they may be critical of their flirtation with violence. But their attempts to influence the current debate about the legacy of the German Student Movement are hampered by the very fact that they were part of the movement, and their attempts to fill the holes of our collective memory will necessarily also continue to feed the 'myth of 68'. While they can offer the reader a (limited) guarantee of authenticity, their sense of loss is a personal, not necessarily a collective one, unless the reader is already receptive to the aims and objectives of the German Student Movement. To the general reader, the intense ruminations over the accidental death of a student and the attempted assassination of another student do not automatically signify that the events have become part of German cultural memory. Paradoxically, it is the next generation of writers who hold the key to this process.

With his striking 'detective novel' *Das Magische Jahr* (The Magical Year, 2008),[24] the author Rob Alef, born in 1965, provides a satirical view of what might have happened had the 68ers won. In this alternative history, the revolution *has* happened, but the irony is that nothing much has changed. People continue to phone in to radio stations to request a dedication to their grandparents, only now they ask for the songs of the revolution. Everybody has a job, but only because the under-qualified are employed to act as human info booths, reeling off useless information to passers-by. Schoolchildren are brought in to theatres to learn about Marxist dialectics in a Punch and Judy show, and visit museums to study the history of the revolution. Like schoolchildren in the real world, they are bored by the attempts of their (equally bored) teachers to convey to them the significance of the 'historic events' that led to the revolution.

The peace and quiet of the fictional post-revolutionary Berlin is shattered when the internet dealer Prometheus Praumann is brutally murdered. Praumann, once a key member of the movement in this alternative universe and a close associate of the great student leader Richard Dubinski (similarities to real persons with the same initials are intentional), has turned his revolutionary past into a goldmine. He sources and sells 'historically important' memorabilia to keen collectors, for example Theodor Adorno's hole-puncher for €2,000 or Ulrike Meinhof's toothpick ('authenticity guaranteed').

In this alternative world, 'things had shifted, and everything had changed' (MJ 29) in 1968. The event that turned the tide was 'the battle for Tegeler's fleece', when the students won a major confrontation with the police and public opinion turned in their favour (in reality, the *Schlacht am Tegeler Weg* was the final convulsion of the German Student Movement). The other crucial difference to real events is that Dubinski was shot dead by an assassin. As a consequence, he is revered as a patriotic hero and martyr,

24   Rob Alef, *Das Magische Jahr* (Berlin: Rotbuch Verlag 2008), hereafter: MJ. All translations my own.

and every year there is an official victory celebration, when the fleece (nothing more than the seat warmer in a police car belonging to a police sergeant
called Karl-Heinz Tegeler) gets paraded around the streets of Berlin as
the 'birth certificate of our new community' (MJ 64). Only when three
further former members of the commune are killed does the investigating
detective realise that the murderer is looking for a photograph to prevent
a long-held secret becoming public: contrary to official history, Dubinski
had not been in Berlin on the decisive day, but, an avid fan, had travelled
to Hamburg to watch the Beatles play.

In the end, it doesn't really matter what happened forty years ago.
Different events may have altered the course of history, but, as Alef points
out right at the beginning, rivers will never flow upstream. The old order
may have been overthrown (MJ 139), but the world is the same. Of course,
the reader is in on the joke that the 68ers have had their day, that their
continuing attempts to define their legacy have led to a myriad of realities.
At times, Alef undercuts the alternative 'reality' by surreal and magical
elements: it is deep winter in June, the chief inspector collects snowflakes
that do not melt, prostitution is a public service (in the *Kamasu-Tram*),
there are daily organised demonstrations on the frozen Müggelsee (benefit
claimants get free skates and banners), and the inspector is rescued by a
group of *Schneenotrettungsdienst* (snow emergency rescue service) manned
by Penguins (MJ 203) who speak a Gaelic dialect and are exceedingly fond
of whiskey. Even the message of the novel, hidden in a sequence of letters
linked to each chapter and revealed at the end, is that DER SCHNEE VON
GESTERN IST DIE LAWINE VON MORGEN (yesterday's snow is tomor-
row's avalanche, MJ 319), a slogan profoundly uplifting for readers of a
revolutionary turn, and absolutely banal for everyone else.

Utopian moments as 'lieux de memoire'

So what are we to make of the recent texts about the German '1968'? Has time healed the wounds, can cultural memory be created out of the experience of conflicting magic and tragic moments? The first thing that the analysis has shown is that in recent German literature the key events of the German Student Movement are generally remembered more sombrely, and in the context of recent debates about the 'war on terror'. Indeed, conservative critics have argued that the West cannot stand united against Islamic extremist violence while condoning violence at home (even if it occurred 40 years ago) as a means of effecting change. We can also note that as the former activists turned writers get older, they find the courage to ask different, more difficult and personal questions. The tragic shootings and the collective sense that history may have turned out differently if these had not happened have turned Benno Ohnesorg and Rudi Dutschke into mythical figures. They have become *Widergänger* (ghosts) that continue to haunt the 68ers and with them the rest of German society.

Michael Stolzke has pointed out that *Der Freund und der Fremde* depends on personal recollections, but goes beyond them by describing the collective experience and the effect of the murder on a generation[25] when Timm concludes: 'He has moved things a lot – as a victim.' (FF 117) The passage continues:

> These are images that sink into our consciousness. They demonstrate a highly condensed situation that speaks for itself and thus emotionally charge rational insights and appeal to our own ability to act. They represent a powerful blow that does not require constant rational renewal but has long-term impact: You have to change. You have to do something. (FF 117)

I would argue that by investing the dead with a potential that can still lead to action, Timm is balancing the tragic moment (a similar case could be

25   Michael Stolzke, 'Generation 1967: ein Nekrologium', 19 February 2007, http:// www.einseitig.info/html/content.php?txtid=548 [accessed 26 March 2008]

made for the film student / terrorist Holger Meins),[26] with the life-affirming utopian anticipation that preceded it. Writing about 'their' 1968 is a delicate undertaking for Timm, de Roulet and Schneider. It means going head to head with one's former self – a literary device recently employed to dubious results by the German writer Günter Grass in his autobiographical text *Beim Häuten der Zwiebel* (2006; transl. *Peeling the Onion* 2007)[27]. The rebellious self in these writers wishes to romanticise the events and feelings of their youth, while the older, wiser self queries the validity of the motivation and exuberance and describes this state of mind as 'delusion'. It is at this point that a younger generation of writers begins to question the dominant narrative, to poke fun at the 68ers fascination with their own history. Rob Alef's satirical novel *Das Magische Jahr* has provided a much-needed antidote to collective self-delusion.

'1968' is slowly becoming part of cultural memory in Germany, but we are still not sure what place it will eventually occupy. '1968' has been included in and allocated a 'place of memory' (Erinnerungsort) in the German equivalent to Pierre Nora's *Les lieux de memoire*.[28] Within this *Erinnerungsort*, the figures of Benno Ohnesorg, the innocent bystander, and Rudi Dutschke, the charismatic student leader, stand out. The historian Wolfgang Kraushaar has described the shots on them as 'unforeseen dynamics' that have changed the trajectory, character and impact of the movement.[29]

The texts discussed in this paper personalise a collective experience and give the reader a helpful insight into the mindset of German 68ers that is missing from the many histories of '1968'. The tragic moments surround-

---

26 See Carrie Collenberg, 'Dead Holger. On an Iconic Image and its Legacy', in: Gerrit-Jan Berendse / Ingo Cornils (eds), *Baader-Meinhof Returns. The History and Cultural Memory of German Left-Wing Terrorism* (Amsterdam / New York: rodopi, 2008), 65–81.

27 See Stuart Taberner, *The Cambridge Companion to Günter Grass* (Cambridge: CUP 2009), 1–2, 139–150.

28 Heinz Bude, 'Achtundsechzig', in: Etienne Francois / Hagen Schulze (eds), *Deutsche Erinnerungsorte* Band 2 (München: C.H. Beck, 2001), 122–134.

29 W. Kraushaar, *Achtundsechzig. Eine Bilanz*, 156.

ing Benno Ohnesorg and Rudi Dutschke are revisited as magic moments, the Holy Grail (even in Rob Alef's pythonesque parody) of the German Student Movement. As far as their utopian dream of an alternative reality is concerned, it lives on because these writers refuse to let it die.

IRENE FENOGLIO-LIMÓN

Reading Mexico 1968:
Literature, Memory and Politics

1. Mexico 1968 and memory

On the fortieth anniversary of the student movement of 1968 in Mexico, several political and cultural activities were organised in Mexico City to commemorate the event. The leftist newspaper *La Jornada*, for example, published a series of articles on important dates of the movement.[1] Meanwhile, the Memorial del 68, a museum inaugurated in October 2007 and dedicated to preserving the memory of 1968, held a series of cultural activities that ranged from public conferences by former leaders of the movement, writers and academics, to radio programmes, movies, music concerts, and dance shows. Several periodical publications issued special numbers dedicated to commemoration and analysis of 1968 (a case in point is the special issue of the weekly *Proceso*).[2] Standard works dealing with this emblematic event of Mexico's recent history were reprinted. During September and October 2008, the walls of the Facultad de Filosofía y Letras of the UNAM – the National University – were replete with posters narrating the history of the movement and inviting the public to a wide range of activities, from conferences to political meetings and demonstrations. As was the case in previous decades, several marches took place to commemorate the killing of civilians in the Plaza de las Tres Culturas in

---

1   *La Jornada* dedicated a section, 'A 40 años', to remembering and recounting especially significant dates in the history of the student movement.
2   'Tlatelolco 68, la impunidad', *Proceso*, special ed., Oct. 23, 2008.

Tlatelolco on October 2 of that year. These are only a few instances that show that the memory of 1968 is still active in Mexico.

There is little doubt that the student movement and its sequels – which still have effects in the present – profoundly marked Mexican society. Today, 1968 is generally invoked as the beginning of a new political and psychological crisis among the Mexican public that led to the emergence of democracy in the country, since it made evident the huge rift between the government's rhetoric of political modernisation and the actual stagnation of State institutions. At the time, this meant breaking away from the PRI (Institutional Revolutionary Party) government, which was held to be a direct heir of the foundational Mexican Revolution. But also, for a whole generation 1968 represents a time of thwarted possibility, a wasted conjuncture in which changes might have been brought about but were cut short by repression. Although 1968 is remembered as a traumatic period during which the government revealed its authoritarian nature, it has also served as a point of cohesion for many discourses of resistance, including political, cultural, social, and artistic ones, among others. Many words and images have been dedicated to this event: films, speeches, documentaries, essays, newspaper and magazine articles, academic studies, novels, poems, memoirs, short stories, testimonies ... the list is long and diverse. It is evident, then, that the memory of the student movement is part of the social, cultural and political imaginary of the country.

Over the years, the movement of 1968 has been construed in such a way in the social imaginary that it has come to symbolise much more than what it is in itself. It has become a symbol of resistance and a historic origin of modern democratic struggles. In general, it is a signifier onto which diverse kinds of social and political representations and demands have been grafted. One reading of the movement sees as one of its gains the democratic turn that allowed, for example, the ousting of the PRI from government in 2000 after decades of party dictatorship. On the other hand, this signifier has condensed, symbolised or represented a series of unresolved demands by different social organisations in the country. The 'failure' of the student movement is usually linked not only to the armed struggle that took place in Mexico during the first half of the 1970s, but also, in a way, to the formation of the Zapatista Army of National Liberation in Chiapas in the

1980s and its public appearance in 1994. So when demonstrators marched in 2008 from the Plaza de las Tres Culturas crying 'el 2 de octubre no se olvida' ['October 2 is not forgotten'], the appeal to maintain the memory of 1968 meant not just that literally, but protesters also voiced a general demand for justice.[3]

Paco Ignacio Taibo II, one of the major writers about 1968, said recently referring to that phrase that condenses the memory of the tragedy at Tlatelolco: 'The words "October 2 is not forgotten" have been socialised, they are national heritage ... "68 is not forgotten" is the heritage of those Mexicans who have turned memory – whether true or false, one's own or borrowed – into a source of pride to support and maintain resistance'.[4] This quote condenses two relevant themes that are central to my argument. The first is the idea that the memory of 1968 belongs – or is the responsibility of – not only the people who, forty years ago, participated in the movement and who were directly or indirectly implicated in it, but that it belongs to the whole nation, who have inherited 68 not only as a historical event but also as a political responsibility. The second theme is the clear link established between memory and resistance. I will be touching upon both these ideas below.

This chapter is located within the discursive space opened by the idea that the unofficial, collective memory of 1968 – especially literary memory – has been a condition of possibility for leftist politics in Mexico, supplying it with an origin of failure and therefore of possibility, a counter-history, and the imaginary of a viable democratic nation. Specifically, I want to

3   An example of this are the marches held in 2008, where the commemoration of October 2 was joined by several resistance organisations. Their demands for social and political justice are easily likened to the ones of the students in 1968 in so far as they all sought, in general terms, that government repression against social movements stops. For an account of the organisations that joined the march, see G. Castillo, M. Norandi and E. Olivares, 'Castigo a los responsables del 2 de octubre, clamor popular', *La Jornada* Oct. 3, 2008, retrieved Oct. 9, 2008, <http://www.jornada.unam. mx/2008/10/03/index.php?section=politica&article=008n1pol>.
4   P.I. Taibo II, 'Casi 40 años y no se olvida', *La Jornada* Oct. 2, 2007, retrieved Sept. 14, 2008, <http://www.jornada.unam.mx/2007/10/02/nota1.php>.

talk about the ways in which literature has constituted itself as a 'para-historical' narrative of the events of 1968 in Mexico.[5] My objective is to ponder two related questions, without necessarily offering an answer: What is the role of literature in constructing our social and cultural imaginary of the student movement? What is the potential of the memory of 1968 as a source of opposition to power, as a foundational imaginary for a real political movement towards justice and equality in Mexico?

It is important to spell out, first, that in this chapter the limits of the word 'literature' are necessarily more open than the orthodox understanding of the term. Thus, my definition seeks to be much more inclusive and 'democratic' by incorporating any text from any genre, which is written with aesthetic intention, strategy or effect. Thus, when I use the word 'literature' I will refer not only to traditional genres such as the novel, poetry, and drama, but also to those two very contested hybrid ones, *testimonio* and the chronicle.[6]

It is also pertinent to clarify the rationale for choosing the texts that will be dealt with here. In the first part of the study I will address works written shortly after the Tlatelolco massacre, texts written between 1968 and

5   I will be using the term 'para-historical' without much rigor to refer to accounts of the movement and its sequels which are not strictly historical in a disciplinary sense (such as a history textbook or an academic article by a historian would be). Thus, hybrid genres such as *testimonios* and chronicles, or testimonial works in general, would fall within this category. Literary texts are 'para-historical' narratives in so far as they construe or account for the movement and its repression.

6   Here I will understand the term 'testimonio' in line with John Beverley's definition: 'By testimonio I mean a novel or novella-length narrative in book or pamphlet (that is, printed as opposed to acoustic form), told in the first person by a narrator who is also the real protagonist or witness of the events he or she recounts, and whose unit of narration is usually a "life" or a significant life experience' (J. Beverley, *Testimonio. On the Politics of Truth* [Minneapolis and London: University of Minnesota Press, 2004], 30–31). John Beverley's discussion of the *testimonio* goes far beyond a simple definition of the genre. Among other things, for example, he argues that this kind of 'postfictional form of literature' questions the canonical Western understanding of literature itself.

1973,[7] which have circulated widely enough to help define that discursive formation we refer to as '1968'. These are authoritative texts that construe a memory of 1968 that undermines the version of events imposed by the government and that have produced, as I will argue here, a number of themes regarding this period that have been incorporated in the social imaginary. The second part of this study deals with two novels published more recently, *La guerra de Galio* (1988) and *El fin de la locura* (2003), which offer a revisionist reading of the student movement which, by contrast with the first group of text studied here, disables the possibility of any leftist opposition in Mexico.

2. The student movement and its sequels

The movement of 1968 in Mexico, although similar in many ways to other student movements, was quite different from what happened in countries such as France or the United States. Luis González de Alba, for example, deliberately makes a point in discussing this difference in his novel *Los días y los años* (1971), where he fictionalises a dialogue between the narrator (himself), Roberto Escudero, and a couple of German activists. One of the latter declares:

> There is a huge difference between the demands made by the Mexican students and the ones upheld in other countries. We cannot understand that you defend the Constitution. In Germany we are not struggling to defend our Constitution, but rather to do away with it. The same thing happens in France and Italy, where students reject their regimes and the laws that support them.[8]

---

7   The only exception to the five-year period I mention is Paco Ignacio Taibo II's essay *68*, which was first published in 1988 as *Fantasmas nuestros de cada día*. The book *68* is a longer version of that essay and was published by Planeta in 1991. A second, updated version was published in 2008. Notwithstanding the period difference with the other works, *68* shares the same spirit and demands.

8   L. González de Alba, *Los días y los años*, rev. ed. (Mexico: Planeta, 2008 [1971]), 42.

The difference is reaffirmed in the dialogue by the narrator when he explains what the Mexican students are struggling to change in contrast to what other students were doing elsewhere:

> I agree with you that ... the students' demands in other countries are very different and apparently much more radical. On the contrary, ours are purely reformist demands [democratic freedom and respect for the Constitution]. The truth is that in our country such demands are deemed not only very progressive but moreover openly revolutionary with regards to their consequences.[9]

On the other hand, as Paco Ignacio Taibo II has noted, the difference between remembering 1968 in Mexico and in other countries has to do with the fact that what is usually commemorated in the former are not the potential *successes* of the movement but its *failures*.[10] Although some Mexican writers have made an effort to draw attention to the creative, powerful and enabling force of the movement itself, to a large extent the memory of 1968 is defined by the repression of civilians and by the death of a yet undisclosed or unknown number of civilians in Tlatelolco.[11] In a way, as I claim here, this *failure* has been a condition of possibility not only of the memory work woven around 1968 (again, 'October 2 is not forgotten'), but also of the leftist political engagement it mobilises. Much like the figure of the ghost coming back to haunt the disjointed site of our

9   González de Alba, 43.
10   P.I. Taibo II, 'Casi 40 años y no se olvida'.
11   After military, police, and intelligence documents related to Tlatelolco were unclassified in 2002, Kate Doyle and *Archivos Abiertos* undertook an investigation in order to determine the number and identity of the dead on October 2 1968. In her report, Doyle explains that, despite the fact that such documents had been officially released, an accurate count and account of the dead was impossible due, mainly, to the strategic material inaccessibility of the archives. The conclusion of the investigation is the following: 'To date, we have found records confirming the deaths of 44 men and women in the archives of the dirty war. Thirty-four of the victims are identified by name. Ten more people are listed as "unknown"'. (K. Doyle, 'The Dead of Tlatelolco', IRC Americas Program, International Relations Center, Silver City, NM, Oct 13, 2006, p. 4, retrieved Oct. 10, 2008, <http://americas.irc-online.org/am/3600>.

present, the memory of 1968 haunts the Mexican political scene demanding a solution to the unresolved exigencies upheld by the movement.

The student movement in Mexico cohered around a series of demands that defended fundamental political rights contained in the Constitution, most notoriously addressing the fact that there was a repressive apparatus at work which suppressed the students' rights to dissent.[12] While the students protested in order to open more spaces of democratic participation, the government ignored their demands and responded viciously against them, breaking up demonstrations, public meetings and marches, and, notably, invading university campuses, thus violating the principle of autonomy of Mexican public universities. Many people were hurt, killed or incarcerated during these months. The repressive response of the government is usually linked with its paranoid reading of events,[13] which was catalyzed by two contextual circumstances: the Olympic Games, scheduled to take place in Mexico on October 12, and, in a larger and more profound way, the Cold War.

The violence against the students reached its peak on October 2, when a massive rally in the Plaza de las Tres Culturas, in Tlatelolco, was brutally repressed. There have been conflicting versions of the bloody events of that evening, since the account published in most newspapers the following day and the reports from witnesses contradict each other in significant ways. Moreover, the number of acknowledged deaths varied significantly: the official tally admitted fewer than a dozen, while other, unofficial versions mentioned around 300 casualties. Forty years after the massacre, the events of that night have not yet been fully explained, the exact number of deaths is unknown, and responsibility for the fatal repression has not been adjudicated.

Despite the façade of normality that ensued, hundreds of people linked to the movement were incarcerated. The repressive environment against

---

12 For an account of the student movement and the context in which it took place, see Claire Brewster's chapter earlier in this volume.

13 C. Monsiváis in J. Scherer and C. Monsiváis, eds. *Parte de guerra II. Los rostros del 68* (Mexico: Aguilar and UNAM, 2002), 154.

dissidents and critics of the political *status quo* continued. This was so much so that the first student demonstration taking place after Tlatelolco – a few years afterwards, on 10 June 1971 – was also brutally repressed by the government in turn and scores of people were killed.

To this day officials have systematically kept information surrounding the movement either a secret or virtually inaccessible. Because successive administrations have kept silent about this – and moreover, because, as recent investigations have shown, some of the officials directly responsible for the repression have since then occupied high government ranks – the truth about what happened during the student movement, and especially in Tlatelolco on October 2 1968, has only very recently and very slowly been made public, despite, for example, the creation of *ad hoc* truth commissions which have achieved very little in this respect.

3. Literature and the quest for historical truth

A clear discursive regularity found in the statements about Mexico 1968 was – and in some respects still is – the search for the *truth* of what took place during the student movement and, especially, on October 2, all of which is directly related to a demand for justice. With rare exceptions, from the beginning the ideological state apparatuses (especially the media) were complicit with the regime's attempts at slandering the movement and, later, at erasing all traces of its repression by obscuring figures and facts. In the aftermath of October 2, virtually all major newspapers aligned themselves with the version of the State, according to which, at Tlatelolco, clashes had erupted between the military and 'terrorists' or, alternatively, that the military had protected the unsuspecting population from cross-fire between snipers and soldiers.[14] To this day, the quest to determine once and for all

---

14   J. Volpi, *La imaginación y el poder* (Mexico: Era, 1998), 327–332; E. Poniatowska, *La noche de Tlatelolco*, rev. ed. (Mexico: Era, 2002 [1971]), 164–166.

the number of casualties and to elucidate the crimes committed in order to punish those responsible has served to keep the memory of 1968 alive.

Notwithstanding this lack of facts and the official denial of responsibility, as well as the actual hindrance of access to public documents, from the beginning testimonies, images and narrations of all kinds from witnesses and participants have challenged the official version – and the official silence – surrounding the events. They have constituted the documental sources for the reconstruction of the student movement.

The main premise of my argument, then, is that, because of its nature and potential repercussions, there is no *official* historical account of the student movement or of its sequels which could be accepted as legitimate, and that, therefore, the history of the movement and its repression has to a large degree been produced by and through 'para-historical narrations'. Thus literature, as a sort of counter-memory, is closely interwoven in the existing social imaginary of 68, precluding the obliteration of the memory of these events.[15] In other words, fiction, which has produced a collective memory of the student movement, has taken the place of official history as an authorised discourse.

Here I would like to invoke Pierre Nora's notion of the 'event' to support the idea that the literature about the student movement, especially because of the specific conditions in which it emerged, 'eventalised' 1968.[16] By using this term I am referring to the process by which an event becomes meaningful or important – an idea that, in this case, is linked to underscoring that of keeping the memory of the injustice alive – by representing it or reinterpreting it in an authorised and valued medium (the printed text). But, moreover, I use the term in relation to the fact that, because of the way in which it has been reconstructed, the history – or, to

15   See, for example, Gonzalo Martré's introduction to his anthology *El movimiento popular estudiantil de 1968 en la novela mexicana* (Mexico: UNAM, 1998), where he states that the memory of 68 would have already faded 'had it not been for the literature produced from right after the events occurred all the way to the present' (9).

16   P. Nora, 'La vuelta del acontecimiento', *Hacer la historia. Vol. III. Objetos nuevos*, J. Le Goff and P. Nora, dir. (Barcelona: Editorial Laia, 1980), 221–239.

put it another way, the *historical imagination* – of the student movement is to a large extent determined by the way in which these fictional accounts have produced it. The literary works that have been sources of truth about 1968 have challenged the relation between literature and the representation of reality due to their hybrid narrative techniques, both questioning the dividing line between historic and fictional narratives, and establishing new and productive connections between them. With regard to this specific point, I contend that the events of 1968 gave rise – taking up Michel Foucault – to an 'insurrection of subjugated knowledges'[17] not only in the sense that what was brought to light were events and perspectives altogether marginalised or erased by the official account, but also because non-orthodox forms of historical narration, such as *testimonios* and chronicles, emerged as alternative and, to a certain extent, *legitimate* accounts of the past. *Los días y los años*, *Días de guardar*, and *La noche de Tlatelolco* are among such works.[18]

Los días y los años (1971) is a testimonial novel by Luis González de Alba, a former student leader from the Facultad de Filosofía y Letras of the UNAM. This text was written while the author was in jail for participating in the student movement. The work is relevant because of its testimonial nature and because it was published shortly after the events it describes. Although created with a clear literary intention – that is, under the assumption that it *is* a work of fiction – it records with minute detail, from an insider's perspective, the organisation and development of the movement

17   In the sense of Foucault's second definition of subjugated knowledges offered in the first of his 'Two Lectures': 'a whole set of knowledges that have been disqualified as inadequate to their task or insufficiently elaborated: naive knowledges, located low down on the hierarchy, beneath the required level of cognition or scientificity'. They are, thus, 'disqualified, popular knowledge'. (M. Foucault, *Power/Knowledge. Selected Interviews and Other Writings. 1972–1977*, ed. Colin Gordon, trans. Colin Gordon *et al* [New York: Pantheon, 1980], 82, 83.)

18   L. González de Alba, *Los días y los años*, rev. ed. (Mexico: Planeta, 2008 [1971]); C. Monsiváis, *Días de guardar* (Mexico: Era, 2006 [1970]); E. Poniatowska, *La noche de Tlatelolco*, rev. ed (Mexico: Era, 2002 [1971]).

as well as the time the author served in the Lecumberri prison. Although the sole author of the novel, González de Alba takes great care to include in the plot the fact that the book was originally a common project between several student leaders serving time and that the information that the novel reveals was at least double-checked with other direct participants.[19] This novel has usually been considered an important source in the reconstruction of the history of the student movement, the events at Tlatelolco and the illegal imprisonment of dissenters in Lecumberri.

In 1970, Carlos Monsiváis published *Días de guardar*, a collection of chronicles from the year 1968. His account of the movement and of Tlatelolco is notable because, through the use of literary strategies, it incorporates not only an objective rendering of events but also the subjective perspective and the spontaneity of the experience of *being there*. Moreover, it mobilises a polyphonic form of narrative which accounts for the diverse actors who participated in the movement. Monsiváis succeeds both in making the chronicle an authorised narration of the events of 68, and in innovating the genre, usually considered minor because of its hybrid nature (since it is neither a strictly historical account nor a purely literary story).

A third work of utmost importance as a source of memory is Elena Poniatowska's *La noche de Tlatelolco*, published in 1971, which is an experimental collage of fragments of voices from people that experienced the event in one way or another. The first part of the book deals with the student movement itself, while the second is dedicated to the massacre of October 2. The relevance of this text is that it incorporates hybrid

---

19   See, for example, the following paragraph: 'I spent a while in my cell reading some notes on the events of September 1968 ... I was missing some information and there was no way that I could get it anytime soon ... We had thought about the possibility of writing a joint account among several of us in order to recover the experience of 1968 as it was lived from within' (González de Alba, 26). Later on he narrates that he was working on this project with at least Gilberto Guevara and Raúl Álvarez, two of the most renowned student leaders (González de Alba, 26, 28). He also talks about this in 'Morir sin conocer el mar Egeo', in *Pensar el 68* (Mexico: Cal y Arena, 1988), 209–213.

narrative strategies from different disciplinary genres (literature, history, journalism) in order to narrate the movement from diverse perspectives, thus producing an inter-subjective and polygonal discourse intimately linked to a more democratic sense of historical accuracy. In *La noche de Tlatelolco* we can hear the voices of different sectors of society (included the President, the police and the media, as well as the students, the parents, and intellectuals) referring to the same events. The value of the work as a source of truth resides not only in its textual content, but also in the set of photographs that precede it, which provide a visual correlate of what happened during those months. This work, then, constitutes a written oral and visual reconstruction of the student movement. *La noche de Tlatelolco* is a truly courageous book that challenged the univocal version sustained by the Mexican government.[20]

Because of the emphasis placed on their referential nature, these works have had a notable influence on the construction of the memory of Mexico 68, since they have been read as sources of factuality. Also, because they are literary texts which work on the basis of narrative strategies, they are well accepted and circulate widely, thus impinging on the way 1968 is read and understood. The first edition of *La noche de Tlatelolco*, for example, was reprinted on 55 occasions; the second, revised edition had been reprinted five times by 2002. These figures reflect the wide acceptance of the book by Spanish-speaking readers. However, the book has been translated into several languages and has circulated enormously in different countries.

---

20   The accuracy of *La noche de Tlatelolco* was questioned in 1997 by Luis González de Alba, who accused Poniatowska of plagiarism of his own work and of distorting passages of it. Poniatowska had to modify the content of several lines of the book, so she had to prepare a second, revised edition.

4. 1968: Literature and Justice

Although the existence of a genre or subgenre called '1968 literature' could hardly be sustained in the Mexican case, it is true that the event has opened up a discursive space that has operated as a continuous literary and cultural reference for decades. In what follows, I will examine a few themes present in this literature which articulate, in my opinion, the injunction for truth and justice that I explained above, and which ultimately constitute an exigency of/for political engagement.[21]

One theme that is recurrently stressed in much of the literature written within a few years after the events of 1968 is the idea that the historical account of it is incomplete and inadequate because, among other things, as we have seen, the official version is intentionally false and misleading, and because the body count of Tlatelolco has not been established. Haunted by the question of numbers, of who counts, and what really counts, literature itself has assumed the responsibility of telling the real and truthful history of the student movement. This is especially relevant in relation to the cultural and social imaginary obsession with keeping alive not only the memory of the violence and the injustice of the attacks on innocent victims who were struggling to articulate a new kind of democracy, but also the government's attempt at erasing all traces of the viciousness with which it responded. Octavio Paz,[22] for example, in his famous poem 'México:

---

21   The theme of 1968 has been treated in several literary works of different genres, of which only a small fraction are commented here. My intention is not quantitative but qualitative: to show how literature articulates certain images around 1968. For other literary works dealing with this theme, see D. Young, 'Mexican Literary Reactions to Tlatelolco 1968', *Latin American Research Review* 20.2 (1985), 71–85; M.A. Campos and A. Toledo, comps., *Poemas y narraciones sobre el movimiento estudiantil de 1968* (Mexico: UNAM, 1998); G. Martré, *El movimiento popular estudiantil de 1968 en la novela mexicana* (Mexico: UNAM, 1998).

22   Octavio Paz was critical of the student movement. As he expressed in his 'Postdata' to *El laberinto de la soledad*, he thought that 'their criticisms are real, their actions are unreal. Their criticisms hit the nail on the head but their actions cannot change society' (O. Paz, *El laberinto de la soledad*, ed. Enrico Mario Santí, 9th ed. [Madrid:

Olimpiada 1968' – the very first literary manifestation against the fatal events of 1968, written to protest against the government's repression of students and sent as a refusal to participate, as was scheduled, in the Cultural Olympiad – emphasises the erasure of evidence from the Plaza de las Tres Culturas on the dawn of October 3: 'Municipal employees / clean the bloodshed / in the Plaza of Sacrifices'.[23] Also stressed in other poems is the government's programmatic effort to keep the facts of the massacre secret. Rosario Castellanos, in 'Memorial de Tlatelolco', writes: 'Who? Nobody. The following day, nobody ... Do not look for what there is not: traces, bodies ... Do not dig in the archives since there is nothing on record'.[24] One last example is Paco Ignacio Taibo's essay *68*, where he asks: 'Where did they dump our dead ones? Where did they drop our dead ones? Where the fuck did they dump our dead ones?'[25] As can be observed in these instances, through the very gesture of denouncement, then, literature posits itself as an authorised enunciation against the officially falsified account of events.

Despite the ethical responsibility and the post-traumatic need to write about Tlatelolco evinced in many of these writings, there is, too, an awareness of the paradoxical impossibility implied in the task. This theme can be observed in the aforementioned poem by Paz, which undoubtedly inaugurated the tone of much of the literature about 1968 written afterwards. This poem expresses the tension rising between the *responsibility* of literature to register the event so as to dispute the untruthful versions spread in the media and buttressed by the government, and the intrinsic *inadequacy* of

---

Cátedra, 2002], 371). Although Paz's political posture at the time of the movement can be considered far from leftist, the fact that he renounced his post as ambassador to India and that he was the first – and one of the very few – government employees to publicly declare his condemnation of Tlatelolco have traditionally been seen as courageous acts in defense of democratic values. For a discussion of this refer to Claire Brewster's chapter earlier in this volume.

23   O. Paz, 'México: Olimpiada de 1968', *Ladera este* (México: Joaquín Mortiz, 1970), l. 17–19.

24   R. Castellanos, 'Memorial de Tlatelolco', in Poniatowska, 163–164, l. 13, 22, 25.

25   P.I. Taibo II, *68* (Mexico: Planeta, 1991), 13.

literature to satisfactorily complete the task. Paz writes: 'The untaintedness / (it is probably worth it / to write it on / the whiteness of this page) / is not untainted)'.[26] As it is expressed in this poem, writing on the cleanliness of the white page is an act of ignominy, since it has already been marred; the page is always already stained by the bloodshed in Tlatelolco. The whiteness of the paper is as spurious and equivocal as the cleanliness of the Plaza on the aftermath of the massacre. By *writing* about Tlatelolco, Paz cancels the possibility of the very act so that it becomes a mere *gesture*. Or rather, the poem itself 'poetises' the deadlock of accounting for the massacre: despite its obligation to write about it, to register the horror of it, poetry cannot fulfill its mission since writing indeed risks hiding or misrepresenting the event itself: 'Look now, / tarnished / before having said anything / worthwhile, / the untaintedness'.[27] According to this poem, then, all literature written after 1968 is marked by the unaccounted-for violence of the massacre. Writing thus becomes an act haunted by a specter that precedes it. The issue that arises is how literature may come to terms with the events of 1968 without 'aestheticizing' death and violence, and 'anesthetizing' all future efforts to struggle against injustice or loss.

Another recurrent theme expressed or implied in many of these writings is how the memory of the student movement – especially the memory of Tlatelolco – should influence our personal and political responsibility in the present. One possible answer is that this event should not simply find its proper, pacified place in the nation's historical archive, nor should the past be recovered, following Santayana, to ensure that the same atrocities will not happen again. Jaime Sabines, for example, writes in his poem 'Tlatelolco, 68': 'Tlatelolco will be mentioned in the years to come in the same way we now talk about Río Blanco y Cananea'.[28] By referring to these two moments in Mexican history where, as in Tlatelolco, the government illegally and fatally acted against citizens, Sabines marks a regularity that links the Mexican Revolution and the student movement,

26   Paz, 'México: Olimpiada de 1968', l. 1–5.
27   Paz, 'México: Olimpiada de 1968', l. 20–24.
28   J. Sabines, *Recuento de poemas. 1950/1993* (Mexico: Booket, 2007), 229–231, l. 7–8.

helping to construct a reading that is common in various interpretations of the latter, where the occurrence of 1968 is explained as the result of an unsolved excess or remainder of the Mexican Revolution.[29] Moreover, if we stretch this idea a little further, we can also find a thread that would take us all the way from the Mexican Revolution to the Zapatista rebellion in Chiapas. Thus, 1968 is integrated within the same unresolved demand for justice that has traversed the history of modern Mexico.

Another part of the answer to this question refers to our responsibility to make sure, in line with Tzvetan Todorov's assertion,[30] that the memory of the wrongs of 1968 be not misused in order to make a 'legitimate' use of violence in the present. This theme has been uncomfortably explored by Gerardo de la Torre in the short story 'El vengador' (The avenger), in which a politicised and frustrated worker of the oil industry who supported the student movement justifies his sexual assaults on young, beautiful, higher-class girls as a form of revenge: 'I am convinced now, we have to fight from within. From within the vagina ... I was accomplishing a mission.'[31] This story problematises the possibility of perpetuating violence as a way of dealing with social resentment and political frustration.

There are two literary images that condense a demand for oppositional engagement as an answer to the question of what to do with the memory of 1968 in the present: the specter and the tree. The specter appears, through a double rhetorical operation (a metaphor and a metonymy), linked to the unaccounted-for deaths of Tlatelolco and to an unremitting demand for justice.[32] A paradigmatic construction of this figure is found in Paco Ignacio Taibo's essay *68*, in which the ghost is a melancholic apparition that is regularly conjured up by a nostalgic generation as a source of strength

29   See, for example, H. Aguilar Camín and L. Meyer, *A la sombra de la Revolución mexicana* (Mexico: Cal y Arena, 1989).

30   See T. Todorov, *Los abusos de la memoria* (Barcelona: Paidós, 2000).

31   G. de la Torre, 'El vengador', in *Poemas y narraciones sobre el movimiento estudiantil de 1968*, M.A. Campos and A. Toledo, comps. (Mexico: UNAM, 1998), 267.

32   For a deeply political and enabling reading of the ghost in relation to Mexico 1968, see B. Bosteels, 'Travesías del fantasma: Pequeña metapolítica del 68 en México', *Metapolítica* 3.12 (1999): 733–768.

that feeds resistance in the present. Taibo says: 'then I discover that we seem to be condemned to be ghosts of 68',[33] and he adds: '68 ... produced enough epic gasoline to feed twenty years of resistance'.[34] Moreover, Taibo construes this specter as a responsibility that is handed down from one generation to the next. In this book, as in Paz's poem invoked above, writing about the movement of 1968 always emerges from a failure to account for and give an account of the event. However, this inheritance implies a political demand, an ethical duty to write which goes beyond the personal wish to save memory, since, as he concludes, 'there are love relations that last enough even for those who were not involved in them'.[35]

On the other hand, in the Sabines poem cited above, the poet writes, referring to the obliteration of evidence from the Plaza de las Tres Culturas: 'One would have to wash not only the ground: also memory ... But blood takes root / and grows through time like a tree'.[36] Here, the blood of the dead of Tlatelolco nurtures a metaphorical tree that should, just as memory should, extend its branches into the present. A comparable metaphorical tree appears in one of Subcomandante Marcos's texts, where he writes: 'memory is not a date that marks the beginning of an absence, it is rather a tree that was planted in the past and that rises towards the future'.[37]

In these instances, the appeal to memory involves a political responsibility to not forget the social injustices that traverse Mexican contemporary history. As I have tried to show in my reading of these texts, the literary memory of 1968 has in general underscored the relevance of reading the past in a way that enables political action in the present.

33   Taibo, *68*, 116.
34   Taibo, *68*, 10.
35   Taibo, *68*, 15.
36   Sabines, l. 29, 33–34.
37   The quoted words by this rebel-intellectual of contemporary Mexico and spokesman for the Zapatista Army – a movement whose concerns, rhetoric and imagery owe much to 1968 – come from an open letter (published in *La Jornada* national newspaper on 18 April 2000) addressed to the family members of the abducted victims of the dirty war waged in Mexico for decades after 1968.

5. Narratives of failure

A few months before the thirtieth anniversary of the student movement, Héctor Aguilar Camín asked the following question in an interview: 'Is 68 part of our past or our present? Is it recent history or current politics?'[38] Although he asserted that he believed that 1968 should be considered an event of the past (that is, that it should be turned into history), there is no doubt that for many others it is still very much alive in terms of the political engagement it demands. If 1968 is still, in some degree, part of our present in the sense that it enables or produces a certain kind of political commitment, then the way it is *read* is still relevant.

I want to suggest that we can trace two lines of interpretation of 1968, which ultimately call for two very different kinds of political intervention in the present day. On the one hand, as we have seen, there is the literary memory of Tlatelolco written a few years after its occurrence, which generally – although not exclusively – recovers the event as an unfinished matter from which a new kind of political engagement should emerge. On the other hand, however, in recent years a number of novels have been written that revisit the events of 1968 and posit them as a failed enterprise that was undertaken for all the wrong reasons and that led nowhere. These narratives of failure around 1968 produce what John Beverley has recently called a 'paradigm of disillusion' in so far as they depict 68 and its sequels negatively and within a narrative of progress that situates this year as part of an immature, adolescent stage.[39] These texts address 1968 in order to represent it as a closed matter and as an error, with the political

---

38   A. Jáquez, 'Toda la verdad sobre la matanza del 68, y fin de la impunidad, reclaman Aguilar Camín, Semo y Monsiváis', *Proceso* 1109 (1 Feb. 1998): 7.

39   In 'Rethinking the Armed Struggle in Latin America' [forthcoming, *boundary 2*, 36.1 (2009)], Beverley uses the term 'paradigm of disillusion' to describe those interpretations which see the armed struggle in Latin America as a mistake and which equate historical with personal development in such a way that the 1960s and 1970s correspond to a 'romantic adolescence'. I thank the author for kindly sending me the unpublished text.

consequence that they appear to prove that the left is not a viable political project in present-day Mexico. Thus, in a number of novels, such as *La guerra de Galio* and *El fin de la locura*, there is a shift in the representation of the importance of 1968 which understands that year and its sequels as a point of (negative) rupture between the past and the present. This type of writing explains the present retrospectively by making 1968 the point of departure, dealing with the analysis of contemporary political, social and cultural issues in order to show that 1968 is the source where the explanation of current national stagnation is to be found.

La guerra de Galio, written by Héctor Aguilar Camín, was published in 1988.[40] The protagonist of this novel represents the generation of young Mexicans who had to deal with the shattered hopes raised by the student movement after it was violently crushed. This text explores the cultural, political and social options available to young people after the traumatic failure of 1968. The main character is a young historian who, influenced by historical materialism, inaugurates a pioneering interpretation that demythifies the orthodox history of the Mexican Revolution and the post-revolutionary nation. Indeed, in his novel Aguilar Camín fictionalises through this character an actual trend that took place in Mexican historiography especially in the 1960s, which questioned orthodox historical readings of the Mexican Revolution and which tried to demonstrate the complicit relationship between these readings and the perpetuation of the party in government. Through the fictionalisation of two apparently contradictory historiographical theories used to explain the present in relation to the past, this novel sets out to demonstrate that social movements are always already doomed to failure and that adopting a sustainable leftist political project after 1968 was – and is – virtually impossible. This novel shows (in a partial but universalised manner) a horizon of stagnation after 1968, where none of the options of the left (neither revolutionary nor political) are viable projects.

40   H. Aguilar Camín, *La guerra de Galio* (Mexico: Cal y Arena, 1988).

El fin de la locura, by Jorge Volpi, was published in 2003.[41] This novel narrates the history of the revolutionary left beginning with the student movement in France and ending with the fall of the Berlin Wall in 1989. It deals with Maoism in France, urban guerrilla movements, the Cuban and Chilean revolutions and, in Mexico, the emergence of a new civil society after the earthquake of 1985, the electoral fraud of 1988, as well as the emergence of the Zapatista National Liberation Army. This work concentrates on the international political context after May 1968 and later extrapolates it to the Mexico of the 1980s.

The history of the left narrated here coincides with the life of the protagonist, Aníbal Quevedo, who goes from rejecting the student riots at the beginning of the novel to adhering to all subsequent revolutionary movements. Later, he grows disenchanted with the revolution in general and becomes a leading leftist intellectual in Mexico during the 1980s. The protagonist's involvement with the left begins in May 68 and ends with his political ruin and suicide on the day the Berlin Wall is being torn down. His engagement with the left, however, is never wholly honest, since it is always mediated by his fascination with Claire, his elusive lover, a 'real' revolutionary who wholeheartedly embraces increasingly radical causes. The author makes a case of explaining revolutionary engagement always in terms of madness, a theme that may be observed through the analysis of Claire's psychosis, which in the novel is explained in Lacanian terms. Thus, any action against the State is explained in terms of psychological disequilibrium, never as a reaction to or a strategy against social or political injustice. According to this novel, what began in May 1968 and ended in November 1989 was utter madness and failure. As in *La guerra de Galio*, all the options available to the left are minutely exposed as undesirable or impossible.

41   J. Volpi, *El fin de la locura* (Barcelona: Seix Barral, 2003).

6. Conclusions

In these pages, I have tried to show that the literary memory of 1968 produces a sort of archive (in the Foucaultian sense) that itself determines not solely the manner in which this event is construed or remembered and the statements that may or may not be enunciated about it, but also, in a more profound and significant manner, the way in which society and leftist politics, as well as literary and historical writing have been posited and practiced ever since. Many of the works written shortly after the student movement represent the event as a matter without closure, and Tlatelolco is transformed into the ground from which issues such as demands for democracy, and social and political justice should be articulated. On the other hand, in recent years a conservative trend has gained ground that depicts 1968 as a failed and closed event that should be transcended and left behind. By exploring the connection between the student movement and leftist politics, these latter works explore the history of the second half of the twentieth century in order to underscore the violence, the madness and the immanent failure that all revolutionary acts (whether in politics, art, theory, or literature) inevitably carry. By establishing a close link between 1968, failure, and leftist politics, these novels perform a sort of political dissuasion, or dissuasive politics, since they help to naturalise the idea that the left is in no case a viable project and, more importantly, that the notion of equality as a form of utopia should be discarded in the name of the only real form of political participation, that is, representative democracy.

CHRIS HOMEWOOD

Have the Best Ideas Stood the Test of Time?
Negotiating the Legacy of '1968' in *The Edukators*

During a key scene in Hans Weingartner's *Die fetten Jahre sind vorbei/The Edukators* (2004) two of the film's protagonists, Jan and Jule, mourn the decline of the revolutionary energy of the youth amidst a cultural climate which has seen potent symbols of rebellion, such as the Argentinean-born communist firebrand Che Guevara, appropriated and repackaged as a depoliticised capitalist brand. As Jan opines, 'rebellion is difficult now [...] what was considered subversive then you can buy in shops now: Che Guevara T-shirts or anarchy stickers',[1] thus begging the question of how current youth cohorts can channel their discontent when the radicalism of previous generations now lives on as a manifestation of the very capitalist consumer ideology it sought to undermine. The commodification of protest which, as Martin Klimke argues elsewhere in the volume, is one way that a global collective memory of '1968' has been kept alive can be witnessed in a variety of sources: from the European fashion retailer *Ringspun's* 'allstars' range (which saw Alberto Korda's iconic image of Guevara reproduced on boxer-shorts and t-shirts) to the 'Che Guevara Revolution Hero 12" Action Figure' (complete with pistol, hand grenade and cigar accessory that can be placed in the doll's mouth) by the Hong Kong company *How2Work Toys*, the recent trend for 'radical chic' the western world over has seen global icons of active participation return as products of passive consumption.[2] The same tendency has also taken hold of the memory of the Red Army Faction

---

1   All cited dialogue is taken from the subtitles to the Pathé international DVD release of *The Edukators*.

2   See the *How2Works Toys* website <http://www.how2worktoys.com/main.html> [accessed on 12 March 2006].

(RAF), the aberrant terrorist organisation which rose from the ashes of the West German 68er movement and was better known to eyewitnesses as the Baader-Meinhof group. The RAF lives on in the nation's cultural memory as a 'pop'-based lifestyle product for the youthful 'Generation Berlin', to borrow Heinz Bude's tag:[3] Warhol styled prints of leading terrorists Andreas Baader and Ulrike Meinhof available for sale on *e-bay.de* and the 'Prada-Meinhof' fashion label launched in 1999 seemed to confirm the declaration by glossy lifestyle magazine *Max* that 'die Zeit ist reif für RAF-Popstars' (the time is now for RAF popstars).[4] Thus deferring to Fredric Jameson it would seem that 'refracted through the iron law of fashion change and the emergent ideology of the generation'[5] (which would appear to be rampant consumerism) 1960s-based protest has not only been conflated with an amorphous, dissident heroism but also a glamour and star potential which is highly sought after in today's cult of celebrity.

However, in the vast majority of cases, any sense that the icons, signs and symbols of revolution are being deployed within youth culture as a direct response to the aims and ideals of '1968' or its wider legacy is lacking. 'Radical chic' is informed by a highly selective process of remembering and forgetting which at once decontextualises and depoliticises the political legacy of icons such as Guevara and is often ignorant of the uncomfortable historical facts that surrounded groups such as the RAF (such as the 'executions' committed in the name of its nihilistic worldview). Instead, an aestheticised fascination with what Niels Werber terms 'die existentielle Erfahrung […], die Intensität' (the existential experience […], the intensity) of this past is privileged.[6] And as Stefan Reinecke makes clear,

3   See Heinz Bude, *Generation Berlin* (Berlin: Merve, 2001).
4   See Andreas, *Karl-May-RAF*, April 2001 <http://www.salonrouge.de/raf-pop.htm> [accessed on 29 June 2005]. Unless otherwise stated, all translations are the author's own.
5   Fredric Jameson, *Postmodernism, or, The Cultural Logic of Late Capitalism* (London & New York: Verso, 1991), 19.
6   Niels WERBER, *Vom Glück im Kampf: Krieg und Terror in der Popkultur*, <http://homepage.ruhr-uni-bochum.de/niels.werber/Antrittsvorlesung.htm> [accessed on 28 July 2006].

in the example of Germany's home-grown terrorists, 'was die RAF war, was sie wollte, was sie tat, rückt in den Hintergrund. Die Geste zählt, nicht der Inhalt' (what the RAF was, what they wanted and what they did all fades into the background. The gesture counts, not the substance).[7] Thus divorced from their socio-political context all that counts is the gesture; a vague, stylised expression of rebellion, provocation and an assumed yet false sense of authenticity which can also be expressed in terms of another famous dictum that would doubtless carry more weight with the wearers of 'radical chic' slogan t-shirts – *Nike*'s 'just do it!' Thus, for a minority that *is* politically motivated and wishes to challenge the accepted status quo, the situation appears dire. Returning to *The Edukators*, in Jule's view the return of 60s rebellion as market commodity is symptomatic of its failure: 'that's why there aren't any more youth movements. Everyone has the feeling it's all been done before. Others tried and failed. Why should it work for us?' In this chapter then I examine how *The Edukators* seeks to address this question by posing the question of how a minority can hope to make a difference when it all appears to have been said and done, and failed. The chapter will consider how Weingartner's film problematises the commodity memory of '1968' as a fashion accessory devoid of a political core in a bid to inspire an otherwise apathetic youth to action. However, the director's decision to engage with this question at all might seem surprising given recent developments surrounding the legacy of '1968' in his own cultural context, and to which we now turn.

The beleaguered memory of '1968' in Germany

By the early 1990s the legacy of '1968' in Germany had largely settled around the term 'successful failure', a consensual if abidingly uneasy dual view of the '68er movement' and its utopian belief in radical social upheaval as,

7   Stefan Reinecke, 'Das RAF-Gespenst', *die tageszeitung*, 5 September 2002.

to cite Ingo Cornils, a 'short-term political failure' but with 'long-term
socio-cultural effects': the students failed to replace capitalism with a more
equal system, but their protests arguably led to the creation of a more liberal society. As Cornils goes on to note, 'each side could claim victory: the
68ers for conquering the imagination, the conservatives for conquering
reality.'[8] But in 1998 the advent of a new government with its roots in the
radical ferment of the 1960s, namely the Red/Green coalition fronted by
former student activists Gerhard Schröder and Joschka Fischer, saw this
fragile accord face increased scrutiny. In 2001 Fischer's past as a militant
street fighter was dissected by conservative opponents in a media frenzy
intended to tarnish the then Foreign Minister's reputation[9] and in the
same year the legacy of this era of protest came under attack from one of its
own number when former 68er Gerd Koenen published *The Red Decade*
which sought to revise the status of '1968' as watershed moment by linking
it to a decade of terrorist violence at the hands of the RAF that culminated
in the infamous 'German Autumn' of 1977.[10]

Moreover, the increasingly beleaguered memory and reputation of
'1968' has suffered a further attack in the first decade of the new millennium
from post-'68 cohorts in Germany, not least the youth-led 'generation of
'89' whose members came of age in the years immediately following the
fall of the Berlin Wall and to which director Hans Weingartner belongs.
Regarded as concomitant with the 'lost' American 'Generation X', this is
a cohort for whom the utopian optimism, energy and ideals which characterised the 1960s have been replaced, and seemingly quite willingly so,

8   See Ingo Cornils, 'Successful Failure? The Impact of the German Student Movement
     on the Federal Republic of Germany', in Stuart Taberner and Frank Finlay (eds),
     Recasting German Identity (Rochester: Camden House, 2002), 105–112. The dual
     view of the German student movement as 'Erfolgreich gescheitert' was introduced
     in 1988 by Wilhelm Bittorf but Cornils suggests that the term's consensual accept-
     ance was first cemented in Matthias Kopp's film essay of the same name. See ibid,
     and Bittorf, 'Träume im Kopf, Sturm auf den Straßen', *Spiegel* 14–21 (1988).
9   In 2001 *Stern* magazine published pictures showing Fischer beating a policeman at
     a rally in Frankfurt in 1973.
10   See Gerd Koenen, *Das rote Jahrzehnt: Unsere kleine Deutsche Kulturrevolution* (Köln:
     Kiepenheuer & Witsch, 2001).

by the capricious fads of consumerist pop-culture, discussed above, as well as private absorption and lifestyle issues. As Rupa Huq maintains in her study of western youth subculture, it is not that current youth cohorts are incapable of dissent. On the contrary they are 'disenfranchised' and see 'themselves as facing a world of diminished possibilities', but nonetheless 'ostensibly satiated' by the consumer distractions that this world also offers them.[11] Echoing the American 'Slacker' ethos[12] a youth survey of Germany's home-grown '89ers' in 1994 concluded:

> They scrutinise everything, but don't do anything; when they do take action, they only do it for themselves; they don't want to change anything – apart from themselves; they don't want to be rebellious because they feel it is more defiant not to be rebellious. They want to rid themselves of this stupid, arduous role which the youth has played since the fifties.[13]

Seemingly then, when the 89ers have mobilised it is only to militate against the critical perspectives and the onerous legacy of the '"Yesterday's heroes" of "1968"',[14] a clear indication of which comes in the form of 89er pop-author Florian Illies's book *Generation Golf.* In an oft-quoted passage Illies

11   Rupa Huq, *Beyond Subculture: Pop, Youth and Identity in a Postcolonial World* (London and New York: Routledge, 2006), 21.

12   The term 'slacker' was made popular by American director Richard Linklater's 1991 film of the same name and became synonymous with the 'stereotype of the post-beatnik idler who spurned career, ambition and political activism in favour of just hanging out.' See Rob Stone, 'Between Sunrise and Sunset: An Elliptical Dialogue between American and European Cinema', in Paul Cooke (ed.) *World Cinema's 'Dialogues' with Hollywood* (Palgrave: Basingstoke, 2007), 218–287 (219).

13   'Sie durchschauen alles, aber sie tun nichts; wenn sie was tun, tun sie nur für sich; sie wollen nichts verändern – außer sich selbst; sie glauben an nichts mehr – außer an sich selbst; sie möchten nicht rebellisch sein, weil sie es rebellischer finden, nicht rebellisch zu sein; denn sie möchten diese alberne, anstrengende Rolle loswerden, die Jugendliche seit den Fünfzigern zu spielen haben.' Taken from *Spiegel* 38, 1994 (58) and cited in Claus Leggewie, *Die 89er: Portrait einer Generation* (Hoffman und Campe: Hamburg, 1995), 25.

14   Cited in Stuart Taberner, 'Introduction: German Literature in the Age of Globalisation', in Taberner (ed.), *German Literature in the Age of Globalisation* (Birmingham: Birmingham University Press, 2004), 10.

sardonically turns the West German Student Movement's attack on the alleged 'mould of a thousand years'[15] back against the protest generation: 'Enough already with the stories of '68, enough with the culture of scepticism, enough with an identity built around a *Lebensgefühl* ('sensibility for life') and politics, enough with the mould of twenty alternative years. Simply enough.'[16]

In the light of such comments, the dialogue which the 89er Weingartner sets up with Germany's radical past is perhaps surprising. *The Edukators* follows the lives of three Berlin-based twenty-somethings who, unlike the majority of their peers, yearn for political change and the liberation of their own 'sensibility for life.' Moreover, for the would-be revolutionaries Jan, Jule and Peter, the ideas and ideals of the legacy of '1968' act as an ideological signpost that might in fact allow them to channel their dissent. With *The Edukators* Weingartner interrogates the current state of political idealism among his generation but poses a question of international significance, namely 'wie man als junger Mensch noch politisch aktiv sein kann' (how one can be young and politically active) when once politically charged subject matter has been revised or remodelled for superficial, fad-driven consumption in the global market.[17] This question has a dual concern, and is aimed at two strata in youth culture. On the one hand Weingartner points to an apparent void in his own culture, asking how one can reinvigorate and remobilise a political engagement that is simply

15   An attack on the alleged ideological residue of Hitler's failed thousand year Reich, the slogan 'Unter den Talaren, der Muff von Tausend Jahren/Under the academic gowns, the mould of a thousand years' featured on protest banners across Germany universities. For a picture of one such banner see Burkhard Spinnen, 'Helmut B., Jahrgang', in Christiane Landgrebe and Jörg Plath (eds), *'68 und die Folgen: Ein unvollständiges Lexion* (Argon: Berlin, 1998), 44.

16   'Also Schluß mit den Geschichten von 68, Schluß mit der Mißtrauenskultur, Schluß mit der Identität von Lebensgefühl und Politik, Schluß mit dem Muff von zwanzig alternativen Jahren. Einfach Schluß.' Florian Illies, *Generation Golf. Eine Inspektion* (Berlin: Argon, 2000), 181.

17   See Dietmar Kammerer, 'Die private Revolte ist nie privat (Gespräch mit Hans Weingartner)', *tageszeitung*, 25 November 2004 <http://www.taz.de/pt/2004/11/25/a0120.1/textdruck> [accessed on 17 July 2006].

lacking among the majority of his generation which has seemingly been interpolated by 'the system' and on the other hand how a resistive minority which is at least attempting to be politically engaged can focus and sustain its nascent activism when icons of rebellion have been swallowed up by the neo-liberal capitalist machinery and can therefore no longer be said to represent genuine resistance. As we shall see, in both cases the answer, for Weingartner, rests with an ambivalent relationship to the 'generation of 68' and their legacy.

Where has the revolutionary energy gone?

After she is fired from her job as a waitress at an exclusive restaurant for smoking in the kitchen, a despondent Jule surveys the Berlin cityscape from the rooftop of a high-rise building with her new friend Jan. Divorced from the frenetic bustle of administered life down below, and aided by a rapidly diminishing bottle of wine, they wax lyrical about patterns of thought and behaviour in society. Jan, posited by the narrative as the leading ideologue of the three friends, comes to the pessimistic conclusion that neo-liberal capitalist economics have penetrated all areas of public life, indoctrinating the masses in their attitudes towards the establishment and negating the possibility of true individual freedom. In many ways, Jan's unmistakably Marcusian portrait of modern life should come as no surprise. As Douglas Kellner remarks in his introduction to the 2007 reprint of the second edition of *One-Dimensional Man*, Herbert Marcuse's 'important work of critical social theory [...] continues to be relevant today as the forces of social domination that Marcuse dissected have become even stronger and more prevalent in the years since he wrote the book.'[18] Further adopt-

18   Douglas Kellner, 'Introduction to the Second Edition', in Herbert Marcuse, *One-Dimensional Man: Studies in the Ideology of Advanced Industrial Society*, 2nd edn. (Routledge: London and New York, 2007), xi–xxxviii (xii).

ing Marcuse's critique Jan singles out television which he refers to by the vernacular 'Glotze' or 'idiot box', that is as a mechanism deployed by consumer capitalism to integrate the individual into its world of thoughts and behaviour. For Jan television is a drug which indoctrinates the populace intravenously with the opinions of its makers in order to assure a numbing state of conformity: what hope is there for revolutionary thoughts in the face of quiz shows?[19]

Given the importance of Marcuse to the 68er movement in Germany, it is therefore unsurprising that, as film critic Martina Knoben commented, 'when Jan argues about the alleged capitalist dictatorship it sounds like it came from a 68er dictionary.'[20] A diegetic explanation for Jan's 'memory' of '1968' is not forthcoming. Rather it would seem that his knowledge and ideological allegiance to the aims of this period are derived from the biography of the director for whom Jan is an alter-ego of sorts. Weingartner (b. 1970) was himself one of the minority whose profound sense of dissatisfaction with administered society compelled him to seek out alternatives. Speaking in interview the director has suggested that 'Ich hatte auch in meiner eigenen Geschichte immer wieder dieses Gefühl gehabt, ich müsste rebellieren, es müsste sich alles ändern, und ich wusste nicht wie' (In my own narrative I'd also always had this sense that I just had to rebel, that everything had to change even though I didn't know how). [21] In the 1990s this unfocused compulsion saw the then twenty-something move from his native Vienna to Berlin to live 'off the grid' with friends in one of the city's few remaining communal squats even if 'es gab keinen Überbau bei uns' (we didn't have a political superstructure).[22] Jan's own clear determination to develop a political superstructure in a Marxist sense might therefore be

---

19   The demagoguery of television was developed by Weingartner into a full length feature. See his *Free Rainer – Dein Fernseher lügt/Free Rainer – Reclaim Your Brain* (2007).

20   Martina Knoben, 'Die ratlosen Rebellen', in *epd Film* 12 (2004).

21   R. Gansera and F. Göttler, 'Die Liebe in Zeiten der Matrix', *Sueddeutsche Zeitung*, 23 November 2004, <http://www.sueddeutsche.de/kultur/artikel/462/43419/print. html> [accessed on 17 July 2006].

22   Ibid.

said to develop the director's unfinished radical trajectory. Thus regardless of the source of his ideological convictions, Jan is more than a hollow appropriator of this past and is unlike the majority of his peers who have militated against the culture of scepticism embodied by the 68ers. Jan has immersed himself in and truly believes in the thoughts and values of '1968' and continues to ask many of the still unanswered questions posed by the radicalised youth of the sixties, such as what right we have to exploit the developing world and why there is so much inequality in a country with so much wealth. '1968' becomes a symbolically-charged moment which, for Jan at least, might point the way out of the protest malaise and stifling socio-economic conditions of the Berlin Republic.

Someone who has firsthand experience of the overpowering weight of capitalist economics is Jule, who has been financially crippled by an impossible €100,000 debt after she crashed her uninsured Volkswagen into a company Mercedes. As she explains to Jan she is now in effect owned by her creditor – the wealthy CEO Hardenberg whose car she wrote off. Although Jule views her financial subjugation to a man for whom the debt represents small change to be morally reprehensible, she has not been able to overcome what Jan, again echoing Marcuse, views as the censorship of the repressive reality principle; Jule has resigned herself to the fact that, in the eyes of the dominant system at least, she was in the wrong and that there is nothing she can do about it. For Jan, capitalist manipulation has overwhelmed Jule's attempt at self-determination, her resignation being indicative of the way the established system has colonised her consciousness, successfully imposing it rules upon her. She explains to Jan that 'actually I just wanted to live wild and free', but much like the coherence of youth subculture in the new millennium, her attempt to construct her own *Lebensgefühl* or 'sensibility for life' has, in Dick Hebdige's terms, 'dissolved under the pressure of material constraints.'[23]

---

23 Dick Hebdige, *Hiding in the Light: On Images and Things* (Routledge: London, 1988), 35.

Nonetheless, Jule is a committed if directionless activist, and so a regular at anti-globalisation rallies where she demonstrates against the sweat-
shop practices which produce the expensive, branded lifestyle trainers that
her peers voraciously consume. However, Jule's efforts appear unsuccessful
and the protesters are quickly dispersed by the police who are posited by
the film as a form of external oppression which compounds Jule's sense
of internal repression. Such prescribed forms of protest have long since
come to be easily absorbed by 'the Establishment.' The social situation that
director Weingartner depicts reverberates with Marcuse's contention in
his essay 'Repressive Tolerance' that 'those minorities which strive for the
change of the whole itself [...] will be left helpless and harmless in the face
of the overwhelming majority, which militates against qualitative social
change'.[24] Even before the police intervene the wider public is seemingly
disinterested in the dubious origins of its fashion trainers and Jule recognises
that playing by the rules of sanctioned protest is ineffective, thus leading
to the sense of political and social 'Orientierunslosigkeit' (disorientation)
which Weingartner feels characterises his generation.[25] Jule craves political change but does not know where to begin, reflecting what the director
referred to as the 'Grundproblem meiner Generation, dass wir in einem
System fundiert sind, bei dem wir nicht wissen, an welchem Punkt wir
es angreifen sollen' (fundamental problem of my generation, that we are
established in a system and yet don't know at which point to attack it).[26]
Jule's dissatisfaction lacks exactitude, much like recent attempts at youth
protest as Huq suggests:

24   Herbert Marcuse, 'Repressive Tolerance', in Robert Paul Wolff, Barrington Moore,
     Jr and Herbert Marcuse, *A Critique of Pure Tolerance* (Boston: Beacon Press, 1965),
     81–123 (94).
25   See Katja Nicodemus, 'Denn sie wissen, was sie tun', *Die Zeit*, 25 November 2004,
     <http://zeus.zeit.de/text/2004/49/Fette_Jahre> [accessed on 17 June 2006].
26   See R. Gansera and F. Göttler, 'Die Liebe in Zeiten der Matrix', *Sueddeutsche Zeitung*,
     23 November 2004, http://www.sueddeutsche.de/kultur/artikel/462/43419/print.
     html.

the anti-globalisation protests of the early twenty-first century are examples of [...] highly politicised groupings that would once have been termed 'subcultures' but are difficult to conceive of today. Their case is interesting because their message arguably lacks coherence as they are rather more *against* global capitalism than *for* any clearly defined set of aims of objectives.[27]

It is therefore not surprising that during their roof-top conversation Jule tells Jan 'the problem is I can't find anything I really want to believe in.' Through the example of '1968' however, Jan believes that he has struck on a way to exceed the 'repressive tolerance' of 'the system' and its ignorance of the real needs and desires of the individual. This vociferous supporter of West Germany's protest legacy advocates its values, asserting to the disillusioned Jule that even though previous youth movements might have failed, 'for all revolutions one thing is clear – even if some didn't work the most important thing is that the best ideas survived.' Specifically, Jan and his partner in activism, Peter, have looked to the memory of '68, to an example which pays homage to aspects of the 68ers political radicalism and might revitalise revolutionary energy in a politically directionless, even apathetic youth and, they hope, liberate themselves from the suffocating peril of administered society.

'All power to the imagination' ... again!

Supposedly out fly-posting at night, Jan and Peter have in fact been engaged in the 'education' of Berlin's bourgeois elite by breaking in to their luxury piles. But these self-styled 'Edukators' do not steal nor do they carry out mindless destruction in their protest against the rich/poor divide and other perceived social ills.[28] Rather they perform very careful 'vandalism', rear-

27 Huq, *Beyond Subculture*, 21.
28 The name the group gives to itself offers a response to the 'ironical question' posed by Marcuse in his essay on 'Repressive Tolerance', namely 'who educates the educators

ranging their victims' furniture as a form of political statement: designer chairs, sofas and tables are stacked on top of each other, high-end stereo equipment finds its way in to the fridge and expensive Meissen pottery turns up in the toilet. Notes are left as part of this politicised act for the occupiers to find upon their return, stating either 'die fetten Jahre sind vorbei' (your days of plenty are numbered) or 'Sie haben zu viel Geld' (you have too much money).

In many ways, the protest of the 'Edukators' seems a very contemporary gesture with a clear international resonance in so far as it is evocative of the current youth-based 'culture jamming' movement which, in the words of Christine Harold, 'seeks to undermine the marketing rhetoric of multinational corporations, specifically through such practices as media hoaxing, corporate sabotage, billboard "liberation," and trademark infringement.'[29] Examples of so-called billboard 'liberation' include the modification of the globally recognizable *Nike* slogan to read 'Just do it … or else!' in a comment against the multinational's alleged sweat-shop practices as well as the defacement of advertisements for television programme's around Toronto which saw a spate of actor's faces amended to look like skulls with the added demand – 'Kill your TV!' Jan and Peter's imaginative attempts to subvert capitalism's cultural images and values are certainly evocative of 'culture jamming', only writ large. They quite literally turn the cultural system of capitalism on its head, transforming the way these objects are experienced by their owners and thus subverting the comfort that the elite gain from their consumer wares into disconcertion.

But although this politicised gesture speaks the cultural language of an 89er pop based protest, it has its roots firmly in a 68er sensibility: the guerrilla form of communication which characterises the international phenomenon of 'culture jamming', as well as Jan and Peter's personal spin on it, is indebted to the anti-authoritarian protest tradition of the 1960s

---

(i.e. the political leaders)' in a society where decisions affecting the masses are ultimately decided by an elite minority from above. See Marcuse, 'Repressive Tolerance', 104.

29 Christine Harold, 'Pranking rhetoric: "culture jamming" as media activism', *Critical Studies in Media Communication*, 21:3 (2004), 189–211 (190).

in Germany, specifically evoking the 'Spaßguerilla' concept forged by the so called political clowns of West Berlin's infamous *Commune I* whose members pioneered a humorous, self-styled brand of praxis which, to quote Rob Burns and Wilfred van der Will, advocated 'the taunting of authority by non-violent means of argument, demonstration and symbolic action.'[30] The satirical content of *Commune I*'s so-called 'political happenings' – such as the theatrical 'Pudding-Assassination' of US Vice President Hubert Humphrey in 1967 – went beyond prescribed forms of protest and were designed to expose the absurdity of those who held positions of authority and social influence in order to 'create contexts of political enlightenment.'[31] In the case of Jan and Peter they seek to shatter the moral authority of the commodities they rearrange, playing them against the very cultural system and consciousness that they are supposed to safeguard.

Furthermore, Peter and Jan's creative violation of the rules of sanctioned protest evokes a clarion call of the 68ers: *Phantasie an die Macht!* or 'All Power to the Imagination!', which as Sabine von Dirke notes 'calls for the transformation of imagination into revolutionary energy and aims at overcoming the repressive reality principle on the individual as well as collective level.'[32] In the case of Weingartner's 'Edukators' it would appear to be a case of 'All Power to the Imagination'... Again: for Jan, Peter and Jule, their own imaginative infringement of the accepted rules of engagement has a liberating potential, both on an individual and, they hope, a collective level.

In an early scene we witness Jan's sense of isolation at the hands of capitalist rationality. In one of the film's numerous and scathing critiques of the increasing gulf between the 'haves' and 'have nots' in German society, Jan becomes embroiled in a conflict with state officials following their somewhat excessive handling of a drunk yet passive vagrant who is riding

30   Burns and Van der Will, *Protest and Democracy in West Germany*, 109.
31   Ibid.
32   Von Dirke, *All Power to the Imagination! The West German Counter Culture from the Student Movement to the Greens* (Lincoln and London: University of Nebraska Press, 1997), 38. For a more detailed exploration of the importance of 'imagination' to the Student Movement, see ibid, 37–43.

the tram without a ticket. After Jan hands the tramp his travel card the inspectors turn on him for his act of solidarity, pursuing him after he leaves the vehicle in what threatens to become a violent exchange. Powerless to make a difference, and so left feeling impotent, Jan retreats to the proto-commune he shares with Peter. Slamming the door to his room behind him, Jan plays thrash metal at full volume before hooking himself up to an oxygen machine. Although the scene is played with a humorous touch, the implications of this gesture are nonetheless clear; the apparent destruction of human solidarity and Jan's own evacuated sense of individual subjectivity have become a suffocating peril for this twenty-something. Jan's reaction follows Weingartner's belief that 'when I, as a person, have this feeling that something isn't right with the world, then I'm unhappy, I'm furious. This feeling must come out and be translated into action, otherwise you will feel ill.'[33] However, there is an antidote to this illness – the creative remodelling of the homes of the wealthy elite gives Jan the focus he needs to channel his feeling of outrage, and liberate his previously repressed life instincts or energies. Jan's sense of anger and power of imagination is transformed into a productive force which he feels has emancipated him from his psychic incarceration within the established system. His remodelling of luxury homes allows him to come up for air without the aid of an oxygen machine; after a successful mission with Peter, both young men are energised and Jan strips his shirt off before screaming at the top of his lungs from the window of their beaten up camper-van in a display of pure euphoria.

However, rather than reading the film as an attempt at emancipation, individual or otherwise, there was a commonly held opinion among sectors of Germany's print media critics that Jan and his companions were leading nothing more than a private campaign against the rich, motivated mainly by social jealousy.[34] Weingartner, in a somewhat tit-for-tat riposte suggested that '"Social jealousy" is a battle cry of the financially well-to-do social classes' before, in a more measured response, going on to insist that 'Breaking into the villas of the rich is a symbolic action.' Evocative of *Commune I*'s

33   See Kammerer, 'Die private Revolte ist nie privat'.
34   Ibid.

embracing of the motto – 'the private is political!' – Weingartner consolidated his defence by insisting that 'a private revolt is, in truth, never private but rather it has social dimensions.'[35] Although Peter and Jan's colourful form of activism is still in its infancy when we join the narrative, the duo is building towards a collective social statement. Peter is overjoyed to discover that their nocturnal activities have made newspaper copy, even if only a few column inches have been devoted to them, and hopes that they will ultimately inspire imitators. Jan, however, has much larger ambitions. The break-ins only represent the first stage of their programme and at the end of the film we see the trio travel to a remote Mediterranean island with the intention of disabling one of Europe's main television transmission hubs. Although we never see the outcome, with this operation the film ends on a utopian note as the three friends seek to halt the supply of an apparent technological drug. Admittedly naïve in its inception this final action nonetheless moves beyond a mere desire for individual liberation to the hope of collective enlightenment.

Paradoxically then, Jan looks back to the memory of a 'failed' revolution in order to come forward and work toward a revolution of his own. But this does not prove problematic for the director who views '1968' in Germany less as 'eine glücklich gescheiterte Revolution' (happily failed revolution), to use Claus Leggewie's famous label, than one which was too quick to concede its countercultural aims and play by the rules of the game.[36] Specifically, for Weingartner: 'the 68er revolution changed a lot but didn't go far enough. That's the bottom line. The movement fell into the long march through the institutions too quickly. The basic principles of the capitalist system haven't changed.'[37]

35 Ibid.
36 Claus Leggewie, '1968 ist Geschichte', *Politik und Zeitgeschichte* 22–23 (2001), 5.
37 Kammerer, 'Die private Revolte ist nie privat'.

'Your time is up manager':
when the ideal of '1968' confronts its socio-political outcome

As such, it is interesting that the trio comes into contact with an old-68er in the film – Jule's wealthy creditor Hardenberg whom the friends kidnap when the remodelling of his home goes horribly wrong. Coshed, gagged and then bound, Hardenberg is dumped in the back of their van as they desperately try to conceive of a way out of a criminal situation of their own making. Echoing the terrorists of the RAF for whom as Jeremy Varon notes, the urgency of survival increasingly took precedence 'over ideological and moral considerations', from this point on the three would-be revolutionaries are 'driven not by any grand design but by the pressures of illegality' which threatens not only their desire for political legitimacy but also their increasingly fraught friendship.[38] Whereas the trio's earlier protest gesture had been *structurally* terroristic yet ultimately mirthful their action now threatens to descend into very real and violent terror as they race to save their own skins. Although Weingartner exonerates '1968' as a symbolic moment of utopian potential it almost seems inevitable that his protagonists' search through West Germany's radical past for liberating forms of protest thus brings them into contact with the 'Achilles heel' of the 68er legacy, that is the 'armed struggle' of urban terrorism which fol-lowed in the temporal wake of the Student Movement.[39] Before we move on to consider the part Hardenberg has to play in detail it is first necessary to briefly examine the encounter of the 'Edukators' with the memory of urban terrorism in Germany.

---

38   Jeremy Varon, *Bringing the War Home: the Weather Underground, the Red Army Faction, and Revolutionary Violence in the Sixties and Seventies* (Berkeley, Los Angeles, London: University of California Press, 2004), 209.

39   See, for example, Cornils, 'Joined at the Hip? The representation of the German Student Movement and Left-Wing Terrorism in Recent Literature' in Gerrit-Jan Berendse & Ingo Cornils (eds), *Baader-Meinhof Returns. History and Cultural Memory of German Left-Wing Terrorism* (German Monitor) (Amsterdam / New York: Rodopi, 2008), 137–155.

From a cabin hide-away in the Austrian Tirol that quickly comes to represent a *Volksgefängnis* ('people's prison'), Jule berates their captive for amassing 'large, expensive things' with his €3.4million salary when Threshold Nation workers cannot afford the bus to the neighbouring town to find employment. For Jule and her friends the solution is idealistically simple – wipe out the international debt owed by the poorer countries. Hardenberg, however, remains adamant that this would cause the collapse of the world financial system and refuses to justify his spending habits which are his democratic right. The terrorisation of Hardenberg points to a qualitative difference between the previous actions of the trio and its subsequent violent form of coercion. Reproaching his young captors for redeploying the terrorists' methods of spreading fear and anxiety through kidnapping, Hardenberg denounces them as 'the RAF of the new millennium.' Such a reproach is not eased by Peter's suggestion that they hang a sign around his neck declaring his status as a prisoner of the 'Edukators', tape it and send it to the press, clearly recalling both the 'political' kidnapping of CDU mayoral candidate Peter Lorenz by the *Bewegung 2. Juni* and the subsequent kidnapping of Hanns Martin Schleyer by the RAF. Jan, Jule and Peter, then, find themselves staring into a precipice that might signal the descent from provocative but peaceful activism into the violent underground of a nascent terrorism of their own making whereby, as Varon notes of the RAF, 'violence of an increasingly destructive sort would be required to sustain the illusion of power.'[40] Although he claims to have been joking, Peter's suggestion that 'we put him [Hardenberg] in the morgue' points to a very worrying possibility of escalation as they struggle to remain in control and so a possible replay of the shift from counter-cultural, playful provocation to the nihilistic worldview of the Baader-Meinhof generation of terrorists. Ultimately, however, this flirtation with the choices offered by West Germany's legacy of urban terrorism is firmly rejected by the director after a dialogue is established with Hardenberg as both sides seek to make the best of their present situation. Having apparently warmed to his captors, the imprisoned CEO softens his earlier reproach, and while he maintains

40   Varon, *Bringing the War Home*, 206.

that 'I don't think it's right what you're doing to me' he concedes 'but your idealism ... I can respect that.' Hardenberg's attitude here mirrors that of another 68er, namely filmmaker Volker Schlöndorff whose *Die Stille nach dem Schuss/The Legends of Rita* (2000) explores his belief that the 'politics [of the RAF] were wrong, terrorism didn't lead anywhere. But the basis of the rebellion, and their urge to build a bridge to the third world and bring that struggle to the urban West, well, in the '70s that sounded like a valid idea.'[41] But unlike Rita whose violent pursuit of a better world leads her to take a life, Weingartner's trio does not cross the same fatal line, thus allowing them to take a step back and attempt to rediscover their 68er-influenced idealism.

The seemingly deadlocked ideological incompatibility between Hardenberg and his captors is at once eased *and* complicated by Hardenberg's shock-claim to be a former student radical, a member of the very generation whose worldview had formed the backbone of the trio's earlier protest gesture, and which to these young activists seems an inconceivable point of origin for a man who is now a top-capitalist. Hardenberg, as far as he maintains, is not just any 'old-68er' either; affiliated with the upper echelons of the Socialist German Student Federation (SDS) the activist turned top-manager claims to have been a close personal friend of the charismatic student leader Rudi Dutschke, the most potent icon of '1968' in the cultural context of Germany.

Given the recent fraught reputation of the radical past in Germany it would seem deeply ironic that a former 68er should have become the target of a 'political' kidnapping in Weingartner's film; here the left-wing interrogators of the 1960s are now themselves being interrogated over their past actions in light of generational shifts. Unlike the Fischer controversy mentioned earlier however, Jan and his companions are not troubled by what Hardenberg might have done during his alleged radical past but rather what he has become, that is one of the many countercultural 68ers

---

41   Miller, 'An Interview with German Filmmaker Volker Schlöndorff', *World Socialist Web Site*, 13 February 2001 <www.wsws.org/articles/2001/feb2001/schl-f03_prn. shtml> [accessed 06 July 2005].

who set out to change the world but who have long since been integrated, and ostensibly happily so, into 'the system'.

According to Weingartner, the decision to make Hardenberg a former student activist was a matter of cinematic realism, an attempt to break the cliché of the rich CEO as a mere one-dimensional caricature of state power: 'das gehört eben zu den Herausforderungen der Realität – dass ein Topmanager nicht so ein mieses Schwein ist, sondern ein kultivierter Mensch. Der als Student irgendwie ein wilder Hund war [...]' (that belongs simply to the challenge of reality: that a top-manager isn't necessarily a lousy pig, but rather a urbane individual who was a wild student [...]).[42] Evocative of the now ubiquitous neologism 'Joschka's wild years' coined by the German current affairs magazine *Spiegel*, Hardenberg (Burghart Klaußner) certainly bears more than a passing resemblance to Fischer, albeit before the Foreign Minister took to the streets again, only this time with his now famous running shoes instead of anti-capitalist slogans in a bid to shed excess weight. '1968' and the utopian idealism of its 'wild years' posits a generational confluence between Hardenberg and his captors through which, for a time at least, Weingartner's narrative might even be said to establish a liminal space of generational reconciliation between the '"Yesterday's Heroes" of "1968"' now carrying the state, and those who would designate them so, namely the 89ers who feel that the enduring legacy of the former student radicals might threaten their own significance.[43] Indeed, the tension between the 'new' and 'old' radicals soon thaws and before long they are trading stories over communal spliffs and playing cards together. Hardenberg who, paradoxically, begins to feel increasingly free through his captivity comes in to his own and seemingly assumes a paternal, even guiding role in the running of what quickly moves from being a *Volksgefängnis* to a new proto-commune in the wilderness. This burgeoning sense of family, which might offer its own utopian enactment of a generational reconciliation, is consolidated when the group travels to

---

42   Gansera and Göttler, 'Die Liebe in Zeiten der Matrix'.
43   Cited in Taberner, 'Introduction: German Literature in the Age of Globalisation', 10.

a telephone box in the nearest village so that Hardenberg can call home to explain his prolonged absence. We share the apprehension felt by Jan, for whom close-ups of villagers' faces hold accusatory glances and the risk of discovery. But Hardenberg or 'Hardi' as Peter has taken to calling him plays his part brilliantly, credibly passing off Jan as his son when a local resident becomes too friendly and thus creating a generational imaginary of a harmonious 68er/89er family album.

Hardenberg, for whom the kidnapping becomes a holiday of sorts and allows for a nostalgic revisitation of his past life, is revitalised and feeds off the familiar idealism reawakened in him by the young 89ers. He relishes his relocation and a simpler way of life freed from the strictures of his stressful career which he claims to have often considered abandoning in favour of a teaching post in the countryside with his wife. Mirroring the place previously occupied by Jan and his companions, the euphoric Hardenberg hangs out of the window of the camper van and sings out loud now that his long since repressed life instincts have been let out for a well needed vacation. However, that is all Hardenberg's revisitation of his past ever amounts to – a vacation. This highly ambivalent character who has since traded in his radicalism for a quick march up the corporate ladder is ultimately unable, perhaps even unwilling to recuperate his former worldview in a sustained fashion. Any symbolic gesture of reconciliation is itself quickly nullified when, returned to his bourgeois life and self, 'Hardi' turns on his new 'friends' making one last visit to the trio at their Berlin proto-commune but in his 'true' identity of a high-powered industrialist with the state apparatus at his disposal. Indeed, flanked by a massive police swat team in a scene which recalls the excessive state reaction to dissent depicted in Volker Schlöndorff and Margarethe von Trotta's *Die verlorene Ehre der Katharina Blum / The Lost Honour of Katharina Blum* (1975), the former 68er's excessive response says less about the potential for terror posed by the 'Edukators' than safeguarding the hegemonic system which now forms the backbone to his identity. The radical past is ultimately an inaccessible foreign country for the former 68er whose previous life has been rigidly colonised by the capitalist epithets he had claimed to feel trapped by.

Conclusion: it makes sense to be engaged

Weingartner certainly had a clear aim in mind for *The Edukators*, stating: 'Ich wollte, dass die Zuschauer aus dem Kino gehen und sagen: Es macht Sinn, sich zu engagieren, es kann auch durchaus Spaß machen, es kann mich politisch weiterbringen' (I wanted the spectators to go to the cinema and say: it makes sense to be engaged. It can even be fun too and can bring me further politically).[44] The importance, it would seem, lies in the attempt. Evoking Linklater's calling-card for his American cult film *Slacker*,[45] Weingartner motions that 'every action is a positive action, even if it has a negative result.'[46] The director wants simply to motivate and where possible inspire his otherwise apathetic peers, thus echoing the aims of his fictional protagonists who hope to inspire imitators. In a case of life imitating art Weingartner's wish was seemingly granted. Described by the director as his happiest moment of the year, in May 2005 a group of masked protestors stormed the exclusive Hamburg restaurant Süllberg in a protest against Germany's 'two-class society'.[47] Armed with oversised cardboard knives and forks the protesters helped themselves to the expensive buffet and distributed flowers to the diners, as well as flyers which attacked the working conditions at the restaurant and its manager:

This Action is directed against working conditions. For the majority of temporary workers in this restaurant, unpaid overtime is the rule. Since the formation of a workers union has been blocked, the employees must work long hours to afford the manager's new car. Simply put, you, the restaurant patrons, can't afford to eat here![48]

---

44 See Gansera and Göttler, 'Die Liebe in Zeiten der Matrix'.

45 Weingartner served as a production assistant on another of Linklater's films, *Before Sunrise* (1995).

46 See Gansera and Göttler, 'Die Liebe in Zeiten der Matrix'.

47 Cited in Christiane Peitz and Jan Schulz-Ojala, 'Radikale brauchen Humor' (Gespräch mit Dani Levy, Volker Schlöndorff und Hans Weingartner), *Tagesspiegel*, 7 July 2005.

48 'Diese Aktion richtet sich gegen die Arbeitsverhältnisse. Im Hause Hauser sind unbezahlte Überstunden für die zumeist nur aushilfsweise beschäftigten Arbeitskräfte die

If the political sentiment here seems familiar that is because the protesters were directly influenced by Weingartner's film – as well as distributing
flyers they all wore t-shirts with the words 'Die fetten Jahre sind vorbei'.
But unlike the slogan t-shirts discussed in the introduction which alluded
to a radical gesture that was in fact lacking, Weingartner's imitators had
a clear political agenda underpinning their statement. Although the aesthetic strategy which informs *The Edukators* might be said to speak to the
'pop' sensibility of a consumerist youth-driven society, it is a 'pop'-based
protest with content: the productive dialogue which the director sets up
with the beleaguered memory of '1968' ultimately challenges a prevailing
trend towards its commodification by restoring its significance as a politically symbolic episode. The Süllberg episode might not amount to the
director having restored the revolutionary energy of the youth but it is
perhaps a small step in the right direction. While critical of what many of
the 68ers have become Weingartner valorises '1968' as a symbolically laden
moment of utopian potential which might continue to offer productive
options for subsequent generations which are otherwise struggling to find
their critical voices.

Regel. Da ein Bertriebsrat verhindert wurde, müssen die Angestellten für Hausers
neuses Auto länger arbeiten. Sie alle können es sich nicht leisten, hier essen zu gehen.'
See Wiebke Strehlow and Olaf Wunder, 'Mundraub im Gourmet-Tempel', *Hamburger
Morgenpost*, 2 May 2005, <http://archiv.mopo.de/rewrite/show.php?pfad=/
archiv/2005/20050502/nachrichten/hamburg/panorama/hmp2005050118314003.
html> [accessed on 18 July 2006].

PART 5

Decentring 1968

SOFIA SERENELLI-MESSENGER

1968 in an Italian Province: Memory and the Everyday Life of a New Left Group in Macerata

1. Introduction

In March 1971, when the Italian '1968'[1] had already developed into widespread socio-political movements reaching the most remote and provincial areas,[2] the small, isolated and rural town of Macerata (c.a. 40,000 inhabitants), in the Marche region of central Italy, also began to be affected by the dynamics of the political struggle. Previously unstudied, this local 1968 inevitably maintained most of the characteristics of the social and cultural context from which it was derived.[3] This was particularly the case with regard to the role of the family, which was traditionally the basis of the structural and cultural identity of this province: structurally, in its roots in the long tradition of sharecropping, and culturally in the prevail-

---

1   Rather that as an 'event', in this paper '1968' is considered as a 'process', i.e. the series of social movements from the mid 1960s through the middle of the following decade. When referred to as the year 1968, the inverted commas are not used. On the Italian debate on the nature of 1968 See S. Urso, 'Il lungo decennio: l'Italia prima del '68', in N. Fasano and M. Renosio (eds), *I giovani e la politica: il lungo '68* (Turin: Ega, 2002), 18–25.

2   On the large and conflicting variety of the 1968 social movements see G. Crainz, *Il Paese Mancato. Dal miracolo economico agli anni ottanta* (Milan: Donzelli, 2003), 288–293.

3   See especially P. Connerton, *How Societies Remember* (Cambridge: Cambridge University Press, 1989).

ing Catholic and solidly Christian Democrat political orientation.[4] This chapter reconsiders the local 'revolution' of '1968' by analysing whether the form of the family was subverted or, conversely and perhaps paradoxically, reinforced and employed as part of the political struggle. It will do so by focusing on 'memories' of everyday life within the local branch of the important Manifesto group, a far-left formation which still survives as a daily newspaper. It will also examine the impact of feminism within the Manifesto group, looking at how it affected the political group's inner dynamics.

What is at stake is the complex relationship between '1968' and the institution of family which, in the ample historiography of 1968, still persists as one of the main historiographical 'holes.' Innovative recent studies have delved into the anthropological and cultural aspects of 1968, which, along with the proliferation of memoirs, constitute new attempts to broaden the historical concept of this movement.[5] However, the same tendency of the student movement, as in the socialist tradition, to leave the family behind in favour of the 'political' struggle has rendered the 'private' side of '1968,' as Paul Ginsborg writes, 'buried history, ... implicit, not explicit, [which is] to be teased out and uncovered from different sources. In the case of 1968 they emerge from oral history very forcefully, but only if the specific ques-

---

4   S. Anselmi (ed.), *Economia e società. Le Marche tra XV e XX secolo* (Bologna: Il Mulino, 1978).

5   For the main comparative studies taking into account the Italian context see A. Marwick, *The Sixties. Cultural Revolution in Britain, France, Italy and the United States, c.1958–1974* (Oxford: Oxford University Press, 1998); R. Lumley, *Dal '68 agli anni di piombo. Studenti e operai nella crisi italiana* (Florence: Giunti, 1994) and R. Fraser, *1968. A Student Generation in Revolt* (London: Chatto & Windus, 1988). Among the Italian studies see especially G. De Marino, *Biografia del Sessantotto. Utopia, conquiste, sbandamenti* (Milan: Bompiani, 2004); P. Ortoleva, *I movimenti del '68 in Europa e in America*, 2nd edn (Rome: Editori Riuniti, 1998) and L. Passerini, *Autoritratto di gruppo* (Florence: Giunti, 1989). See also testimonies from various marginal militants in F. Crocchi (ed.), *Un anno durato decenni. Vite di persone comuni prima, durante, dopo il '68* (Rome: Odradeck, 2006).

tion is posed.'[6] Nevertheless, the family has now been claimed as a crucial space in historical dynamics,[7] and it is precisely during the course of the 'long '68' that we find, both in Italy and in the broader European context, a crucial transformation of sociological models, socio-cultural concepts and the legal status of the institution of the family itself.[8]

Through a micro-historical case study such as Macerata, this chapter also highlights the relevance of the socio-cultural context in the experience and memory of the movement, and this might bring new insights into our general understanding of 1968. Indeed, the majority of historical studies have concentrated primarily on the main urban centres,[9] and therefore

---

6   P. Ginsborg, 'Measuring the Distance: the Case of the Family, 1968–2001' (2002) *Thesis Eleven* 68–71, 47.

7   See P. Ginsborg, 'Family, Civil Society and the State in Contemporary European History: Some Methodological Considerations' (1995) 4 *Contemporary European History* 3, 249–274.

8   See F. De Singly and V. Cicchelli, 'Contemporary Families: Social Reproduction and Personal Fulfilment', in M. Barbagli and D.I. Kertzer (eds), *Family Life in Twentieth Century* (London: Yale University Press, 2003), 311–349.

9   Only sporadically, and more recently, have there been attempts to reconstruct the more provincial and marginal contexts, and then often through collections of personal memories rather than historical analyses. See N. Fasano, 'Giovani ad Asti: voci dalla provincia', in Fasano and Renosio, *I giovani e la politica*, 161–204; O. Bo, 'Il '68 dei contadini', in Fasano and Renosio, *I giovani e la politica*, 205–221; P. Clemente, *Triglie di Scoglio* (Magiari: Cuec, 2002); M. Ceriani (ed.), *Che cosa rimane. Racconti dopo il '68* (Milan: Jaca Book, 2001); M. Becchetti (ed.), *Parma dentro la rivolta* (Milan: Punto Rosso, 2000); G. Sacchetti, 'Il Sessantotto aretino/la provincia italiana negli anni della rivolta' (1998) *Per il Sessantotto* 14–15, 75–85; A.M. Zanetti, *Una ferma utopia sta per fiorire. Le ragazze di ieri: idee e vicende del movimento femminista nel Veneto* (Venice: Marsilio, 1998); L. Passerini, *Storia di donne e femministe* (Turin: Rosemberg & Sellier, 1991), 96–123; A. Orsi, *Il nostro Sessantotto: 1968–1973, i movimenti giovanili studenteschi e operai in Valsesia e Valsessera* (Vercelli: Istituto per la Storia della Resistenza Cino Moscatelli, 1990); S. Distefano, *'68, che passione! Il movimento studentesco a Catania* (Catania: CUECM, 1988); A. Stramaccioni, *Il '68 e la Sinistra: movimenti e culture: l'esperienza umbra 1966–1972* (Perugina: Protagon, 1988); R. Rovetta, *Brescia Sessanta. La cultura: gruppi, iniziative e protagonisti, 1960–1968* (Brescia: Grimau, 1984) and G. Fiori, "68. Il movimento studentesco nella provincia, Marginalità, spontaneismo e organizzazione', in P. Sorcinelli (ed.),

the multifarious features of the Italian movement are still to be researched, both in terms of its particular characteristics in specific contexts and with regard to the nature, methodologies and dynamics of its dissemination.[10] Memories are inevitably affected by the '1968' local dynamics and are indicative of the '1968' experience in specific areas and of its continuing effects. Macerata is just one regional case study among many others, yet detailed investigations of the various legacies and experiences of 1968 can provide more concrete assessments of its complexity and plurality as a phenomenon which, in Peppino Ortoleva's words, was at the same time both 'local' and 'global'.[11] This also tells us much about the 'centre' of the 1968 movement and about the extent, and limits, of its vast experiment to change the institution of the family and society.

2. Methodology: Micro-history and oral history

This study is based on the life stories of more than thirty participants in the local political movement, which developed in Macerata in 1971 with the first appearance of the extreme left groups. Interviews have been conducted in a number of sessions between the spring of 2005 and the winter of 2007,[12] and the 'memories' are mainly from the ten to fifteen militants that founded and participated at different levels in the inner hierarchy of

---

      Marginalità, spontaneismo, organizzazione. 1860–1968 uomini e lotte nel Pesarese (Pesaro: Iders, 1982), 93–118.

10   Cfr. A. Mangano, 'La geografia del movimento del '68 in Italia', in P. Poggio (ed.), *Il '68: l'evento e la storia* (Brescia: Fondazione Luigi Micheletti, 1990), 231–256 and M. Grispigni and L. Musci (eds), *Guida alle fonti per la storia dei movimenti in Italia (1966–1978)* (Rome: Ministero per i beni e le attività culturali, Direzione Generale per gli Archivi, 2003).

11   Ortoleva, *I movimenti del '68 in Europa e in America.*

12   See S. Serenelli, *1968 in provincia. Famiglia, spazio e la memoria della vita quotidiana a Macerata, 1960–1980*, PhD diss., University College London, 2008.

the local Manifesto group. Although a section of the other main extreme left group 'Lotta Continua' had also been founded in Macerata, most of the protagonists of the local movement converged in the Manifesto political formation, rendering the Manifesto group of particular interest to our understanding of 1968 in this region. Memories have also been compared with the wealth of unpublished material collected during the course of field-research.

Research on oral history and micro-history has emphasised the importance of looking at individuals within their life contexts and at the way in which they subjectively experience and metabolise events, as a way of reaching a closer understanding of historical phenomena.[13] Oral history always implies a complex interaction between past and present, with recollections of the past being affected by the image of the self that each individual wishes to convey in the present. This entails ellipses, omissions, and even silences that, on the basis of a shared cultural substratum, make representations of the past harmonious with the resulting identities in the present.[14] Micro-history has also shown that there is sometimes scarce correspondence between the 'macro' and at the 'micro' level. In the case of Macerata, in fact, myths that have crystallised the 'collective image' of 1968 either do not apply or assume specific connotations. This also applies to the silences and elliptical narratives that in the historical debate have been suggested as forming the basis of the 'unwritten' history of the Italian 70s, such as violence and the ultimate defeat of the extreme left's political project.[15]

13 G. Levi, 'A proposito di microstoria' in P. Burke (ed.), *La storiografia contemporanea* (Bari: Laterza, 1993), 111–147; G. Prins, 'La storia orale', in Burke, *La storiografia contemporanea*, 111–166.

14 L. Passerini, *Fascism in popular memory: the cultural experience of the Turin working class* (Cambridge: Cambridge University Press, 1987), 23. On memory of everyday life see especially P. Jedlowski, *Storie comuni. La narrazione nella vita quotidiana* (Milan: Mondatori, 2000).

15 See A. Cento Bull and A. Giorgio, 'The 1970s through the Looking Glass' in A. Cento Bull and A. Giorgio (eds), *Speaking Out and Silence* (London: Legenda, 2006), 1–8. See also E. Palandri, 'The Difficulty of a Historical Prospective on the 1970s', in Cento Bull and Giorgio, *Speaking Out and Silence*, 115–120.

In memories and oral histories on the Italian '1968', a movement that brought the first challenge to the family institution since the birth of the Italian Republic,[16] the metaphor of a 'family' has seldom been used in relation to the extreme left groups[17] and only with reference to their collective lifestyles. In her work on the 1968 in Turin, Luisa Passerini relates memories of the 'private' side of the movement to psychological strategies of coping with the sense of defeat ex-militants have felt following its eventual demise. Guido Viale, leader of the 1968 movement in Turin, is one of the few ex-68s to mention the family in relation to the extreme left groups. In his view, the re-appearance of the 'family' as the structural foundation of the extreme left parties parallels the conventional division of 1968 between the initial, genuine phase and the radical upheavals represented as the defeat of the 'original' movement.[18] The association between the political groups and the 'family' is referred to more often in feminist writings, but only with negative connotations regarding their 'patriarchal structure' and the quality of interpersonal relationships within the groups.[19] In brief, both memories and historiography have emphasised the 'return', within the extreme left parties, to 'patriarchal' forms of relationships and hierarchies, with the critical impact of feminism as the cause for the end of the extreme left parties as well as for the break-up of many couples. The 'family', therefore, has always constituted a 'negative' reference, and 'positive' references have been made only to lifestyles which were alternative to it.

Conversely, in memories from Macerata the collective recollection of the political group is mostly rendered through the widespread employment of family tropes, while the assimilation between the Manifesto group and

---

16   P. Ginsborg, *A history of contemporary Italy: society and politics, 1943–1988* (London: Penguin, 1990), 304.

17   See A. Cazzullo, *I ragazzi che volevano fare la rivoluzione: 1968–1978: storia di Lotta Continua* (Milan: Mondatori, 1998), 166. For the absence of any comparison between the family and the party in political theory see for example P. Pettit (ed.), *Contemporary Political Theory* (Toronto: MacMillan, 1991).

18   G. Viale, *Il Sessantotto: tra rivoluzione e restaurazione* (Milan: Mazzotta, 1978), 181.

19   L. Grasso, *Compagno padrone* (Florence: Guaraldi Editore, 1974).

the family is often not only metaphorical but related to its actual structure and is never negatively associated with a sense of defeat. The crucial role of the family typifies both the 'amnesia indigenous to feminism',[20] in other words the silences which have been regarded as the reason for the missing history of Italian feminism,[21] and the collective representation of the local extreme left group. This entails differences in ways general issues such as 'violence' in the 'public' and 'private' spheres[22] and the collective sense of 'grief' for the political defeat[23] are negotiated and historicised. The oral-history and micro-historical focus on the margins, therefore, also enrich the complexity of '1968' in its multifaceted subjective and contextual plurality and in the complex interaction between ideology and everyday life practice.

3. The local Manifesto group and the ideological view of the family

The local Manifesto group was founded by a core group of about ten people that since the end of 1968 had constituted the small avant-garde of the local 'generational movement'[24] and emerged as the leadership of the local

---

20   See L. Passerini, 'Memory for Women's History: Problems of Method and Interpretation' (1992) 3 *Social Science History* 16, 671.

21   A. Rossi Doria, 'Ipotesi per una storia che verrà', in T. Bertilotti, A. Scattigno (eds), *Il femminismo degli anni Settanta* (Rome: Viella, 2005), pp. 1–24.

22   A. Bravo, 'Noi e la violenza. Trent'anni per pensarci' (2004) 3 *Genesis* 1, 17–56 and L. Passerini, *Storia e memoria degli anni settanta* (2005), www.societadellestoriche. it.

23   L. Passerini, *Autobiography of a generation: Italy, 1968* (London: University Press of England, 1996), 127–135.

24   Along with the distinction between the 'sociological generation' and 'political generation' see A. Cavalli, 'Generazioni' (1998) *Parolechiave* 16, 17–33. In this chapter only the political phase of the movement is taken into account. Before 1971, the 'movement' in the Macerata province was characterised by the local fascination with

university occupation in March 1971. As the founders of the local branch of the Manifesto group, this core group of leaders and their female companions were at the top of the local Manifesto hierarchy. In 1973, with the diffusion, on a national level, of the 'Collettivi femministi comunisti' founded by 'double militants' (i.e. women who were militants both in the extreme left and in the feminist groups),[25] the women of the Macerata group were also inspired to form an associated feminist group. With the local spread of the political movement from 1971 onwards, the Manifesto core group became a point of reference for at least 400 militants among young people locally. Rather than a 'regression' from the 'image of a fan opening to infinite possibilities'[26] and from the collective discovery of subjectivity[27] during the first phase of the movement,[28] here the extreme left militancy coincided with the 'beginning' of direct participation. On the ideological level, the foundation of the Manifesto core group coincided with the emergence of a critical view of the family institution amongst its members. This channelled the generic discomfort and will of an alternative which was dispersed among the local youth. The local militants eventually came to share the view of the family held by the national Manifesto group. In contrast with the other extreme left formations, whose reflection upon the family was only in response to the Divorce Referendum in 1974, the Manifesto group opened the debate on the family institution as early as 1971 to counter the 'threat' of feminism being gradually embraced by militant

---

the American hippy culture and with the poets of the Beat Generation. This phase is separated from the 'political' phase also by its being driven by a small avant-garde among the local youth.

25   See M. Fraire, *Lessico politico delle donne: teorie del femminismo* (Milan: Franco Angeli, 2002), 124. See also A. Calabrò and L. Grasso (eds), *Dal movimento femminista al femminismo diffuso: storie e percorsi a Milano dagli anni '60 agli anni '80*, 2nd edn (Milan: Angeli, 2004).

26   See Passerini, 'A Memory for Women's History', 681.

27   L. Passerini, 'Utopia and Desire' (2002) *Thesis Eleven* 68–71, 11–30.

28   On the distinction of three different phases in the Italian 1968 see M. Flores and A. De Bernardis (eds), *Il Sessantotto*, 2nd edn (Bologna: Il Mulino, 2003), 194–195.

women within the Manifesto organisation.[29] Given the heterogeneity of the cultural framework typical of the first phase of the student movement, the adoption of a Marxist perspective raised the expectations of a 'scientific' understanding of the structural function of the family in contemporary capitalism. But it restricted de facto the theoretical and practical exploration of alternative models. With Engels' *The Origin of the Family: private property and the state*[30] as the main theoretical reference, the nuclear family, the main instrument for the preservation of property, was held to survive in a 'mystified role.' Once it had lost the structural status of an economic unit, it only retained the psychological function of subjecting the individual to the conservation of capitalism. The family was, as the Manifesto national leader Luciana Castellina wrote in 1974, 'the only island ... where the inner solidarity among blood-relatives is the other side of the brutal egotism towards the outside and of the withdrawal on its own, narrow privatism.'[31] However, with the concentration on structural aspects rather than on the inner site of psychological oppression, the adoption of a Marxist perspective also gave the issues of family and private life a theoretical secondary role.[32] Absolute priority was given to the political struggle, and a new model of the family was regarded as naturally consequential to the economic and social order that originated from the abolition of ownership. Rather than being examined in the complex variety of its concrete forms, functions and conditions during that phase of dramatic change,[33] the family was

29   See Fraire, *Lessico politico*, 123. See also D. degli Incerti (ed.), *La sinistra rivoluzionaria in Italia: documenti e interventi delle tre principali organizzazioni: Avanguardia operaia, Lotta Continua, PdUP* (Rome: Savelli, 1976), 205–280.

30   F. Engels, *L'origine della famiglia, della proprietà privata e dello Stato* (Rome: La nuova sinistra, 1973).

31   L. Castellina, 'La vertenza famiglia', in L. Castellina (ed.), *Il Manifesto. Famiglia e società capitalistica. Quaderni del Manifesto-1* (Rome: Alfani, 1974), 269.

32   On the ideological view of the family in the socialist tradition see M. Casalini, 'La famiglia socialista. Linguaggio di classe e identità di genere nella cultura del movimento operaio' (2005) *Italia Contemporanea* 241, 415–447. On the view of the family in the Communist Party see Ginsborg, *A History of Contemporary Italy*, 197.

33   L. Balbo, 'La famiglia degli anni '70', *Il Manifesto*, 5 May 1974. This article is among those collected by the local feminists and kept in private archives.

considered by the extreme left only as an ideological nuclear model. The only theoretical indications for an alternative kind of family did not go further than 'a humane couple' – as the other extreme left group of Lotta Continua wrote in its Journal in 1971 – 'formed by the union of free and equal human beings.'[34]

Even the local feminists who, like the 'Collettivi femministi comunsti' on a national level, subscribed to traditional Marxist precepts did not go so far as to elaborate a theoretical alternative to the family and to protest against the institution of the couple. Imported by extreme left female militants that were mainly concerned with the priority of the 'political revolution' and of their extra-parliamentary affiliation, feminism drew attention to the 'private sphere' of gender relationships.[35] However, although the ideological view of the family was enriched by its recognition as the first site of 'sex oppression' specific to women,[36] the lack of a theoretical reflection on alternative models was explicitly lamented in documents from the same feminist group. 'On the level of the family and of women's liberation we have not until now been able to find a strategic alternative,' feminists from Macerata wrote in 1974;[37] while, in most of the article by the feminist and Manifesto leader Luciana Castellina kept in private archives, militant women were insistently urged not to 'consider themselves as separate' from their male counterparts.[38] Therefore, with regard to the family, the local feminist theoretical positions tended to shift between the need for its destruction and, more likely, as it was made clear in most of their writ-

---

34   Anon., 'La donna, la famiglia e la rivoluzione' (1970) 1 *Comunismo*, 75–82.

35   See S. Piccone Stella, 'Introduzione. Femminismo e sociologia della famiglia', in M. Fraire (ed.), *Lessico politico delle donne. Sociologia della famiglia, sull'emancipazione femminile*, vol. 4–5 (Milan: Gulliver, 1979), 6–33 and P. Jedlowski and C. Leccardi (eds), *Sociologia della vita quotidiana* (Bologna: Il Mulino, 2003), 94–99.

36   See C. Saraceno, 'La contraddizione uomo-donna tra movimento femminista e sociologia della famiglia', in Fraire, *Lessico politico delle donne. Sociologia della famiglia*, 66–74.

37   Collettivo Femminista, 'Documento del collettivo femminista maceratese', Macerata, 1974, in Fondo Luzi, Biblioteca Mozzi Borgetti, Macerata.

38   L. Castellina, 'Bisogna evitare a tutti i costi di considerarci una corporazione', *Il Manifesto*, 8 March 1974.

ings, the call for its transformation in terms of equality within the couple.[39] In conclusion, rather than a 'family utopia' the Manifesto group, like every other extreme left party, was a 'political utopia' which regarded 'family utopias' such as the communes as unwanted diversions from the political struggle. However, at Macerata, it also constituted a 'new kind of family' where the new collective lifestyle and the feminist emphasis on 'subjective liberation' stimulated the experimentation with new models of the family. Ingrained traditional family cultures come into conflict with the emergence of new concepts of family and alternative family practices, furthering the complexity of ongoing processes of change. This dialectic and its effects are still implicit in the collective recollection of the political group through the different use of family models, as well as in individual and collective memories of the impact of feminism on the group's everyday life and inner relationships.

4. Memories: the party as a 'family'

'I remember when we set up our base: we worked together and restored the place ... It was all-absorbing and we used to live together all the time. ... Even now, in memory, I cannot distinguish between the family and the group: to me, group and family were a single unit.' This account from Palma, a feminist leader and one of the founders of the Manifesto group, is representative of the way in which the Manifesto militants from Macerata describe the political group. Compared to memories of the collective lifestyle typical of extreme left groups where 'the way of being together' was likened to 'a way

---

39   L. Castellina, 'Lettera aperta ai compagni del Manifesto', In B.M. Frabotta (ed.), *La politica del femminismo, 1973–1976* (Rome: Edizioni Savelli, 1976), 228. See also the degree thesis by one of the female interviewees, P. Loi, *Charles Fourier critico della civiltà moderna*, BA diss., Università degli Studi di Macerata, 1974.

to constitute a family,'[40] memories from Macerata are firstly distinguished
by the frequency of family tropes as the main means to describe the group.
Secondly, they are distinguished by the qualitative implications of the use
of these family tropes. According to Luisa Passerini, the concentration on
the 'positive aspects of everyday life attitudes and cultures of the movement' constituted a strategy of defence against the confrontation with the
responsibility for 'violence' and with the 'grief' associated with political
defeat.[41] Therefore, the stressing of the collective quality of everyday life has
been a constant in memories, and this has been the only way in which the
'family' has been rescued as a 'positive' metaphor for the political groups.
At Macerata, by contrast, almost all the members of the Manifesto group
refer to the political group through the use and overlapping of different
family models, both metaphorically and with reference to the intrinsic
structure of the group. Moreover, the 'family' here is often referred to as a
positive concept, associated with a sense of group belonging, 'cohesion' and
'affective solidarity.' Although asserted most forcefully by the ex-militants
at the top of the group's inner hierarchy, this image of the political group as
a cohesive 'family' represses memories of the authoritarian and hierarchical
nature of relationships inside the group.

The frequency of family tropes is implicit in the (male) recollection
of the foundation of the group. This is evident from Lapo, a university
student in the bigger but still provincial city of Bologna and a member
of the Manifesto's National Committee, in charge of the diffusion of the
Manifesto organisation in the Marche Region; and from Tardo, a leader of
the local university occupation in March 1971. Both their descriptions use
the metaphor of family figures, implicitly alluding to the gerontocracy of the
sharecropping family model still widespread in the local countryside.[42]

40   Cazzullo, *I ragazzi che volevano fare la rivoluzione*, 166. See also A. Grandi, *La gen-
      erazione degli anni perduti: storie di potere operaio* (Turin: Einaudi, 2003).

41   Passerini, *Autobiography*, 132.

42   Most of these militants' families moved from the local rural areas to the town of
      Macerata during the post-war migratory phenomena. These families were rarely
      nuclear but mostly still extended, with strong economic and social relations to the
      local countryside. See A. Adversi, 'L'economia contemporanea', in A. Adversi, D.

Tardo ... addressed me as if he was my son, and then he discovered he was one year older than me!! (Lapo).

I told Fernando:[43]'I think we should open a Manifesto section at Macerata!' and he replied: 'how can we do that? We are all little boys!' I said: 'look, there's one from Recanati[44] who is older' ... That was Lapo, who had already turned grey! (Tardo).

Interestingly, the foundation of the extreme left groups is also symbolised by the passage to maturity, as a sort of coming of age. 'After the University occupation, at the end of January 1971, I'm a man of the movement', explains Tardo, defining himself for the first time in the course of his life-story as a 'man'. Both the allusion to the asymmetric family relations implied by the old-young hierarchy and the symbolisation of the extreme left militancy as the first coming of age are peculiar characteristics of this local 1968. This 1968 began at a very late stage in the national and international movement, when the climate had already profoundly changed from the time when students used to write not 'to trust anyone older than thirty' on the Parisian walls. Participating in extreme left militancy meant the formation of a new collective identity and the rupture of provincial isolation through the sense of belonging to a larger revolutionary project. Therefore, if the typical use of family tropes to describe the political group implied a taken-for-granted acceptance of hierarchy, this was also due to the specific features and dynamics of 'a 1968' whose late beginning impeded the differentiation between the reappearance of 'old' forms of authority[45] and the antiauthoritarian essence[46] of the movement in its first stage.

Cecchi and L. Paci (eds), *Storia di Macerata*, 5 vol. (Macerata: Biemmegraf, 1977), 428–451.

43   Fernando was the former leader, together with Tardo, of the University occupation in 1971 and now one of the founders of the local Manifesto group.

44   Recanati is a small district of Macerata where the first local section of the Manifesto group was founded six months before the Macerata section.

45   Ginsborg, *A History of contemporary Italy*, 312.

46   See R. Lumley, 'Spazio dei movimenti e crisi d'autorità. La definizione delle identità collettive' (1999) 1 *900. Rassegna di storia contemporanea*, 99–108.

Descriptions of the political group as a 'family' come mainly from
militants who became closest to the leadership of the group. Tardo, his
partner Frida and other cadres at the top of the hierarchy, as well as the
other leader Fernando and his partner Palma, began to share houses that
were frequented by militants, and it is mainly in this core group of at
least ten people that the image of the family overlaps structurally with the
Manifesto group. Besides, in a tiny town such as Macerata, these militants
were also related by long-standing friendships and everyday acquaintances
preceding the time of political militancy, and this boosted the structural
coincidence of the political group with a 'primary group' of friends and
couples.[47] Among these militants, explicit references to the group as a
'family' are mostly made by men, generally through a family model that
is implicitly patriarchal, but whose asymmetry is explicitly unnoticed,
hidden by the stressing of the kind of 'intimacy' which is sociologically
regarded as typical of the 'symmetrical family' model.[48] In doing so, the
cadre Blasco, for example, also stresses the structural role of the couple at
the foundation of the group:

> Well, the Manifesto group was in fact like a family: Tardo and Frida mum and dad,
> and then the children ... Frida was the feminist leader, Tardo was the leader of the
> Manifesto group, and then there was a network of numerous children, everyone with
> his own specialisation. ... However, as far as I remember, the mum and dad of this
> political family didn't rule over individual behaviours. In addition, my relation with
> them was mostly political: I used to talk only about politics with them (Blasco).

> With regard to relations, ... the Manifesto group had represented my own family.
> Inside the group, we established a kind of humane relations that maybe was too
> 'ideologised,' but that at least brought us to live together. ... Tardo, for example, is
> like a brother to me, even though we've lost touch and we don't see each other very
> often (Uto, Manifesto cadre).

47   See F. Mattioli, *Introduzione alla sociologia dei gruppi* (Rome: Seam, 2000). See also
     Passerini, *Autobiography*, 129–130.
48   A. Giddens, *The Transformation of Intimacy* (Cambridge: Polity Press, 1992).

In these memories from the top of the hierarchy, a certain amount of reading between the lines is required to tease out information about the rigidity of the pecking order as well as to grasp the nature of relationships ruled by the efficiency of political militancy. Examples are seen in Blasco's account, where some images conform less with that of a 'family' than with a 'militarised party' ('the mum and dad of this political family didn't rule over individual behaviours'); and also in Uto's remark about the ideological essence of relationships. For the rest, comments on the hierarchical structure and on the 'objectified' quality of relationships inside the political group are never explicit. Instead, what prevails, in both male and female accounts, is the focus on the inner solidarity, 'cohesion' and 'informal' structure of the group:

> I remember when we set up our base: we worked together, we did every single thing, we even restored the building! It was all-absorbing, we used to live together twenty four hours a day! We used to eat together, study together, go to university together. Then meetings, leaflets to print, things to organise ... We, women, we couldn't feel discriminated against: there was a strong spirit of comradeship (Palma).

> There was a strong acceptance of the leadership deriving from recognition of the leaders' competences and authoritativeness, including their ability in public speaking. ... I'd never been in competition and accepted the leadership. Plus the group was extremely close-knit, with friendly relationships common place (Ambretta, Manifesto cadre and feminist militant).

This is particularly evident in descriptions of the leadership, where images from the local sharecropping family model are used (and sometimes distorted)[49] not to underline the hierarchical structure but to enhance the

---

49   On the functioning and inner hierarchies of the local family model see especially S. Anselmi, 'Padroni e contadini', in Anselmi, *Le Marche*, 265–267. For more complex accounts focused on the subjective level, although not specific of this area, see C. Papa, *Dove sono molte braccia è molto pane: famiglia mezzadrile tradizionale e divisione del lavoro in Umbria* (Foligno: Editoriale Umbra, 1985) and especially G. Contini, *Aristocrazia contadina: sulla complessità della società mezzadrile. Fattoria, famiglie, individui* (Siena: Protagon, 2005).

sense of belonging and cohesiveness of the group. Rather than a 'patriarch',[50] the leader Tardo is generally described as a family-figure, an 'elder brother' or an affective 'father', assuming the traditional 'pillar of the community' role.

> My image of Tardo is that of a father-figure, someone who mediates and organises the others. What strikes me is that with time he's been able to win everybody round. Now he's an authority at Macerata: he's a reference point for my cousin, for my brother, who he used to play with in 1963, and now he tells them stories ... (Lara, feminist militant from Milan).

> There was not a proper leader but decisions were agreed upon by all. It was like a typical family from this area. In this province there's always been a sense of family as a group rather than as a site of patriarchal authority: the sharecropping family used to work as a single unit (Tardo).

This might also hint at a charismatic influence still affecting memory, especially in the context of a small town where the old dynamics of social control are partially still in place (Tardo is actually an influential figure on the local political scene). In fact, the radical feminist Lara (a former militant from Macerata, who moved to Milan and has not been involved locally for some time) is the only voice which makes explicit the dynamics of competition and the arbitrary selection of the leadership: 'they caused me much pain. Stelvio[51] was basically forbidden to be part of the local Manifesto because of his former political experience in the Pci and Psiup. ... This is the story they invented: "we belong to a group!"'. In order to find local memories that somehow mirror the widespread criticism of the hierarchical and objectified relationships typical of most historical accounts and memoirs

---

50   See M. Diani and P. Donati, 'L'oscuro oggetto del desiderio: leadership e potere nelle aree di movimento', in A. Melucci (ed.), *Altri codici: aree di movimento nella metropoli* (Bologna: Il Mulino, 1984), 315–348. On the organisation of the Italian extreme left parties see G. Vettori, *La sinistra extraparlamentare in Italia. Storia, documenti, analisi politica* (Rome: Newton Compton Editori, 1973). On the Manifesto group see S. De Bartolo, *I temi politici della sinistra extraparlamentare negli anni '70. Il caso del Manifesto* (Ferrara: CDS, 1998).

51   Stelvio was Lara's partner and one of the leaders in the 1971 University occupation.

about the extreme left groups,[52] it is necessary to turn to memories from base-militants, the most marginal and remote from the core group of leaders. In all the other cases, aspects such as lack of democracy, inclusiveness and social control, even when pointed out, are softened by emotive considerations; and responsibilities are never attributed to specific individuals (usually the leader, as in the case of the most marginal militants) but to the impersonal entity of the 'group.' This also stems from the accounts of ex-militants, such as the former leader Fernando, who have developed a strong discontinuity with their past.

> The political group was somehow like a family. For example, if you said: 'let's go out for pizza', then you had to go as twenty people! Twenty people out for pizza, twenty people to the cinema, twenty people going on holiday ... I was critical and disagreed with such conformism. Once Palma and I had an intimate New Years Eve in a cave in the mountains, and we became the object of the group's criticism: 'they are isolating themselves!' I remember that Palma cried ... It was exactly like a family, with the obligation to spend time with your relatives (Fernando).

Only in descriptions from former base-militants does the concept of family re-acquire the negative connotation it has in leaflets and newspaper articles collected in the private archives. In these cases, the political group is still described through the use of family tropes, but in the model of a 'patriarchal family' regulated by a compulsory system of control negating the possibility of individual 'private' life.

> Belonging to the political group made you feel observed because you had to behave in accordance with the other people in the group. If you had different attitudes, then you could emerge as different: when you belonged, you belonged. [...] Externally, they professed individual freedom, but you couldn't be free inside. There was no freedom at all (Lana, Manifesto cadre and feminist).

---

52 S. Voli, *Quando il privato diventa politico: Lotta Continua 1968–1976* (Rome: Edizioni Associate, 2006).

It was enormously difficult to mediate between the individual and collective side for me. I've always been accused of being changeable and immersed in my own private life. The idea was that, when you do politics, you have to do it fulltime and that personal life was an impediment to political militancy (Ubaldo, Manifesto cadre).

In the case of women, this system of control is often related to dynamics of love and sexuality and, implicitly, to the political exploitation of the female body.[53] With respect to this, the family-based structure of the political group is even more forcefully reasserted. Besides the implications on the changing cultures and practices of family, it is pointed out that the structural role of the couple was crucial for the group's inner stability and balance.

It was very difficult to say 'no, I can't go with you because I don't fancy you!' or 'because I love someone else ...' You couldn't: this was part of the rules. (Lana)

When I came back to Macerata I had a brief love affair with Tardo and I wrote him letters from Milan. Then, I learnt that these letters had been read publicly in the political group. The fact that the group – which I didn't know personally! – sat down in a round table and read my letters, I define as a violence against individual privacy. [...] Our relationship was analysed in its effects on the political group because it concerned the leader couple (Lara, feminist from Milan).

Finally, the structural and symbolic centrality of the 'family' in representations of the Manifesto group from Macerata is also highlighted by the recollections of ex-militants, who are the most external and critical of the group. Referring to single members of the group by name rather than to the group as an impersonal single entity, their criticisms still use images from the local family tradition. Yet, in this case, the sharecropping family model is not distorted to symbolise cohesiveness and equality, but rather used as a means to describe the rigidity of the pecking order and the oppressiveness of social control. The functioning of the party is even more clearly related to the family and kinship structure anthropologically typical of the rural

53   Voli, *Quando il privato diventa politico*, 52–55. See also Lara's testimony about a female militant in the local Manifesto group: 'S. ... was a "free spirit", one of the women who regarded sexual intercourse with workers as part of the revolution.'

village, with this system of control being exerted through the traditional means of 'gossip' in separate gender spheres.[54]

> It was like a theatrical 'drama'. The couple Fernando-Palma displayed a sort of piece of theatre where, forcing their private and public behaviours, they attempted to appear 'different' from what they were. Their house had become an 'agorà', both a private habitation and a section of a party that, to be honest, did not really exist!! This couple worked as a sort of civil court: all behaviours were defined by them as being in conformity or not being in conformity with the revolutionary ideology. [...] The other couple was Frida-Tardo: they were the court of appeal (Santa, Manifesto sympathiser).

In brief, the peculiarity of this strong use of family tropes in the collective memory of the local Manifesto group is a clear trace of a 1968 which, although ideologically involved with the widespread criticism of the family institution, in practice was itself an expression of the local strength of family networks and family cultures. In particular, this is evident from the way these family tropes are used. As far as the militants outside the Manifesto group are concerned, associations between the political group and the 'family' maintain the negative connotations they had in most feminist criticism of the quality of relationships and the system of power inside the extreme left groups. This is in contrast to the core group of leaders, for whom the idea of family is always used with positive implications. The different historical family models (i.e. the 'sharecropping family' from the local tradition, the 'patriarchal family' ideological model and the subsequent model of the 'symmetrical family') are used interchangeably and are sometimes distorted, to retrieve an image of group cohesiveness and unity. Therefore, the key processes by which the family is remembered in the Manifesto group are firstly, the influence of the socio-cultural context on the specific experience, memory and legacy of this '1968'. Secondly, the crystallisation of a collective memory that is itself an emanation of the

---

54   Cfr. S. Delamont, *Appetites and Identities: an Introduction to the Social Anthropology of Western Europe* (London: Routledge, 1995) and F. Ramella, 'Reti sociali e ruoli di genere. Ripartendo da Elizabeth Bott', in A. Arru (ed.), *La costruzione dell'identità maschile in età moderna e contemporanea* (Rome: Biblink Ed., 2001), 79–88.

strength of family affiliations. Thirdly, and most importantly, the local impact of feminism on the group's inner dynamics as a potential challenge to the overriding image of unity of the group.

5. Inner dynamics: Feminism and the Manifesto group

It has already been noted that local feminists maintained a position that was complementary rather than in opposition to their political affiliation. This is also the case of many other feminist collectives founded by political militants, but only in their early stages.[55] As a consequence, the ideological attitudes of this kind of feminism were much less extreme than the ones of radical feminists, both towards the family and the political group. 'Feminist militants from the Manifesto group were more moderate and closer to the position of the UDI,'[56] Palma, one of founders of the local feminist group, explains. 'It was an ideological discourse on gender equality and on women's rights and discrimination, but we'd never challenged the man-woman personal relationship.' Although the 'specific' gender oppression of women was theoretically affirmed,[57] it was not believed that men, in the words of the leading feminist theorist Carla Lonzi, were objects to be 'despised' and

---

55   See A. Pasquali, 'Dentro e fuori il femminismo. La doppia militanza', in A. Crispino (ed.), *Esperienza storica femminile dell'età moderna e contemporanea*, vol. 2 (Rome: La Goccia, 1982), 145–158.
56   The UDI (Unione Donne Italiane) was the organisation of women affiliated to the Communist Party, adhering to the principles outlined by the traditional theory of women's 'emancipation'.
57   This was in contrast with theoretical positions prevalent among extraparliamentary 'double militants' from Lotta Continua, maintaining the priority of 'class oppression' over 'sex oppression'. Cfr. Fraire, *Lessico politico*, 57–65. On the different Italian feminist groups cfr. Calabrò and Grasso, *Dal movimento femminista al femminismo diffuso*.

'insulted'.[58] In many articles on the Manifesto journal by Luciana Castellina which were underlined and collected by most of the local feminists, men were considered to be allies in the battle against the common enemy, the capitalist system, ideologically regarded as the origin of the oppression of women.[59] However, most of these articles were also dedicated to theoretical reflections on problematic issues such as 'double militancy' in the feminist and political groups. Double militancy was generally argued to be the cause of unsolvable subjective contradictions between militancy in the extreme left groups and collective self-discovery and horizontal and qualitative relationships within the consciousness-raising groups.[60] One of these articles published within the Manifesto journal, 'The tragedy is to look for a party and to find a family', describes 'double militants' from the group Coordinamento Romano denouncing the quality of relationships that, inside their political groups, were 'selective,' 'competitive' and imbued with 'the confusion between the criticism of individualism and the negation of the individual.'[61] Therefore, even the less radical forms of feminism turned out to have subjectively affected female militants such that feminism was both among the main causes of the collapse of extreme left groups and shaped the historical collective memory of the later stages of the movement. At the same time, experiments with sexual freedom and new demands for 'qualitative' relationships had a disastrous effect on the survival of many couples,[62] stimulating the transition to new family structures and cultures[63] in a profound and complex process of change.

58   C. Lonzi, 'Sputiamo su Hegel', in R. Spagnoletti (ed.), *I movimenti femministi in Italia* (Rome: La nuova sinistra, 1974), 94–124.

59   M. Gramaglia, 'Referendum e liberazione della donna', in Castellina, *Famiglia e società capitalistica*, 55. See also Fraire, *Lessico politico delle donne*, 85–94 and 110.

60   L. Lilli and C. Valentini (eds), *Care compagne. Il femminismo nel Pci e nelle organizzazioni di massa* (Rome: Editori Riuniti, 1979).

61   Coordinamento Femminista Romano, 'Femministe nel partito. Il dramma è cercare un partito e trovare una famiglia', *Il Manifesto*, 31 March 1977.

62   G. Viale, *A casa* (Naples: l'ancora s.r.l., 2001), 94–95.

63   E. Forni, 'Coscienza femminista e rapporto di coppia', in E. Forni (ed.), *Essere donna oggi: ricerche sulla formazione dell'identità femminile* (Trento: Unicoop Trento, 1978), 119–155.

However, in the collective memory from Macerata, the tendency is to diminish the importance of feminist militancy as well as its impact on the political group. In the individual memories, feminism is generally defined as a determinant for subjective self-discovery: 'feminism was a crucial experience, not only for me, but for most of the other women. It gave us the chance to approach what you felt deep inside, which wasn't related to the class struggle but maybe just to the problems you had with your boyfriend!' (Lara, feminist and Manifesto militant). Yet, in the collective memory,[64] neither is the feminist group described in terms which reflect the subjective and collective experience of a new kind of 'politics' (i.e. horizontal relationships, collective self-discovery, etc ...), nor are there references to issues, such as the subjective impact of the 'double militancy', that were potentially threatening for the unity of the affiliated Manifesto group.

In recollections of the feminist militancy, memories firstly concentrate on inner rivalries and on the aggressive attitudes of the most influential members, especially with regards to the controversial debate on the priority of sex-struggle over class-struggle. Secondly, they concentrate on the importance of visibility at local level: 'dressing the same, taking to the streets, make the movement visible: this was important at Macerata!' (Ambretta, feminist and Manifesto militant). Finally, memories sometimes focus on the subjective difficulty of conforming to ideological behaviours so much in contrast with the culture of their socialisation: 'I experimented a lot with the ideology of sexual freedom, but this made me feel a sort of "schizophrenia" between these new sexual practices and my own feelings' (Lana, feminist and Manifesto militant). In this respect, as well as with respect to the objectified references to the feminist leaders through the same schemes of 'competency' and 'efficiency' as in the extreme left groups,[65] it is evident that the local practice of feminism did not create an 'alternative sisterhood'. Significantly, this is made explicit only by the radical feminist

64   On reflections on the 'unwritten' history of feminism that are centred on the difficulty to verbalise the consciousness-raising processes see A. Rossi Doria, 'Ipotesi per una storia che verrà', in T. Bertilotti and A. Scattino (eds), *Il femminismo degli anni Settanta* (Rome: Viella, 2005), 1–24.

65   Voli, *Quando il privato diventa politico*, 36–43.

from Milan, Lara, while in Macerata there is no trace of past reflections on themes related to the specific condition and identity of women inside the political groups:

> There was an inner hierarchy, even though it wasn't looked for. But we had very strong political leaders, some of them also very charismatic. Among the executives, Palma was the most skilled one in sustaining confrontations in meetings, etc. Me, for example, I tended to be on the side ... She, on the other hand, was part of the group, she was competent, she was better at talking politics and at intervening in debates (Ambretta).

> Once we went on holiday together, one summer, we slowly became friends and got a little bit more relaxed. Also, when I happened to live for a while in the house shared by the Manifesto group, there was never a real feminist confrontation with Frida about the relationship with male comrades in the movement: on our difficulty to speak, for example, and on the fact that we were always behind the organisation of public debates but never at the forefront (Lara).

In recollections of the impact of the theoretical constructs which were approached, further aspects of the local feminist memory show the absence of a subjective and collective sense of separateness from the rest of the political group. The 'double militancy', for example, is in most cases affirmed to be 'lived without deep subjective conflicts' (Ambretta) and feminism itself is said neither to be 'addressed against the political group' nor to be 'inspired by the refusal of men' (Palma). In brief, there is no trace of past reflections on what Stefania Voli defines as the 'double annihilation', both in terms of power as well as of gender identity, female militants underwent in the extra-parliamentary groups.[66] What mostly stems from the local feminists' memories is instead the minimisation of the impact of feminism in order to preserve an image of cohesiveness and unity within the Manifesto group.

> Feminism was not really directed against the unity of group. [...] I was convinced that I was not subordinate to the males in the group: feminism did not come into the group, the group remained something very united (Palma).

66   Ibidem, 32.

The only explicit references to an impact of feminism on relationships and group dynamics are to be found in male memories, although some attempt is still made to ensure the perpetuation of the image of inner solidarity. Some of the most politically focused accounts, such as the one by Tardo, repeat the classic themes of the confrontation between the political parties and feminist 'double militants.'[67] Male accounts, the most focused on subjectivity, however, unveil the renegotiation of inter-gender relations and gender identities caused by the impact of feminism.[68] This is clear, for example, from men's insistence on the sense of loss caused by censorship of their language[69] and, more dramatically, by the loss of control over their 'private' sphere. The main cause of the feeling of displacement among men was the discussion of their private lives, in their absence, during feminist consciousness-raising sessions, where all the most intimate aspects of their personal relationships and behaviours were laid bare and analysed.

> The local Manifesto group had always been very open to the feminist experience. Their mistake was to destroy the Udi and to refuse its theory of emancipation. [...] We didn't have any conflicts. This is a quiet place, without a tradition of strong political conflicts and extremism, and this has an influence on everyday life and relationships (Tardo).

67 I.e. the theory of 'emancipation' in opposition to the theory of 'liberation'. See anon., 'Un gruppo di compagne del centro romano del Manifesto', in B.M. Frabotta (ed.), *Femminismo e Lotta di Classe in Italia* (Rome: Edizioni Savelli, 1973), 227–248, and anon. 'Esperienze del collettivo femminista comunista', in Frabotta, *La politica del femminismo*, 39–47.

68 Although still lacking specific research, reflections on the changing concepts of masculinity during the age of social movements can be found in S. Bellassai, 'Verso il '68. La cultura del movimento operaio e il mutamento sociale (1958–1970)', in L. Baldissara (ed.), *Un territorio e la grande storia del '900. Il conflitto, il sindacato e Reggio Emilia. Dal secondo dopoguerra ai primi anni '70*, vol. 2 (Rome: Ediesse, 2002). See also S. Bellassai, 'Mascolinità, mutamento, merce: tre emme per un'indagine', in P. Capuzzo (ed.), *Genere, Generazioni, Consumi: l'Italia degli anni Sessanta* (Rome: Carocci, 2003), 105–138 and P. Capuzzo, 'Mascolinità e relazioni di genere nella cultura politica comunista (1947–1956)', in S. Bellassai and M. Malatesta (eds), *Genere e mascolinità. Uno sguardo storico* (Rome: Bulzoni Editore, 2000), 267–316.

69 G. Lepschy, 'Language and sexism', in Z.G. Baranski and S.W. Vinall (eds), *Women in Italy: essays on gender, culture and history* (London: MacMillan, 1991), 117–138.

The feminist group used to gossip about men. I remember that once I was with a friend of mine. You know, when the women had their meetings we were wondering what they were doing and it was also a bit scary! This friend of mine managed to listen in, and then came back and said: 'no worries guys, it's female gossip!!' [...] You obviously had to pay attention to your behaviour and especially to what you were saying to make sure it wasn't discriminatory. God, if by chance you happen to say something wrong they went wild against you! It was like committing a mortal sin! (Fernando)

In brief, what is striking is the contrast between these and female memories, where recollections of sources of conflict within the group are either silenced or repressed. Rather than on the 'episodic memory'[70] peculiar to feminism, this contrast seems to depend both on the local kind of feminism and on some contextual features of the Macerata province. On the one hand, one of the causes for this less pronounced radicalism was, as Sapegno points out, the 'strong resistance, by women whose full involvement in politics gave for the first time the self-perception of being empowered as individuals and so they were reluctant to admit to being oppressed inside their own counter-culture.'[71] This also related to the practice of a kind of feminism that subscribed to old Marxist precepts which rendered it difficult to understand the gender specificity of the new female 'subjects.'[72] On the other hand, this overshadowing of the experience of conflicts[73] between men and women in the Manifesto group is the sign of a sense of emancipation deriving not so much from the practice of feminism as from the condition of 'militants,' together with their male comrades, inside the political group. In the little town of Macerata, the deep-rooted Catholic conservatism constituted a strong factor of gender segregation, with most

70   Passerini, 'Memory for Women's History', 671.
71   See M.S. Sapegno, 'Tra Nuova Sinistra e autocoscienza. Roma: 1972–1974', in A.M. Crispino (ed.), *Esperienza storica femminile dell'età moderna e contemporanea*, vol. 2 (Rome: La Goccia, 1982), 99 and Pasquali, 'Dentro e fuori il femminismo', 152. See also P. Zumaglino (ed.), *Femminismi a Torino* (Milan: Franco Angeli, 1996), 40.
72   Pasquali, 'Dentro e fuori il femminismo', 100.
73   On the dynamics and outcomes of the feminist confrontation within the Manifesto group see Fraire, *Lessico politico*, 126–127.

memories insisting on the novelty of these women's public presence and emancipated attitudes (i.e. going out at night). It is not by chance that the sense of equality inside the Manifesto core group is usually stressed through the comparison of the male comrades with authoritarian family-figures: 'maybe because of the comparison with the way I was treated by my father, I felt comfortable inside the group and did not feel either excluded or downtrodden' (Palma). In the conservative narrowness of the Macerata province, in fact, the sense of group cohesion and solidarity was partially due and certainly enhanced by its constituting both a means and a 'nest' for the experimentation of alternative lifestyles.

6. The Manifesto group. A 'new kind of family'?

The opening of houses and the sharing of domestic spaces implied a significant change in everyday life attitudes: 'we really didn't have the exigency of privacy as a couple: we were comfortable with being many people, something that now would be incompatible with me!! The way you feel comfortable in a couple, we felt comfortable in a group' (Palma). However, feminist concepts and practices of 'sharing' went beyond their material forms. It included the sharing of private interiority as well as of affections through the attempt to erode, through sexuality, the institution of the couple. Also in memories from Macerata women appear to be the keenest on the search for alternative ways of life, which, in contrast to male memories, are described through reference to experimentations with intimate relationships.

> The fact of being in a close rather than in an open couple, without being involved in other relationships, this is what we considered 'castrating' for a woman: also for men, but mainly for women. [...] Having other relationships while being in a couple was something we considered as sexually and mentally liberating: the fact that you opened up to other experiences, to other things ... And this created real pain because such things could never succeed. I mean, we made repeated attempts, but in the end jealousies always came out (Frida).

We experimented like crazy. Just to tell you, cheating on someone – which is something I had to cope with later and caused me great pain – at that time was just normal: 'why? What's the problem? He can sleep with me, and then with another one, he can love two people at the same time!' Simone De Beauvoir was our guru and we practiced this sexual freedom, with great experimentation. When we got married, to me it was logical that, if he fancied someone else, he could sleep with her, because it was part of his own freedom (Palma).

It has been noticed how the spread of feminism transformed private homes into political meeting places for women,[74] where new forms of consciousness were collectively elaborated, undermining the stability of the existing families and giving rise to radical experiments of cohabitation among women.[75] Beside feminism, practices of free sexuality were diffused among the extra-parliamentary militants, where – as it has already been said – the female body often became an instrument of political struggle. Love dynamics, strictly endogamous, are often recalled as being aligned with, and changeable according to, the political hierarchy within the group.[76] Therefore, although without an overriding ideological project of overcoming the family institution, this complex web of feminist ideologies and extra-parliamentary practices inevitably impinged on the stability of the existing family models.

In memories from Macerata, although references to the diffusion of these practices are frequent, especially in the case of women, there is no mention of the changeable nature of love dynamics between the Manifesto militants. Moreover, the image of stability of the couples at the centre of the political group is never contradicted. References are made to the subjective difficulty to adapt to ideological behaviours which were emotionally incompatible with the cultural models of previous socialisation. Explicit mention is also frequently made of the case of the couple Palma-Fernando,

---

74 Passerini, *Storia di donne e femministe*, 163.
75 See Lara's memory on her experience in Milan: 'I left Stelvio and went to live with a group of feminists for a few months. There were women who left their families arriving at any time day or night, women who were ashamed to admit they had husband and children.'
76 Voli, *Quando il privato diventa politico*, 50.

whose collapse has become the only reference, in collective memory, to the difficulty of overcoming the tradition of romantic love.[77] Only in the external memories from Lara, however, is the unstable nature of most relationships, including the leader couple, explicitly hinted at ('Frida was firstly with Fernando and suddenly became Tardo's partner', she says, while also recalling her short love affair with the leader Tardo). In all the other memories from inside the Manifesto core group, the system of couples is instead crystallised in the inner hierarchy to the extent that the couples and the hierarchy seem to legitimate and to correspondingly reinforce each other. Other than as a site for the experimentation of alternative lifestyles, the Manifesto core group is often remembered as a means to 'contain' the tensions that the ideological practices of new sexual mores created within the couples. Again, this is associated with images from the traditional rituality of the rural village in traditionally separated gender spheres:

> At Macerata there's always been a sort of dilution of tensions thanks to the group's support. If the couple was in crisis, there was the group of women who sustained the woman, affectively, and the problem was dulled [...] There was this sort of ancient ritual, men with men and women with women (Lara).

Therefore, in recalling the Manifesto core group as a new kind of family, only those recollections that least challenge the conventional view of family, such as the newness of collective lifestyles, are explicitly brought to the surface. Besides that, although some women's memories reveal diffuse attempts at 'liberating' the experience of sexuality from the institution of the couple, the collective image of the political group seems to stand unaffected by the profound cultural changes entailed by these experiments.

To sum up, the stability of the Manifesto group is rendered through conventional concepts of family as the only legitimate site for the experience of sexuality and through the traditional immobility of emotional and sexual relationships. Silences in memory might be voluntary or involuntary and depend on different factors. When voluntary, as opposed to

---

77   Ginsborg, 'Measuring the Distance', 64.

involuntary causes such as those associated with trauma,[78] individual and collective silences often derive either from a relationship of discontinuity with the past or from a selective memory that is in conformity with present identities and values.[79] In the case of Macerata, therefore, memories of alternative lifestyles are not edited only for modesty's sake, understandable when talking about such private subjects as sexuality, they are retrieved in ways in which they preserve traditional concepts of family, as a means to legitimate and reinforce the image of cohesiveness and stability within the political group.

7. Conclusion

In dealing with ways in which 1968 has been recalled, forgotten and misremembered, this chapter attempts to show the peculiarity of a local experience and memory of 1968 in the micro-context of an Italian province. In particular, it has taken into account the ways in which the main subject of the local '1968' political struggle within the extreme left group Manifesto has been described through the widespread use of family tropes. In a rural context where the Catholic subculture and sharecropping tradition has placed the institution of family at the centre of local identity, images from the family institution also become crucial in the structural and cultural representation of the political group. In the collective memory of this 1968, different historical models of the family institution are used to convey an image of stability and cohesiveness of group. Despite the generalised

---

78   L. Passerini, 'Ferite della memoria. Immaginario e ideologia in una storia recente' (1988) 2 *Rivista di storia contemporanea* 17, 165–190. On traumatic memory see especially C. Caruth, *Trauma: explorations in memory* (London: University Press, 1995) and C. Caruth, *Unclaimed experience: trauma, narrative and history* (London: Johns Hopkins University Press, 1996), 1–24 and 91–112.

79   See A. Portelli, 'Oral History as Genre', in M. Chamberlain and P. Thompson (eds), *Narrative and Genre* (London: Routledge, 1998), 23–45.

ideological criticism of the institution of family, the local '1968' could not free itself from the 'family' as an enabling structural and cultural basis of the 'movement' itself.

Although specific to micro-historical contexts, local case studies such as Macerata are also relevant to the 'core' of 1968 and the historical comprehension of its complex nature. Firstly, the fact that '1968' reached rural provinces such as Macerata proves what a broad and widespread phenomenon it was, at the intersection, even in the most marginal areas, of crucial processes of change. Secondly, the 1968 movements were deeply influenced by contextual aspects which, notwithstanding the universal aims and purposes of the movement, imply a multiple definition of the movement in relation to its various experiences and effects. At Macerata, the 1968 as a mass political movement spread late, coinciding with the mass diffusion of the movement and of the extreme left parties at national level, and without the subjective experimentation historically acknowledged as the distinctive characteristic of its initial phase. As a consequence, this local memory illustrates the variety of meanings and effects associated with '1968'. One of the main 'devices' and 'defences' of memory, Passerini writes, is 'to periodise'.[80] Rather than as a defeat of the original spirit of 1968,[81] the local spread of the extreme left groups is subjectively and collectively regarded as an achievement of a place in the 'making of history', with explicit reflection on issues such as inner democracy and gender equality giving space to the importance of falling into line with the national movement.

In conclusion, for men and women from Macerata, 1968 was mainly an emancipatory experience of participation, and this accounts also for the collective emphasis on the importance of the sense of a 'group'. Although underlining a certain amount of discrepancy between ideological discourses and everyday life practices, the collective reference to the local family tradition was also a means to legitimate the local movement through the image

---

80   Passerini, *Authobiography*, 126.
81   See G.R. Horn, *The Spirit of '68. Rebellion in Western Europe and North America, 1956–1976* (Oxford: Oxford University Press, 2007).

of 'cohesiveness' and 'stability' within the Manifesto group. In brief, through this plurality of local perspectives, it may be argued that there are many 1968s. Without questioning the essence of 1968 as a 'global' experiment in individual and collective emancipation, this plurality can tell us much about the complexity of the movement and its legacy today.

Notes on Contributors

DANIEL BENSAÏD was a leading activist during the May 1968 events in France and at the time, he was a student at Nanterre and a member of the Trotskyist grouping, *Communist Revolutionary Youth*. Until his death on 12th January 2010, he was Professor of philosophy at Université Paris VIII and recognised as a major intellectual and activist on the French Left. He authored 28 books and his recent work includes *Marx, mode d'emploi* (La Découverte 2009), *Prenons parti pour un socialisme du XXIe siècle* (Mille et Une Nuits 2009) and *Démocratie dans quel état* (co-authored) (La Fabrique 2009).

CLAIRE BREWSTER is a lecturer in Latin American history at Newcastle University. She is a member of the Society of Latin American Studies and the Newcastle-based Americas Research Group. Her publications related to this research include *Responding to Crisis in Contemporary Mexico* (University of Arizona Press 2005); (with Keith Brewster) *Representing the Nation: Sport, Control, Contestation and the Mexican Olympics* (Routledge 2009); and 'Changing impressions of Mexico for the 1968 Games' in *Reflections on Mexico '68*, ed. K. Brewster (Wiley-Blackwell 2010).

TIMOTHY S. BROWN is Assistant Professor of History at Northeastern University and a member of the Boston German History Workshop. He is the author of *Weimar Radicals: Nazis and Communists between Authenticity and Performance* (Berghahn 2009). Other recent publications include '1968 Performance in East and West: Divided Germany as a Case Study in Transnational History' (*American Historical Review*, February 2009), and 'Music as a Weapon? Ton Steine Scherben and the Politics of Rock in Cold War Berlin,' (*German Studies Review*, February 2009). He is co-editor of the forthcoming essay collection *Between the Avant Garde and the Everyday: Subversive Politics in Europe, 1958–2008* (Berghahn 2010), and is currently working on a monograph for Cambridge University Press entitled '1968: West Germany in the World'.

INGO CORNILS is Senior Lecturer in German and Head of the Department of German, Russian and Slavonic Studies at the University of Leeds, UK. Among his publications are the volumes *Hermann Hesse Today / Hermann Hesse Heute* (with Osman Durrani, Rodopi 2005), *(Un-)erfüllte Wirklichkeit: Neue Studien zu Uwe Timms Werk* (with Frank Finlay, Königshausen 2006), *Baader-Meinhof Returns: History and Cultural Memory of German Left-Wing Terrorism* (with Gerrit-Jan Berendse, Rodopi 2008), and *A Companion to the Works of Hermann Hesse* (Camden House 2009).

IRENE FENOGLIO LIMÓN is Professor of Literary Theory in the Literature Department at Universidad Autónoma del Estado de Morelos, in Mexico. She has published on the relationship between politics and literature in contemporary Mexican authors and translated several books into Spanish.

JOHN FOOT is Professor of Modern Italian History at the Department of Italian, University College London. His publications include *Milan since the Miracle. City, Culture and Identity* (Berg 2001), *Modern Italy* (Palgrave 2003), *Calcio. A History of Italian Football* (Fourth Estate 2007) and *Italy's Divided Memory* (Palgrave 2009).

DANIEL A. GORDON is Senior Lecturer in European History at Edge Hill University, Chair of the Association for the Study of Modern and Contemporary France – North West, and has held visiting fellowships at St Antony's College, Oxford, and the University of Nice. His publications include articles in the journals *Modern and Contemporary France*, *Past and Present*, *Dissidences*, *Historiens et Géographes*, *Cahiers de la Méditerranée* and *Migrations Société*, as well as contributions to volumes of essays.

STUART J. HILWIG is Professor of History at Adams State College in southern Colorado. His main areas of research are contemporary Italian history with a focus on oral history, the media, and politics. He is the author of several articles on the Italian '68 and his book, *Italy and 1968: Youthful Unrest and Democratic Culture* (Palgrave Macmillan) will appear on bookshelves in January 2010.

CHRIS HOMEWOOD is Lecturer in German and World Cinema at the University of Leeds. Recent publications include 'The Return of "Undead" History: The West German Terrorist as Vampire and the Problem of "Normalizing" the Past in Margarethe von Trotta's *Die bleierne Zeit* (1981) and Christian Petzold's *Die innere Sicherheit* (2001)', in Stuart Taberner and Paul Cooke (eds) *German Culture, Politics and Literature into the Twenty-First Century: Beyond Normalization* (Camden House 2006) and 'Making Invisible Memory Visible: Communicative Memory and Taboo in Andres Veiel's *Black Box BRD* (2001)', in Gerrit-Jan Berendse and Ingo Cornils (eds) *Baader-Meinhof Returns. History and Cultural Memory of German Left-Wing Terrorism* (Rodopi 2008). He is currently co-editing the volume *New Directions in German Cinema* for I.B. Tauris and working on his first monograph exploring filmic representations of the Red Army Faction.

MARTIN KLIMKE is Research Fellow at the German Historical Institute, Washington, DC and at the Heidelberg Center for American Studies, University of Heidelberg. Among other publications, he is the author of *The Other Alliance: Student Protest in West Germany and the United States in the Global Sixties* (Princeton University Press 2009), the co-editor of *1968 in Europe: A History of Protest and Activism, 1956–77* (Palgrave Macmillan 2008), *1968. Ein Handbuch zur Kultur- und Mediengeschichte* (Metzler 2007), and the publication series 'Protest, Culture, and Society' (Berghahn Books).

WOLFGANG KRAUSHAAR is a political scientist and since 1987 a researcher at the Hamburg Institute for Social Research. In 2004 he taught as a visiting professor at Beijing Normal University. He is a member of the Association of German Scholars. His main research interests are: protest and resistance movements in the history of the Federal Republic of Germany and the German Democratic Republic (1949–1990), in particular the 1968 protest movement and the Red Army Faction. His most recent publications are: *Achtundsechzig. Eine Bilanz* (Propyläen 2008) and, as editor, *Die RAF und der linke Terrorismus* (Hamburger Edition 2006).

SUSANNE RINNER is Assistant Professor of German Studies at The University of North Carolina at Greensboro. Her research focuses on twentieth-century and contemporary German literature, film, and culture. Her research and teaching interests include the sixties; protest movements and terrorism; cultural memory; and the transnational and transcultural relations between the US and Germany. She has published several articles on the representation of the sixties student movement.

SOFIA SERENELLI-MESSENGER is a postdoctoral research fellow in the Department of Italian Studies at Reading University. Her UCL PhD is entitled '1968 on the Periphery: Family, Space and Memories of Daily Life at Macerata, 1960–1980'. Since January 2008 she has been conducting research in Predappio for the AHRC project 'The Cult of the Duce' which includes research into various aspects and features of the cult of Mussolini from the fascist era until the present day.

SARAH WATERS is Senior Lecturer in French Studies at University of Leeds and author of *Social Movements in France. Towards a New Citizenship* (Palgrave/Macmillan 2003). She has published widely on the theory and practice of French social movements and recent articles include 'Situating Movements Historically. May 1968, Alain Touraine and New Social Movement Theory' *Mobilization* (March 2008) and 'Globalization, the Confédération paysanne and symbolic power' *French Politics, Culture and Society* (forthcoming 2010). She is currently completing a monograph on globalisation, opposition and French identity.

LAN YANG is Lecturer of Comparative Linguistics and Literature at the University of Leeds. His current research focuses on the language style of contemporary Chinese literature. He is the author of *Chinese Fiction of the Cultural Revolution* (Hong Kong UP 1998), *A Study of Gong'an Dialect* (The Great Chinese Dictionary Press 1992), *The Dialects of Hubei Province* (Hubei People's Press 1997), and co-author of *The Concise Encyclopaedia of China* (Sichuan Dictionary Press 1994).

Index

CULTURAL HISTORY AND LITERARY IMAGINATION
EDITED BY CHRISTIAN EMDEN & DAVID MIDGLEY

This series promotes inquiry into the relationship between literary texts and their cultural and intellectual contexts, in theoretical, interpretative and historical perspectives. It has developed out of a research initiative of the German Department at Cambridge University, but its focus of interest is on the European tradition broadly perceived. Its purpose is to encourage comparative and interdisciplinary research into the connections between cultural history and the literary imagination generally.

The editors are especially concerned to encourage the investigation of the role of the literary imagination in cultural history and the interpretation of cultural history through the literary text. Examples of the kind of issues in which they are particularly interested include the following:

- The material conditions of culture and their representation in literature, e.g. responses to the impact of the sciences, technology, and industrialisation, the confrontation of 'high' culture with popular culture, and the impact of new media;

- The construction of cultural meaning through literary texts, e.g. responses to cultural crisis, or paradigm shifts in cultural self-perception, including the establishment of cultural 'foundation myths';

- History and cultural memory as mediated through the metaphors and models deployed in literary writing and other media;

- The intermedial and intercultural practice of authors or literary movements in specific periods;

- The methodology of cultural inquiry and the theoretical discussion of such issues as intermediality, text as a medium of cultural memory, and intercultural relations.

Both theoretical reflection on and empirical investigation of these issues are welcome. The series is intended to include monographs, editions, and collections of papers based on recent research in this area. The main language of publication is English.

Vol. 1   Christian Emden & David Midgley (eds): Cultural Memory and Historical Consciousness in the German-Speaking World Since 1500. Papers from the Conference 'The Fragile Tradition', Cambridge 2002. Vol. 1. 316 pp., 2004. ISBN 3-03910-160-9 / US-ISBN 0-8204-6970-X

Vol. 2   Christian Emden & David Midgley (eds): German Literature, History and the Nation. Papers from the Conference 'The Fragile Tradition', Cambridge 2002. Vol. 2. 393 pp., 2004. ISBN 3-03910-169-2 / US-ISBN 0-8204-6979-3

Vol. 3   Christian Emden & David Midgley (eds): Science, Technology and the German Cultural Imagination. Papers from the Conference 'The Fragile Tradition', Cambridge 2002. Vol. 3. 319 pp., 2005. ISBN 3-03910-170-6 / US-ISBN 0-8204-6980-7

Vol. 4   Anthony Fothergill: Secret Sharers. Joseph Conrad's Cultural Reception in Germany. 274 pp., 2006. ISBN 3-03910-271-0 / US-ISBN 0-8204-7200-X

Vol. 5   Silke Arnold-de Simine (ed.): Memory Traces. 1989 and the Question of German Cultural Identity. 343 pp., 2005. ISBN 3-03910-297-4 / US-ISBN 0-8204-7223-9

Vol. 6   Renata Tyszczuk: In Hope of a Better Age. Stanislas Leszczynski in Lorraine 1737-1766. 410 pp., 2007. ISBN 978-3-03910-324-9

Vol. 7   Christian Emden, Catherine Keen & David Midgley (eds): Imagining the City, Volume 1. The Art of Urban Living. 344 pp., 2006. ISBN 3-03910-532-9 / US-ISBN 0-8204-7536-X

Vol. 8   Christian Emden, Catherine Keen & David Midgley (eds): Imagining the City, Volume 2. The Politics of Urban Space. 383 pp., 2006. ISBN 3-03910-533-7 / US-ISBN 0-8204-7537-8

Vol. 9   Forthcoming.

Vol. 10 Alasdair King: Hans Magnus Enzensberger. Writing, Media, Democracy. 357 pp., 2007. ISBN 978-3-03910-902-9

Vol. 11 Ulrike Zitzlsperger: ZeitGeschichten: Die Berliner Übergangsjahre. Zur Verortung der Stadt nach der Mauer. 241 pp., 2007. ISBN 978-3-03911-087-2

Vol. 12 Alexandra Kolb: Performing Femininity. Dance and Literature in German Modernism.
330pp., 2009. ISBN 978-3-03911-351-4

Vol. 13 Carlo Salzani: Constellations of Reading. Walter Benjamin in Figures of Actuality.
388pp., 2009. ISBN 978-3-03911-860-1

Vol. 14 Monique Rinere: Transformations of the German Novel: *Simplicissimus* in Eighteenth-Century Adaptations.
273pp., 2009. ISBN 978-3-03911-896-0

Vol. 15 Forthcoming.

Vol. 16 Ingo Cornils and Sarah Waters (eds): Memories of 1968: International Perspectives.
396pp., 2010. ISBN 978-3-03911-931-8